DOMINIQUE NASTA

contemporary romanian cinema

The History of an Unexpected Miracle

WALLFLOWER PRESS
LONDON & NEW YORK

A Wallflower Press Book
Published by
Columbia University Press
Publishers Since 1893
New York • Chichester, West Sussex
cup.columbia.edu

A complete CIP record is available from the Library of Congress

ISBN 978-0-231-16744-4 (cloth : alk. paper)
ISBN 978-0-231-16745-1 (pbk. : alk. paper)
ISBN 978-0-231-53669-1 (e-book)

Cover image courtesy of:
Filmex (*Niki and Flo*), Mobra Films (*4 Months, 3 Weeks, 2 Days*), Mandragora
(*The Death of Mr. Lazarescu*) and Strada Films (*How I Spent the End of the World*).

Columbia University Press books are printed on permanent
and durable acid-free paper.
This book is printed on paper with recycled content.
Printed in the United States of America

c 10 9 8 7 6 5 4 3 2 1
p 10 9 8 7 6 5 4 3

contents

Dedicated to my husband and my sons

In memory of Alex Leo Șerban (1959–2011)

Acknowledgements

The main acknowledgement goes to Romanian film historian, archivist and critic Bujor Rîpeanu. My debt to him is immense: without his invaluable written contributions, constant advice on bibliographic sources, film copies made available while he was head of the Romanian Film Archive, numerous discussions and insightful commentaries on versions of the manuscript, this book would not exist. My wish is that translated versions of his outstanding contributions to Romanian historiography reach the widest international audience as soon as possible. My deepest thanks also go to film critic, Romanian Film Archive editor and Balkan film authority Marian Țuțui, for having contributed essentially to my research by providing more than a hundred copies of Romanian films, from the early years to the present. I would also like to thank him for sharing his knowledge on films I was not familiar with: most chapters of this book could not have been completed without the films Marian helped me uncover or rediscover. I also wish to thank Yoram Allon at Wallflower Press, whose enthusiasm, confidence, patience and unrelenting editorial support for this project helped me bring the book to completion; he was always available to answer my questions and to extend deadlines, allowing me to update material in accordance with the constant metamorphoses of contemporary Romanian cinema.

The academic and administrative staff at the Université Libre de Bruxelles Faculty of Philosophy and Letters and its Film Studies department enabled me to combine teaching with research time in the best possible ways. I therefore wish to thank successive Faculty Deans Jean-Pierre Devroey, Didier Viviers and Manuel Couvreur for their unflinching support. I also wish to thank my long-time collaborator and colleague Muriel Andrin for carefully re-reading the manuscript and for helping with many academic issues, relieving me from administrative burdens, allowing me to spend the necessary time on the manuscript, and enduring my doubts and hesitations with intelligence and good humour. Anne Gailly, Myriam Billon, Aurélie Lachapelle, Marta De Oliveira, Frédéric Dhantschotter and Marc Jamgotchian helpfully provided assistance and technical support all the way through. This book has also gained from stimulating discussions with students over many years. Special thanks go to three Romanian M.A. students studying in Brussels: Lucian Marinescu, Vlad Nedelcu and Alexandra Grigorianu. Lucian helped with various re-readings of the manuscript, and Vlad's contribution to the iconography proved essential. Jeremi Szaniawski helped substantially, copy-editing parts of the text.

I am particularly indebted to the Belgian Film Archive, to its former outstanding curator Gabrielle Claes and to her entire experienced staff: they generously gave me unlimited access to all existing material in relation to Romanian films and filmmakers and enabled me to organise the first retrospective entirely dedicated to Romanian cinema, in September 2007. Many academics helped me shape this book and encouraged me to pursue my goal. I sincerely thank Irène Bessière, Daniela Berghahn, Gian Piero Brunetta, Nevena Dakovic, Marc Dominicy, Thomas Elsaesser, Dina Iordanova, Daniel Lindvall, Bruno Mazzoni, Giovanni Spagnoletti, Christina Stojanova, Marc Vernet and Christian Viviani, for giving me the opportunity to present lectures, teach courses and seminars, attend international conferences, and publish chapters from encyclopaedias, essays and dictionary entries on Romanian films and directors. Distinguished film theorist and friend David Bordwell offered insightful comments on earlier versions and persuaded me to cover the widest range of films from a cinematic sphere seldom approached before. Film director and colleague Luc Dardenne always manifested a lot of interest in Romania's emerging New Wave and constantly encouraged me to pursue and finalise my work.

The Romanian film community at large has helped me substantially, providing material, answering my emails and spending a lot of time on the telephone. My debt to my long-time friend the late Alex Leo Şerban cannot be measured: his untimely death is still something I cannot come to terms with. If Romanian cinema had a distinctive, encyclopaedic and highly ironic critical voice that was heard worldwide, this was Leo's: almost every chapter in this book is here to prove it. Critic Cristina Corciovescu invited me to the first 'Romania on the Movie Map 2008' Bucharest conference and enabled me to watch a lot of features and meet and interview most New Wave directors. I thank her for contributing to the manuscript with interesting information and ideas. My thanks go equally to Romanian directors Nae Caranfil, Radu Gabrea, Lucian Pintilie and Corneliu Porumboiu for answering my questions. I am very grateful to Mircea Daneliuc's experienced film editor Maria Neagu, for our long telephone conversations. Screenwriter and director Răzvan Rădulescu provided invaluable information about issues related to the Romanian New Wave. So did editor Cătălin Cristuțiu on the work of the late Cristian Nemescu, and cinematographer Oleg Mutu on his experiences with Cristian Mungiu.

Several relatives and friends require special thanks for helping in various ways: Marina Baconsky, Nel Bădescu, Mircea Deaca, Florin Draşcaba, Dana Duma, Ruxandra and Wolfgang Enzensberger, Ileana Ghiţulescu, Oana Lungescu, Philip Mosley, Adrian Niculescu, Natalia Noussinova, Mara Pigeon, Sanda Ripeanu, Achille Tramarin, Marietta Ujică and Ion Vianu. Last but not least, I want to thank my mother, Marguerite, and my father and intellectual guide, Professor Mihaïl Nasta, for their love, sustained help and support in all circumstances. I am also grateful to my brother Marius, who provided some useful assistance. Above all, my husband Alec Cunescu's invaluable love, intellectual involvement and practical assistance were pivotal at all stages of the preparation of the manuscript. He and our wonderful sons Stéphane and Pierre endured it all for more than four years, watching the same Romanian films over and over again, while also laughing whole-heartedly at Romanian jokes and at previously censored scenes and dialogue. I can only respond to them with my endless love.

Preface

On 14 July 1984, our family and friends drove me and my father to Bucharest's Gara de Nord, the railway station where we embarked on a two-day journey. We were bound to reunite, after a two-year forced separation, with my mother and brother, who had fled to Belgium on a tourist trip. I had mixed feelings. I was persuaded my future husband would manage to join me very soon, but I experienced the terrible fear of not seeing him and our other friends and relatives ever again: they all lived in a prison, the keys of which were in the hands of those who served the dictatorship. I was about to cry, but at the same time I was elated, enthusiastic, full of hopes and so relieved to say goodbye to this country that definitely was not mine any more. The concept of home-land, *patrie* in Romanian, had clearly become a foreign one to me. How could I ever identify with a country where liberty was non-existent, where every move was spied upon, where you had to queue for hours in order to get basic foods, where there was just one black-and-white television channel glorifying Ceaușescu and his wife day in, day out, and where all the street lights went off at 8pm?

Once in Brussels, I clearly decided to consider all this a bad dream and start a new life. Five years later, while I was finishing my PhD in Film at the University of Brussels, on 22 December 1989, history brought back my bad dreams in a more than unexpected manner. The same Ceaușescu was to be seen on television sets all over the world. There was no glorifying left, only a corpse surrounded by blood, filmed and framed as no dictator had been before. Later I recognised familiar faces among those proclaiming, in the derelict Romanian Television studio, that revolution had won. From the moment I realised my native country's spectacular upheaval was being written with images, most of which had been filmed by the Romanians themselves, the concept of homeland suddenly struck hard. It helped me clearly understand one thing: for my compatriots, most of whom had been deprived of liberty for more than forty years, the key which opened the prison doors most certainly had the shape of a camera.

Romania's name was back on world maps, and a few years later so was its cinema. But had the latter ever existed? Actually, did anyone know anything about the cinema of this distant, miserable, ex-Soviet satellite? Dictionaries and film history chapters were filled with errors and misinterpretations. Back in 1990, was anybody able to quote just one representative Romanian film? Had such a thing as a Romanian film school similar to the Soviet, Polish, Hungarian or Czechoslovak ones ever existed?

Answering this set of questions is one of the aims of the present book. The necessity of providing a comprehensive answer amidst the constantly changing trends of contemporary world cinema is no coincidence at all. For the last ten years, the Romanian New Wave has brought forth an unprecedented number of extremely talented filmmakers, performers, screenwriters, editors and cinematographers. They have been producing so many internationally acclaimed short and feature films that it has become difficult nowadays for any film connoisseur to affirm that the names of Cristian Mungiu, Cristi Puiu, Corneliu Porumboiu or Radu Muntean are unfamiliar meteorites.

Nonetheless, these people did not emerge from nowhere: retracing the origins of their inspiration before discussing their own films proved a highly challenging enterprise, both on an intellectual and on a personal level.

Dominique Nasta
July 2013

Introduction

The entry on 'Romania' in the *Handbook of Soviet and East European Films and Filmmakers*, published in 1992, opens with the following assessment:

> Like Romania itself, Romanian cinema has remained obscure. The sparse international distribution of its films has made it remote and unfamiliar. Until recently, it has been aesthetically insignificant, adhering rigidly to the somehow formulaic necessities imposed by film's illustrative and ideological functions in a totalitarian regime. For these reasons, Romanian cinema has not gained the world stature of other Eastern European cinemas. (Roof 1992: 309)

Some twenty years later, things have changed radically. Not only has Romanian cinema gained an indisputable global stature over the last ten years or so, but it has miraculously managed to catch up with and even outdo in output and quality other Eastern European cinemas.

With Romanian contemporary cinema present for more than a decade at important film festivals over the world, winning prizes and being an identifiable part of European co-production, distribution and training circuits, the appropriate moment has come to look at Romania's film history, in an attempt to explain and analyse those aspects that have shaped and made it relatively unique today. Although essays published in specialist journals, cultural institute programmes and international conferences have tackled the issue of the

Romanian New Wave on a regular basis, what has been lacking is a complete overview of the Romanian film phenomenon. So far, interesting, original and exhaustive books have unfortunately only appeared in Romanian (as can be seen in the bibliography here), so their accessibility has been extremely limited. Such a situation is due both to the extremely severe rules implemented for more than four decades by a Stalinist regime and a Communist dictatorship and to the fact that Romania has lacked a cultural policy for showcasing its domestic output and preserving films from the past.

The period covered runs for roughly a century, from the difficult beginnings of the Romanian film industry in 1911 to some very recent productions. Unlike other books concentrating on the history of a national cinema, this overview of Romanian production focuses not only on periods and trends, but also on isolated directorial outputs. Here, some general chapters concentrate on periods and trends, while many others are dedicated to specific directors who have been influential upon the development and positioning of Romanian film at home and abroad: Dan Pița, Mircea Daneliuc, Lucian Pintilie, Nae Caranfil, Cristian Mungiu and other important representatives of the Romanian New Wave. The book also contains additional information regarding Romanian migrant and diasporic film artists, with a particular focus on Radu Gabrea, a director whose versatile career spans from the early 1970s to the present.

The emphasis here is both on the socio-historical background that has conditioned the emergence of specific trends (e.g. film minimalism) and on cinematically relevant and – contrary to Judith Roof's assertion quoted above – aesthetically significant characteristics of individual works. Thus, essential directors and landmark films illustrative of a certain period or style have been purposefully given detailed attention through in-depth analyses. Art cinema has obviously received more attention in the present book than commercial cinema; no doubt a lot remains to be said about popular sub-genres showcased by Romanian cinema over the years, such as historical super productions, comedies, and action and adventure movies, and so one hopes that other researchers will continue these explorations.

In the interests of developing a better understanding of both Balkan and Latin features particular to Romanian films, some chapters include concepts drawn from sociology, philosophy, ethnography and literary theory. Translating pieces of dialogue, poems, puns and jokes from Romanian into English has not been easy, considering that some terms do not have equivalents; I have therefore sought paraphrases as close as possible to the initial meaning. And as explained at various points in the book, soundtracks often prove as important for decoding a film as visuals; this is why lyrics from apparently insignificant credit songs have been translated and commented upon.

CHAPTER 1

Difficult Beginnings

HISTORICAL AND CULTURAL LANDMARKS

A Latin island set in a sea of Slavic neighbours, Romania is a country that has consistently felt close to identities and sources that were somehow out of reach. The issue of national identity has always been at the centre of socio-political debates, numerous invasions having left the country with little energy to catch up with the rest of Europe. As Catherine Durandin rightly notes:

> Romania's history is related to its frontiers. Situated at the extreme frontier line of the Roman Empire, Romania borders the Byzantine Empire, close to the Ottoman invasion line, and finally acts as a frontier line between the Russian expansion and its Western opponents, the Austro-Hungarians in the nineteenth century. (1995: 19; author's translation)

Dina Iordanova similarly argues that

> If one looks from the West, the Balkans are perceived as homogeneous; if one looks from within, they are often perceived as diverse and heterogeneous. [...]

3

> It is a specific feature of the Balkan situation that each one of the countries pre-
> fers to look at some West European country for cultural identification rather
> than to any of its Balkan neighbours: Romanians look traditionally to France,
> Bulgarians to Germany and Slovenes to Austria and Italy. Unlike the imperial
> legacy of Austro-Hungary which is considered to have boosted social progress,
> Ottoman rule is considered as a major interruption and as an impediment to fulfil
> European goals. (2001: 8)

A beautiful country with a balanced natural potential, Romania has many ethnically configured ancestral traditions represented in its oral folklore. Artists
of all kinds have long manifested an unusual propensity for lyricism by way of
original poems and songs. In terms of defining categories, the main Romanian
symbolic paradigm is to be found in the archetypal tale of *Mioritza*. Romania's
most enduring cultural text has mixed ethnic origins: a shepherd boy from
Moldavia is warned by his beloved ewe (*mioară* in Romanian), diminutively
called *the little lamb*, *Mioritza*, that his fellow shepherds – coming from
Wallachia and Transylvania – plan to murder him and take his envied flock.
He accepts his fate without resisting. The only thing he asks the lamb before
he dies is to tell his own mother a different story: that he married a king's
daughter, and that all natural elements were witnesses to the magical wedding. Consequently, the ewe will not tell a story of death and betrayal, but a
beautiful, almost metaphysical tale.

In a definitive essay significantly called *The Mioritic Space* (1936), Lucian
Blaga, a well-known Romanian poet from the 1930s, delineates the ballad as
some kind of geography of the Romanian poetic imagination, but also as a
philosophical attempt to explain the Romanian spirit through landscape, which
he saw as a stylistic matrix of Romanian culture. Blaga insists on establishing
a distinction between the effects of the natural environment on the collective
spirit on the one hand and on the personal subconscious on the other (see
Durandin 1995: 25). In a similar vein, reputed philosopher Mircea Eliade sees
Mioritza as a collective answer to the terrors inflicted by history: the ballad's
hero finds a meaning in his tragic fate because he does not consider it a personal event, but rather a mythical happening. The shepherd thus provides an
answer to an otherwise absurdist situation, countering death and misfortune
through a nuptial fairy tale. The cosmic marriage from *Mioritza* is a mythical
one, an example of cosmic Christianity – part pagan, part Christian – clearly
dominated by nostalgia for nature (see Pavel 2006: 5). Several critics have suggested that this tale might account for the tendency of the Romanian people
to suffer oppression passively, hence the fatalistic *Weltanschauung* implicit in

Mioritza. As many case studies of significant past and present films will try to show, fatality is indeed at the core of the Romanian psyche, precisely counter-balanced by a lot of black humour, spontaneity and ironic wit.

Mid-way between a form of fatalistic resignation and the tragicomic absurdist dimension present in a number of filmic productions over the decades, the Romanian cultural realm has always manifested an obvious penchant for reinterpreting major historical events. Such a tendency has resulted in a deliberate mixture between what French philosopher Paul Ricoeur has called the *time of fiction* and *historical time* (1990, III: 180). This aspect will prove crucial for decoding themes and styles conveyed by Romanian culture in general and by fiction and non-fiction cinema in particular, before and after 1989. I suggest that Romanian contemporary fiction films are extremely close to Ricoeur's re-definition of Aristotle's three-fold mimesis as developed in his seminal survey *Time and Narrative*: *time of fiction, historical time* and audience reception time all mix into one coherent signifying entity. Ricoeur's considerations surprisingly fit the contents and style of several past and present Romanian films. According to Ricoeur:

> We find a basic indication of the way in which the fictive experience of time relates in its own way to lived temporality and time perceived as a dimension of the world in the fact that the epic, the drama and the novel never fail to mix historical characters, dated and datable events, and known geographical sites with invented characters, events and places... Nevertheless, we would be sorely mistaken if we were to conclude that these dated or datable events draw the time of fiction into the gravitational field of historical time. What occurs is just the opposite. From the mere fact that the narrator and the leading characters are fictional, all references to real historical events are divested of their function of standing for the historical past and are set on a par with the unreal status of the other events. (1990, III: 129)

Aristotle's, hence also Ricoeur's, mimesis is three-fold: after *mimesis 1 (prefiguration)*, which tries to understand human action in its semantics and temporality, *mimesis 2 (configuration)* opens the kingdom of 'what if?' and creates narrative configurations which are precisely meant to be antonyms of historically validated, true stories. For Ricoeur, *narrated time* constitutes (and this point will prove extremely relevant to our purposes here) an alternative to the classical representation of time as flowing from the past towards the future. Thus, when approaching *mimesis 3 (refiguration)*, meaning the reading/interpretive process, what interests Ricoeur is not only the process of restoring the author's intention behind the text, but also 'the movement by which the work of art unfolds, as it were, a world ahead of itself' (1990, I: 70).

A relevant case in point from a totally different cultural domain is the *Balada Conducătorului* (*Ballad of the Dictator*, a.k.a. *The Song of Revolution*, 1990), composed and performed only a few weeks after the fall of Ceauşescu by the world-renowned Roma band Taraf de Haïdouks. The ballad is close in style and mode of address to the already-mentioned *Mioritza*, yet the content differs drastically. Working out a pre-existing melodic plot, it tells the true, chronological story of the uprising and of the subsequent short trial that toppled the 'tyrant who has destroyed Romania', obviously inspired by images shown on television. Lead singer/composer Nicolae Neacşu uses a highly oral expression and non-grammatical verbal forms, distorting his violin's sound with horsehair tied to it, to great emotional effect. He describes nature's 'green leaf, flower of the fields' as the shepherd speaks to his ewe-lamb in the original ballad:

> Green leaf, a thousand leaves...
> On December 22
> Time caught up with us
> ... So what did the students do?
> Once in Timişoara
> ... They shouted: no more tyrant
> To Bucharest they headed, shouting
> Let's wipe out dictatorship ...
> Ceauşescu heard their shouting ...
> And what did the police do?
> Brought him back to Bucharest
> Locked him in a room
> Took his pressure before the trial
> And the judges said to him
> Tyrant, you have devastated Romania.[1]

A further comparison between the *Ballad of the Dictator* and the paradigmatic *Mioritza* may invite new ways of understanding the Romanian psyche and its subsequent translatability into film. The *Ballad* has maintained the poetic, rhetorical mode of address to a natural element because it obviously needs an extension, an escape from a very concrete, albeit violent, reality, about a man who destroyed a whole country and who will have to pay for his deeds. The 'green leaf' issued from a common natural landscape is nonetheless a passive listener, not an active messenger as was the case with the ewe-lamb from *Mioritza*. In *The Ballad of the Dictator*, reality, history and sung narratives are reunited; they become, for a short time span, a homogeneous entity. This explains why one line of the ballad reads 'time has caught up with us', or, in a literal translation, 'time has returned'.

It is not only Romanian contemporary cinema which has used the 'fall of the dictator' paradigm as a main point of thematic reference to great effect. Earlier films focusing on real and/or historical facts from Romania's past share this recurrent integration of ongoing events and recounted ones. Besides, the different types of socio-political and economic upheavals which have prevented Romanian filmmakers from expressing themselves freely and fully demonstrating their craft have paradoxically engendered, as in many other neighbouring countries in the Soviet sphere, codified modes of expression. Different spatio-temporal lines co-exist inside such films: their common ground often lies in a joke, a song or a poem.

THE UPS AND DOWNS OF A FALTERING FILM INDUSTRY

Romania's highly problematic socio-political situation as a monarchy led by the Hohenzollern dynastic line during the first two decades of the twentieth century, after centuries of Ottoman, Greek or Russian occupation, did not prevent the country's Byzantine heritage from prevailing. Nor did it diminish the impact of the French spirit in Wallachia and Moldavia and the inevitable Austro-Hungarian way of life in Transylvania. This myriad of European influences had both positive and negative effects on the way film as a new invention was turned into a bankable industry.

Positive effects, confirming Romania's intention to bridge the cultural gap between Oriental and Western parts of Europe, include very early screenings of Lumière films (in Bucharest in May 1896) and the presence of foreign cameramen shooting on location their Romanian shorts, the *'vues roumaines'*, concentrating exclusively on local topics. The earliest known operator of a motion-picture camera in the Balkan region was Paul Menu, who filmed a military parade in Bucharest in May 1897. A Bucharest-based optician and photographer with French origins, Menu subsequently shared his filming experience with Lumière and Pathé cinematographers. Romanian journals from the early twentieth century also mention the quick connections established for distribution purposes with European countries benefiting from important film production rates such as France, Germany and, to a lesser extent, Italy. In 1908 and 1909, many theatres equipped to show newsreels and fiction films

7

alternating with vaudeville numbers began to be built, first in Bucharest and later on in other important economic and cultural cities in the rest of the country such as Iași, Cluj and Sibiu (see Cantacuzino 1968: 98).

While most films from the early years of the century have disappeared due to bad preservation conditions, the most important Romanian feature film produced in 1912, *Independența României* (*The Independence War*, Grigore Brezeanu/Aristide Demetriade), has been preserved and has even served as a screening subject for Nae Caranfil's more recent epic *Restul e tăcere* (*The Rest Is Silence*, 2007), to be discussed in a subsequent chapter. It depicts the different kinds of wars Romania had to wage for its independence in the nineteenth century, after several centuries of mainly Ottoman domination.

A jack of all trades with a hunchback, the son of renowned actor Ion Brezeanu, raised and known for innumerable accomplishments inside the theatre world throughout his brief life, Grigore Brezeanu co-directed and co-scripted the film with his close collaborator, director and actor Aristide Demetriade. Both had already directed two films produced by the Pathé-Bucharest subsidiary, which are considered the first fiction features ever produced in Romania: *Amor Fatal* (*Fatal Love*, 1911) and *Inșir-te Mărgărite* (*Spin a Yarn*, 1911), neither of which has been preserved, unfortunately. Brezeanu employed a cast that included celebrated figures from the Bucharest stage such as Constantin Nottara and Aristizza Romanescu, as well as *émigré* actress Elvire Popesco in her screen debut, in order to convincingly impersonate important Romanian historical figures. Three years before D. W. Griffith's *Birth of a Nation* (1915), the film featured hundreds of extras provided by the Ministry of Defence and was almost entirely shot on location in the outskirts of Bucharest. Historical war scene revivals filmed by French camera operator Franck Daniau skilfully alternate between visual and verbal (intertitles with excerpts from odes and poems) celebrations of Romania's representative assets (that is, peasants dancing in national dress on the battlefield).

Leon Popescu, a theatre owner and manager with influential contacts in the world of high finance, co-produced *The Independence War*: he continued over subsequent years to develop his film business via his company Filmul de Artă Leon Popescu. Mainly genre films, these eventually proved pale copies of the Pathé-distributed series 'Films d'Art' (see Rîpeanu 2004: 24–5). They did not succeed in setting up a real national filmic output: the production rate was extremely slow, and films did not fare well commercially, lacking any international appeal. Furthermore, the economic effects of World War I on the Balkans had a far-reaching impact on the industries of Romania; the local subsidiaries of Pathé and Gaumont ended their business in 1915, and theatre owners were forced to rely on national productions. The most prolific wartime studios were in Cluj (then called Kolosvar and part of Hungary), where from 1914 to 1916 several directors contributed to an impressive output of sixty-two films.

During the first two decades of Romanian cinema's existence, production teams used well-known literary figures as screenwriters, adapting their novels, plays or short stories but also asking them to re-write pieces of dialogue to provide a cinematic framework for their themes and styles. Such is the case of Liviu Rebreanu, the essential representative of the Naturalistic trend, whose work would actually span more than sixty years of cinema, but also with Mihail Sadoveanu, who specialised in historical novels, and Victor Eftimiu, a poet and playwright. However, the most frequently adapted author remained Ion Luca Caragiale. His feature film and television longevity was greater than that of Rebreanu: his tragicomic, sarcastic depiction of Romanian society has left its mark on classical film directors such as Jean Georgescu through to contemporary auteurs of the twenty-first century, such as Corneliu Porumboiu.

A highly original example from the silent era, *Manasse* (Jean Mihail, 1925), an adapted play about a dramatic event from the Jewish community, proved an exception, with no sequels in subsequent years: it told the story of an impossible love in a Jewish traditionalist family which refuses a mixed marriage, somehow echoing the storyline of Alan Crosland's *The Jazz Singer* (1927). As in many other Eastern and Central European countries, the transition to sound was slow and difficult, requiring technical production equipment that was obviously lacking. The late 1920s nonetheless saw the emergence of action melodramas about *haidouks*. These half-bandit, half-hero Balkan musketeers were known in the Western world thanks to the exotic-flavoured prose of Romania's wandering exile writer Panaït Istrati. The most notable director of such products was Horia Igiroşanu, whose only preserved film is *Haiducii* (*The Outlaws*, 1929). Aiming to exalt nationalist feelings, the post-Stalinist era recuperated such commercially viable characters, changing them into entirely positive heroes.

A Lubitsch-like lyrical and burlesque comedy still preserved in the Romanian archives, *Maiorul Mura* (*Major Mura*, Ion Timuş, 1928), produced by Jean Georgescu, helped pave the way for the first comic talkies which were real box-office hits. But this was clearly an exception, most mediocre co-productions demonstrating the industry's inability to develop its own craftsmanship when it came to introducing sound, dialogue and/or music. Romanian critics and audiences alike received the multiple-version film wave that struck most European countries during the transitional era with much scepticism, since everything seemed terribly false and artificial. Thus, interesting realistic novels by Liviu Rebreanu such as *Ciuleandra* (1929) and *Venea o moară pe Siret* (*The Mill on the River Siret*, 1931) were brought to the screen by German director Martin Berger but proved to be complete flops. Later, French silent cinema director Camille de Morlhon shot *Roumanie, terre d'amour* (*Romania, Country of Love*, 1931) on location; French critics lampooned it on account of the ridiculous fact that Romanian peasants were leading their cattle in French.

Only sixteen films were produced during the first decade of sound films, and genres did not undergo renewal. Famous Romanian-born actors and directors lost hope in real careers and left their native country for clearer skies, while businessmen were tempted to accept foreign films based on Romanian subjects but with dialogue in French or German. As usual, there emerged some notable exceptions, mostly co-productions with Germany or France. For example, *Visul lui Tănase* (*Tănase's Dream*, Constantin Tănase/ Bernt Aldor, 1932), co-produced by Tobis-Melofilm (Berlin), was an intriguing comic talkie showcasing a very popular music-hall director and actor, Constantin Tănase. The latter is invited to act in a German film unfolding in the Berlin studios with lots of hilarious situations, versatile though quite vulgar dialogues and quid pro quos in three languages: Romanian, French and German (see Sava 1999: 119). Eventually the audience discovers all this was just a dream; he is seen waking up after having watched his embedded dream in a movie theatre. Buster Keaton's thematically similar *Sherlock Jr.* (1924), made a few years earlier, could have served as an influence. Another quite successful co-production of that period was *Trenul fantomă* (*Phantom Train*, a.k.a. *Ghosts on the Train*, 1933), directed by Jean Mihail as the Romanian version of an eponymous Hungarian film, initially based on a British play by Arnold Ridley. Interesting sound effects coming from sources such as a mysterious radio and dialogue filled with sardonic Anglo-Saxon humour reveal the macabre though laughable fears of travellers on a frontier US train filled with bootleggers.

Romania's socio-political context from the 1930s and early 1940s was the theatre of alliances and positions that still perplex today's historians. Though marked by its Byzantine heritage and unique capacity to introduce the French spirit in a Balkan environment, Romania was trapped by nationalist tendencies teaming up with the German fascist model. The tendency to celebrate the country's Orthodox taste for religious rituals while simultaneously verging on anti-Semitism in adhering to Germanic ideals drove many Romanian intellectuals and politicians to conclusions and acts most of them later deeply regretted. The violent legionary movement that also originated from these circumstances perpetrated terrible crimes; the most notable were the pogroms from Moldavia between 1940 and 1942, ordered by their head, General Antonescu, with Hitler's support (see Durandin 1995: 267).

As expected, economic alliances with the Third Reich brought some long-awaited capital; the press and part of the educational system were controlled and censored, while films were most naturally meant to showcase the national assets. Initially devoted to promoting the country's treasures via documentaries focusing on folkloric propaganda, the first National Film Office (ONC) was thus created as late as 1938. As a consequence, an unprecedented amount of acclaimed documentaries but also some salient feature films were produced; among them, Paul Călinescu's precious ethnographic piece *Ţara Moţilor* (*The Land of the Motzi*, 1939) won the Best Documentary Prize at the Venice Film Festival.

However, the first internationally acclaimed Romanian box-office hit produced by the ONC was *O noapte furtunoasă* (*A Stormy Night*, 1942), made by the versatile Jean Georgescu, an artist of humour and irony in the authentic vaudeville vein. One of the most successful stage comedies by Caragiale, *A Stormy Night*, tells the hilarious story of two amoral sisters, a cuckold husband and an absent-minded dandy, Rică Venturiano. Romania's authentic Molière, the writer dismantles hypocrisy and provincialism through unique, untranslatable lines and situations, including typically Balkan *joie de vivre* moments and some highly ironic interludes. While the cast included fabulous actors from the Romanian stage, the technical staff assisting Georgescu was partly international: Swiss cameraman Gérard Perrin and French editor Yvonne Hérault clearly contributed much to ensure the film's highly dynamic syntax (see Cantacuzino 1969: 198).

Private initiatives which could not get state funding and were produced by independent companies (such as Ciro Film and Dacia Film) fared quite well at the domestic level, and included two genre products depicting city life by Ion Şahighian, a director with roots in the theatre and having already directed successful comedy shorts. *O noapte de pomină* (*A Night to Remember*, 1939) is a contemporary variant on the aforementioned *A Stormy Night*, relying on effective dialogue quid pro quos by playwright and screenwriter Tudor Muşatescu; *Se aprind făcliile* (*Torches Are Lighted*, 1939) was a melodrama now sadly lost (see Sava 1999: 130). Collaborations with right-wing regimes other than the German one also enabled the production of two war melodramas and a romantic comedy through Cineromit, a short-lived company co-financed by Mussolini's government. *Cătuşe roşii*, a.k.a. *Odessa in fiamme* (*Odessa in Flames*, 1942), was directed by popular Italian director Carmine Gallone and starred a famous opera singer, Romanian-born Maria Cebotari. *Escadrila Albă*

(*The White Squad*, Ion Sava, 1942) – featuring a key figure from the Romanian theatre world, Lucia Sturdza Bulandra – has not been preserved. The production of the third one, *Visul unei nopți de iarnă* (*A Midwinter Night's Dream*, Jean Georgescu, 1944), another Mușatescu screenplay by the versatile author of *A Stormy Night*, was delayed by wartime restrictions, but the film ended up being completed and approved by the censorship board in 1946 (see Nasta 2000: 1474).

GROUND ZERO?

On 23 August 1944, a military coup led to a radical change in the course of history: Romania finally joined the anti-Nazi alliance. As in most Eastern European countries, the Soviet Union imposed Communism on Romania, leaving the country with no other possible political alternative. From February 1947, the Communist takeover assumed an increasingly rapid and violent pace, forcing the abdication of the king and the proclamation of the People's Republic. In 1947 Petru Groza's regime centralised the economy, and on 11 June 1948, the Romanian People's Republic completed the major part of its reorganisation: the government nationalised all industrial, transportation and mining enterprises along with banks and insurance companies and banned all kinds of private property. Romania worked on implementing its five-year plans: the emphasis was on heavy industry and collectivisation in agriculture. Russian Stakhanovism reigned; the study of Russian became compulsory in schools. Members of the old *bourgeoisie* and intellectuals with cosmopolitan tendencies were arrested, put on trial and imprisoned for several years. This left indelible marks on thousands of individuals whose lives and careers were completely destroyed (see Durandin 1995: 381).

In her survey *Cinema of the Other Europe*, Dina Iordanova opts for a post-World War II film periodisation that includes five distinct periods. The first period, characterised by totalitarianism and isolation, begins in 1949, the time when the Communists in the region consolidated their power and managed to control all aspects of social, political and cultural life. The period ends in 1956, a year that is important for two occurrences – the official end of Stalinism and the failed anti-Communist Hungarian uprising (see Iordanova 2003: 9).

According to Michael Stoil, in Romania as in Bulgaria and Albania, where national industries had not been established, film distribution was immediately placed under Communist political supervision: in all three cases directors were sent to the Soviet State Film Institutes and given large doses of ideological indoctrination, along with training in Socialist film techniques (see Stoil

1974: 104). The same scenario as in all Soviet satellite countries unfolded in the Romanian film industry. Stalinist dictatorship actually made film historians declare the year 1950 the zero level of Romanian film. Antonin and Mira Liehm note in their chapter 'Romania: Starting from Scratch, 1945–55' that

> After 1948, Romania's cinema was less favoured than its counterparts, and its development was slower. The artistic community, decimated by purges and emigration saw film as a prolonged arm of an unpopular regime. [...] Romanian film created its own style based on realistic bathos of commercial silent films, on dialogues of socialist-realist jargon. (Liehm & Liehm 1977: 139)

Răsună valea (*The Valley Resounds*, 1949), directed by Paul Călinescu, was heralded as the first film of 'a new world', in spite of its very low technical qualities. The film portrays peasant brigade members working on building sites and fighting against ex-landowners. All this was carefully wrapped into the social-realist jargon inspired by the Soviet model: the film ended with a quotation from First Secretary Gheorghiu Dej announcing that 'nothing will stop our heroes'. The credit song, a march bearing the same title, was played on building sites all over the country.

Film directors such as Dinu Negreanu, Marieta Sadova and Victor Iliu appeared on the scene, while old veterans such as Jean Georgescu and Jean Mihail resurfaced directing sheer propaganda such as *În sat la noi* (*In Our Village*, Jean Georgescu, 1951), *Brigada lui Ionuţ* (*Ionuţ's Brigade*, Jean Mihail, 1954), *Mitrea Cocor* (Victor Iliu, 1952), *Desfăşurarea* (*The Development*, Paul Călinescu, 1954) and *Nepoţii gornistului* (*The Bugler's Grandsons*, Dinu Negreanu, 1953). There were small exceptions, such as a more 'bourgeois' comedy adapted from successful playwright Mihail Sebastian, *Afacerea Protar* (*The Protar File*, Haralambie Boroş, 1955), the first Romanian film ever to be selected for the Cannes Film Festival.

A spirit of criticism inherited from de-Stalinisation pervaded Eastern Europe starting in the late 1950s. It heralded the birth of the intellectual reaction against state-directed orthodoxy in both politics and the arts. After Stalin's death in 1953, the most important film school founder and auteur was Victor Iliu. A teacher and director inspired by Eisenstein's pioneering theories on film, he directed his own films but also trained future filmmakers of a short-lived, isolated 'thaw', such as Liviu Ciulei, Lucian Pintilie and Radu Gabrea, each of whom will be discussed in separate chapters later in this volume. Iliu's *La moara cu noroc* (*Mill of Good Luck*, 1956) is undoubtedly the best film of the decade, ranking as a second 'classic' after *A Stormy Night* in Romanian film histories. The director aimed to create an original, auteurist screen adaptation of an important nineteenth-century writer from Transylvania. Never adapted before, Ioan Slavici's naturalistic prose was unique in its depiction of tragic passions in the rural milieu. Expressionistic lighting techniques, innovative handling of the actors' physiognomy and a non-conventional editing rhythm sustain the archetypal portrayal of an eternal triangle: the weak-willed inn-keeper, his beautiful young wife and her lover, Lică Sămădău – a handsome haïdouk-outlaw who promises everybody easy money.

Trained as an architect, a set decorator and occasionally an actor who ended up as one of Romania's most prominent stage directors, Liviu Ciulei left a distinctive imprint on the propagandist 1950s, carrying out different ideological assignments before recognition in Cannes with his masterpiece *Pădurea Spânzuraților* (*The Forest of the Hanged*, 1965). His debut, *Erupția* (*The Eruption*, 1957), convincingly features an oil derrick which is miracu-lously re-activated and unfolds in a hostile, volcanic environment: it presents characters with atypical destinies separated and reconciled, within a narra-tive set-up that insidiously refuses the ongoing Soviet diktats. *Valurile Dunării* (*The Danube Waves*, 1959), the story of a steersman, played by Ciulei, who sacrifices his life and marriage for the anti-fascist cause, received an important prize at the Karlovy Vary International Film Festival in 1960. The film is reminis-cent of Andrzej Wajda's World War II chronicles in its realistic yet highly lyrical rendering of a perilous war journey on the Danube.

This ideology-infested decade also witnessed the emergence of the first generation of graduates from the newly born state-subsidised Institute for Theatre and Film (IATC), some deciding to work and write their films in tan-dem, such as Manole Marcus and Iulian Mihu. Their psychological war-time epic in the vein of Wajda's *Kanal* (1956), *Viața nu iartă* (*When the Mist is Lifting*, 1958), is quite classical in subject matter, but its editing is reminiscent of *nouvelle vague* pioneers such as Alain Resnais. The hero, Ștefan, is a young journalist badly wounded during World War II: he recollects his own past and his handicapped father's itinerary before World War I, trying to answer essen-tial questions about the meaning of so much bloodshed. War is presented as a permanent state of affairs, in which past and present are constantly blended through flashbacks. The film was heavily censored and its premiere was delayed for more than a year, as it was judged too pacifist and much too strictly invested in form.

Mass film genres also timidly emerged in the late 1950s, consisting mainly of animated films, thrillers, comedies and sketches drawn from short stories and plays by the durable writer Caragiale, and last but not least, domestic but co-produced adaptations of authorised classics directed by foreign filmmakers. However, because of their poor quality, screenings of the majority of these films were not well attended, while those that rose above mediocrity were quite successful with domestic audiences.

In terms of subjects adapted from literature, the case of Romanian-born writer Panaït Istrati is worth mentioning at this point. Born in the Danube port of Brăila and having left home at the age of twelve, self-taught Istrati eventually became a long-time protégé of left-wing writer Romain Rolland and started writing in French without any training. After gaining international recognition for his authentic and uniquely colourful depiction of life in the Balkan area and becoming well-considered by left-wing authorities, he visited the Soviet Union but ended up denouncing Stalinist crimes before his premature death. His case is more interesting because of the unusually widespread critical reception of his work in the West than because of the film adaptations, which have been quite mediocre so far, with many not passing the test of time. The Balkan Gorky left a considerable amount of semi-autobiographical fiction and non-fiction; not only Romanian but also more general Eastern European characters mostly from a rural, marginal environment acquired mythical appeal and were recycled by other less-acclaimed writers and film directors.

Fragments of his work as an exile writing in French on Romanian topics were first approached during the silent era and later adapted twice during the 1950s. Films such as *Ciulinii Bărăganului* (*Bărăgan Thistles*, Louis Daquin, 1957) and *Codin* (*Codine*, Henri Colpi, 1963) bear the signature of French directors obviously interested in collaborating with Eastern-bloc regimes. In the latter, an ex-convict who served ten years for murder, Codin, cannot refrain from committing more murders and is despised by his own mother, while a young boy, Adrian Zografi, witnesses the misery and decay of this milieu.[2]

Filmed on location on the outskirts of Istrati's native Brăila with a predominantly Romanian cast and crew, the film features unconvincing performances from French actresses dubbed into Romanian. Screened at the 1963 Cannes Film Festival, Colpi's version of *Codin* was awarded a prize for its Franco-Romanian screenplay and technical qualities, but the film is closer to television standards than to those of theatrically distributed feature films. *Bărăgan Thistles*, Daquin's version of another rural drama by Istrati about the famous 1907 peasant uprisings, did not receive many positive responses; it did not showcase any international star and the foreign direction of a Romanian cast seemed far-fetched and artificial (see Liehm & Liehm 1977: 258).

Ion Popescu-Gopo, the leading figure in Romanian animated film, directed the most notable exceptions to this poor-quality output (see Cantacuzino 1968:

204). They proved pioneering in Europe at the time and were intended as anti-Disney minimalist cartoon creations. *Scurtă istorie* (*A Short History*, 1956), *Homo sapiens* (1960) and *Allo, Hallo* (1963) had two thematic constants: the advent of humanity represented by Little Man and an overtly poetic dimension. Story-wise, Little Man proves very daring and wanders through the entire universe, the globe image being a recurring device in most Gopo animations; Méliès' work also often appears as an overt reference. Gopo's work was much less censored than the average Romanian film production; his soundtrack mixed languages and various noises in surprising counterpoints and the music by Dumitru Capoianu was atonal and jazzy. *A Short History* won Romania's first big international prize, the Cannes 1957 Short Film *Palme d'Or*.[3]

During the four decades covered by this chapter a sum of adverse socio-economic and historical conditions consistently prevented Romanian cinema from surfacing worldwide with an identity of its own until the late 1950s. The next chapter aims to show how some bright intervals facilitated by the East-European Thaw allowed the emergence of noteworthy genres and auteurs.

CHAPTER 2

Bright Intervals
Romania's Short-lived Thaw

For Dina Iordanova, the 1956–1968 period between two revolutions (in Hungary and Prague) coincides with Khrushchev's Thaw in Russia and corresponds to a process of liberalisation in terms of themes and style. The transition that ultimately led to the emergence of the 1968 Prague Spring, but was suppressed the same year by the invasion of Warsaw Pact forces, only occurred on a minor scale in Romanian cinema. The recognised and internationally acclaimed New Waves were Polish and Czechoslovak. Important isolated auteurs came from the Soviet Union, Yugoslavia, Bulgaria, Hungary and Romania (Iordanova 2003: 9).

In the late 1950s Romanian Prime Minister Gheorghe Gheorghiu Dej rejected the Thaw theses adopted by neighbouring countries, arguing that Romania had already de-Stalinised its general politics by removing the ancient Communist hard-line faction. Possible positive consequences of the Thaw were downplayed and nationalistic propaganda took over. This happened notwithstanding the fact that Dej eventually also criticised Stalin: he banished the Moscow hard line as early as 1952. The ideological upheaval, which took place during the late 1950s in cultural circles in Hungary and Poland, supported by factions from their respective ruling parties, had no equivalent in Romania. There was only a brief Thaw stimulated by the rehabilitation of some previously unauthorised cultural elements (e.g. shelved writers), followed by a new wave of repression where many intellectuals and members of the intelligentsia were put on trial and marginalised for absurd reasons. Dej, who rallied the Soviet cause, strongly criticised the Hungarian 1956 uprising, which was supported by isolated groups of intellectuals and students who wanted to join the Imre Nagy supporters. According to historian Vlad Georgescu, Dej's loyalty was rewarded by a unique phenomenon in Central and Eastern Europe: a complete Soviet troop withdrawal from Romania in 1958. Bucharest's intention was to bring about Romania's release from Soviet control and gradual return to the family of democratic nations (Georgescu 1985: 5).

As a close collaborator of Dej, Nicolae Ceauşescu became, as early as 1961, one of the keenest defenders of the nationalist line. Cultural propaganda, directed by hard-line ideologist Leonte Răutu, had already fomented a nationalist myth, refusing any foreign influence and criticising the 'decadent' bourgeois representatives. Western European and United States observers hoped the Bucharest move would 'stimulate passive resistance to communist ideology and Kremlin control', which the politics newcomer Ceauşescu helped ensure for quite a while (Harrington 1991: 143). His election as Secretary General right after Dej's death did come as some sort of surprise: a comrade from the early Communist and anti-fascist years who had also shared a prison cell with Dej, Ceauşescu first seemed a mere shadow of the other more charismatic leader. Nonetheless, he worked out his own bourgeoning authority in ways that did not betray his subsequent despotism and destructive paranoia. Gaining the public's confidence, Ceauşescu took a clear stand against the 1968 crushing of the Prague Spring by Soviet troops. After a visit paid by an enthusiastic Charles de Gaulle earlier the same year, Ceauşescu's daring public speech in August deeply impressed the population. In the opinion of Vladimir Tismăneanu,

> The 'balcony scene' in August 21, 1968, when Ceauşescu addressed a crowd of over 100,000 and angrily condemned the Warsaw pact intervention [...] was nothing but a masquerade but it worked [...] Many Romanians from the intelligentsia who had been skeptical about his politics joined the Communist Party, confident in a brighter future. (Tismăneanu 2003: 202)

On a different plane, once Ceauşescu started his reign, Russian disappeared from schools as a compulsory language, Latin identity was rehabilitated and a period of apparent domestic and foreign progress followed: a new economy flourished, immigration to Israel or the United States was rendered less difficult, more freedom was guaranteed to artists and writers and intellectuals in general. Many political prisoners were freed. New opportunities to travel and arrange collaborations with partners from West European countries previously banned re-surfaced, translations into Romanian of noteworthy works were authorised anew, while important cities such as Cluj, Timişoara, Craiova, Constanța and Iaşi, were modernised so as to properly welcome foreign visitors. People also witnessed the return of Romanians from abroad: essential figures from the international scene such as Ionesco, Brâncuşi and Eliade were partly rehabilitated and appeared again on the national scene.

Catherine Durandin fully understood the different shades of the brief Romanian Thaw. She explains to what extent a ghetto survived in socialist Romania and what its main characteristics were. In *A New Beginning: The Golden 1960s* she helps draw the delicate line between the new Communist elite, ready to serve the ongoing politics under any circumstances, and the representatives of the old world (Durandin 1995: 403). Their children or grandchildren were still taught French, English and German at home, managed to get foreign books and journals from friends and family abroad, were nostalgic about the past and preferred their old, badly kept pieces of furniture and some precious objects to the modern ones. This social minority did not mix with the politically correct ones, which enabled it to be somehow preserved. By letting this minority have access to values of the Western world, the illusion of open doors was as close as it could be to reality, while remaining clearly remote. Thus, very few people refusing allegiance with the current power were authorised to travel abroad, while the new Communists and their children had permanent visas for travel.

The result was that people travelled with their minds through books, magazines and screenings for cinephiles at the Romanian Film Archive (founded in 1957), but also by having limited access to foreign Cultural Institutes, such as the French, Italian and American ones. The latter often set up film days and retrospectives and helped organise concerts and theatrical performances. The richly illustrated Romanian monthly film magazine *Cinema* also proved very instrumental in keeping filmgoers and film fans well informed.[1] This meant covering not only the domestic but also the international film scene, though most of the discussed films were actually never shown in cinemas.

In Liehm's opinion, Romania clearly lagged behind the other East European film industries. Only in 1965 did they manage to produce eighteen films, with craftsmanship and themes being more varied. Film production in the mid-1960s 'amounted to 15 fiction films, 25 cartoons, 76 newsreels, 150 documentaries, mostly stereotyped comedies, mysteries, antifascist tales about the unflinching heroism of Romanian soldiers' (Liehm 1977: 353). Almost half of the film production in the late 1960s and early 1970s consisted of adaptations of established literary authors such as I. L. Caragiale, Liviu Rebreanu and Mihail Sadoveanu, as well as more recent ones such as Mihail Sebastian and Ion Agârbiceanu.

In *Balkan Cinema: Evolution after Revolution*, Michael Stoil distinguishes between various sub-genres that apply to Balkan cinema in the 1960s and include Romanian films. *Tudor* (Lucian Bratu, 1964) represented the historical film: the focus on a nineteenth-century revolutionary allowed for the incorporation of both socialist and nationalist traditions. Tudor was an entirely positive character, while other characters were portrayed as essentially one-dimensional, lacking human complexities. The proto-revolutionary film dealt with the early Romanian Communist Party and emphasised the anonymous workers of the clandestine cells of the 1930s. *Duminică la ora şase* (*Sunday at Six*, Lucian Pintilie, 1965) and *Cartierul veseliei* (*The Gaiety District*, Manole Marcus, 1967) lacked an optimistic spirit and did not depict dramatic victories for the early Communist movement: they collectively offered an impression of isolated Marxists constantly losing members to betrayal in a near-hopeless attempt to raise class-consciousness. The audience is made aware the character has been assigned a mission, but the mission is never described. The anti-fascist film produced in Romania downplayed the Soviet role in the liberation of Romania. Thus, in *Porţile albastre ale oraşului* (*The Blue Gates of the City*, Mircea Mureşan, 1973), the seizure of the Bucharest airfield was depicted as an entirely Romanian operation, in which soldiers helped the advancement of the Red Army (Stoil 1982: 78–96). Most of the thriller sub-genre remained similar in content to the classical espionage film, featuring the violence of gunfights between spy rings and security forces, exciting chases and fistfights directed by specialist Sergiu Nicolaescu (e.g. *Cu mâinile curate/With Clean Hands*, S. Nicolaescu, 1972), but it also included highly popular humorous crime stories such as *Aventuri la Marea Neagră* (*Adventures at the Black Sea*, Savel Stiopul, 1970) and *Astă seară dansăm în familie* (*Tonight We Dance at Home*, Geo Saizescu, 1972). Moreover, a series of five feature films, *Brigada Diverse în acţiune* (*Brigade Miscellaneous*, Mircea Drăgan, 1971–72), depicted such crimes in a satirical, almost surreal fashion, with alleged criminals being pursued by inept police.

Professionals benefited from exclusive state funding and witnessed the creation of the future Balkan Cinecitta, the Buftea studios. Prestige co-productions with Italy, France, Britain and West Germany became realities: huge-scale heritage films were made, such as *Dacii* (*The Dacians*, Sergiu Nicolaescu, 1966) and *Columna* (*Trajan's Column*, Mircea Drăgan, 1968). Retracing the struggles of their Dacian ancestors led by King Decebal to establish hegemony over the Roman invaders resulted in *simili-peplums*, with artificial dialogue featuring dubbed foreign actors such as Pierre Brice, Antonella Lualdi and Marie José-Nat. However, fairly professional cinematography, lavish set designs and costumes, and action scenes featuring thousands of extras filmed on location with a quite acute sense of organic Hollywood-style editing guaranteed acceptable domestic box-office entries. Cloak-and-sword romances such as *Haiducii* (*The Haidouks*, Dinu Cocea, 1965) and *Răzbunarea haiducilor* (*The Revenge of the Haidouks*, D. Cocea, 1968) also resurfaced, five sequels having been produced from 1965 to 1968. They featured musketeers who take from the rich and give to the poor in the already mentioned nationalist-flavour style of the 1930s.

During the second half of the 1960s Romania offered cheap production costs to West European mainstream directors who shot their films on location inside the Buftea studios: such was the case with René Clair's *Les Fêtes Galantes* (1965), Jean-Paul Rappeneau's *Les Mariés de l'an II* (1970) and Terence Young's *Mayerling* (1967). East German filmings of successful youth TV series such as *Winnetou*, *The Last of the Mohicans* and *Tom Sawyer* (1968), were also welcomed. Henri Colpi struck back with *Mona, L'Etoile sans nom* (*The Nameless Star*, 1966) starring Marina Vlady, adapted from a successful Romanian play by Mihail Sebastian (Nasta 2000: 1480).

Light comedies, animated films and adaptations of authorised writers were produced at a constant pace with poor results in terms of quality, given that censorship had continued to be very active and no great liberty in subject matter or dialogue was granted to filmmakers. A handful of atypical filmmakers did not make concessions to the commercial strain of imposed genre films. Two of them made highly original films that were shown in the European festival circuit and became internationally acclaimed classics: the already mentioned Ciulei, also very active in theatre, and Lucian Pintilie.

The point of departure for Liviu Ciulei's *The Forest of the Hanged* was the homonymous novel by Liviu Rebreanu. The Transylvanian-born writer had a flair for dense portrayals of characters in both intimate situations and collective ensembles, linking their relationships to historical events. His prose had always represented a seemingly inexhaustible treasure for screenwriters and directors alike. The story, unfolding during World War I right before the dismantling of the Austro-Hungarian Empire, was inspired by a true tragedy, the death of the writer's brother, Emil, himself a deserter. The plotline roughly consisted of the tragic fate of a Romanian officer from the Austro-Hungarian front, young Apostol Bologa (Victor Rebengiuc), who realises the absurdities of war and refuses to kill his Romanian kinsmen. He faces the death penalty after a long-prepared desertion. Bologa's destruction of an enemy searchlight results in his promotion and transfer to fight against Romanian enemies: he rejects the proposal and tries to desert but is wounded and hospitalised, before being subjected to an anti-Romanian court martial again and attempting desertion. His anticipated death by execution will occur on a hill with barren trees, the 'forest of the hanged' seen in the first shots of the film.

Ciulei's adaptation of the novel is very innovative: all the 'I' narrative disappears and is changed into subjective audio-visual flashes; images of the front and discussions in headquarters are depicted with an extraordinary gift for expressive details. Screenwriter Titus Popovici also introduced episodes which are not in the novel. Discussions led by Captain Klapka – played by Ciulei himself – prove faithful to the novel and become self-reflexive. Klapka, who had also planned to desert while on a previous front, teaches Bologa how to live, forget, pretend and lie, and how to try to build a family while there is war.[2] Nationalist issues at stake in a region with a mixed population were rendered as faithfully as in the novel: thus, Apostol first despises Hungarians, then befriends Hungarian officer Varga (Andrei Csiky), and eventually ends up falling in love and marrying a beautiful Hungarian peasant, Ilona (Ana Szeles), the daughter of the regiment's grave-digger. As Marian Țuțui has noted, though only Romanian is spoken, various accents corresponding to actors with mixed origins (Hungarian, German, Moldavian) are heard in the film (Țuțui 2006: 33–41).

The black-and-white camerawork by veteran documentary cameraman Ovidiu Gologan is remarkable, featuring beautiful light contrasts and many highly expressive close-ups. The editing favours discontinuity, thus proving highly modernist: Ciulei passes from ensemble long shots and collective scenes to very intimate lighting and vivid ethnic settings. The film's syntax is often complex, with frequent movement between time periods and recurring subjective visions, alternating with long shots from the war front. The 'last supper' scene is quite unique, including a semi-dissolve in which Bologa's fiancée Ilona is desperately staring both at him and into the barbed wire which separates them from the 'forest of the hanged'.

Fig 1. *The Forest of the Hanged*: the 'last supper'

At the Cannes Film Festival the film was awarded the prestigious Best Direction Prize. French critics wrote 'Romanian cinema has finally accomplished its coming of age' (De Baroncelli 1965). Nonetheless, lacking the liberty in creation he craved, Ciulei returned to the stage, where he maintained very high standards of creativity, and never directed a film again. In the early 1980s he left Romania and continued to direct prestigious theatre productions in Germany and the United States.

Interestingly enough, another adaptation of a Rebreanu popular novel, *Răscoala* (*The Uprising/Blazing Winter*, 1965) by Mircea Mureşan, about the largest peasant uprising in recent Romanian history, won the Opera Prima prize in Cannes one year later. This director would actually specialise in high-profile adaptations: he also brought to screen an almost mythical piece of fiction, *Baltagul* (*The Hatchet*, 1969) by realist writer Mihail Sadoveanu. Though it cannot stand comparison with Ciulei's masterwork, *The Uprising*, despite artificial dialogue and an inability to depict in true colours the feudal-like Romanian class system, displays some obvious cinematic qualities, especially in ethnographic sequences revealing everyday life in very authentic locations. Moments echoing through images the Romanian literary penchant for naturalism include the abuse of a peasant girl by a perverse *boyar* and the fiery discourse in Parliament of an isolated landowner. The film's montage, constantly alternating collective scenes with more intimate ones, is particularly astute, though at times the quality of the image is quite mediocre and the score too pervasive.

The Hatchet, an adaptation project aborted in turn by Ciulei and Pintilie, was eventually directed by Mureşan as a co-production with Italy. An indisputable schoolbook classic by prolific writer Sadoveanu, it is a tale of murder and revenge in the fatalistic folklore line of the already mentioned *Mioritza* ballad. What distinguishes it from many other subjects/topics of the same kind is the fact that the main character seeking revenge and securing justice is a woman, probably one of strongest feminine figures in the whole of Romanian literature. Part of the co-production agreement no doubt required that an Italian actress play the part, and Margarita Lozano delivered an outstanding performance (though quite badly dubbed in Romanian), over-shadowing qualified Romanian actors, whose acting seems artificial and far-fetched. She is Victoria Lipan, now fierce, stubborn and determined in her unflinching quest for her husband murdered by his fellow shepherds, now sweet, sensual and maternal in her recounting of their long-time love story, her fits of jealousy and the affection she manifests towards her children. The second Italian choice, for the opposite part, that of Bogza, the husband's killer, was famous character actor Folco Lulli. He appeared only briefly towards the end of the story, and the poor dubbing made him look almost ridiculous in an ethnically connoted context, where other badly cast actors also seemed to hesitate between theatricality and an almost documentary, highly realistic acting style.

The Hatchet was highly criticised for this lack of consistency in the dramatic handling of the dense original story: it definitely should be reconsidered in terms of its very accurate and diversified filmic depiction of the Romanian ethnic puzzle, in the line of Ciulei's *Forest of the Hanged*. Victoria's vengeful journey includes discussions with Orthodox priests amidst prayers and choruses in a wonderful medieval monastery with perfectly kept biblical frescoes; a sale of her belongings to a Jewish merchant, David, who also introduces her to his Jewish wife and converses in Yiddish; a visit to an old Moldavian fortune-teller who reads from tarot cards; talks with Hungarians and Germans she comes across in Northern Moldavia (she asks whether they have seen her husband); and a typical funeral feast with a gargantuan meal preceding the disclosure of the murderer.

Fig 2. The monastery frescoes from *The Hatchet*

The film adopts the ethno-mythical tone of Sadoveanu's story, and the natural environment becomes a character, as Lipan constantly dreams about it, questions it and refers to it. The fatal revelation of the announced murder also has a wonderful winter setting as sole witness. It is marred by Maurice le Roux's far too intrusive score, yet another Italian production requirement (Rîpeanu 2004: 165).

As in the other East European emerging 'film waves', new kinds of films were released offering a non-schematic perception of contemporary topics. Incidentally, these films were released more or less in the same year: they include Andrei Blaier's *Diminețile unui băiat cuminte* (*Mornings of a Sensible Youth*, Andrei Blaier, 1966), *Meandre* (*Meanders*, Mircea Săucan, 1966) and *Un film cu o fată fermecătoare* (*This Charming Girl*, Lucian Bratu, 1966). Supposed emotional dramas such as the mediocre *Gioconda fără surîs* (*Gioconda Without That Smile*, Malvina Urșianu, 1967), which was praised by domestic critics as one of the first films made by a female director, were infested with post-Stalinist catchphrases and featured usually gifted performers acting in an unbearably artificial way.[3]

Mornings of a Sensible Youth, the first auteur film after some mediocre commercial products by young director Andrei Blaier, avoids the 'work site' stereotype in a quite interesting way. The film's main character, Vive, was played by Dan Nuțu, still a student at the time; he subsequently became Romania's paradigmatic 'angry young man' on stage and screen over more than a decade.[4] Vive initially works as a welder but suddenly refuses to stick to 'socialist integration'; he is reluctant to deal with the responsibilities of real life and prefers to follow his own atypical path. Some kind of light-heartedness characterises Vive and his friends: they reunite at street corners and in record shops in a very casual way, separate, and meet again without entering 'serious' relationships or engaging in moral debates. Audiences also witness scenes never shown onscreen before: violent quarrels between old-fashioned parents and their emancipated children, suicide attempts and even the death of an old factory worker addicted to alcohol. Echoing a Czech New Wave classic on the same theme, Evald Schorm's *Návrat ztraceného syna* (*The Return of the Prodigal Son*, 1966), the film features freeze frames and blurred images, jazz music, voice-overs and elliptical montage.

Part of the first generation of theatre and film school graduates from the late 1950s, Lucian Pintilie is the author of the highly modernist and sophisticated *Duminică la ora şase* (*Sunday at Six*, 1965) and of Romania's essential contribution to the cinema of the 1960s, *Reconstituirea* (*Reconstruction*, 1969). Pintilie's entire filmic output will receive close scrutiny in a chapter entirely dedicated to him.

The name of Mircea Săucan is less familiar than Pintilie's to both domestic and foreign audiences. Yet he was a product of the short-lived Romanian Thaw, as he directed two very daring, highly atypical films in the late 1960s and early 1970s, *Meanders* (1967) and *Suta de lei* (*One Hundred Lei*, 1973). These were first accepted, though largely transformed, then heavily censored and ultimately shelved, leading to Săucan's subsequent exile to Israel in the early 1980s. A film about missed meetings, *Meanders* obviously lacks coherent story value, undoubtedly because it has been cut and revised many times. An adulterous triangle features a mature intellectual woman, Anda (Margareta Pogonat), who refuses to follow her initial feelings for ex-partner Petru (Mihai Pălădescu) and returns to reason, as represented by her elder second husband, Constantin (Ernest Maftei). The younger generation, represented by her stepson Gelu and his girlfriend Lia (Dan Nuţu and Ana Széles), proves less dependent on moral constraints. The adults act and speak very artificially and the audience will have difficulties in distinguishing between the poetic realm and the allegedly real situations. The style is however highly modernist: the film was conceived as an audio-visual elegy, including chiaroscuro lighting effects and discontinuous editing via jump-cuts. There are embedded lyrical interludes featuring mysterious horses with an atonal musical background. Săucan obviously favoured art for art's sake: he filmed dancers on the train platform, couples revolving in bizarre architectural settings, youngsters erring on the beach at dawn, and so on. Foreign critics who had the opportunity to see the film drew comparisons with Alain Resnais's modernist films (Rîpeanu

2004:143). *Meanders* was briefly shown at different intervals during the late 1960s and early 1970s but only within the domestic sphere: its international premiere only took place after 1989.

The 1960s obviously offered the Romanian film industry a unique opportunity to develop and diversify, thanks to the considerable increase in film production, the establishment of a National Film Archive, the emergence of a monthly film journal, the generalisation of professional training in all related areas and, last but not least, the possibility to team up with West European partners. Unfortunately this period was very brief and soon directors and screenwriters had to find alternative ways to avoid censorship for obscure, often absurd, reasons.

CHAPTER 3

Romanian Cinema in the 1970s

Versatility on the Menu

THE OFFICIAL LINE: GENRE FILMS WITH A NATIONALIST FLAVOUR

The end of the Romanian Thaw – which lasted less than a decade – was characterised by two events. On the one hand it was specified in the 10th Party Congress Report in August 1969 that the new society would be superior to capitalist societies from all perspectives, overtly criticising former established contacts with the Western world. On the other, after a trip to China and North Korea in May 1971, Ceauşescu was highly tempted to introduce methods of indoctrination used by Mao's Cultural Revolution. The politicised media thus initiated the publication of the famous July 1971 Theses. Liberalisation movements were contained and a personality cult was installed, so as to consolidate Ceauşescu's position as a unique Communist leader among those active in the East European bloc (Tismaneanu 2003: 206).

Film, more than any other cultural field, had to align itself to this new line. Thematic and structural changes were most perceptible in the historical sub-genre and in productions inspired by ideologically related past and present topics. Two main concepts dominated the Romanian cultural context. The first stressed Romania's territorial continuity since time immemorial. The slogan 'We have been here for two thousand years' lasted for more than a decade and infested all cultural domains from literature to film, including poetry, song, dance and painting. The second insisted on the fact the Romanian artist was meant to create works with strong political/ideological connotations.

The July theses also brought the obligation of setting up ideological standards among critics, writers and filmmakers active in the field. Such debates could be read in the *Cinema* monthly; reconsidering them with a fresh view leaves a terribly bitter aftertaste, as most of the artists involved used an incredibly neo-Stalinist jargon. Thus, on the occasion of a round table about the necessity of creating political films, one can read about the climate of stimulating responsibility and of relevant requirements which pervaded during the last meeting between artists and 'our Secretary General, Comrade Nicolae Ceaușescu' and about 'all kinds, all genres of films, be they historical or about contemporary issues, needing to attain the status of political films'.[1]

As was the case during the 1960s, two cinematic trends co-existed during the 1970s, developing this time not within one single system (Centrala România Film, subordinate to the Ministry of Culture) but divided between seven film studios, within four separate 'production houses' (Stoil 1982: 53). An official trend in accordance with the Party line included genre films, historical epics and adaptations, innocent comedies, the anti-fascist thrillers mentioned earlier and films formatted for children and/or adolescents. A more peripheral trend focused both on heritage films and on films with more daring contemporary topics. Alongside established filmmakers, this trend showcased a new generation of fresh graduates from the IATC (National Film and Theatre Institute) which would prove pivotal in the next years: Dan Pița, Mircea Veroiu, Stere Gulea and Dinu Tănase.

The handling of storyline and dialogue within the official line had one common denominator: the figure of one of the few professional screenwriters, Titus Popovici. Popovici, yet another example of longevity in the Romanian film industry, started writing for the cinema in the late 1950s (co-adapting with Iliu *The Mill of Good Luck*) and managed to stay on until the early 1990s. His case is intriguing because it proves, once again, to what point directors, and implicitly audiences, were manipulated by the tenants of the regime's cultural brainwashing strategies. Two major achievements by Popovici for the official line have marked the Romanian 1970s and, to a lesser extent, the following decades in very ambiguous ways. The first was a prestige historical epic about an essential national hero, *Mihai Viteazul/Michael the Brave* (1970; alternative title *The Last Crusade*), the most expensive Romanian film in the Communist era, directed by Sergiu Nicolaescu, the same genre maverick who had started the *peplum* Cinecitta revival with *The Dacians* in the late1960s.

The film deals with a brief period of national history (1593–1601) when Prince Mihai started a war of liberation against Ottoman domination and managed to momentarily unite three provinces that are now part of Romania – Wallachia, Moldavia and Transylvania – before being murdered. Hollywood-scale production statistics include the production period (two years), the number of locations (many regions of Romania, Persia, Istanbul, Rome and Vienna), the number of extras (30,000), and the number of actors and stunt-men (250 and 200, respectively). A four-hour spectacular in two parts, echoing Sergei Bondarchuk's Soviet epics from the same period, it reveals very impressive camerawork, shot in beautiful Eastman colour, large-scale set pieces and a dazzling array of period costumes. However, the screenplay appears quite simplistic, heavy-handed and artificial in terms of dialogue, while crowd scenes are often covered by Tiberiu Olah's pompous score, including choral ensembles. Good actors deliver rather theatrical performances with sentences that seem to come directly out of history manuals. A huge Romanian box-office hit, *The Last Crusade* was highly acclaimed by Ceaușescu and became the model for the new nationalist epic trend, to be perpetuated by directors such as Doru Năstase, Malvina Urşianu and Constantin Vaeni. As Anne Jäckel notes in an essay, *The Last Crusade* 'fully endorses the idea of the Daco-Roman continuity' argued for by the July 1971 theses (Jäckel 2006: 77). Sergiu Nicolaescu was at that time an important Party official for Romania Film and managed to set up a deal with Columbia-Warner, dubbing the film into English and distributing it in forty countries and on eighteen TV channels. As in many other genre films he directed during the next three decades, Nicolaescu played a role in the film, that of a Turkish *pasha*.[2]

The other major achievement by screenwriter Popovici undoubtedly was *Puterea şi Adevărul* (*The Power and the Truth*, 1972), directed by Manole Marcus and considered a pioneering political masterpiece among governing ideologists and critics alike. Recent Romanian sources reveal that Popovici was asked to write a semi-autobiographical story first staged as a play that would evoke the itinerary, combats and achievements of Ceaușescu in a codified way (Rîpeanu 2005: 41). The hero supposed to impersonate him, activist Duma (Ion Besoiu), stood for the new generation of Communist leaders, whose mentality proved less rigid than that of the first hard-line Stalinist defenders. As a matter of fact he often challenged his superior within the Party hierarchy, Stoian, inspired by the figure of Gheorghiu Dej and played by imposing actor Mircea Albulescu, a kind of Romanian Marlon Brando with a lot of masculine charisma and a stentorian voice. Dej was presented as a womaniser whose behaviour is quite brash. He rejected the line represented by the first hero of illegal Communism,

Lucreţiu Pătrăşcanu, who was falsely accused of treason, sent to prison and murdered. Amza Pellea played Pătrăşcanu's equivalent, Petre Petrescu.

The Power and the Truth could be seen as a sequel to *The Valley Resounds* twenty years later, the former a vibrant hymn to Dej and Lenin, the latter a clear tribute to Ceauşescu and his trajectory. The celebrated hero is now part of a new society, which seemingly refuses the personality cult and opts for a collective consensus, a bridge between several experienced generations of Communists. Thus, entire parts of the film, suffused with Tiberiu Olah's far too emphatic film score, consist of newsreel inserts and flashbacks evoking the advent of nationalised enterprises and of numerous building sites swarming with enthusiastic workers. As in most East European and Soviet-era war epics and revivals, the scenes depicting attacks, factory arson and crimes perpetrated by the malevolent old regime were shot in a very realistic way.

What is interesting to note is that at different moments in the film, physical violence is laid bare and there is a refusal to water down situations that had never been shown this way before. The dialogue written by Popovici is much more straightforward then in any other ideological film from that period, while still remaining very orthodox. Intimate moments and erotic subtexts are also revealed in unexpected ways. Thus, at the party thrown by Stoian/Albulescu for Duma's wedding to a very charming young girl (Irina Gărdescu, supposedly standing for young Elena Ceauşescu), Stoian is openly flirting and dancing with the bride. The music they are dancing to sounds like some kind of Luis Mariano-like Romanian crooner, whose translated lyrics are: 'Senorita, your body is a feline snake / Your breasts are a sublime treasure'.

Nonetheless, the film's most spectacular sequence is an embedded *mise en abyme*. During an official meal, a very young girl proudly wearing her pioneer uniform[3] recites a patriotic poem in front of an audience, which includes a costumed Santa Claus invited to join the different party officials. One of them, presumably drunk, suddenly asks for a gun and simulates shooting ('Poc, poc'). A small boy dressed as a pioneer takes away the gun from him, saying: 'Give me the gun, uncle, I want to kill the enemy of our class'; he then shoots for good and almost kills somebody accidentally.

Romanians were fascinated by this hole in the censorship curtain that allowed them to learn, among other things, how Communist leaders were selected, how specific lodgings that belonged to the bourgeoisie were allotted to them and how their wives were carefully chosen according to strict ideological criteria. No wonder the ending to such a comprehensive fresco needed to be highly demonstrative, a stereotyped triumphalism, with a long shot revealing the open road to the creation of bright socialism.

Some hybrid genre films from the 1970s, mid-way between the official and the peripheral trends, were barely shown in festivals during the 1970s and had very limited distribution outside the East European circuit. Other genre films, such as thrillers directed by director for all seasons Nicolaescu including *Cu mîinile curate* (*With Clean Hands*, 1972) and *Ultimul cartuş* (*The Last Bullet*, 1973) and children's films and comedies such as the highly popular *Păcală* (Geo Saizescu, 1974), fared well on the national level but had little if any impact on the real evolution of Romanian film. Musicals, more than animated cartoons or television shows, clearly represented a sub-genre East European film industries had difficulties in handling, given the unusually high production costs involved in such projects.

The Romanian exception was Elisabeta Bostan, a key figure in the world of film for and about children and later an appreciated film teacher. She started her career in the late 1950s with documentaries and short films conceived as films of bestsellers for children, gaining national and somehow also international acclaim. In the early 1970s, Bostan made her most famous musical triptych, *Veronica* (1972) and its sequel *Veronica se întoarce/Veronica Is Back* (1973) followed by *Ma-ma/Rock 'n' Roll Wolf* (1974), a co-production involving Romania, the USSR and France, which still fascinates the audience every time it is shown on domestic television. Both *Veronicas* have aged and seem a bit dated to a present-day audience: purposefully nationalistic scenes are meant to showcase Romanian folklore, while a quite unconvincing little girl with an unpleasantly shrill voice is projected into a world of magic, where animals sing and dance. *Ma-ma* is on the contrary extremely watchable in terms of narrative content and style, featuring beautifully choreographed ballets on the set and on ice and quite inventive songs. The storyline is based on the Romanian classic by Ion Creangă, a variant of the Brothers Grimm tale about the big bad wolf and the seven goats. The wolf is plotting to kidnap the goat's children for a bag of gold while she goes to the fair. Her children have been told not to open the door, but one of them disobeys as he also wants to visit the fair, so everything goes wrong. The mother needs justice to be done and the wolf to be caught and roughly punished for his deeds. The Soviet contribution is quite outstanding. The two main parts, the mother (Ludmila Gurchenko) and the wolf (Mikhail Boyarsky), act very convincingly, acrobatic dances are close to rock 'n' roll, and ravishing special effects delight the eye. The French contributed some inspired musical score (by Gérard Bourgeois).[4] However, the major work comes from Bostan herself: by having the film co-scripted by a

Russian and a Romanian, she managed to harmoniously combine casts from two different countries and cultures. There are quite a lot of singing children and Romanian theatre and vaudeville stars (e.g. Florian Pittiş as the parrot and George Mihăiţă as Petrika the donkey) who perform highly inspired musical numbers.

As might be expected, there were very few melodramas in the Romanian production of the 1970s: the pathetic vein had nothing glorious to showcase and losers, whether men or women, were not well regarded. An exception was *Drum în penumbră* (*Through Dusky Ways*, 1972) by Lucian Bratu, written by Petru Popescu. The latter, a modernist poet and writer, had only one screenplay produced in Romania before he fled to the USA and started working in Hollywood. The subject he imagined is quite daring and unusual. A man and a woman in their forties meet during a brief late summer vacation on the Black Sea. They fall in love without knowing much about each other and meet again in their daily life, but special circumstances finally prove their relationship has no future, so they eventually part. Compared to films dealing with similar topics in neighbouring Eastern Bloc countries, the film clearly lacks homogeneity and seems to have suffered from some drastic cuts, as confirmed by recent exegesis (Rîpeanu 2005: 52). However, more than half of the picture has no ideological or moral message to deliver, just intimate moments on the beach, in restaurants and in hotel rooms, in the line of Claude Lelouch's *Un homme et une femme* (*A Man and a Woman*, 1965). Monica (Margareta Pogonat) and Radu (Cornel Coman) refuse to reveal anything to each other about their past life, indulging in a transitory existence which almost contradicts the principles of Communist destinies.

The melodramatic strain is palpable during the second half of the film, when Monica, after refusing to give her phone number to Radu, is found by him and eventually reveals the realities of her daily life. A typist for university staff members and exhausted by her routine work, she is divorced and shares her small flat with two spoiled teenage children and an exasperating mother. She is unable to sort out her two lives, constantly hesitating between her love for Radu and her duties as a working mother in a hostile environment. Fate knocks on her door after a visit to an eccentric female friend (Ileana Stana Ionescu), who tells her fortune from a coffee cup, a typically Romanian superstition. She has a car accident while driving at night to meet Radu, and her ailing mother dies at home during her absence. Another melodramatic twist throws a young soldier into her path, during the most poetic scene in the film, echoing Agnès Varda's *Cléo de 5 à 7* (1962). A few hours later, the camera reveals her head dozing on the soldier's shoulder inside a bus: Monica steps down hastily and runs back home. After her mother's funeral she has a last discussion with Radu at the cemetery and realises he won't be able to cope with her complex existence, so she leaves him. The ending is definitely an unorthodox one.

Actorul si sălbaticii (*The Actor and the Savages*, Manole Marcus, 1974) is a rare example of a musical biopic focusing on a critical moment in recent Romanian history. Indeed, the character depicted in the film, famous actor and vaudeville theatre director Constantin Tănase, was at the peak of his career during the right-wing pro-fascist years and died just one year after the Soviet occupation. Toma Caragiu, probably the best comic actor of the Romanian scene of the early 1970s, plays him in the film.[5] Official line screenwriter Titus Popovici clearly changed facts from Tănase's life to fit the Communist requirements: in real life Tănase was not so critical about the pro-fascists as he was of the Russians, lampooning them in sketches and rhyming lines that became famous. In the film, Caratase is a declared anti-fascist, performing virulent sketches that will almost cost him his life. The film constantly alternates moments of comedy in the best Romanian comic tradition with pure vaudeville musical interludes. Composer George Grigoriu and choreographer Cornel Patrichi mix modern music and dance with jazz and swing standards of the 1940s in a manner highly reminiscent of Bob Fosse's *Cabaret* (1972).

There is also an ideological subtext made up by Popovici so as to highlight the plague represented by the nationalistic and anti-Semitic elements of the Iron Guard. Caratase, though famous and protected by high-ranking authorities, receives constant threats both from the King's messengers and from Iron Guard 'tough guys'. His Jewish lyricist Ionel Fridman (Mircea Albulescu) is beaten and harassed, but manages to write the Santa Claus sketch Caratase will perform before almost dying onstage of a heart attack. This contrived version of historical facts is symptomatic of Communist-era falsifications and has little in common with the real Tănase. However, the film's final sketch, written by Dan Mihăiescu and Grigore Pop, is an anthology piece of vaudeville. Caratase, dressed as Santa Claus, makes his appearance while a glockenspiel plays 'Silent Night' in the background. One notices that he is wearing the Nazi uniform under his Christmas attire, and he is quickly surrounded by a group of young men.

'Guten Abend meine Liebe Kinder Kamarade' says he; 'Heil, Crăciun, Führer' (*Crăciun* means *Christmas* in Romanian) is their salute to him. He then identifies each boy dressed in German *lederhosen* (playing trousers). The text plays upon words and combines Romanian and German, creating brilliant puns such as 'Ich adus pușculițen', which initially means 'I have brought moneyboxes'. But the word 'pușculiță' is also the dimininutive for a gun: the

Fig 3. *The Actor and the Savages*:
Caratase as a Nazi Santa Claus

boys all like the rifles and simulate shooting, while Santa Claus invites them to sing other special carols and to play hide and seek. The second time they shoot it is for real.

The film confronts us with an interesting editing counterpoint in the best thriller tradition: at the same moment a hired killer from the audience points at Caratase, he is prevented from doing so by police inspector Toma (Mircea Diaconu). Santa quickly abandons his disguise to portray a vicious caricature of Hitler, wearing a moustache and constantly giving orders in military cadence. He wishes much happiness to Romania, explaining that 'we Germans' take all the assets from the country and give all cities German names. Caragiu sounds like a political spokesman when he finally takes off his second disguise and addresses both the audiences: 'You've laughed / I'm glad you did / It's a good thing to laugh, about ridiculous savages / When I'm dead you need to keep laughing / But maybe laughter is not enough / You need to stop them / They want to sell our country to Hitler and turn it into a concentration camp / Stop the green plague if you want to go on laughing'. Then he collapses and almost dies of a heart condition. Film fiction clearly becomes a complex vehicle, both entertaining and didactic, true to the spirit of the transitional 1970s and to the official line. Caragiu has a real Shakespearian stature; his versatile changes in tone and mode proved he could impersonate almost anyone. It is high time foreign audiences became more familiar with his pivotal though brief contribution to Romanian film and theatre.[6]

EXPERIMENTS IN DOCU-FICTION AND HERITAGE FILM ADAPTATIONS

The peripheral trend's ringleaders from the 1970s were Mircea Veroiu and Dan Piţa (to whom a separate chapter will be dedicated), co-authors of *Apa ca un bivol negru* (*Water Like a Black Buffalo*, 1970), a remarkable semi-documentary manifesto.[7] Actually a collective project set up by final year students from different sub-sections of the Romanian Film and Theatre Institute, the film's credits also feature other young directors and screenwriters such as Andrei Cătălin Băleanu, Petre Bokor (documentary director), Youssouf Aidabi (Ethiopian film student), Stere Gulea (film director), Roxana Pană (film critic), Iosif Demian (cinematographer and future director), Dinu Tănase (cinematographer) and Nicolae Mărgineanu (additional camera operation). The main idea sticks to the general line of a documentary, but its treatment is much closer to devices used in fiction films: several crews decide and are authorised to record on film the terrible consequences of the disastrous floods which affected different regions of Romania. In May 1970 the water levels of some rivers in Transylvania began to rise in a worrying manner: 160 people died in the town of Lipova and rainwaters overwhelmed 1,445 houses.

Water Like a Black Buffalo (subtitled *Of Men and Waters*, May 1970) is a rare jewel, cinema at its best with a running time of less than one hour. In interior sequences echoing Agnès Varda's 'snapshot' technique from *Daguerrotypes* (1974), survivors of the catastrophe address the camera in frontal shots and freeze-frame family portraits. Their voices are heard commenting on images more often *off* than *on* screen, so that their personal misfortunes, handed over from one sequence to the other, gradually turn into a big collective assessment. A superstitious old woman asks 'why God has brought such a misfortune': she actually provides the key to the film's title, explaining that 'the water came over like a wild beast, some kind of buffalo', while we are watching sepia images

of floods at dusk. Another peasant's story is interrupted by a girl's tale of the floods: she is briefly shown on a see-saw at different moments in the film, providing some visual rhyme.

The film inevitably but sparingly features comments with ideological hints: thus a marble name plate indicates that all this was done thanks to Comrade Nicolae Ceauşescu, Romania's Secretary General. The setup changes from one region to another, with shots of poverty-stricken people

Fig 4. A visual rhyme in
Water Like a Black Buffalo

living in makeshift houses. In some places only the house walls are left, such that people admit their life is almost over since they have lost everything. The film ends with images of young boys passing bricks from one to another, suggesting the people's willingness to rebuild the future amongst ruins.

Water Like a Black Buffalo also offers moments of elaborate lyricism, with repeated tracking shots in a corn field and a strikingly vivid rendering of flooded roads, trees, houses and men from all generations. The camera becomes an all-encompassing mirror, revealing a universe transformed by wild waters. Besides unusually complex editing strategies, the film features a soundtrack that alternates musical quotations from Bach or Albinoni with very realistic sound effects, including an unidentified deafening noise. The chromatic scheme is also polymorphous, oscillating between shades of sepia, black-and-white and full colour. According to the Romanian retrospective catalogue edited in 2000 by the Trieste Film Festival, the film was criticised and partly censored: 'Too human to be appreciated by the censors, *Water like a Black Buffalo* was criticised for paying too much attention to aesthetics and had to undergo some changes. A section was added to the film's opening scenes, which showed the positive aspects of the environmental disaster: the reconstruction of a condominium dedicated to Nicolae Ceauşescu' (Grmek Germani 2000: 188).[8]

Nunta de piatră (*Stone Wedding*, 1971) by the Piţa/Veroiu duo is an adaptation of two short stories, *Fefeleaga* and *La o nuntă* (*At a Wedding*), by Transylvanian writer Ion Agârbiceanu. An impoverished widower who has already mourned the loss of two of her children, Fefeleaga (played by acclaimed theatre actress Leopoldina Bălănuţă) works hard in the Western Carpathians goldmine region of Roşia Montana to support her only daughter, who happens to be terminally ill. When the latter dies, her mother symbolically puts her to earth, in a wedding dress she has painstakingly managed to buy after selling her only horse. Fefeleaga is a Greek tragedy character, silently following her predetermined path and accepting her fate without resentment, fully aware one cannot fight destiny in the line of the paradigmatic shepherd from the quintessential *Mioritza* ballad. Her life seems to be a series of mechanically performed duties, cyclical movements and routines. As in the ballad, the heroine portrays her daughter's passing away as a marriage with the natural surroundings. The soundtrack further sustains this symbolic undercurrent, each natural sound being foregrounded. A kind of equivalent of a voice-over commentary on the event is provided by different choral occurrences, a capella songs by Dorin Liviu Zaharia: conceived as ballads, these songs contain both a foretelling and a confirmation of Fefeleaga's tragic fate:

Under the dragon's sky
At the ravine brink
Having no one in the world
Blind and nameless only her horse listens to her
(Töke 2006: 132)

Fig 5. Fefeleaga and her horse in *Stone Wedding*

Romanian critics from the 1970s have argued that the storyline is too minimalistic and does not go beyond day-to-day gestures and physiognomies (Potra 1979: 143). Paradoxically, here lies the film's power and originality, particularly for 1970s Romania, in a context where artificial, imposed dialogue lines had been prevailing for the last twenty years. The tableau, pictorial, silent-cinema-like quality of the interior but mostly exterior location shots serves the depiction of highly evocative landscapes, stone walls, water mills, deserted hills and tortuous medieval city streets.

The acknowledgment of an anticipated death re-appears in the second part, At a Wedding, but this time the scope is rather collective: this part deals with the sacrifice of a well-to-do musician having to face the savagery of participants at an arranged wedding. The opening long shot shows a bunch of soldiers on a deserted hill, one of whom proves a deserter. The latter meets a musician on his way to a wedding and proposes to accompany him. Mircea Diaconu is the soldier, a strong personality full of wit and candour, and Radu Boruzescu, the film's set decorator, plays the musician. The couple of newly-weds (played by Ursula Nussbacher and George Calboreanu Jr.) are welcomed by a group of peasants reciting another rhymed popular poem about an arranged marriage, the film thus re-assessing the importance of oral tradition. The wedding looks more like a funeral, with guests eating in silence, until the musicians arrive and one of them falls for the bride. In a significant mise en abyme sequence, the soldier puts on a marriage veil and sings an anticipatory ballad about an eloping bride. The police catch and kill the deserter. The musician leaves the place and takes the bride along at dawn, framed in a wonderful long shot. Says the inner sung voice: 'My wedding was not a maiden's / Our guests seemed turned to stone'.

For Lilla Töke, the film is constructed around significant binary symbolism. The most obvious is the repeated coupling of the themes of death and wedding. Life and death, wedding and bereavement are inextricably connected. The young lovers may escape, but this happens in parallel with the innocent soldier's demise. The wedding clearly is one of the key tropes of Balkan cinema (Töke 2006: 133). Only eight copies of the film circulated within the domestic distribution circuit, while around 400,000 people saw it: the average number of copies for a film was about twenty. This proved once more the lack of confidence the state-subsidised film industry had in the art-house cinema (Rîpeanu 2005: 38).

The same duo that made Stone Wedding directed another set of adaptations of Agârbiceanu. The shooting of Duhul aurului (Lust for Gold, 1974) started in 1971 at approximately the same time as Stone Wedding, but the film only came out in 1974, with a few additional scenes: there was never any explanation for the delay. The plotline for both stories (Mîrza and Lada/The Chest) centres around the lust for gold in a region where its discovery, exploitation and trade have been common practice for centuries. Agârbiceanu is part of a writers' lineage including the already discussed Slavici and Rebreanu. Most of his short stories made ideal subjects for films. In the first story, the climactic scene is the capture by the police of Mîrza, the main hero, after a long pursuit perfectly orchestrated around the steep cliffs of the region. Underplaying characterises the performances. The film was shot on location, like *Stone Wedding*, in the Apuseni Mountains, in the same district of Roşia Montana, and Iosif Demian produced some very sophisticated and stylish black-and-white photography. There is a very elaborate set design, close to photographic tableaux, again by Boruzescu and Stürmer. Many reframed, embedded frontal long shots stress the importance of this type of staging, not present elsewhere in Romanian cinema.

The Chest, directed by Piţa, contains naturalist elements echoing Emile Zola or Frank Norris. It focuses on an old widower (Ernest Maftei), who is sought by young girls for his alleged fortune, kept in a mysterious big chest. The chest is actually full of heavy stones, and each young bride dies while trying hard to open it: the old husband outlives all his victims. In a macabre irony, the first epilogue shows the widower proudly hanging all his wedding portraits, one next to the other. This device resembles the rhetorical trope called 'chiasmus', as every wife who thought to bury and inherit from the older husband eventually became his victim.[9]

Felix şi Otilia (*Felix and Otilia*, Iulian Mihu, 1971) is a three-hour heritage adaptation quite different from other stiff, didactic and neo-nationalistic historical films. George Călinescu's source novel *The Secret of Otilia* is the story of an unresolved romance between Felix (Radu Boruzescu) and Otilia (Julieta Szöny), who prefers the material comfort offered by Papadopol (Sergiu Nicolaescu).[10] The other characters corresponding to authentic landowners and petty bourgeois upstart types are well played by experienced character actors such as Gheorghe Dinică as Stănică Raţiu, the latter playing the unscrupulous lawyer who steals the family's remaining fortune. Some dialogue is surprisingly uncensored, displaying a liberty in tone and content. The film remains a landmark in terms of set and costume design, by Miruna and Radu Boruzescu. The stylish, refined settings are highlighted by the graph-colour technique used by cinematographers Gheorghe Fischer and Alexandru Întorsureanu, with almost Méliès-like chromatic impacts. Thus, a very unusual sequence includes a cinema session with excerpts from a colonial film, followed by a slapstick clip and later on by a quite interesting comment about the miracle of film as an incipient art. The highly melodramatic ending unfolds during World War I, when all characters meet again in tragic circumstances, when it is too late for them to reunite.

Mircea Veroiu's *Dincolo de pod* (*Beyond the Bridge*, 1976) is an accomplished adaptation of *Mara*, yet another important novel by Ioan Slavici. The film was conceived in a much lower key than the novel. The story of Mara (Leopoldina Bălănuţă), a strong-willed widower who backs up her daughter Persida (Maria Ploae), eventually estranged and abused by German-born husband Hans (Andrei Finţi), is rather peripheral, leaving room for a lot of additional material.

The Hungarian reign over Transylvania, with a purely Romanian popula-tion fighting to strengthen its position before the 1848 revolution, had been a long-standing reality. The film reveals that German and Hungarian-born retailers and landowners had a much greater advantage in terms of social and religious status. Although the subject is socially and ethnically relevant, Veroiu does not always manage to sustain its topicality, especially in the second part of the film, with exaggerated slow-motion scenes of killing between ethnic Transylvanians and Romanians. Filmed on location in the pivotal medieval sur-roundings of Sighişoara, the film does feature outstanding cinematography by Călin Ghibu, with Vermeer-like visual compositions. One example is the opening point-of-view shot from the monastery window from which a nov-ice, Sida, is watching Hans, her future husband.[11] There is also good acting from the usual stock of actors coming from theatre: Bălănuţă as the title hero-ine Mara, expressive Irina Petrescu as Catholic Mother Aegidia, Ion Caramitru as priest Codreanu, and famous theatre actor Petre Gheorghiu as a money-hungry neighbour. Though physically attractive, the main heroes, Sida and Hans Huber, are unconvincing in their parts. The unaccomplished quality of some scenes is probably due to Veroiu's wanting to focus on too many sit-uations. However, most Romanian critics considered the film 'a great event' and stressed Veroiu's unusually personal contribution to a modernist, more socially oriented adaptation of a classic (Căliman 2000: 248).

Mircea Veroiu further specialised in visually arresting adaptations through-out the late 1970s and the early 1980s (*Intre oglinzi paralele/Between Facing Mirrors*, 1978, from a novel by Camil Petrescu, *Adela*, 1985, inspired by the work of Garabet Ibrăileanu). He also directed a powerful war drama, *Să mori rănit din dragoste de viaţă* (*To Die Wounded by Love for Life*, 1983). After a brief period of French exile, he returned to Romania in the early 1990s and died pre-maturely, but unfortunately his last films have not stood the test of time.

Înainte de tăcere (*Before There Was Silence*, 1978), Alexa Visarion's debut feature after a good start in the theatre, is probably one of the best heritage adaptations from the 1970s. A very inspired reworking of a famous Ion Luca Caragiale naturalistic novella, *În vreme de război/In Times of War*, it takes place during the Independence War against Turkish domination. A psychological drama develops within the limits of a family triangle, allowing outstanding acting performances: Stavrache (Liviu Rozorea) the innkeeper, his brother Iancu (Ion Caramitru), an ex-priest turned burglar, and Ana (Valeria Seciu), the innkeeper's wife coveted by both of them. After falling in love with her brother-in-law, Ana learns he has died on the front but refuses to accept the idea: she becomes obsessed with him and oscillates between realistic daydreams and nocturnal hallucinations. She gives birth to a stillborn child and gradually becomes more and more distant and aloof from her husband, who will end up mentally deranged. The main action is surrounded by interesting secondary plots involving war deserters tortured on a huge wheel, famine-stricken peasants asking for more liberties and a dumb 'fool of war', convincingly played by Mircea Diaconu. There are some unforgettable moments: the imaginary return of the dead brother who shares the marital bed and talks to the couple, and the scene where jealous Stavrache looks for his wife's broken necklace among the cows from the muddy barn. The film's general tone often echoes theatrical staging, despite frequent naturalistic outdoor scenes: chiaroscuro tableau-like shots with candle lighting, synaesthesia states enhanced by a challenging sound design, and so on. There is no additional music, only some authentic folklore purposefully sung in a false key.

Moromeții (*The Moromete Family*, 1987) was directed by Stere Gulea a decade later than the above-mentioned adaptations. However, it is an interesting adaptation of Marin Preda's *Moromeții*. His best-known novel redraws in two volumes published in 1955 and 1967 the dissolution of a peasant family. The story is inspired by the writer's father's life and takes place in the Danube plain a few years before World War II. Ilie Moromete has been married twice and has six children to support and deal with, in both the private and the public sphere. Land taxes accumulate and he and his family have to consistently fight an inflexible tax collector. The three elder sons do not get along with his new family and want to sell a plot of land so as to split the sum and start a new life in Bucharest, running away with the family's stolen horses. Moromete eventually sells the land and pays the tuition for his youngest son, Nicolae.[12]

Spectacular scenes are worth mentioning: in the presence of a dumbfounded crowd, a huge acacia tree is brought down by Ilie Moromete (Victor Rebengiuc), who needs to sell it. The episode is further inspired by an autobiographical short story Preda had published before his famous novel. Catrina (Luminița Gheorghiu), his second wife, is a devoted mother but also a caricature of a bigot, superstitious and pragmatic at the same time, capable of sudden tenderness and caustic humour. Nonetheless, playing real peasants is not an easy task: much of the dialogue sounds quite artificial, unnatural. Allusions to the ongoing military extremist dictatorship and different government issues are far-fetched and sound as unnatural as in all films from that period. Many scenes are devoid of any plot progression, consisting mainly of discussions among middle-aged peasants surrounding Moromete, who indulge in heavy drinking, swearing and loafing around: they do not seem very relevant to a non-Romanian audience. The film's second half and final part about the family tragedy of coveted land seem too long, with falsely pathetic domestic scenes, creating the same difficulties of comprehension for a foreign audience. The lyrically relevant ending, with Moromete leaving the countryside for the town with his young son in the midst of a barren land is a strong reminder of a similar scene from Ciulei's *The Forest of the Hanged*. The film is one of the few peasant movies in Romanian film history that could be labelled as anti-propagandistic. The story is an eternal one, its characters to be found nowadays in similar situations, the social system in the countryside not having changed a lot.[13]

STRANGE FOREBODINGS: DEVIANT EVERYDAY TOPICS ON FILM

Ceaușescu's obsession with industrialisation and the politics of austerity enhanced by his 1980 decision to pay the entire foreign debt, as well as his profound hostility to market-oriented reforms, led to the dramatic decline of living conditions and to the growth of collective discontent. Unorthodox initiatives in the field of external politics were meant to cover up from the West the growing domestic repression of the late 1970s. The economic situation worsened after 1975 and accelerated the country's economic and social decline. From 1972 onwards members of the Ministry of Culture regularly visited all cultural events: they provided indications and suggested changes. Theatre and film studios, concert and opera houses, and recording and publishing companies were also rigorously controlled. Screenplays were discussed and negotiated for months, sometimes years, such that the final results were disappointing because too many changes and compromises had been made. Many films were shelved or delayed waiting for changes to be completed. The ubiquity of censorship had serious consequences for artistic creation in general: on the one hand there was the constant temptation of self-censorship that drove gifted artists to give up sincerity. On the other, the same artists aimed at complicity with an audience whom they could satisfy by means of parabolic, encoded hints about the ongoing absurdist situation.

The plot of Mircea Săucan's second highly controversial film, *Suta de lei* (*One Hundred Lei*, 1973), focuses on the Cain/Abel relationship between Andrei Pantea, a successful Bucharest actor in film and TV (Ion Dichiseanu), and Petre, his younger brother (Dan Nuţu). Approached again by Săucan after *Meanders*, playwright Horia Lovinescu comes up with an allegorical, more real-istic screenplay than the one written for *Meanders* six years earlier: it reveals the hypocrisy of a counterfeit society in Communist times. Andrei the upstart has access to foreign alcohol and cigarettes. Petre, an occasional poet, has run away from home and refuses to go to university or get hired for a suitable job, preferring to loaf around, steal and ask for money from his brother. Besides, he has learned some puzzling things about his father, a high-ranking Communist official. After falling in love with one of his brother's female fans, Dora (Ileana Popovici), Petre is ready to commit suicide, following a last missed settlement with his brother.

There is the same concern with very elaborate avant-garde and experimen-tal audio-visual discourse as in *Meanders*. Images change and have a whole range of black-and-white shades, under- and over-exposed grain, freeze-frames and jump-cuts; authentic, unusually true-to-life dialogue alternates with voice-over poems, songs, recurring metaphors and TV broadcasts. The soundtrack assuredly is one of the most innovative of the Romanian 1970s: Săucan asked avant-garde composers Anatol Vieru and Richard Ochanitzky to produce an ensemble of musicalised noises, atonal clusters, recycled music from classical composers and ethnic music, thus establishing a double diegetic discourse.

The same censorship problems faced by *Meanders* arose for Săucan with *One Hundred Lei*, but the effects were far more devastating. Shooting started in 1972 and was finished quickly but was constantly delayed, because the director was obliged to make numerous changes and cuts (Rîpeanu 2005: 79). Thus, all references to foreign products had to disappear and the angry young brother had to be saved in the end. Some critics received the film in very severe terms, stressing the fact that the meaning of many scenes was totally unclear and vague, and this was highly frustrating in terms of viewer response. Săucan left Romania for Israel after a serious mental breakdown due to the failure of such a controversial project. A copy of the initial, uncut version was shown in 1990 in Bucharest and in European festivals over the world dur-ing retrospectives.

More than thirty years before Cristian Mungiu's ground-breaking *4 Months, 3 Weeks and 2 Days*, Andrei Blaier's *Ilustrate cu flori de câmp* (*Postcards with Flowers*, 1974), from his own screenplay, was probably the first Romanian film about an abortion and its tragic consequences. Opening images with ongo-ing credits are shown via binoculars, supposedly from a big merchandise ship in the Black Sea harbour region, with a working site in the proximity of the

Danube-Black Sea Channel. The same images will actually be part of the closing sequences, as if someone had told the story from the ship/cruiser, on an
occasional visit to this provincial town. This will be soon confirmed by the fact
that one of the film's main characters, Victor, is a sailor and will sail away at
the end. From the very beginning the narrative effectively presents three subplots by way of suspenseful cross-cutting means: 1) An ongoing provincial
wedding with lots of ethnic music, eating and chatting, and harsh, naturalistic
accents, the guests including a number of perverted upstarts; 2) The arrival
in town of Laura (Carmen Galin), a young girl victim of an adulterous affair
who explains right away to the young Irina (Elena Albu) that she has come to
have an abortion; and 3) The wanderings of Victor (Dan Nuţu), a young sailor
having left the wedding and spying on his ex-fiancée Irina, who is actually the
daughter of one of the midwives.

Irina's sinister mother (Eliza Petrăchescu) will serve as a link between the
three sub-plots, as she will come and go from one place to the other, pretending she is very concerned with the future victim of the abortion. The direction
stresses the naturalistic aspects of provincial 'hyenas', echoing scenes from
Pasolini's classic *Mamma Roma* (1961). Thus the second midwife, Draga
Olteanu, who specialised in vulgar, self-assured and cynical characters, is
heard uttering harsh comments about the imminent abortion: 'in two hours
we'll say bye-bye to this little thing, we just have to throw it out and forget
about it'.

Laura gets worse, turns pale and feverish, and finally dies. A first conclusion
shows Irina arriving at the wedding in despair, being caught in a frantic dance
and turned into a fake bride by her fiancé before breaking the news to the
abortionists. 'We're good for prison', the latter declare in a highly naturalistic
shot, where they are seen lying among stuffed birds. They will attempt to dis-
simulate the murder, burying the body in the dark during a sinister, barely lit
scene. Irina talks to Victor in a hotel room and tries to confess to the murder
but concludes by declaring that nobody can be trusted. Before committing
suicide, she sends a letter to Victor in which she reveals everything in a personal, utterly sincere testimony: 'what I did not have the courage to do, I leave
it to you. This crime should not remain unpunished. Please send me postcards
with flowers from all your trips.' When he reads the lines it is too late: the final
shot shows his almost immobile, confused face in a freeze-frame.

In his essay on the film's production, Rîpeanu notes that its ideological mission was more than transparent: reveal the tragic consequences of an illegal
abortion so as to reinforce the demographic politics honed by Ceauşescu, at a
moment when sanctions were extremely severe (Rîpeanu 2005: 86).

Films by women directors appear as exceptions in the Romanian film industry context. *Stop cadru la masă* (*Snapshot Around the Family Table*, 1979), directed by Ada Pistiner, is actually her first feature film after a career in documentary filmmaking. The film features an odd adulterous couple played by popular folk and variety singer Anda Călugăreanu (Nuşa) and Soviet film star Alexander Kaliaguin (Filip), dubbed in Romanian by a 'copy' of him in real life, character actor Marin Moraru. Explicit adulterous scenes occupy a large section of the narrative. Both mistress and wife are unusually real and touching, impersonating interesting alternatives for the same middle-aged, frustrated man. Wife Clara (Dorina Lazăr) seems totally unsophisticated, while Nuşa, the young architecture student, is more sarcastic and ironic. Closure inevitably brings the husband back home for a snapshot around the family supper. Heavy censorship seems to have been applied to the film, as apart from two or three kisses, no sex is shown. The film's general tone is close to that of a shelved female Soviet author from the 1960s, Kira Muratova. It was rated as 'a superb film' by the London National Film Theatre programme edited on the occasion of the Romanian Film Week in September 1981.

The first feature film by newcomer Alexandru Tatos, *Mere Roşii* (*Red Apples*, 1976) is a lighter, more comic variation on the cinema of 'moral concern' from the Romanian 1970s. A positive, unglamorous hero tries to change the world on a small, unspectacular scale, and manages to persuade the others and, implicitly, the audience that he is right. Mircea Diaconu is anti-conformist surgeon Mitică Irod, terribly fond of red apples and fighting against career-obsessed colleagues. The hospital milieu allows unexpected transgressions of the official line. A documentary-like immediacy reveals people and places with a lot more authenticity than most other films from the same decade.

However, the director's most outstanding achievement proved to be *Secvenţe* (*Sequences*, 1982): it was rated as fifth best in the 2008 Top Ten Romanian Films of all time and is considered a milestone for contemporary directors such as Cristi Puiu. The film is yet another variation on the same paradigm, that of 'revealing while filming'. There is also very realistic dialogue, an exception within a national production stuffed with artificial lines full of lies and exaggerations.

In his posthumously published *Diary*, Tatos explains how the sketch *Four Slaps* was filmed in eight days and was subsequently structured as a portmanteau project. Consisting of three episodes, each of which features the same characters and filming crew, the film was finally called *Sequences* and came out after numerous cuts and revisions. Numerous entries in his diary contain sentences of the type: 'Thank God, they accepted this new version', 'They finally agreed to leave it as I planned it', and so on (Tatos 1994: 330). The three episodes, *The Phone Call*, *The Restaurant* and *The Rehearsal*, are full of very interesting details of Romanian everyday life under Communism.

The film's intertextuality is unusually dense. Propagandistic newsreel footage is watched and commented on by the real director and crew of the film in a half-ironic, half-serious tone, and the image grain and type (16mm, Super 8, TV) is constantly shifting from one category to another. The crew is extra- and intra-diegetic: they both act in the fictionalised story and comment upon it as external witnesses. The film's opening shows a newsreel about 'August 23, A milestone in the history of our country', commented on by the voice of a newsreader who covered the news on Romanian Television for a long time. Then the director is heard detailing his script: 'our film has two periods, Matei's past as an illegal fighter and the present life of his children'.[14]

The Phone Call is about people queuing to make a phone call in a deserted bar, while others eavesdrop. Situational humour derives from issues relating to food shortage. Later on the director himself is seen giving directions. The events are inspired by the popular Romanian TV weekly programme *Reflector*, which had a mission to reveal everyday society problems via

Fig 6. The embedded newsreel from *Sequences*

direct interviews. In *The Restaurant*, the crew decides to continue shooting the story of the Socialist hero and embarks upon a bus journey to a remote destination. The main stopover is a restaurant run by Costel (Mircea Diaconu), the ordinary guy nobody cares for, who compensates for his lack of masculine charisma with a high dose of sarcastic humour. He is the half-cuckold, occasionally drunken husband, harassed by an unfaithful wife. Before leaving, the crew visits his apartment and discovers the wife (Luminiţa Gheorghiu) sitting shyly on the sofa, Diaconu explaining that he did not have the guts to chase her off. In a hilarious moment, the crew admires Costel's collection of pencil sharpeners. Everything looks quite miserable, revealing an economic situation Ceauşescu sought to hide and minimise for Western observers.

Four Slaps focuses on the shooting of a film called *Happiness*, about an illegal father hero who dies in prison, while his daughter is revealing the truth about his past. The film is a directorial *tour de force* here in terms of reflexive reframing of the action. As in Truffaut's *La nuit américaine* (*Day for Night*, 1973), Tatos gives precise indications to the actress playing the part of the daughter (Emilia Dobrin Besoiu), while different groups of actors chat in the wings. The camera shifts from one group to another and finally stops briefly to film a discussion between two old actors supposed to be stand-ins for an official dinner. One of them realises that the person sitting opposite him is in fact his prison torturer, but the latter refuses to admit it:

- How many years passed?
- A man's life, you don't recognise me, do you?
- How could I, I never knew you.
- Could be, I only recognised you because you do the same gesture with your handkerchief as you used to when you hit me in prison.

The torturer finally confesses: 'I only slapped you four times', a line that explains the film's first working title. Eventually, Tatos, who also plays the director, gets angry and tells the victim and his torturer to shut up because they are only props. The closing credits unfold with the camera revealing all levels of action by means of an all-encompassing crane shot.

CHAPTER 4

Dan Piţa
A Filmmaker for All Seasons

Though Dan Piţa's ground-breaking debut in docu-fiction as well as his films co-directed with Mircea Veroiu have been discussed earlier in relation to the peripheral trend of the 1970s, his polymorphous, almost paradoxical oeuvre does call for a separate chapter. Piţa remains an extremely interesting figure in the context of Romanian cinema. There are several reasons justifying this status. First, there is his unusual longevity: his career has spanned more than thirty years, starting in the early 1970s and continuing well into the first decade of the twenty-first century. Second, there is his highly versatile nature. He has approached and dealt with all cinematic genres: shorts (his final degree film *Viaţa în roz/Life in Pink*), important docu-fictions, realistic films dealing with everyday topics, heritage films, television series, Romanian-style westerns, encrypted (metaphorical) cinema and less inspired post-Communist natural-istic films on controversial topics.[1]

In terms of the contemporary zeitgeist, Piţa's *Filip cel Bun* (*Filip the Kind*, 1974) is probably one of the most comprehensive chronicles of Romanian city life on film. The screenplay is by Constantin Stoiciu, the author of *Mornings of a Reasonable Boy* (1966), made by Blaier ten years earlier. There are variations on the same *Bildungsfilm* theme: a young hero refuses to stick to society and family requirements and prefers to go his own way. Diverse layers of society are represented, in relation to the complex personality of unglamorous yet witty and engaging Filip (Mircea Diaconu). Stalinist times seem awkwardly close, though the action is set in the early 1970s. Deceptively sophisticated opening credits feature inserts of antiques and are backed by an eclectic musical score by Dorin Liviu Zaharia. The film's narrative immediately introduces us to Filip's everyday life. With the exception of the father, a factory employee, the members of this dysfunctional family seem either unemployed or busy doing some unofficial work at home.

Filip's refusal to follow the traditional university training path leads him to most unusual experiences, ranging from a tragicomic dog vaccination session in a deserted storehouse to an occasional job in a Communist market hall. The viewer thus has access to a bleak, miserable Romanian city life, where the black market is alive and flourishing and Communist mafiosi already constitute the most prosperous layers of society.[2] Despite his troubled professional life, Filip's love life is quite active: Angela, the girl he is dating, is played by the same fresh and juvenile Ileana Popovici from *One Hundred Lei*. Her female friends include occasional hookers who specialise in seducing Italians, the quintessential coveted Westerners in the 1970s. During a sequence that miraculously escaped censorship, Filip is seen having a drink in a restaurant with his father, while at the neighbouring table Angela's friends are questioned by the Romanian KGB, the much-feared *Securitate*. We overhear phrases such as: 'Do you still meet with that Italian guy', such activity usually leading to sanctions such as the rejection of applications for a passport for travelling abroad or getting specific jobs.

The film's conclusion was clearly imposed on Piţa and Stoiciu. After repeated visits to his father's factory followed by discussions in the demonstrative Stalinist line (e.g. 'Is this the kind of world you fought for, Father?'), Filip decides to integrate into the worker's community, leaving behind a more intellectualised, far-fetched universe where he does not seem to fit in. In what appears to be an open ending he packs up and leaves home on a bus for an allegedly brighter future. Recent sources mention that censor Dumitru Popescu from the Party's Central Committee dictated compulsory changes in the profile, focus and *dénouement* of the initial story (Rîpeanu 2005: 84).

Piţa's less accomplished *Tănase Scatiu* (*A Summer Tale*, 1976) was adapted from a very popular turn-of-the-century novel by Duiliu Zamfirescu, close to the spirit of Tolstoy. The main hero is a rough, violent, bad-mannered provincial upstart with Greek origins, who breaks up a sincere love story by imposing an arranged mismatch to a decaying landlord: he is eventually killed by rebellious peasants he was aiming to further exploit. As Scatiu, Victor Rebengiuc is perfect, while the other actors are often typecast or wrongly cast. Despite beautiful cinematography by future director Nicolae Mărgineanu, featuring pictorial compositions which echo paintings by classic nineteenth-century Romanian painters such as Nicolae Grigorescu and Theodor Aman, the action is highly non-naturalistic in places. Many sequences seem to have been censored, as dialogues are highly artificial, as if taken from a Communist history textbook.[3]

Dan Piţa directed and wrote the screenplay for *Concurs* (*Contest*, 1982), a film that was definitely part of the encrypted cinema trend. The film took two years to reach the country's screens, the orientation contest organised for a group of employees being a pretext for depicting a totalitarian society dominated by an absurdist bureaucracy, very much in the line of Czech New Wave director Jan Nemec's *O slavnosti a hostech* (*Report on the Party and the Guests*, 1967). As in Nemec's film, the woods are purposefully filled with traps. The participants lose control over their own situation to the point of not knowing who they are any longer. A closed universe in the Kafkaesque tradition is obviously ideal for proving to what point the individual is trapped, unable to go beyond the limits of an imposed territory: if he does not stick to the rules he might die, commit suicide, be eliminated or become a mere shadow. The young rebel, played by acting student Claudiu Bleonţ and nicknamed 'puştiul' (the kid), is unwilling to obey, a dissident at the periphery of society, unable to impose his own truth and perpetually ambiguous: he also heralds a final apocalyptic event.

The competition serves as a starting point for a fable-like narrative: the majority of participants are confronted by the young boy, who reveals all their shortcomings. The opening scene is quite breath-taking, featuring a tracking shot through a rain-filled path in the woods, very similar to shots revealing the flooded roads in *Water Like a Black Buffalo*. The kid, dressed in a flashy yellow raincoat, leads the way on his bike, sometimes offering mysterious looks towards the camera. Synthesised electronic music composed by regular Piţa collaborator Adrian Enescu perfectly fits the synaesthesia feeling of entering a strange world. Before the credits and the bike journey end, the figure of the East European paradigmatic white horse appears and catches up with the cyclist.

Fig 7. *Contest*: **the mysterious boy with a bike**

As soon as the bus passengers from 'The Planning Team' step down, they reveal their personalities as high-profile figures who do not fear exposure. A voice from a loudspeaker inside some kind of police car gives precise indications about the do's and don'ts, but nobody really pays attention. The film's parallel subplots include an adulterous affair between the bus driver and the wife of a contest leader, as well as a group of unidentified people arriving with a helicopter and announcing they will do some tests on a work site, so everybody should clear the place in the evening, otherwise 'a tragedy might occur'. A ridiculous loudspeaker holder framed in extreme close-up delivers his message: 'orientation is man's tool in conquering nature… You all know orientation means finding your way through an unfamiliar setting.' A surrealist encounter with a flock of hens they take along on their trip results in a surprising visual interlude, feathers invading the whole screen and generating strange attitudes. The kid embarks upon some kind of rite of passage: he prevents the others from walking under falling trees, helps them jump over abysses, plunges into muddy waters, saves participants from small and big incidents. Strange female shouting from an unidentified place in the woods makes them think some kind of rape is going on. The journey degenerates, they start arguments, fight and fake death. During a final questioning the kid will confess his name (Vasile) and social status (worker). A very impressive final sequence reveals the body of a naked dead woman after a rape in the woods. This is a quite daring scene for a Romanian film in the early 1980s. A big explosion occurs and all contenders stare from inside the bus, imagining the young boy as the victim. He nonetheless turns up again: the trip members mysteriously follow him into the mist while the closing credits unfold.

Different readings of the film reveal the advantages of an encoded, parabolic cinema. In an interview for *Libération* in 1990, Piţa himself explains he had used metaphor to avoid censorship:

> Behind each contest participant here looms a member from the Ceauşescu government. The one walking around with a broken compass stands for the Five Year Plan chief, the one who fakes death as the Minister of Justice. Besides, they all make a lot of mistakes finishing the contest in a totally inglorious manner.[4]

The director's next film, *Faleze de nisip* (*Sand Cliffs*, 1983), is both a challenging exercise in theme and style and a quite unique case of ideological censorship and denigration in the history of Romanian cinema before 1989. The storyline, adapted from *Zile de nisip/Days of Sand* (1979) by Bujor Nedelcovici, is actually quite a simple one: different quite valuable objects are stolen from a beach and the victim, a reputable doctor from a Bucharest establishment, falsely accuses an innocent person. The latter is a brash, outspoken young carpenter who strongly resembles the real thief but who refuses to admit to something he is not responsible for. A long and painful enquiry follows, paradoxically allowing the accused to prove stronger and more enduring than the accuser, who will eventually succumb to psychological pressure. A rare response to the bleak context of an ever-growing cult of personality, the film was withdrawn from the distribution circuit a couple of days after its first screening and had its real premiere in 1990.

The opening credits of *Sand Cliffs* unfold according to the same pattern as *Concurs*, and yet another young boy (Gheorghe Visu, also called Vasile) is heading towards an unknown destination in barren, late autumn woods next to a Black Sea beach. While the credits roll, the young boy is seen walking casually on the beach, playing with a dog at dusk. A quick, Hollywood-style action set-piece ensues: we see a loving couple on the beach, a middle-aged man, Doctor Hristea (Victor Rebengiuc), dozing near them, and the young boy next to an attractive girl with black and curly hair. Then another tourist lying next to the couple tells them the young boy stole some things. The accusation is quickly followed by a cut to a police station questioning room, where the police inspector (Valentin Uritescu) is extremely aggressive. While the report is being dictated, a flashback is inserted revealing in extreme close-up the doctor and his mistress (Carmen Galin) in blinding daylight on the same beach.

The suspenseful, strange atmosphere of the beach investigation scenes somehow echoes the mystery which derives from the arrival of the young man in Roman Polanski's *Noz w Wodzie* (*Knife in the Water*, 1962). Gradually, the enquiry becomes a show that the other characters watch with an undisguised pleasure. Things degenerate and a lot of verbal violence ensues, the police inspector trying to persuade the young man he is responsible for the crime. Eventually the child is found dead and the same Vasile is accused of murder. The doctor becomes so obsessed with the suspected thief that he gradually loses control over his own mistress.

The inquiry takes them to Vasile's house, to his work place, and to some experienced fishermen on the beach: they learn that his father is a tramp collecting bottles on the beach and that his family situation is critical. They also meet a Roma woman who is convinced Vasile is a thief. Her daughter Amira (Oana Pellea) starts a dance, her transparent blouse attracting all the men's looks, and tells the Major, 'I don't know his name, but tell him I'll be waiting for him'.

Back in the questioning room, Vasile proves extremely perceptive and gives an honest appraisal of the situation when addressing the doctor. This particular piece of dialogue is highly critical of the way human relationships evolve in

Socialist Romania. The film's second half reveals to what point Doctor Hristea has become psychologically unstable. Despite being promoted to hospital director, he keeps having mental flashes of Vasile stealing and hiding on the beach. When Hristea and Vasile meet again, a spectacular sequence summarises crucial moments from the past, interrupted by visuals and noises of machines from the warehouse, while the two men engage in a new physical combat, followed by an outdoor pursuit along the same beach. In the very last scene the doctor is running on the beach, asking Vasile to stop running, while the kid is framed in the same position as in the opening, seemingly untouched by what is going on. Another far more ambiguous shot is an extreme close-up of Rebengiuc, a fallen, destroyed, exhausted man, his face covered with sand, a strange rhyme with the film's less sombre beginning.

Interviewed about the film's re-issue, Piţa explained that *Sand Cliffs* was meant to be decoded in the same way as *Contest*: 'The young hero kills the Communist Establishment, as represented by the doctor'.[5] *Sand Cliffs* was roughly criticised by Ceauşescu in person on the occasion of the Mangalia Conference which took place in August 1983. The conference marked a new peak in the history of neo-Stalinist absurdity: most of the leader's discourses centred around the nationalist issue of the perfect Romanian worker, free of any moral or psychological impurity. Interestingly enough, the August issue of the Romanian *Cinema*, from the same year, published the whole political and educational working session led by Ceauşescu. Some passages are worth mentioning at this point:

> Film industry needs to accomplish important missions. We need good films that should portray real models for life and work. But comrades, I have just watched a film that not only misses this point: it also presents elements from the periphery of society that should never be shown by filmmakers and screenwriters. [...] The film I'm talking about is portraying a young worker from the Black Sea coast who has nothing to do with present day workers [...] The director and screenwriter of this film are not familiar with today's heroes. Such films should not be produced. [...] How come the ideological Commission hasn't done its work properly? How come such a distorted image of our working class has been authorized? We do not need such a film, we need an art that should portray our new man, the man we are building nowadays... Our present-day reality is wonderful and needs to be highlighted.[6]

The plot of *Pas în doi* (*Paso Doble*, 1985) is quite close to an allegory of Shakespeare's *Love's Labour's Lost*. Mihai Rotariu (Claudiu Bleonţ) and his older, more average, colleague Ghiţă (Petre Nicolae) are both turners in the same factory and share the same bachelor hostel room. Their free-time activities seem quite sophisticated for average workers, as they include evening classes, fencing, boxing, disco dancing and playing music in a band led by one of their foremen, Anton (Mircea Andreescu). Irresistibly young and charming, Mihai steals away Ghiţă's girlfriend Maria (Ecaterina Nazare), a single mother, while still in love with and almost proposing to beautiful, charming Monica (Anda Onesa).[7] As announced by the title, he will oscillate between these two loves during the whole film, ending up alone. *Paso Doble* is thus an authentic eulogy to the spirit of Truffaut's *Jules et Jim* (1962). As played by Claudiu Bleonţ, the fallen angel from *Contest*, the amoral Mihai is extremely engaging.

Despite portraying extremely bleak times – the last years of Communist dictatorship – this is an unusually free film, close to the modernist trend of the factory world seen as a surrealist universe. The socialist overpowering contest paradigm is called here 'Skilful Hands', but it is rendered peripheral. The winner of the contest is Gheorghe Tena/Ghiţă, but his will prove a bitter victory. He learns that Maria has left for another work place after having fallen in love with his best friend: in a scene that appears to stress in an alternative way the 'water' theme, he talks to himself in the shower, rehearsing his speech and asking Maria to come back. Dialogue exchanges between characters are sometimes far-fetched, but there are also very many daring innovations in theme and style heralding a postmodern vein. Thus, the constant use of filters and deforming lenses (cinematography by Marin Stanciu) and the mix of electronic music and music by Joseph Haydn help create an audio-visual universe where emotion prevails over any form of reality. Haydn's positive message about a better world remains an encrypted allegory.

There are many light, visually enthralling moments depicting everyday life both at the factory and inside the hostel: a pillow fight with feathers invading the whole screen space; a surrealist *intermezzo* where the band led by Anton plays different instruments in different registers, only to be submerged in water as if in a swimming pool; an unexpected, almost ludicrous karaoke song session by Ghiţă and Mihai, and so on. Much closer to contemporary standards of explicit erotic scenes than any other film from that critical historical period of bleak totalitarian times, *Paso Doble* also unveils the amoral side of the characters without representing any obvious ensuing moral sanctions: Mihai kisses young Monica in the shower in a very 'hot' scene set to Haydn, only to fantasise sexually about the older Maria at the public library a few scenes later. Ecaterina Nazare is emotionally convincing in the role of the emancipated, liberated Maria, raising a child whose father is obviously unable to assume his role, in love with both Mihai and Ghiţă, unable to make up her mind.

As oneiric but less metaphoric and encoded than *Contest*, the film nonetheless contains lots of openly mystical references of the kind often inserted by East European directors. Mihai thus finds and wears a crown of thorns at the beginning of the film, leaning against a boxing pillow and simulating some kind of crucifixion. The film's ending is quite tragic and has hysterical overtones: Mihai is beaten up by every one of his victims (Monica, Maria and Ghiţă) for not having been able to make up his mind. We see the same corridor as in the opening, symmetrically displaying a cross-like illuminated window, what critic Eugenia Vodă has described as an 'altar to non-being' (Vodă 1995: 250). Corridors, paths and infinite roads seem to be a recurrent motif in Piţa's cinematic universe. The camera tracks over shiny, transparent, almost surreal paths, suggesting to the audience that they are entering some miraculous, almost unreal universe.

Piţa managed to make two less innovative films during the Communist era, which were produced in 1987 and 1988 respectively, but only got to the screen in 1989. These were *Noiembrie, ultimul bal* (*November, the Last Ball*), a costume drama based on a novel by Mihail Sadoveanu, and *Rochia albă de dantelă* (*The White Lace Dress*), a contemporary melodrama featuring a terminally ill working mother confronted by moral dilemmas. Like most directors who worked under Communist pressure for quite a while, the post-Communist transition was not an easy one for Dan Piţa. Romanian critics considered that he had lost his touch and could not face the change of paradigm. However, at least two of his films from the early 1990s, *Hotel de lux* (*Luxury Hotel*, 1992) and *Pepe şi Fifi* (*Pepe and Fifi*, 1994), fared quite well on the national and international circuit and remain milestones for their indisputable power in conveying Romania's zeitgeist after Ceauşescu's long-expected fall. He often quit his creative laboratory during this transitional period in order to join the leaders of the new cinema, heading newly created film units and obtaining budgets for production and technical equipment via his position as Head of the National Centre for Cinematography.

As would be the case with many East European directors, Piţa obviously plunged into a kind of affected naturalism, with deliberately perverted characters in desolate locations, the apocalyptic mood being a common denominator of humans alienated by years of dictatorship. Awarded the Silver Lion at the 1992 Venice Film Festival, *Luxury Hotel* is a nightmarish parable aiming to unveil the mechanisms of dictatorship in a challenging, albeit irritating, way.

For Yoram Allon, the film is a daring portrayal of the totalitarian repression soon after the fall of the regime, 'vomiting the vitriol welling up for decades' (Allon 2002).

The film introduces us to a young waiter, Alex (Valentin Teodosiu), the newly promoted manager of a mysterious restaurant in a gigantic hotel. The hotel is actually an allegory of the State and was partly filmed on location in the pharaonic 'People's House'. Alex wants to change the sinister atmosphere reigning everywhere, but the windows have wooden barriers, such that the place looks like a concentration camp. A prison-like barred elevator leads him from the upper floors of some kind of high-brow society to a highly exploited and terrorised mass of undefined workers echoing Fritz Lang's subterranean crowd in *Metropolis* (1927). The waiter's mother (Irina Petrescu) also works in the basement: she soon reveals to her son that the malevolent tyrant (Ştefan Iordache) heading this hotel dominated by violence, lies and perversion is actually his father. The waiter is also confronted by a Dantesque, Orwellian universe where people are constantly filmed and spied upon by hidden cameras and microphones, the recorded inquiry and torture scenes being embedded and shown again on a mini TV screen in the dictator's hidden refuge. The embedded fragments include scenes of non-dissimulated violence, but also quite a lot of prostitution, sex and nudity, taboo issues for more than forty years in Romanian film. Luxury seems nonetheless to be built on human misery, such that the masses from 'The People's House', some of whom are handicapped, finally emerge from the infernal circles: rebellion against megalomaniac dictatorship is imminent, the victims becoming hangmen. Piţa used a large number of extras from the army, the Ministry of Interior and even a handicapped people's association to increase the verisimilitude of scenes often difficult to watch.

One senses a great amount of professionalism in the work of a filmmaker whom critics salute as being an experienced auteur, with a particular gift for creating a fascinating audio-visual universe and directing actors. However, the film has aged quite badly, and the Romanian dialogue sounds highly artificial. The general feeling is that it describes a nightmare while mixing up different narrative codes (realistic, symbolic, absurd), without really making an assessment of it.

Piţa's *Pepe şi Fifi/Pepe and Fifi* (1994) has been justly described by Romanian critic Alex Leo Şerban as a 'requiem for dead innocence'.[8] It could be also labelled as a kind of Balkan *La Dolce Vita*, depicting the destiny of siblings in a tough world of prostitutes, beggars and dealers of all kinds. The cynical nature of character depiction and the naturalistic narrative echo several post-

Communist East European films of the same category. Both Fifi (Irina Movilă), an occasional prostitute who falls for a gay procurer, and Pepe (Cristian Iacob), an aspiring boxer who turns into a Mafiosi heroin dealer, are extremely gifted and emotionally engaging characters. Other secondary parts include an extra-lucid handicapped youngster and a beggar burning secret police files, thus completing the picture of Ceauşescu's painful socio-economic legacy. Nonetheless, there are quite a lot of concessions to bad taste and the cinematic syntax is almost entirely based on aggressive sex and violence meant to shock the viewer.

Dan Piţa's other films from the 1990s include *Eu sunt Adam* (*My name Is Adam*, 1996), a highly personal adaptation of several short stories by seminal writer/philosopher Mircea Eliade, and *Omul zilei* (*The Man of the Day*, 1997), another 'slice of life' from neo-capitalist Romania, portraying a vicious politician in a totally perverted environment. Though the brilliant actor Ştefan Iordache dominates both, they do not match up to Piţa's established reputation. The same can be said about the more recent *Second-hand* (2003) and *Femeia visurilor* (*The Dreamt Woman*, 2005), which, as was the case with the earlier films, did not reach any international distribution circuit via festivals, owing to their surprisingly low quality, didactic message and unconvincing scripts. Critics subsequently concluded that the filmmaker for all seasons should have stopped creating before being caught up in the 'tyranny of success'.

Mircea Daneliuc
Romanian Cinema's Rebel with a Cause

Mircea Daneliuc unquestionably stands as the most important Romanian director of the 1980s, while also proving relatively prolific and thought-provoking
during the immediate post-Communist period (five films from 1991 to 1995).
As was the case with other auteurs, his work has only been partially shown to
non-domestic audiences and still needs to be reconsidered for a number of
reasons. The first and most important one relates to the fact that despite enor-
mous difficulties, Daneliuc's films managed to escape Communist censorship,
while bringing to the fore extremely authentic characters and situations, thus
constituting an invaluable picture of Romanian society. The second one is the
director's uncommon capacity to shift from highly realistic stories to parables
and allegories, while enabling critics and audiences alike to decode them in
inspiring ways. The third is that Daneliuc is probably a unique case of consistent artistic rebellion, having used film as a weapon against a dysfunctional
society, both during and after the end of Communism.

Daneliuc's apprenticeship as a filmmaker is atypical: before being admitted to a filmmaking department, he failed the admission assessment five
times, thus entering the environment much later than his contemporaries. In
the meantime, he read French at university and earned his living as a schoolteacher. Unsatisfied with being just a highly daring director, Daneliuc has
also proved a gifted novelist, playwright, theatre director and actor, playing

main or peripheral parts in his own films so as to feel closer to his own performers.

After a highly successful debut in the mid-1970s, *Cursa* (*The Long Drive*, 1975), Daneliuc achieved a high though problematic production rate in the early 1980s. Thus, four films were out almost at the same time, because their premieres were always delayed due to the director consistently refusing to cut scenes. The other films he directed were more genre-oriented, less auteurist: *Ediție specială* (*Special Edition*, 1977), a thriller unfolding in the 1940s, and *Vânătoarea de vulpi* (*Fox Hunting*, 1980), adapted from the novel by official writer Dinu Săraru. The latter had a lesser aesthetic and thematic impact. Daneliuc was simultaneously active in theatre directing, one production from the early 1980s, like Slavomir Mrozek's *The Immigrants*, having been considered a milestone in the Romanian theatre.

The opening shots from *The Long Drive* herald what will be Daneliuc's constant device: reflexivity. He is seen giving instructions inside what appears to be a factory while he is busy filming, a camera over his shoulders. The novelty resides in his urgency to report on reality and film it at the same time, this simultaneity helping abolish the frontier between fiction and reality: 'Stop', he tells the crew. 'Start again so we can shoot the departure, too bad, we've missed it.' He is interviewing factory workers; then the image is reframed in black and white over a coloured background. His female star and real-life partner, Tora Vasilescu, is shouting at him in her first onscreen appearance at the factory, a love/hate relationship which will become the trademark of a highly atypical couple in the context of Romanian film.

The film is a road movie unfolding inside a spectacular mountain region, the freshly inaugurated Transfăgărășan (1974), conceived as a strategic military route running across the highest sections of the Carpathian Mountains.[1] Three characters, two men and a young woman, come across different events which will modify their *Weltanschauung*, their view of the world: getting to know each other despite regional differences, dancing in a bar and having violent altercations with some young hippies, and visiting old peasant friends from a Transylvanian village.

Maria (Tora Vasilescu), dressed in a flashy red raincoat, smoking and blasé, is invited to join the drive by extrovert Ion (Constantin Diplan). His co-driver Anghel (Mircea Albulescu), one minute silent and cynical, the next hysterical or violent, clearly falls for the girl. The gigantic item – a boiler – they are supposed to be carrying to the work site does not fit on every road, but reaching their destination proves only a secondary concern. The *ménage à trois* is treated in a sophisticated, high-strung way with a lot of dramatic tension. Anghel returns to his native village with Maria: no love scene transpires, just the revelation of a dead wife who had betrayed him with a colleague.

The film's climax is orchestrated with an impressive cinematic command for a debut: during a highly suspenseful sequence, the truck almost runs off the road over a precipice, this being prevented by a superhuman effort from the two drivers. In the meantime, realising Maria has disappeared, they run back to find her. She ends up at her fiancé's place, but he proves a bigamist, whose wife does not understand what this is all about. Drawn to the drivers, the young woman steps back into the truck and asks: 'Where are we heading for?' The ending is thus clearly an open one.

The main plot of *Proba de microfon* (*Microphone Test*, 1980) centres on cameraman Nelu – played by Daneliuc – and television reporter Luiza (Gina Patrichi), who are emotionally involved and are interviewing people caught travelling by train without tickets. As in most films touching on contemporary topics, the train becomes a metaphor for human knowledge, and the station is an extremely complex environment. The reporters seem rather free to choose the interviews that will be actually shown, a quite unusual practice in a system where any information is closely watched. They are also ready to use a hidden camera: the reflexive devices used by Daneliuc are as sophisticated as the ones used by French directors such as Jean-Luc Godard and Michel Deville. Daneliuc is one of the first directors to have used direct sound, recording entire scenes and then mixing them with post-synchronised ones.

The film thus contains a lot of semi-documentary footage along with genuinely natural situations, accents from different parts of the country, rough everyday language, and physical as well as psychological forms of unrest. The credits unfold with the names of the actors while simultaneously introducing the viewer to the heart of the subject: a Super 8 mobile camera catches in close-up unknown faces on the train. Most of them refuse to face the camera: we hear a feminine voice off-screen, describing how she had been sexually abused by an unknown guy.

The film's title is decoded a few sequences later, when Luiza is heard saying off-screen, 'One, two, three, four, five, microphone test'.

On the train, the journalist couple also meet Ani (Tora Vasilescu), a charming young factory worker. Nelu will fall in love on the spot and

Fig 8. *Microphone Test*: the opening credits

have an on and off tumultuously erotic affair with her, with lots of scenes of explicit love-making, without however managing to get to a happy ending.[2]

The often meta-filmic reports are filmed in a fresh, sarcastic way, for example the factory community report with girls waiting to get married and ready to find a husband or the sequence revealing Ani's colleagues busy preparing the only chocolate-filled biscuit available on the market. They strongly echo similar slices of life from Milos Forman's *Lásky jedné plavovlásky* (*Loves of a Blonde*, 1965). Once again, the image of different parts of Romania these fragments reveal is of a poor, derelict country with unsolved economic problems, in terms of employment, housing (many adults still live with their parents or relatives in small apartments) and food supplies.

Ani is an anti-heroine *par excellence*, probably one of the most unusual female characters from the East European Communist context, where the lack of morality was highly unusual and strongly condemned. She lies to Nelu about her real identity, her family history and her past love affairs. We thus learn that she has given up her job after getting involved with different men, among them a dolphin tamer from the Black Sea coast, who is being interviewed at the swimming pool. As in Piţa's *Filip the Kind*, foreigners attracting young girls are mostly Italian, and so are the goods they dream about. Nelu desperately tries to turn Ani into a normal, moral, decent woman before he is eventually sent to military service. When he meets her again she cries and tells him it is too late. Her hair is in a loop and she is expecting a child by another man.

The scenes in which Nelu has his hair cut, tries on his military costume and then integrates into army life appear to portray a spectacular personality shift. They prove to what extent Daneliuc himself was a very gifted performer, capable of unexpected changes in mode and tone. The film was conceived as a self-portrait because many events from Daneliuc's life are there: his tempestuous, sexually charged relationship with Vasilescu/Ani, his hair-cutting scene for military service during his university training and the medical check-up are all autobiographical. Romanian critics' Top Ten listed *Microphone Test* as the ninth best Romanian film of all time (Corciovescu and Mihăilescu 2010: 169). The film was Daneliuc's biggest box-office hit, at home and abroad.

Daneliuc wrote and directed *Croaziera* (*The Cruise*, 1982) while still waiting to get the exploitation visa for a long-delayed project, *Glissando*. Considered as the tenth best Romanian film by domestic critics, the film's general tone is far darker than the preceding one's in terms of colour, outdoor shooting, character behaviour and mode of address (Corciovescu and Mihăilescu 2010: 185). However, there is the same taste for immediacy as in his previous films. Credits unfold on a black screen backed by an 'aural discourse': noises suggesting a departing ship engine and voices of people busy getting together.

'Magdalena', a very vulgar Roma music standard from the 1980s, is heard, and is meant to stress the spirit of the times in the minds of the audience:

- Magdalena tell the truth
  Tell me who bit your breasts
- Yesterday while I was in the garden
  A bee bit me
- Magdalena stop lying to me
  I know bees have no teeth[3]

The plot focuses on young workers who have won important contests in different disciplines (sports, chemistry, hand sewing, poem reciting, and so on) and have received this cruise as a gift. A highly cynical, sarcastic atmosphere pervades: the opening scene reveals the presumptuous organiser and leader of the cruise, Proca (Nicolae Albani), presenting the programme to a young audience who boos and protests on learning that they need to stop the show at nine p.m. Again, the tone is close to Forman films from the late 1960s. Daneliuc and Vasilescu resurface as a recognisable couple. This time she is a blonde with short hair: 'I thought you were a top model', he tells her during an interlude.

The participants visit different Romanian cities and building sites, listening to explanations and speeches with little enthusiasm. The state of those places filmed on location on the Danube coast is quite miserable. The atmosphere on the ship is dominated by frequent quarrels: they reveal their obsession with food, health and material things in the restrictive Communist environment. The leader also invites the most beautiful girls to come and join the ship, while the other participants sleep in collective dorms where strange things seem to happen. Meanwhile all sorts of contests, puzzles and hide-and-seek parties are going on.

After a bout of indigestion due to bad food, the crew's doctor, Velicu (Paul Lavric), suggests 'we send thirty of them home and forget about it', but Proca insists on continuing as if nothing had happened. He eventually turns aggressive and tyrannical. An interesting closure device is accompanied by a long, blatantly contrasting voice-over. We hear Proca reading his 'ship log', while unspectacular images of participants are shown. They are either packing to depart or preparing for the collective photo session:

July 24. Everything worked out perfectly. The weather was not always on our side but we managed to overcome all obstacles. Medical check-up, swimming contest, visiting cultural and historical seminal places, as well as setting up the final dance party, all these went out fine in an atmosphere of undaunted enthusiasm and discipline.

It was a miracle that such a free film went out during bleak times: it was watched by a huge audience, until the Party officials realized that it was harmful and took it out of the distribution circuit. The sarcastic comic line lampooning a dysfunctional society is the same as the one set up by playwright Caragiale almost a century ago.

Daneliuc wrote the screenplay for *Glissando* (1984) as early as 1980. The initial inspiration came from *The Man from a Dream*, a short story by novelist Cezar Petrescu set in the 1930s. The director took over the idea of an inveterate gambler having constant visions and dreams about his past and committing suicide after a series of personal failures. The film's epigraph further contextualises the film's zeitgeist and reads:

> History will condemn and nail down the ones found guilty for this crime against human progress and entire generations, still experiencing the sequels of the terrible pain we have been suffering from, will set a curse on them (Nicolae Iorga, 25 sept, 1939).

Then there is a black screen over which a Nazi swastika metamorphoses into the Romanian Legionary right-wing movement symbol. Daneliuc, who added the epigraph under pressure from the Censorship Commission, thus handles editing and chromatic patterns to suggest a terminal fascist world, engendered by the legionary dictatorship alluded to in the quotation from renowned historian and politician Nicolae Iorga.[4]

In the opening scene, the camera pans over lace curtains which allow daylight to filter in to an otherwise dark room, which is filled with objects, old photos and paintings.[5] This kind of descriptive set-up will be repeated several times in the film as the main hero's paradigmatic space, both his prison and his refuge. We discover Teodorescu (Ştefan Iordache) dozing in his bed, almost unable to get up, faltering in search of his clothes.

The first scenes confirm the hypothesis advanced by the meaning of the title word, *Glissando*. The word comes from the French *glisser*, 'to slide'. Applied to piano and harp, it refers to the effect obtained by sliding rapidly over keys or strings, so that every individual note is articulated, no matter how rapid the 'sliding'.[6] Indeed, Daneliuc introduces narrative cells resembling vignettes, which slide back and forth in time and space. These cells contain streaks of time from the past, such as the one figuring Teodorescu as a young boy, hesitatingly answering questions asked by his history teacher. The mysterious, beautiful Agatha, represented in a family portrait in Teodorescu's room, attends the exam, suggesting a maternal though quite aloof presence. Throughout the film Teodorescu will keep asking the hospital authorities for news about the mysterious Agatha, whose painted portrait will be highly coveted.

The epicentre of these sliding scenes – featuring Teodorescu either as an active protagonist or as a distant observer – is a multifunctional building, initially resembling some kind of Turkish spa. Different floors separated by a labyrinthine staircase also contain a torture prison room, an X-ray diagnosis room, a concert hall, a library, a gambling house and even some military barracks. The inhabitants of this highly ambiguous space range from groups of decrepit old people resembling concentration camp victims to seemingly decadent bourgeois card players of both sexes. Daneliuc used different locations for this building. Complex location shooting also took place in the Bucharest Jewish district and later on in Floreşti, a village next to the city of Ploieşti, as well as in Băile Herculane, a renowned spa resort.

A quite long episode in the film's narrative line unfolds in the countryside. One of the characters present in the Turkish bath, later to be identified as Alexandru Agiu (Ion Fiscuteanu), invites Teodorescu to his place, suggesting a change of air would be highly profitable. Agiu's recently acquired property is an interesting place in terms of social schemes. The owner not only confesses to having bought it recently from a man of noble lineage who went bankrupt, but also proves an impostor, an upstart with bad manners and a deliberately vulgar mode of address. He displays a mixture of admiration and non-dissimulated verbal irony when addressing his children's pseudo-French upbringing, via quite uninspired, almost hysterical quotations of Verlaine and Baudelaire and references to mythical Paris.

Daneliuc's *mise en scène*, the dominant chromatic tonality and the lighting and cinematography used to depict this allegedly idyllic universe constantly verge on a kind of chiaroscuro, where characters are almost shadows and objects are more suggested than fully shown. Teodorescu, though overstimulated by Agiu, seems passive and disenchanted. Agiu tries to persuade him to start an affair with his insipid wife (Rada Istrate), to no avail. In the meantime, the governess Nina (Tora Vasilescu) has started a seduction game with Teodorescu that will end up in an erotically charged love affair in Bucharest.

Glissando phenomena reappear in the countryside, with constant verbal allusions to the dreamer's condition. Teodorescu recollects a strange old man who appears in all his dreams, while Agiu confesses he barely dreams. They visit another spa next to their property: the promenade is filled with people dressed in white, while a military march is heard. Teodorescu eventually comes upon the mysterious man from his dreams, Iorgu Ordeanu (Petre Simionescu), an aristocrat having lost almost all his fortune at cards, an occasional art collector whose portraits strangely resemble the much coveted one featuring the mysterious Agatha.

The film's second half maintains the iterative audio-visual pattern used for the sliding effects. Nina, now sharing Teodorescu's bed, is jealous and has fits of hysteria. Barking voices from an unidentified radio source are manifest echoes of a fascist discourse commenting on a football match, presumably issued by the fascist Iron Guard. The almost barking voices from the radio would have reminded Romanian audiences of Ceauşescu's speeches, where collective hailing and applause turned into an inescapable obligation on the the part of the brainwashed masses. Outside, on the streets at night, there is an unexplained chaos and a mysterious close-up of a distinguished bearded middle-aged man, who is shouting in panic. This anonymous figure, played by expressive theatre actor Gheorghe Ghiţulescu, will turn up again at different moments with no apparent narrative motivation.

Teodorescu's return to the multifunctional Dantesque place is probably Daneliuc's most spectacular *tour de force* in terms of *mise en scène* and editing patterns. The playing den, where the hero will lose and win back his fortune at different times, is so close to the hospital that old men's desperate voices are heard shouting for help. The low-angle views of this apocalyptic prison-like space seem to figure different stages from Dante's nightmarish visions. The last half hour of the film is dominated by a biblical Armageddon intimation, close to what Bela Tarr accomplishes in seminal scenes from *Werckmeister Harmonies* (2000).

The end of the world seems near, as Teodorescu – accused of being an 'Antichrist' – drives Ordeanu to suicide after making him lose his money and his temper. The film's very last scenes, filmed on deserted streets in the Jewish district with an army of half-naked old people led by the hospital doctors and forced to obey military orders, reveal another Dantesque concentration-camp-like set of images. Teodorescu is a silent observer, his hand set on a broken piece of glass before he performs the final suicidal act with a small gun. Details on cars and flags further suggest this is the work of the Iron Guard.

In his extremely personal and tortured diary, *The Torn Cat*, Daneliuc mentions having been summoned innumerable times by Ceauşescu's censors and ministers to cut most of this overtly apocalyptic part: he eventually agreed to make cuts to the copy sent to the Venice International Film Festival. Shown in a shorter version, it curiously won no prize, but its critical acclaim was considerable. After almost two years of delay to the domestic release of *Glissando*, Daneliuc made a costly gesture for dictatorship times: he officially handed back his Party membership card and became estranged from the filmmaking world, with painful economic consequences for his everyday life. He detailed these aspects in his book in a violent, aggressive, ironical tone, changing slightly the names of the real-life characters but also giving ludicrous nicknames to different Communist big shots (Daneliuc 1997: 175-99).[7]

The screenplay for *Iacob* (1988) was approved after a cinematic silence of four years, during which Daneliuc was forced to shoot industrial 16mm documentaries about factory life. Adapted from the short story *The Death of Iacob Onisar* by naturalist writer Geo Bogza, the story recounts the tragic destiny of a middle-aged miner from Transylvania, who eventually falls off a cable car at night and dies. Daneliuc also got inspiration from other stories by Bogza and incorporated them into one unified subject.

The film's prologue starts with a close-up of a man's forehead, the man being seen eating in silence a minute later. The man, Covaci (Florin Zamfirescu), will soon commit suicide. Foregrounded sound effects suggest a Tarkovskian apocalyptic universe. We see a naked and bloody shouting woman in a conjugal bed, as if she had just lost her virginity. There is a window explosion, then a crash at the entrance of a mine and a fade out to the credit '*Iacob*, a film by Mircea Daneliuc'. Credits also allow the sound score to develop, a totally modernist, non-harmonic composition by Anatol Vieru, a frequent contributor of such compositions, suggesting both strangeness and anxiety.

Most scenes were filmed on location inside abandoned gold mines in Transylvania and in the Petroşani area, where a miners' revolt briefly burst out in 1977. Iacob's mining environment echoes many controversial issues in the Romanian psyche. He first appears as a strong, determined, outspoken character, in complicity with his fellow miner Trifan (Ion Fiscuteanu), who will later tempt him into stealing gold. In the following scenes we discover the workers' modest family circle, where widowers find new partners to care for their children and men share gold theft secrets. Trifan's brash young daughter (Cecilia Bârbora) tempts Iacob (Dorel Vişan) at different moments. Daneliuc realistically depicts morose everyday existences caught in the trap of economic misery and human decay from the 1930s. Eventually Iacob and Trifan are accused of theft and sent to another, more remote coal mine. The film's narrative structure sets up a chain of visual symbols the meaning of which will later be clarified, neutral shots of a cable car in the distance, Iacob's first trip testing the cable car at night, and so on. Iacob becomes an alcoholic, having unexpected fits of jealousy and aggressiveness and refusing any form of charity or pity, confronted by a kind of unavoidable decline.

In a brightly directed scene, a mining elevator accident is avoided but some miners still sustain injuries. The film's twenty-minute coda has rightly been considered as one of the most intense and tragic codas ever in a Romanian film.[8] It's Christmas Eve, quite late in the day, chilly and windy outside, with snow covering the whole region. Iacob, who has already contemplated the cable car from afar during previous scenes, decides to get on it, hoping to get home earlier. But times are hard, and energy is expensive, such that at some point, high in the sky, 200 metres above the earth, it stops still. Our character thinks this may be just an accident, and is persuaded it will start again: he talks to himself, sets up a fire, dozes off. Time goes by, and there is no noise around, so he gets up and starts shouting for some help. He swears, implores, says prayers. Almost frozen, he attempts a desperate act, that of jumping off the funicular. A close-up of his hand and then a blood stain on the ground where he has fallen are the two metonymic symbols Daneliuc uses to close his film.

One is hard-pressed to describe Vişan's superhuman performance, the outstanding camerawork (by Florin Mihăilescu), the complex editing (by Maria Neagu), alternating vast ensemble compositions with close shots to create an unbearable tension, the hyper-real sound design (by Horea Murgu) foregrounding silence as the sole answer to fatality. Taking up Bogza's own coinage, Eugenia Vodă describes Daneliuc's enterprise as an act of 'creative exasperation' (Vodă 1995: 365). The film may also be decoded as a variant on the constant Romanian myth, that of the prophetic little lamb Mioritza: the hero's death is clearly inscribed in his suicidal enterprise and occurs in the midst of a wintry natural environment. Another interesting interpretation comes from Mircea Dumitrescu.[9] He refers to the homonymous hero from the Old Testament, Jacob, the son of Isaac and Rebecca: Jacob has a dream in which angels provide him with a ladder leading to Heaven and granting him protection from his ancestral God Abraham. In Dumitrescu's opinion, Bogza's hero attempts to climb up a similar ladder, using the cable car as a sort of manger on Christmas Eve. However, his enterprise proves a complete failure and he is not blessed, but rather condemned to an inevitable, self-inflicted sacrifice. This metaphor of tragic self-confrontation might stand as a moral and political decoding of a dead end, an apocalyptic condition for the Romanian people in general.

Fig 9. Iacob's attempt to get off the funicular in *Iacob*

Iacob was nominated for Best Film and Best Actor at the Berlin European Film Academy Contest in 1988, but no public mention of these nominations was made in Romania.

A 11a poruncă (*The 11ᵗʰ Commandment*, 1991) was Daneliuc's first post-Communist film. It is freely inspired by a novel by dissident writer Paul Goma, about a renowned Communist prison based in the town of Pitesti where torture on a wide scale was a common practice.[10] Nonetheless, the film's immediate subject is not Communist times, as it clearly takes place before the end of World War II. Daneliuc had already written an original screenplay as early as 1980, called *A and E*, the initials of Adolf Hitler and Eva Braun. As was the case with the mysterious sanatorium in *Glissando*, there is a perfectly recognisable allusion to Communist dictatorship with its shamefully coercive and humiliating practices.

Obeying an order of the Allied armies, a group of Germans having similar physical characteristics to Hitler, Eichman, Borman, Goebbels, Göring and Eva Braun are interned in a special prisoner camp somewhere in Europe, so as to be further identified and eventually punished.[11] These people have to go through the nightmare of misrecognition and false accusation. A sudden, unexplained bombing destroys the camp, and only eleven survivors are left. Afraid of being misidentified, they stay together and rebuild a micro-universe where tyranny, grotesque attitudes and mutual hatred prevail.

For more than two hours, they wait for a miraculous outcome: 'maybe God will make something good happen', says one of the characters. They fight, kill, rape and turn into beast-like creatures but finally manage to escape their self-confined post-apocalyptic universe. They only leave behind their ex-leader Heintz (Constantin Dinulescu), who turns insane and does not dare face reality anew. The general atmosphere of the film is very hard to bear on the part of the audience, as there is so much gratuitous violence and insanity.

Sparse critical material has commented on the allegorical side of the film, which alludes to an extension of the Ten Commandments, namely 'Thou shall not get caught'.[12] Passages from the Bible have been reworked by Daneliuc to fit the visual message: they are heard in a voice-over from a commentator reciting with a very monotonous intonation. Also, the musical score compilation features highly appropriate instrumental and classical fragments from Bach's *Passions*, Mozart's *Requiem* and Pergolese's *Stabat Mater*, in the style of a postmodern quotation. The film starts in a highly symbolic register with an establishing shot of a huge barren tree that is pulled down, its branches being afterwards broken and burnt by a group of people speaking German. The voice-over is heard saying:

> At the beginning there was the word. Then there was hatred and despair. And
> then there was the fire that burnt them down and turned them into steam and
> smoke, pure ashes [...]. Fire meant purity.

Symmetrically, the film's closure is structured as an apocalyptic moment. It is
first dominated by human death amidst fire in a glacial winter atmosphere
while the same voice comments: 'The fire burnt out humans, but a bigger
fire started anew'. Despite eschatological visuals, the aural counterpart is not
entirely pessimistic. Daneliuc imagines the return of another cycle, offering
madness as an alternative to death for the remaining prisoner, Heinz.

The 11th Commandment is a film which is hard to ignore when talking about
the history of Romanian cinema. Eugenia Vodă mentions the fact that this production opens up a new period of Romanian cinema, while departing from the
old one, governed by Communist dictatorship. Daneliuc's radical pessimism
filters into every scene: there is no hope left either for individual men or for
humanity in general (Vodă 1995: 370).

The picaresque plotline of Patul conjugal (The Conjugal Bed, 1993) is worth
discussing before getting into other kinds of considerations. In tough post-
Ceauşescu Bucharest, everybody is struggling to make a living: poverty is
more extreme than ever and market economy is a grotesque illusion. Vasile
Potop (Gheorghe Dinică), a deserted movie theatre manager, desperately
seeks money for an abortion for his wife Carolina, as he cannot afford to raise
three children. He tries to borrow from his mistress, attractive ticket seller
Stela (Lia Bugnar), but the latter soon quits her job to become a professional
hooker and occasional porn star under her husband's direction. In the meantime, Carolina (Coca Bloos) initiates a campaign to sell her unborn child to
Western clients, even though her husband persuades her to go to Belgium
and give birth there to a Western baby. Potop tries everything to achieve his
ends, including subletting his theatre to new alternative political parties and
selling a copy of a lavish book honouring Ceauşescu. He gets into all kinds of
trouble and spends some time in a mental asylum. Potop seeks revenge but
fails to club his pregnant wife to death. He then decides to set fire to himself,
but realising nobody really cares, he finally manages to hang himself in front
of a shocked audience in his own theatre.

The epilogue occurs thirteen years later, in 2006, and features Carolina's
abnormal, degenerate son selling empty bottles. The score introduces the
main theme from Richard Strauss's Zarathustra. Mocking usual nationalist
aberrations, the young boy declares his name is Decebal (the first Romanian
Emperor who dared defy the Roman invaders). He meets Stela, now a

decaying, ageing prostitute, and asks her for sexual favours inside his parents' deserted apartment, arguing he can even 'sell his crazy mother' if necessary. Thus the film ends how it started, with a grotesque sex scene in a totally dystopic, degenerate, hopeless universe.

The Conjugal Bed is obviously structured in the allegorical mode. The film's constantly digressive storyline unfolds on three highly distinctive planes. The first plane is contained in Potop's apartment, with its conjugal bed over which a huge mirror has been set. The second is a deserted movie theatre, where unbelievably surreal events take place. When Potop and Stela, his mistress, make love inside his movie theatre, she balances herself naked on a seesaw against images of Ceaușescu delivering his last speech.

Before the epilogue, Potop manages his suicide by hanging himself against the same screen, next to a mummified and crucified naked body. The third space is actually post-revolutionary Bucharest itself, mainly its centre with the now mythical University Square as well as the Palace Square, where a huge stationed helicopter is constantly watched by onlookers.

All narrative spaces are dominated by perversity, violence and hysterical acts, often downplayed by a kind of sarcastic irony highly characteristic of the Romanian psyche. The generalization of evil is Ceaușescu's direct heritage,

Fig 10. Sophisticated visual embeddings in *The Conjugal Bed*

as he had encouraged, via highly restrictive and coercive mechanisms, the development of the traumatic individual and later a highly deranged collective consciousness. Now that most people are out of work or frequently on strike, some of them are nostalgic for the deceased dictator.

In the apartment 'area' cynical reflexivity is another device successfully used by Daneliuc, obviously criticising gratuitous screen horror. Potop, having unsuccessfully tried to stab his pregnant wife, ironically addresses the audience off-screen: 'Look at this, isn't it horrible? I told you it was going to be like that.' Finally, within the city area, the main hero again performs a reflexive act: before attempting immolation he parades as a sandwich man, proclaiming 'Romanians, something great is being set up for you'.

Daneliuc's consistent follow up to *The Conjugal Bed* was *Această lehamite* (*Fed Up*, 1994), a film difficult to understand beyond Romanian frontiers. It features a typically domestic vision of, on the one hand, the disastrous condition of hospitals in general and of patient treatment in particular and, on the other, explicit forms of sexuality, returning to the screen after decades of implicit ones. Daneliuc got his inspiration from a *fait divers* which had occurred in Germany, where a clinically dead woman had been kept alive so as to try to save the baby she was expecting.

The film's beginning and the ensuing actions show characters who are fed up with their daily life in drab post-Communist Romania. Doina (Ana Ciontea) dies in a car accident. The emergency ward in a derelict hospital confirms her clinical death. The medical staff realise she is four months pregnant, the foetus being kept alive via a unique reanimation unit. One of the female doctors, the much coveted Vali (Cecilia Bârbora), tries hard to keep the baby alive, especially after having met the child's alleged father, Bebe (Horaţiu Mălăele).[13] The latter incidentally falls in love with Vali and declares his feelings during half-comic, half-grotesque telephone conversations. The experiment gradually becomes a common goal for several characters: Vali dreams of being awarded the Nobel Prize for her accomplishment; Bebe is persuaded he could get Doina's apartment by proving he is the father. Doina herself, portrayed in the film as a phantom, hopes to be reincarnated via the child who outlives her. Unfortunately, nobody manages to achieve this common goal: Doina's reanimated body is 'unplugged', as the ward has to be freed for another emergency.

Daneliuc uses devices that are strongly connected with silent cinema aesthetics. Thus, Doina, though in a deep coma, appears systematically by way of superimpositions, providing explanations for the audience or scolding the father of her unborn child. By way of the Romanian title, which literally means 'this state of being fed up', Daneliuc evokes the post-revolutionary society in the same straightforward and cynical way he did fourteen years earlier in *Microphone Test*. Nonetheless, the regained liberty in tone and subject matter reveals a much deeper form of human misery and degradation, palpable at all levels. Vulgarity has replaced kitsch, pulling people's leg and swearing having become the natural way of expressing one's ideas.

Bebe is supposed to act as the epitome of the Romanian 'Natural Born Loser'. He treats the disastrous condition of Romanians with irony. At a certain point he even drops the sentence: 'God, take me to Albania', a country which used to be seen as much worse than Romania in terms of Stalinist dictatorship.

The ending however offers a ray of hope: the wish to give birth to a child, to start a new life over old ashes from the past. Daneliuc's odd couple, after finally having real sex in a car in the middle of a traffic jam, wishes it could be 'blond, very blond'. This is yet another allusion to the West German myth of a much craved form of material prosperity. The musical counterpoint is also interesting: we are symbolically invited to listen to an electronic disco-like version of the national anthem, 'Deşteaptă-te române/Wake Up, Romanian'.

Daneliuc's last post-Communist production worth mentioning is *Senatorul Melcilor* (*The Snails' Senator*, 1995), which was part of the 1995 Cannes Film Festival official selection. Christina Stojanova summarises its plotline in the following way: 'It is about a ubiquitous and invincible *apparatchik*, perfectly adapted to the new, post-communist circumstances'.[14] Alex Leo Şerban considers Daneliuc's film a fable in the line of *Fed Up* and *The Conjugal Bed*, because characters and situations depicted in the film are vehicles for ideas and concepts while also, to a lesser extent than the previous ones, engaging emotions and empathy on the part of the audience (Şerban 2009: 195).

Vicious, arrogant, allegedly cheerful senator Vârtosu (Dorel Vişan, the main hero from *Iacob*) arrives in a forgotten village to inaugurate a hydraulic power station: the plant is intended to put Romania on a level with the West, thus standing for the country's longing for a better place in the world circuit. A Swiss TV crew visits the new plant. Romanians are close to the Swiss and the French language-wise, but not so close in terms of civilised standards.

The film's title is explained during one of the subplots: an invitation to the senator and the foreign guests to eat snails collected by the exploited villagers. The search is a bit absurd, as the snails do not seem to be available in great quantities, but again this is a pretext for moving away from the comic vein and unveiling some tragic ethnic issues. Romanians and Hungarians but also, inevitably, Roma people indulge in occasional stealing and raping. While they are busy collecting, the senator is enjoying a typical Balkan lifestyle in one of the numerous resorts that belonged to Ceauşescu. Between copious eating and drinking parties backed by folklore music, he even reproaches one of the servants for the fact that she has been faithful to the party for forty-five years.[15]

As in most Daneliuc 'fable films', the ending is highly metaphorical, far from any kind of realist story tradition. One hears the hammering sound of an arch being built at the top of a neighbouring hill by some unknown hermit. Daneliuc invites the active viewer to see an intimation of 'paradise lost', once the journey into triumphant transition is over.

Daneliuc's twenty-first-century output, after an eight-year interruption, was dominated by contemporary issues handled with questionable black humour in a cynical, embittered and often aggressive tone (e.g. *Ambasadori caută patrie/Ambassadors Seek Country*, 2003, *Sistemul nervos/The Nervous System*, 2005, and *Legiunea străină/The Foreign Legion*, 2008). This work proved rather disappointing and did not measure up to the outstanding quality of his early production. However, his films from the 1980s, such as those already discussed as well as his trilogy about the moral condition of post-Communist

Romania, definitely constitute milestones in the evolution of Romanian film in the second half of the twentieth century. Critic Cristian Tudor Popescu has rightly argued that 'Daneliuc's films proved a shock and re-shaped the way audiences saw things in Romania'.[16]

CHAPTER 6

The 1989 Moment
Film and History in the Early 1990s

Romania's break from Communist dictatorship engendered by the 1989 revolutionary moment was obviously different from similar phenomena going on in most East European countries. Most importantly, it was almost entirely and sometimes excessively filmed by professional film and television crews and by numerous amateur cameras. In Ricoeur's terms, *time of fiction* and *historical time* for once coincided (Ricoeur 1990, III: 129). Such a situation had very long-term effects on the future history of Romanian cinema. These effects were felt in the early documentaries, domestic and foreign docu-fictions, shorts and feature-length films of the early 1990s and followed their trajectory through the first decade of the twenty-first century, the decade which witnessed the emergence of the Romanian New Wave. This is why a detailed historical reminder is necessary at this point.

After a particularly brief period of liberalisation (1963–1971), the global oil crisis of the early 1970s triggered new sacrifices and restrictions among the Romanian population. The neo-Stalinist heritage took over and the personality cult around the dictator and his entire family was constantly growing. At the beginning of 1977, writer Paul Goma rallied the Prague-born 'Chart 77' dissident movement, protesting against the Romanian state of affairs. During the same year, the miners from the Jiu Valley manifested their solidarity with Goma by going on strike, thus sending a very powerful message to the regime

(Niculescu 2002: 4). Ceauşescu talked to the miners and made promises he never kept. After a fifteen-year reign, Romania was a backward country, below all normal standards: the rural population still represented half of the country, while infant mortality proved unusually high (Dobrincu, Tismaneanu & Vasile 2007: 703-6).

Like most dictators, Ceauşescu was obsessed about what he would leave behind: what would history write about him? Time and the past were his greatest enemies. He wanted to wipe away any traces of the past and turn Bucharest into his town, thus making room for one of the most ambitious construction projects in Europe. He thus ordered the destruction of thousands of houses, of entire districts, monuments, churches and public buildings by renowned architects. According to Andrei Codrescu:

> The presidential palace, built over the three layers of secret tunnels, is the regime's most grimly symbolic building. Its floor space is more than 400,000 square feet and thirteen stories [...] It is three times the size of Versailles [...] Fifty thousand people lost their homes so that the site could be cleared when the construction began in 1984. (Codrescu 1991: 122)

In 1987, Gorbachev visited Romania and wanted to persuade Ceauşescu to start reforms: he faced a categorical refusal. In November 1987 there was another important strike. On the last day of local elections, workers from a Braşov-based truck factory asked for better working conditions. They broke into the Party offices and devastated them, destroying official portraits and shouting: 'Down with Ceauşescu, Down with Communism'. The event recalled similar ones from Gdansk and Budapest. On 10 March 1989, the *New York Times* published the 'Letter of the Six': an open letter addressed to Ceauşescu by six Party veterans. The six reproached the dictator for his not wanting to apply the Perestroika principles in his country and for the general failure of his system. As a consequence, the six signers were marginalised and sent away in forced residence throughout the country. Romania seemed to be at the end of a historic cycle (Tismaneanu 2003: 227).

In 1989, the year of the Eastern bloc downfall, most Communist regimes collapsed at the same moment. Romania lagged way behind, the generalised repression being worse than ever. Says Codrescu: 'The eight Romanian days that shook the world began in Timişoara, a city [in] Western Romania. There, on Friday, December 15, 1989, three hundred Romanians from different ethnic minorities formed a human chain in front of Reverend Laszlo Tökes' house', Tökes having actively been preaching in favour of human rights and democracy (Codrescu 1991: 27). In the meantime, there had been strikes and marches for three days and young people from all over the country took trains to the city to form guards in defence of the city. Following these events Ceauşescu called a huge meeting in the Republic Square, mobilising workers from Bucharest factories. Hundreds of thousands of people came up shouting 'Down with the Dictator' and transforming chants of 'Hurrah' to 'Ura' (meaning 'hatred' in Romanian).

The events going on in neighbouring countries favoured the Revolutionary movement launch. The majority of Communist leaders negotiated with their revolutionary opponents in order to avoid bloodshed. Romania was the only country where the revolutionary process entailed injuries and deaths: 1200 people died between 16 December and 27 December 1989. The huge exaggeration of the number of deaths, 60,000 instead of the above figure, was intended by several Warsaw Pact media agencies to increase international awareness of the Romanian situation. The brutal execution of the presidential couple, immediately after the hasty process the entire world could watch on television, was justified by the necessity of stopping the massacre of the population by terrorists, most of whom were acolytes of the Ceauşescu regime. Only some of those who took up the political leadership had had important positions during the Communist regime. April 1990 marked the beginning of one of the longest meetings in contemporary history: 52 uninterrupted days and nights in the Bucharest University Square. However, in June 1990 miners called up on purpose from different Romanian provinces repressed the meeting. The repression was unprecedented in its brutality, thus constituting a shock for the entire civilised world (Niculescu 2010: 80).

As mentioned earlier, the political events brought about an unprecedented amount of images of all sorts, what might be called the multi-faceted film of the revolution. But this almost natural phenomenon was not the first official chapter of the new cinema. The people from the film industry – whether established filmmakers, newcomers or exiles returning – wanted to start by saving Romanian cinema. Their agenda consisted of innumerable urgent points, among which figured the abolition of censorship and the rehabilitation of a whole range of shelved or banned films from the past. Also, many short or feature debuts had been delayed and were waiting to be screened. Television had always shown a lot of domestically produced films. However, for more than two decades, the Communist reign had produced films meant as collective indoctrination.

As early as January 1990, a Provisional Film-makers Committee consisting of, among others, Dan Piţa, Mircea Daneliuc, Stere Gulea, Alexandru Tatos and actor Victor Rebengiuc met Prime Minister Petre Roman in order to try to set a real political basis in terms of film industry production and distribution. The first proposed measure consisted of the creation of an autonomous entity, the CNC (Centrul Naţional de Cinematografie/The National Centre for Cinema), with no institutional link with the Ministry of Culture. This measure was rejected in the first instance, and a few months later exile director Lucian Pintilie became head of the newly created Ministry of Culture Film Unit.[1]

The Buftea Studios did not remain the only alternative to filming on location, given its old and inefficient equipment. Very soon private initiatives and newly inaugurated studios surfaced, the majority of them backed by foreign investors and/or producers: *Castel Film* (a joint venture with Paramount Studios headed by Vlad and Oana Păunescu), *Filmex* (headed by Constantin Popescu), *Atlantis Films* (a French joint venture) and *Media Pro* (headed by future TV mogul Adrian Sârbu). The newly created structures that emerged thanks to private investments proved more than necessary: they were an attempt to thwart a new type of censorship, the economic one.

Domestic professionals as well as filmmakers having returned from exile with a different kind of know-how strove for the emergence of a new film industry. A decree for reorganising the existing structures and proposals for establishing new legal structures meant to control the production and distribution of new films were concomitant with the above-mentioned private initiatives. There were also state-subsidised and supervised units headed by an institution called Cinerom, including both art house cinema subsidiaries, such as Solaris, supervised by Dan Piţa, and mainstream commercial films, as well as those by the everlasting director Sergiu Nicolaescu. The latter went on producing successful thrillers and historical epics about pivotal characters and periods from Romanian history. Nicolaescu also continued making films in the nationalist vein, including daring portraits of fascist despot Antonescu and his conflict with King Michael (*Începutul adevărului – Oglinda/ The Mirror*, 1993).

Nonetheless, because of difficult economic conditions and obsolete screening facilities, domestic production and distribution was extremely limited: attendance rates in cinemas reached their lowest point. People much preferred watching films at home, on the numerous newly available TV channels. As a matter of fact, nearly a year after the December revolution, Romanian audiences did not see film as an absolute priority. Beside productions dealt with in previous chapters, four categories of art-house films by less familiar or totally unknown directors are worth mentioning at this point:

1) Those still indebted to a metaphoric encoded cinematic language.

2) Those choosing to put it bluntly and reveal the realities of the immediate post-Communist Romania.

3) Those eager to retrace unknown and long-forbidden periods and facts from recent Romanian history, such as the terrible ordeals of Communist prisons or the forced collectivisation replacing private property.

4) Those depicting in a style closer to documentary and television the complex facts of the December revolution and of its immediate consequences.

In the first category, debuts by Bodgan Dumitrescu (*Unde la soare e frig/ Sunny but Chilly*, 1990) and Radu Nicoară (*Polul Sud/South Pole*, 1991), as well as a third feature by Ioan Cărmăzan (*Casa din vis/The House from a Dream*, 1991), were lightweight. Despite some stylish black-and-white photography, gifted performers and modern soundtracks, their scripts were pretentious and uninteresting and their destinies both on domestic screens and on the festival circuit were extremely ephemeral. Similarly, the second category has few titles to boast about in addition to those by established auteurs. As critic Alex Leo Şerban has noted in *4 Decades, 3 Years and 2 Months with Romanian Cinema*, the problem with films wanting to depict reality was that Romanian audiences from the early 1990s did not want to see that reality onscreen (Şerban 2009: 46-7). They clearly preferred commercial, unpretentious productions of ready-to-watch genre films. As a consequence, as in all ex-Communist productions from the neighbouring countries, the contemporary topics shown on film had to contain a lot of violence, sex and rough language in order to attract audiences. Şerban rightly argues that some kind of censorship had to be re-established, in order to avoid mediocrity and vulgarity.[2]

Two films from this sub-section stand the test of time: *Stare de fapt* (*State of Things*, Stere Gulea, 1994) and *Priveşte înainte cu mânie* (*Look Forward in Anger*, Nicolae Mărgineanu, 1993). As will be seen later in this chapter, both directors had previously dealt with early post-Communist times (Mărgineanu's *Undeva în Est/Somewhere in the East*, 1991) and with the pivotal issue of the December '89 revolution (Gulea's semi-documentary *Bucureşti, Piaţa Universităţii/Bucharest, University Square*, co-directed by cinematographers Vivi Drăgan Vasile and Sorin Ilieşiu). After a less than convincing hyperrealistic film about the moral terror reigning in Timişoara during the late Communist period, *Vulpe Vânător/Fox: Hunter* (1993), Gulea was in search of a subject about the consequences of revolution in everyday life. *Fox: Hunter* was co-produced by a German private company and adapted from a story by the German minority-issues novelist and later Nobel Prize winner Herta Müller.

State of Things was inspired by a true story from an idea by Lucian Pintilie. A member of the medical staff from a Bucharest hospital had been falsely accused in the days following the revolution of having stolen some medicine to help cure a young revolutionary. The life experience of Alberta (Oana Pellea) is terribly tough and emotionally challenging. Through her daily work she has access to information about revolutionaries killed with premeditation by the ex-secret police, as well as to the way national television manipulated the information the audience had been watching day in, day out. Alberta is an idealist who becomes a victim of the malevolent secret police, as embodied by officer Mureşan (Răzvan Vasilescu), a cruel and vile individual who beats, slaps and eventually rapes the young woman. Paradoxically, she will want to keep the child, going as far as delivering the news to the rapist's widow. The story ends with an almost unbearable childbirth scene, Alberta shouting her lungs off assisted by a nun. She craves a better future for her child in a troubled transitional period, where many things still need readjusting. Stere Gulea declared in the press that 'if the viewer does not feel hit in his stomach after seeing this film, my work has been useless' (Căliman 2000: 425).

Nicolae Mărgineanu, still active inside the Romanian film industry, had initially trained as a director of photography: he opted for directing in the early 1980s, specialising in biopics (e.g. *Ştefan Luchian*, 1981, about one of Romania's most famous painters) and adaptations, the most accomplished one being *Pădureanca* (*The Forrest Maiden*, 1986). After 1990, his films fared rather well in international festivals and were essential for describing the Romanian post-revolutionary zeitgeist. Such is the case with *Look Forward in Anger*, a very truthful insight into Romania's post-'89 painful transitional period. The story takes place on the outskirts of a construction site on the banks of the Danube, next to the town of Galaţi, where misery, unemployment, black market activities and strikes are the usual lot of workers and of their families.

As in Piţa's *Pepe and Fifi*, the alternative to this highly problematic existence is prostitution, in the case of one of the worker's daughter, and theft, in the case of her younger brother. The main character is their father, Fane Ciucudel (Remus Mărgineanu), whose personality outdoes the usual post-Communist stereotypes. He is an ex-dissident who has lost his job because he has been denouncing the ex-secret police members. Fane (diminutive for Stefan) realises that everything he fought for has fallen to pieces and that people 'have died for nothing'. Hence, he will participate in numerous strikes, trying to survive through occasional, peripheral jobs. He will never hesitate to call a spade a spade, via a lot of harsh language. There are some memorable phrases, like the one he utters to his son when asking him to put on the TV: 'Come on, turn on the lies'. However, his family is only partially dedicated to his cause. His children take up different paths. The boy Nelu (Laurenţiu Albu) ends up a vagabond. His nineteen-year-old sister (Luminiţa Ciobanu), at school in the morning and a cheap brothel employee at night, will indirectly be the cause of the film's most spectacular scene. Seeking revenge for her having become a prostitute, her elder brother (Cristian Iacob) will use a huge crane from the work site in order to literally tear to pieces the ship-brothel and its inhabitants: he will end up in prison. Shot at night with an astonishing craftsmanship, this final Armageddon lingers in one's mind long after the film is finished. *Look forward in Anger* got two international prizes in Italy and one in Portugal.[3]

Mărgineanu also directed two films about Communist times, to be put in sub-category three: *Undeva în Est* (*Somewhere in the East*, 1991), shot immediately after the revolution, and *Binecuvântată fii închisoare* (*Bless You Prison*, 2002). Adapted by the director from a novel by writer Augustin Buzura, *Somewhere in the East* uncovers the crimes committed under the initiative and guidance of the Romanian Communist Party during the collectivisation campaign in the 1950s, which completely destroyed Romanian agriculture. Eugenia Vodă calls the campaign a '*potemkinade*', during which many old and young peasants were imprisoned, destinies sacrificed and village values completely perverted (Vodă 1995: 237). Despite another convincing performance by Remus Mărgineanu and by a few other gifted character actors, the film often seems oversimplified and demonstrative, like some docu-fiction shown in schools. Similarly, *Bless You Prison*, based on Nicole-Valéry Grossu's homonymous bestseller though inspired by her husband's true story, does not stand comparison with other productions about life in Communist prisons.[4]

A more challenging example covering the same topic is a film released in the early 1990s, *Cel mai iubit dintre pământeni* (*The Most Beloved of Earthlings*, 1992) by Şerban Marinescu, another Marin Preda adaptation starring Ştefan Iordache. *The Most Beloved* assuredly was one of the most popular Romanian novels from the 1980s. The novel is a kind of fresco describing the horrors of Romanian Stalinism in a hybrid mode, combining psychology and realism. Director Marinescu did not stick to the letter of the book, incorporating more sex, violence and harsh dialogue than its original source.

Professor of philosophy Victor Petrini (Iordache) is wrongly accused and sent to forced work on minor charges, while having sex in his bathroom with younger wife Matilda (Maïa Morgenstern). After this abrupt prologue, the film moves on many years and is divided into two distinct parts. Part one unfolds mainly in a labour prison dominated by brutal torturers, one of which is attacked and killed by the hero himself in self-defence. Part two reveals to the audience the way Petrini starts over from zero via low-end jobs, ranging from pest controller to bookkeeper. He eventually ends up condemned again after a crime of passion. The film and the book's title allude to the character's passionate nature, wanting above all to be loved by women. Despite many useless thematic interludes and the usual lot of gratuitously vulgar scenes, the film is very well cast.

Trahir (*A trăda/Betrayal*, 1993), a Franco-Romanian co-production by exiled director Radu Mihăileanu back at work in his native country, is also worth mentioning at this point. Indeed, this is yet another film about the controversial Romanian Communist past. Born in Bucharest in 1958, the son of journalist Ion Mihăileanu, who co-scripted Pintilie's *Sunday at Six*, Mihăileanu fled Romania in 1980 after a brief career as a theatre actor at the Bucharest Jewish Theatre. Reaching France via Israel, he trained as an assistant director and worked for television. He briefly returned from exile in the early 1990s to shoot *Betrayal*. Inspired by a true story, *Betrayal* is about the ambiguous relationship between an initially dissident poet, George Vlaicu (played by Belgian actor Johan Leysen), and the famous Stalinist secret police. Vlaicu is forced to serve an inspector (Alexandru Repan) by reporting on the lives of others, in order to escape prison and lead a writer's life.[5] Notwithstanding its interesting socio-political implications in the depiction of a long-ignored period from the Romanian past, *Betrayal* unfortunately appears as a mediocre co-production, difficult to watch and highly artificial. This is mainly due to the fact that it is spoken in French, while it unfolds in Romania and pictures native characters talking a different language than their own, a generalised plague common to most recent Euro-puddings. Besides, obviously for budgetary reasons, Romanian actors were asked to speak French, with sometimes surprisingly implausible results.

The two most important documentary films from category four, those depicting the controversial Romanian December 1989 revolution, were actually collective projects. *București, Piața Universității* (*Bucharest, University Square*, Stere Gulea, Sorin Ilieşiu and Vivi Drăgan Vasile, 1991) and *Videogrammen einer Revolution* (*Videograms of a Revolution*, Harun Farocki and Andrei Ujică, 1992) were produced under different circumstances and in different countries, but their objective was the same: unveiling the multiple perspectives that made up an unprecedented chronicle in recent Romanian history. Their target audience was obviously different. *University Square* was widely distributed in Romania and has been shown on domestic TV at regular intervals, with additional testimonies from those who took part actively in the events. *Videograms* has been literally touring the world and has been the subject of a vast critical enterprise, its two directors being also renowned media scholars. Paradoxically it has become only recently familiar to Romanian audiences.

Bucharest, University Square was the first film of the newly created Cinema Studio of the Ministry of Culture, headed by director Lucian Pintilie, who initiated the project, seeing it as a moral obligation in the Romanian post-revolutionary context. This montage film deals with a very complex event which unfolded over several weeks: the gathering of thousands of people around the university square in spring 1990. According to Codrescu:

> On April 22, 1990, a large demonstration marched on the television station calling for Iliescu's resignation. In a sudden riot police attacked and beat the demonstrators who had spent the night in the University Square. Several protesters began a hunger strike. Iliescu denounced the demonstrators as hooligans. [...] The old Communist style had spontaneously re-asserted itself. A small city of tents appeared and University Square was declared a 'Non-Communist Free Zone'. After the victory of the front, demonstrators manifested and went on strike again. In June, the 'democratic forces' called by president Iliescu arrived with pipes and sticks. They wore blue miners' helmets, were about 5000 and were seen beating men, women, even children. According to different sources, some of these were not real miners but Securitate-trained spies. It was clear that one dictatorship had replaced another. (Codrescu 1991: 189)

The montage aspect allows different opinions to comment on this major event, which explains why important figures of the Romanian intelligentsia are interviewed at several moments in the film: pivotal writers from the revolutionary movement (Mircea Dinescu, Ana Blandiana), ex-dissidents (Doina Cornea), controversial politicians (Silviu Brucan) and most importantly student leaders physically molested and harassed by the miners. As proven by sequences filmed by the directors themselves and by amateur cameras in the square, the interviews are only glimpses of a very complex ensemble that unfolded over several weeks. The edited sequences also include manipulated information relayed on Romanian television: the demonstrators from the square appeared at certain moments as a chaotic mob, which had to be calmed down by some state-driven forces, the miners.

Stere Gulea told the press there was no need to stage events, while the publicity campaign for the film read 'Every citizen a viewer/every viewer a consciousness'. The 'University Square' phenomenon proved to what extent, after forty-five years of dictatorship, there were still battles to fight.[6]

Fig 11. The miners' attack in *University Square*

Not a Romanian film, but clearly a film about Romania, *Videograms of a Revolution* could not have been created without the background of its co-author, Andrei Ujica. Born and educated in Timișoara but having emigrated to Germany in the early 1980s, Ujica proved a versatile intellectual, whose contacts with the Romanian intelligentsia were instrumental in making the polyphonic montage film about the Romanian revolution. He co-scripted his found footage project with German media artist Harun Farocki, whose work in the field of non-fiction and video installations received international acclaim.

A brief overview of the film's structure is necessary at this point. Entirely conceived as a montage of television broadcasts and amateur found footage, *Videograms* is a media-based example of historiography confronting images from different sources, at times showing the same event from different perspectives. However, it does not offer its own definitive solution as to how things really happened during the five days that shook the country. Roughly speaking, the film unfolds on three planes, which are either simultaneous or separated by longer or shorter time intervals. They are related to each other by a commentator's voice and by titles that are not always presented in chronological order (Young 2004: 245; Privett 1999).

1) A whole series of filmed professional or amateur scenes occur around the Central Committee and Presidential Palace headquarters: people are seen heading towards these places. We subsequently watch the famous last meeting occurring on the Central Committee square. Ceaușescu's speech is interrupted by booing and shouting, forcing him and his wife to leave the place. A few sequences later, they are seen fleeing by helicopter from the rooftop of the same building. As a consequence, protesters invade the palace, recalling S. M. Eisenstein's *October* (1927). In the meantime, the terrace from which the dictator was seen delivering his final speech now hosts new speakers: dissidents, well-known writers and actors, politicians, and so on.

2) The other set of recurrent images is related to the televisual sphere in two ways. First, the viewer is systematically shown images broadcast by television. The audience also witnesses episodes unfolding inside the Romanian Free television area, mostly filmed by amateurs and proving to what extent the officially broadcast images are biased or incomplete. The famous Studio 4 turns into a permanent arena, where almost all the important protagonists of the revolution turn up to address the audience and implicitly the whole world.

As Christa Blümlinger argues: 'the television apparatus does not change after the fall of the despot but the event is increasingly reported on the station, taking on the conventions of television' (Blümlinger 2004: 167).

3) The third set of images are of a highly hybrid nature, as most of them are situated mid-way between the official version of the revolution events and the parallel ones. Most of them feature a form of reflexivity: one either sees the person filming in an explicit manner or can easily infer from subjective shots that the camera filming is an amateur one. Eventually, after the much-debated short Christmas Day trial and execution of the presidential couple, with the subsequent extremely crude and shocking revelation of their corpses, an additional film unit films the reactions of people assembled around their television sets, some of them applauding.

As was the case with its prologue, the closing image of *Videograms* favours a mode of address derived from an amateur initiative. One year has elapsed since the revolution and a man from the crowd addresses the audience in a quite pessimistic tone. He seems sceptical about the chances of freed Romania reaching an authentic democracy while old values are still in place. His eyes filled with tears, he does nonetheless wish everybody a Happy Christmas.

Gérard Althabe notes that from *Videograms* on, 'plural images of the same historical event may question its very reality, proving that the image cannot be an autonomous entity any longer' (Althabe 2001: 25; author's translation). Farocki and Ujica ask the viewer to realise to what extent there were trafficked images and political media blackouts, but also a lot of highly realistic, extremely moving ones. The relationship between historical agency and virtualisation of events in the case of the filmed Romanian revolution obviously demonstrates that the country's main challenge in the course of time was trying to establish one truth, not several truths.

Paradoxically, one has to wait for more than a decade for young filmmakers to look this subject straight in the eyes anew. They will proceed in a purely fictional way, using refreshingly black humour and minimalist aesthetics to depict tragic moments from the lives of young people who desperately fought for liberty and for a better world.

CHAPTER 7

Through a Glass, Darkly
Lucian Pintilie as Past and Present Role Model

- Why do you make films, Lucian Pintilie?
- To survive. I know no other way to survive, except making films.[1]

This chapter closely scrutinises the narrative structures and unique style of Lucian Pintilie, the most influential Romanian filmmaker to date. Pintilie miraculously managed to bridge the gap between the short-lived Thaw and the post-revolutionary period, re-integrating into the domestic film industry after a forced artistic exile of almost twenty years.

Part of the first generation of film school graduates from the late 1950s for whom cinephilia was a common practice, Lucian Pintilie made his debut as an assistant to veteran director Victor Iliu,[2] was briefly employed by Romanian national television and directed two important feature films in the late 1960s, while also staging some memorable classical and contemporary plays. Consistently refusing to make concessions to the Communist regime, he entered an artistic exile period as early as 1972. He was granted a privileged, albeit paradoxical status, that of travelling freely to Europe and the US and returning to Romania whenever he wished, on the condition that he did not direct any film or stage any play in his native country. He managed with a lot of difficulties and delays to shoot a film in 1981, without being able to have an official premiere for it. A few months after the 1989 December revolution he was back to work and wanted to make up for lost time, first as a producer and then as a director, his second Romanian career unfolding roughly during the next fifteen years (1992–2007).

Pintilie has depicted Romanian realities using irony, satire and embedded narratives, thus following the lineage of a heritage which has always been extremely familiar to him: the work of playwrights such as Caragiale and Ionesco, known for their taste for black humour, cynicism and the grotesque, alongside philosopher E. M. Cioran's consistent pessimism. Most of his films are adapted from pre-existing literary material, but his imprint as screenwriter makes them all pure Pintilie products. The director has always used cinema as a medium to denounce what he describes as the apathy of a lethargic Romanian society, as well as to criticise both Communism and post-Communism, while exploring metaphysical evil and historical guilt. Pintilie takes over Eugene Ionesco's formula from *The Chairs* (1952), considering the whole world to be a 'tragic farce' (Jäckel 1999: 27).[3]

Lucian Pintilie's first feature film, *Duminică la ora şase* (*Sunday at Six*, 1965), is an authorised love story set against the World War II resistance movement. Co-scripted by columnist Ion Mihăileanu, it is partly based on the latter's personal story. According to Bujor Rîpeanu, Pintilie is explicitly anti-dogmatic and changes the initial storyline, which focused much more on the Communist resistance side, so as to highlight the experimental aspect of the cinematic language (Rîpeanu 2004, I: 131). He uses editing techniques close to the style of Alain Resnais, with mental flashes brilliantly translated on screen through daring cinematography and a very challenging sound score.

Though criticised by hard-line Communist colleagues because of its lack of transparency in depicting the illegal cause, *Sunday at Six* is welcomed as the first Romanian film to apply the aesthetic principles of European modernism. This is confirmed by Pintilie's own remarks: he seems to opt more for an improvised story, edited in an arbitrary way, and refuses to be 'enslaved by a didactic, over-explicit, chronological' narrative. 'I realize I'm organically unable to tell a story fluently', declares Pintilie to film critic George Littera.[4]

The action unfolds in 1940, but its visual aspect is clearly closer to the early 1960s. We are introduced via a freeze-frame to Radu (Dan Nuţu), a clandestine factory worker belonging to an illegal Communist movement. He lives in Bucharest but has to complete an important mission outside the capital. Once he is travelling on the train to complete his mission, we learn he will have to use a new code name. 'Do not forget, your name is Ion Arghir', Maria (Graziela Albini) tells Radu, who is sitting next to her in a train compartment. Noticing he does not listen, she repeats the sentence to no avail. He has mechanically memorised his new identity and is sadly watching a group of noisy youngsters, his melancholy gaze betraying the sadness he is experiencing in realising his life will be different from theirs. Later on his voice-over says: 'Try to forget everything else and remember just one thing, your name is Ion Arghir'. The similitude with Emmanuelle Riva's character from Resnais's *Hiroshima mon amour* (1959) is striking, her on- and off-screen comments focusing on the necessity either to remember or to forget painful personal events (Silvestri & Spagnoletti 2004: 24).

Different flashbacks recompose his love story with young Anca (Irina Petrescu), a student he had met by chance some time ago. In one flash-back they are attending a party packed with young people when a fight with aggressive Romanian fascist officials breaks out; they escape and spend the night together. Neither of them knows the other is a resistance member until they meet on a common mission, called 'Sunday at Six'. Though Radu receives the order not to see Anca again, they meet in secret to spend another night together. She is briefly imprisoned, then freed. They are eventually caught by opponents and the young girl is mortally wounded in front of her lover, who desperately tries to bring her back to life and put an end to her agony. Radu later goes off on another mission, which proves an ambush: he is seen running away on the beach but his days are clearly numbered.

The pioneering use of the *transtrav* technique (combining deep focus and tracking shot), launched by cinematographer Sergiu Huzum, has the effect of both compressing and dilating time, thus faithfully rendering the hero's mean-dering subjectivity. Both in daytime outdoor scenes and in nocturnal indoor episodes, the camera goes back and forth in time and space, trying to prove to what extent the hero needs to take refuge in the past. Memory is like a puzzle waiting to be solved, filled with corridors and hiding places, the back yard filled with people hanging their laundry. We see the couple wandering downtown and fantasising about trips and matrimony. Thus, the wonderful scene, echoing Agnès Varda's *Cléo from 5 to 7* (1962) and showing the wed-ding dress chosen by Anca in a shop, is not only visually but also narratively relevant, as in real life the couple will never be able to get married. During one of their walks Radu and Anca walk next to a tennis court, separated from the court by an iron wire. Anca decides to abolish the distance by uttering an English counting rhyme: 'I have a cat / Her name is Kit / And by the fire she likes to sit'. The metaphor here clearly wants to express the idea of two frail existences which still believe in the liberty to talk and have fun. When the recurring motif of the elevator appears again by way of an arbitrary editing technique, it resembles a guillotine cutting off any form of hope.

Another modernist master Pintilie mentions in interviews is Michelangelo Antonioni. Of interest to Pintilie is not only the way characters and situations relate to objects which stand for their inner states, but also the innovative use of atonal music and synchronous sounds from present and past reminiscences. In the vein of Antonioni's composer Giovanni Fusco, Romanian composer Radu Căplescu and future frequent collaborator sound engineer Andrei Papp design autnomous sounds and symbolic harmonic or non-harmonic music clusters. At some moments they are foregrounded in an almost excessive way, so as to suggest the hyperreal intensity of character situations and sensations, while at others they are barely present, in small but sensible doses, with mental images shifting back and forwards in time.

The film starts in a railway station and ends on the seashore, where the male protagonist, his fake identity betrayed, realises that any attempt to escape would be in vain. Magda Mihăilescu rightly compares him to Antoine Doinel, the teenage hero of Truffaut's *Les quatre cent coups/The 400 Blows* (1959), who turns his back to the sea and faces the audience.

Sunday at Six is the harbinger of a new tendency in Romania, where there had previously been no signs of modernism, as was the case in the other Soviet satellite countries. Critics having seen the film in festivals such as Locarno, Pesaro, Hyères and Cannes appreciated the film's modernist montage, while noting the contemporary undertones of a story supposed to unfold during World War II (Leonardi 2004: 74). Despite critical remarks due to some artificial dialogue imposed by ideological circumstances, the film won two major awards in Romania as well as nine prizes at international film festivals.

Pintilie's second feature, *Reconstituirea* (*Reconstruction/Reenactment*, 1969),[5] has always been regarded on the international scene as Romanian cinema's unique 'dissident' film. It arrived as a real surprise, Romania having lagged way behind the other Eastern bloc new waves. In an interview with the French journal *Positif* published in 1971, Pintilie seems to be unusually optimistic and confident in his country's chance to finally say goodbye to the Stalinist heritage, calling Romanian cinema 'a handicapped child with aluminium legs' (Briot 1971: 49). He also recognises his debt to Romanian and West European masters from Gogol to Caragiale, especially as he feels much more comfortable with subjects written by others.[6] Pintilie admits that his film is an exception in the context of Romanian cinema and belongs to no particular school or film generation (Nasta 2000: 1483, 2004: 51).

Through a daring cinematic gesture, the filmmaker aims to break the mirror of totalitarian conformism: *Reconstruction* centres around an act of juvenile delinquency, meant to be re-enacted so as to serve as an example of what cannot be done. Supposedly filmed in a *ciné-vérité* style, the reconstruction ends in tragedy, as one of the two students is killed due to an absurd technical filming error, the remaining one being violently attacked by a mob walking out of a football match. The film is adapted from a short story inspired by a real event witnessed in the late 1950s by journalist and writer Horia Pătraşcu, who decided to fictionalise it.[7] The real reconstruction took place in 1963 in Transylvania, and Pătraşcu witnessed the filming process. Another member of the film club who attended the real reconstruction was Sergiu Huzum, who became Pintilie's most dedicated director of photography.

The screenplay of *Reconstruction* was first entrusted to Liviu Ciulei, who suggested changes Pătraşcu did not agree with. Pintilie proposed a new treatment, which was debated, delayed and modified by different ideological commissions (Rîpeanu 2004, I: 171). Similarly, after the brief shooting period on location in Sinaia, the film's editing process became unusually long: more than eight months, during which different political authorities argued about reality having been distorted in a flagrant way. Several intellectuals defended the film after having attended a private screening, but Ceauşescu in person refused to authorise its public premiere. Pintilie hung on to his project and went as far as being interviewed by a Radio Free Europe journalist to whom he expressed his indignation. Eventually, under such domestic and international pressure, *Reconstruction* was granted a very limited distribution and there was no official premiere. Though highly successful – there were lines in front of the cinema and windows were broken by those trying to get into the theatre – the film was withdrawn after one month from most Romanian cinemas.

No wonder Communist authorities tried everything to prevent it from being widely seen at home and abroad, since *Reconstruction* is the freest Romanian film of all time. Despite its morose, albeit tragic outcome, it is also an extremely funny film: one laughs whole-heartedly on several occasions. Romanian irony, sarcasm and caustic wit have never been more alive than they are in Pintilie's feature. On the French MK2 edited DVD, film critic Michel Ciment rightly compares it to Jean Renoir's *Partie de campagne* (*A Day in the Country*, 1938): the first half of the story is indeed bathed in an almost blinding late summer light, with fields filled with wild flowers, and woods and magnificent mountains looming in the background. During the second half, skies are menacing, thunder is roaring, and violence is uncontrolled.

Quite common as a Western modernist self-reflexive device but seldom found in East European films of the late 1960s, the prologue eventually proves to be a flash-forward. The Pirandellian *mise en abyme* of a noteworthy event would actually be at the centre of most subsequent Pintilie films, the author fre-quently opting to debunk the filming process. A film clapper insert resembling the one from Jean-Luc Godard's *Tout va bien* (1970) thus signals the beginning and end of the prologue: 'Reconstruction/254/A2' (Nasta 2007b: 2).

Fig 12. Vuică's opening shout in *Reconstruction*

A young boy has just slipped down into a ravine and realises with amazement he has been hurt. An off-screen voice gives him instructions as to how to raise his muddy face and long hair filled with blood from the ground.

The film's title and credits unfold over this scene, which will be repeated at least three times, the only additional sound heard being that of the filming camera. A counter-shot will reveal a group of sun-bathers, the filming crew, and a freeze-frame will capture another young boy later to be identified as the one who has been beaten and hurt. What the audience is really watching is one of the last scenes from a suppos-edly educational film in the tradition of Socialist propaganda. Ripu (Vladimir Găitan) and Vuică (George Mihăiţă) are forcefully led to an isolated mountain bar where they previously celebrated their school graduation: they got drunk and smashed up the bar, while also hurting the bartender. A local magistrate accompanied by a whole staff forces them to re-enact the violent fistfight.

Soon afterwards, the real story setting opens up with a kind of synesthetic feeling unleashed by simultaneous hyperreal stimuli: dialogue, music coming from radio or TV sources, animal and lavatory door sounds, the exasperating sound of the off-screen filming camera. The story has an astonishing visual immediacy, thanks to Sergiu Huzum's outstanding black-and-white photogra-phy. The setting itself is dominated by an Antonioniesque sense of 'being there'. However, the general tone of the *mise en scène* owes a lot to theatrical influ-ences, every pivotal character acting as a meaningful entity (Nasta 2004b: 52).

There are also highly burlesque aspects highlighted by Pintilie's inventive *mise en scène*: the arrival of the jeep containing the story's main protago-nists is a moment of sheer slapstick comedy. We see the driver, the prosecutor (George Constantin), professor Paveliu (Emil Botta), the cameraman (Nicky Woltz) and his assistant, and the two students Vuică and Ripu, getting off one by one, as if the capacity of this jeep were infinite. Later on, the same party tries to stop the car's horn, which seems to be out of order, to no avail. The noise grows more and more exasperating, filling the whole space, until finally somebody manages to stop it. Pintilie is clearly mocking a hierarchical society, where Communist authority should also be having a rough time.

The climate is surrealist, nobody really believing this reconstruction is worth performing. The bar is next to a railway station and a football stadium. The picture is completed by an unknown charming young girl (Ileana Popovici) in a bathing suit. She and Ripu will flirt briefly before the tragic outcome. Though frequently filmed in long shots, *Reconstruction*'s action takes place simultaneously on different spatial planes: the railway platform, the lake, the woods and the vicinity of a stadium. These planes seemed to be related to one another via a stage-like structure, this feature being manifest every time Pintilie shoots from high-angles so as to reveal the scene of the reconstruction.

The military officer, the apparently nonchalant prosecutor and the camera operator – who will eventually discover his camera is not charged and will have to start the whole thing over again – each intend to give orders about the way the reconstruction should be dealt with. Meanwhile, the re-enactment process is constantly delayed and deliberately not finalised. Though it is meant to be a one-day event, the action seems to last forever, somehow following the Theatre of the Absurd conventions, thus creating a kind of *temps mort* effect. A constant, absurdist form of humour turns a ridiculous totalitarian enterprise into a huge metaphor for deranged authority.

Professor Paveliu is the only character to prophesise the tragedy looming behind an ordinary situation: he is horrified by the very idea of the reconstruction and has a premonition regarding the upcoming tragedy. 'Why don't you tell them they are free and pretend they are prisoners?' he asks the prosecutor. The latter had previously declared bluntly to his assistant that he was having an affair with the professor's wife. The professor will eventually drink out his despair in a cynical way. His mortified face staring at the void against the car window at the end of the story reminds one of Dostoyevsky's characters.

The mysterious young girl, to whom several names are assigned, stands at the opposite extreme: she is an unintentional witness to the whole story, walking around aimlessly in her bikini, sunbathing, giggling and miming different gestures, taking a dip in the lake, constantly listening to a small radio, going around almost naked. During one of the numerous reconstruction attempts, the assistants will stare at her

Fig 13. The perceptive professor in *Reconstruction*

symbolically climbing up a huge advertising sign for an instant soup.

The film thus tells one more about state institutions and the adolescent zeitgeist than any documentary or TV report: a new type of formal dissidence suddenly emerges. In a strikingly impudent scene the young boys are asked

Fig 14. *Reconstruction*'s smart girl in a bathing suit

Fig 15. Rehearsing before filming in *Reconstruction*

by the zealous officer to re-enact 'every gesture, fight, every song you sang, every glass you broke'. The whole thing turns wayward as they serenely disobey, ironising the re-enactment by singing daring out-of-tune songs and breaking glasses and bottles on purpose.

The television leitmotif will actually prove a recurring device in Pintilie's cinematic universe. The entire story is going on next to a football stadium, but the building is almost exclusively suggested by off-screen shouts and comments during the whole film. By means of the constantly shown television broadcast from inside the bar, the audience is confronted with a particular audio-visual experience: an ambulance first identified by its off-screen siren is seen heading towards the stadium, both in real fiction time and as part of the television broadcast of the same event (Nasta 2004a: 54).

During a filming pause, Ripu, Paveliu and the cameraman embark on an escapade into neighbouring woods in search of a lost flock of geese. Vuică seizes the opportunity to fake being lost, causing tension and anguish among the whole party, who desperately shout his name. Pintilie thus integrates the forest theme already present as a catalyst for timeless metaphors in the films of his geopolitical neighbours. With the sun irradiating every single leaf, the silence is broken by off-screen crying: it is Paveliu, whose devastated face is again framed in extreme close-up. In the meantime, Vuică is seen commentating on his own on an intervention by firemen in a nearby place and singing an a capella Romanian folk song he resumes at the end of the film.

When Vuică re-appears, they are ready to start shooting the scene from the prologue in which Ripu is supposed to hit Vuică. The former refuses to hit his friend, but is put under such pressure by the prosecutor, the military and the camera operator that he finally starts hitting. Vuică's head is badly hurt when he falls, a scene which clearly echoes the film's beginning. Images from the prologue are now repeated and integrated into a wider context, that of a reconstruction with fatal consequences. Everyone is so satisfied that the reconstruction has finally taken place that nobody really cares about the young man's accident.

During the final sequence, a savage mob coming out of the stadium and filmed via an extreme high angle is aurally backed by a Romanian *variété*

standard, thus creating a strange counterpoint effect: the musical reference exceeds the limits of the visualised screen space (Nasta 2004a: 56).[8]
This magnified vision is immediately followed by a spiral-like return to the
heroes' microcosm, while Vuică, the dying hero, still manages to strike up a
song. Ripu takes his head on his lap and listens to his final words: 'Mă doare,
mă doare in cur' / 'It hurts, it hurts my ass' (meaning 'I don't give a damn').
In the meantime, the skies are looking menacing, and everyone wants to
get back home before the storm. Pintilie resists the temptation to enter the
stadium and films in long shots the crowd, a sinister snake-like procession
which reacts to Ripu's gestures without knowing what has really occurred
previously: these are grotesque and brutal people, victims of a repressive
dictatorship. A crowd is seen coming out of the stadium, some intrigued
by the fact that Vuică has been so badly injured by his colleague. The camera now cuts to a collective close-up of the football fans' faces gazing in
bewilderment at a tragic, albeit absurd event. Though this crowd ignores the
causes of this death it seems to condemn the remaining young man, giving
him a hard time and insulting him. Ripu gets nervous and hits some of them
back. As a consequence, Ripu himself is given a rough time by the others
and falls into muddy ground. The film opened on a freeze-frame close-up
of Vuică, and it ends with a similar freeze-frame close-up of a bedazzled
Ripu. Two innocent men have been massacred, thus relating the film to 'The
Massacre of the Innocents', a biblical theme present in most of Pintilie's subsequent films.[9]

Says Pintilie:

I come from a country where reconstructions were among the most violent means
of mystifying and violating reality. Individuals were tortured in order to follow a
programmed mise en scène [...] These people banned my film mainly because
they did not understand the fact that I was questioning the very principle of
a reconstruction: an abuse of which neither the torturers nor the victims were
actually conscious [...] The second reason for banning it was the tragic finale,
which downgraded the very idea of the educational film, the political act led by
Communist authorities. The third reason came from the image I chose to show of
the crowd, resembling a Greek chorus, exiting the football match at the end of
the story: they are a caricature of humanity, jeered at, marginalised, deprived of
any intuition about reality and its tragic facts. This is one of the darkest scenes of
my entire work. Human bestiality is suggested both by the off-screen sounds of
the football match and by the on-screen final shots. (Silvestri 2004: 25; author's
translation)

Reconstruction was greeted with critical acclaim at the Directors' Fortnight in Cannes, but Pintilie could not attend the screening.[10] In *The Most Important Art: Soviet and East European Film after 1945*, Mira and Antonin Liehm describe *Reconstruction* as 'an allegory about cowardice and indifference [...] absolutely uncompromising in its moral criticism'. They consider it 'the best film to emerge from Romania during the 60s', with 'elements of black humour in the tradition of Gogol and Swift', 'indeed one of the pinnacles of European cinema during that decade' (1977: 354).

My parents happened to be among the happy few to have attended one of the screenings of *Reconstruction*: they kept talking to me about the film as if it were a hidden talisman, a bottle full of liberty, thrown into the mysterious sea of exile. The long-closed bottle containing the only real dissident film from the late 1960s was miraculously found and opened in 1990. The film had barely circulated, so it looked brand new. Considering its revolutionary content and stylistic composition, critics and audiences alike developed a 'year zero' syndrome, unanimously calling it the first real Romanian filmic work of art (Nasta 2007: 2). Critic Eugenia Vodă thus argues in *Cinema and Nothing Else*:

Scenes, dialogues and images from *Reconstruction* are now part of a collective consciousness, they are real memory reflexes [...] the film looks strange because it is so close to our everyday life. With a few minor changes, if you replaced 'comrade' with 'sir', changed the ads and the type of music, and replaced the camera with a more sophisticated video one, everything would seem to stick close to life as it is today. Moreover, the film has a nearly documentary cinematography and an extremely fresh, modern sound (Vodă 1995: 19; author's translation). Indeed, the film's immediacy both at the level of the storyline and from an aesthetic standpoint turned it into a harbinger for the younger post-Communist generation of filmmakers. According to leading contemporary Romanian screenwriter Răzvan Rădulescu:

> At the beginning of the 1990s my generation was unable to name five Romanian valuable films. Watching a film like *Reconstruction* twenty years later meant witnessing the purest perfection, because there is still a dynamite effect provoked by this movie. We decided to look for a master, a green light, a filmmaker who made good choices in terms of acting, editing, sound. Besides, Pintilie was extremely daring, he didn't care about consequences, he wanted to shock and interest the audience in completely different ways.[11]

In October 2008, almost forty years later, *Reconstruction* came first in a top ten of the best Romanian films of all time awarded by domestic film critics

(Corciovescu & Mihăilescu 2010: 9). For its fortieth anniversary at the 1992 Locarno Film Festival, the French journal *Positif* chose five representative films from the modern international circuit: *Reconstruction* was one of them. For Michel Ciment, 'this is one of the major works from the East European cinema context, heralding changes which occurred twenty years later'.[12]

Following his radical refusal to cut scenes from the film and the suppression of his theatrical production of Gogol's *The Inspector General* (considered to contain too many overt allusions to the Romanian Communist regime) after three performances, the director was invited to work for the theatre abroad and was granted a permanent passport. He would not be allowed to direct films in his own country before 1981. Lucian Pintilie became an *'auteur maudit'* whose screenplays were turned down and whose films were shelved for almost twenty years, while he staged very highly praised plays and operas. From 1972 to 1990 he was active in France, Britain, Yugoslavia and the United States. Chekhov, Molière, Ibsen, Ionesco, Mozart, Bizet and Verdi were among the authors he staged, garnering public and critical acclaim.

In 1979 Pintilie shot an adaptation of a Chekhov short story, *Pavillon VI*, for Yugoslav television. The film follows closely the mental confusion of a Russian doctor handling suffering in a mental ward. He strolls in the woods on his own, reads a lot, listens to music and, despite his routine life, believes himself superior to everybody around him. He meets one of his ex-students, Nikita, a political prisoner, but also a rebel spirit who challenges him intellectually and disturbs him to the point of unbalance. He the judge, the leader will become the accused, 'death's servant', finding himself confined to the same ward where his life will end in tragedy. This Faustian pact renders the atmosphere more and more unbearable and proves again a poignant metaphor for life under a repressive regime. The film stars Yugoslav actors, is spoken in their language, and is made with Yugoslav technical staff, such that, even directed by a Romanian director, it cannot be considered a Romanian film. Pintilie himself explains that it was turned into a full-length feature and rated as one of the ten best Yugoslav films of all time. It got a prize from the Catholic Film Office in Cannes in 1979.

The exiled director attempted a filmic comeback in 1981 with *Carnival Scenes/De ce trag clopotele Mitică* (literal translation: *For Whom Do the Bells Toll, Mitică?*). His second film as an exile is a free adaptation based on his own 1977 screenplay of Caragiale's *D'ale Carnavalului/Carnival Scenes*, a play he had already staged successfully for the theatre. The context and the circumstances of the film's delays and eventual premiere are detailed in Pintilie's autobiography, significantly called *Bricabrac* (Pintilie 2003: 320). According to different sources, the production of *Carnival Scenes* started in September 1979 and ended in spring 1981: the film's premiere was not authorised and it was shelved until August 1990, only one original copy being left. Its real premiere thus took place only in 1991. How was it that Pintilie – a half exile – was allowed to start shooting by Communist authorities while his second feature, out ten years earlier, was almost never shown on domestic screens and rarely in festivals? Pintilie explains that he had so many turned-down, 'buried alive' projects that they decided to accept one of them, so as to avoid the external pressure of such powerful media as Radio Free Europe.

Even though it is set at the turn of the twentieth century, a vaudeville structure dissimulates allusions to the destructive madness of power and the violence of social relationships in a contemporary Romania already in a state of decrepitude. The film adapted from Caragiale's play depicts a world of counterfeit passions and dubious morals. Caragiale had always been an officially accepted author, a solid source for the inside and the outside market; however, what the authorities did not realise was that Pintilie wrote a screenplay which took many liberties with subject, tone and mood. Conceived as pure vaudeville, the intrigue of *Carnival Scenes* sets up a carefully planned vengeance plan for a double adultery taking place during a huge carnival party. Pintilie invents scenes and adds material from other short stories by the same author, among the most notable being precisely the paradigmatic character from the Romanian title, Mitică, absent from the initial play (Pintilie 1992: 45). The scenario thus zigzags between dialogue from the play, added fragments from Caragiale's prose and Pintilie's own postmodern self-reflexive elements framing the film. The general tone is far more passionate, hysterical and sexually explicit, but also more sombre, grotesque and cynical, than that of Caragiale's play.

Pintilie explained that there was no censorship during the shooting itself. The completion being delayed, the director wrote a letter to the Ministry of Culture, photocopied 500 times and signed by the majority of the cast. He asked the authorities for permission to go on filming after months of interruption, mentioning that the right to continue belongs to Romanian culture. Under constant pressure, especially from Radio Free Europe, the censors allowed him to finish his film, but as soon as he did so, first he was asked to cut important parts and then it was denied exhibition. For Romanian literary critic Alexandru Călinescu, the censors perfectly understood that boorishness is a permanent state of things, that the spirit of the slums had been carried over into the present, multiplying itself beyond Caragiale's times. The slums of 1880 were those of 1980 (Călinescu 1998: 78).

Framed by a real shooting crew, a self-reflexive device much favoured by Pintilie, the camera relentlessly tracks a hysterical, excessive, gossipy petty bourgeois community obsessed with futile problems. As in *Reconstruction*, the prologue and epilogue deal with filming, while clearly distancing themselves from the limits of theatrical conventions: the viewer is shown the tracking camera's rails, the loudspeaker, the camera operator, the director himself.

The opening scene is a very explicit lovemaking session between two characters whose whispers and moans suggest a long-time complicity. We are further introduced to Pampon (meaning 'bobble'), Pintilie's frequent stage and screen collaborator Victor Rebengiuc, when he comes back from a card-playing party and discovers that his mistress, Didina (Tora Vasilescu), is betraying him with a mysterious man. The latter had inadvertently left a compromising written note which also contained his address. Pampon thus decides to search for him at Nae's (Gheorghe Dinică) place, but there he meets only his assistant, Iordache (Mircea Diaconu). The picture is completed by Nae's larger-than-life mistress Miţa (Mariana Mihuţ), who has also discovered she is being cheated on. Both deceived lovers realise that the note Pampon found at his place comes from Nae and had been written by Miţa herself. They decide to seek revenge.

In a scene highly reminiscent of Fellini's *Otto e mezzo* (1963), Pampon tracks Nae to a Turkish spa. A carnival feast is soon underway and everybody is ready for masquerade and jokes. One of the key figures is that of Mitică (Ştefan Iordache), an immoral character: his sudden death will occur in the midst of a popular feast *par excellence*, where French cancan and Romanian folklore joyously co-exist. Nae takes on a disguise to hide his real identity and so does Miţa. A burlesque pursuit ensues with no real conclusion, and an innocent character who had taken up Nae's disguise is the only real victim. The party finally gets to Nae's house, and the two rival women start another violent fight, but in the end they are all reconciled and start partying again. A distant cry is heard; it is Mitică's mother mourning her dead son: he was mistakenly killed. 'Why do the bells toll Mitică?' somebody asks at one moment in the film. 'Because they have ropes' is the answer, confirming how cruel and mean life is in a world were people lack any real feelings.

Men and women lose their identity, plunged into mud and misery, but their pleasures are paradoxically voluptuous: they seem to enjoy and approve of their own decay, which perfectly fits the carnival atmosphere. Pintilie diversifies the playwright's initial stylistic nuances, in a devastatingly baroque structure in which everybody is perverted and decayed. One party following another, lust for fun turns ferocious. After Mitică's unexpected death, the party, bedazzled by hangovers, backed by some strange music, head in their carriage towards an unknown destination, while Pintilie and his cameraman re-appear to close the self-reflexive paradigm they opened at the beginning of the film (Mihăilescu 2004: 45).

Sylvie Rollet rightly notes that Pintilie's stylistic label is a mechanical rhythm broken by its own ostentatious nature: ellipses are created by means of jump-cuts and successive scenes telescope into each other, creating a feeling of a mad pendulum which will be found in his subsequent post-Communist productions. The multiple spaces are nonetheless related to the theatrical representation because of their fragile, transient nature (Rollet 1997: 27). *Carnival Scenes* is an ensemble of genre scenes comparable to Hogarth's paintings in which the characters' fits of hysteria and outbursts of passion are echoes of a gigantic masquerade. According to Alex Leo Şerban, the film is an apotheosis of *mise en abymes* which multiply at a very fast pace. As a matter of fact, the film's opening quotation from Caragiale is 'I feel enormously and see monstrously'.[13] In the closing scenes, the similarities with Nikita Mikhalkov's memorable adaptation of Chekhov's *Unfinished Piece for Mechanical Piano* (1977) are striking. The similarity lies not only in the similar use of operatic excerpts on a soundtrack which has no pre-composed score, but also in the world-as-a-stage syndrome, the party returning to its daily routine at dawn, nostalgic for its carnival masks.

A very interesting, untitled documentary shot by Horia Lapteş during the filming of *Carnival Scenes* and shown on Romanian television[14] reveals via detailed interviews to what extent the whole cast considered working with Pintilie a unique privilege. It also demonstrates to what extent the film is difficult to grasp for non-domestic audiences. Last but not least, it is a unique opportunity to watch the Romanian director at work: commenting and analysing every scene, looking for the perfect gesture, imitating the part of every character, until the right tone is reached. *Lucian Pintilie's Quest for Perfection* could be an alternative title for this precious document.

Following the fall of the Ceauşescu regime, Pintilie's return to professional life in Romania was heralded as a kind of messianic gesture: he was appointed head of the Film Studio, which was subsidised by the Ministry of Culture. He was in his late fifties and wanted to make up for lost time. The period between 1992 and 2002 was his second 'thaw', and he shot a film every two or three years, mostly French co-productions. He started a rewarding co-production agreement with the influential Marin Karmitz, another Romanian-born émigré producer/distributor who had been active within the French industry for quite a while.[15]

Pintilie's first post-totalitarian opus, Balanţa (The Oak, 1992), has a far wider scope than his previous films, though it is strikingly similar in tone and depiction of morals. It could be regarded as a Romanian variant on Emir Kusturica's Underground (1995): a fast-paced story packed with cynicism and bitter irony and including a few surrealist moments, meant to offer an insight into one of the toughest dictatorships. Adapted from a novel by Ion Băieşu, Balanţa (The Scales), the film's story unfolds in 1988, one year before the fall of Communism. The screenplay offers an alternative title, which is Wake Up, Romanian, also the title of the post-revolutionary national anthem. A semi-official author from the late 1960s, Băieşu had his only 'dissident' novel published in 1985; it was banned shortly after. As Pintilie recounts in his autobiography, he had time to read it and realise to what extent it would make an amazingly dense fresco of Romanian Communist society on film. The director made a wish that this would be the first film he would shoot as soon as he was given the opportunity (Pintilie 2003: 347).

As a novel, The Scales – whose title film critics further read as expressing a delicate balance between an abject world and a better one – has inspired comparisons ranging from Emile Zola to Hieronymus Bosch. Everything, including the army, the secret police, the priests, the hospital milieu and the atmosphere on packed trains, is depicted in a sensational, dense, albeit surreal way. The film remains faithful to this extremely wide narrative scope. According to literary critic George Pruteanu, the novel is an authentic '250 page encyclopedia of disaster': a corpse is stolen from a locked room, a Gypsy is married to a princess, four men rape the main heroine, a priest asks his wife to starve to death their severely handicapped child. The novel's rhythm is close to a piece of hard rock music, as is the accelerated pace of the filmed version.[16] The deconstruction of reality at the core of Pintilie's previous films is here a narrative function, not a goal. Şerban explains that the film unfolds by means of constant audiovisual embeddings and mise en abymes: home movies, Polaroid photos and reconstructed events from the past, culminating with the apocalyptic finale, itself a mise en scène (Şerban 2006: 166).

The Oak's main narrative line is the story of Nela (Maïa Morgenstern), a young schoolteacher who, after the death of her terminally ill father, embarks on an almost self-inflicted apocalyptic journey through a devastated Romania. As in the novel, the film has several other subplots gravitating around Nela's main story, Pintilie wanting to depict a highly complex social fresco of Romanian society.

In the breath-taking opening scene, Pintilie leads us to a shabby, miserable apartment entrance, using a staggering low-angle tracking shot. The music reproduces fragments from Richard Wagner's 'Prelude' from *Lohengrin*: the penchant for musical quotations from operas will remain a constant in Pintilie's subsequent films. It is still heard inside the apartment where Nela, the colonel's daughter, is watching a strange home movie next to her dying father, a former high-ranking Communist official.[17] Pintilie's cinematic discourse revisits the self-reflexive principle from *Reconstruction* in new, highly original ways. A Super 8 home movie starts as a joyful Christmas party featuring Nela as a young girl, wearing the famous pioneer uniform, with her father disguised as Santa Claus, in the company of other officials in military uniforms. It will degenerate into a surrealistic, macabre killing, the girl holding a small gun and aiming at everybody around her. The heroine is subjectively re-infusing her hate and disgust for the Communist regime into reinvented images from her childhood (Nasta 2007b: 2).

We find the same macabre masquerade principle at work in a political vehicle from the early 1970s already discussed, *The Power and the Truth*. However, Pintilie argues that these scenes originate from his having had access to

Fig 16. A very special Christmas party in *The Oak*

Ceaușescu's own home movies.[18] Other insights into this topic are offered by a documentary about the filming of *The Oak* by cinematographer Gabriel Kosuth, *Filmare* (*The Shooting*, 1992). At one point in the documentary, Pintilie is seen giving instructions about the home movie sequence: he is telling the girl supposed to play Nela as a child, 'you should look like Zoïa', actually the name of Ceaușescu's daughter.

Part of the same family of anarchists and disobedient heroes as the ones in *Reconstruction*, Nela tries to commit suicide, swears and uses a macabre kind of humour of which she is inordinately proud, obviously some kind of weapon against an unbearable reality. As in most Pintilie films, death in all its forms acts as a corollary for all human behaviour. Thus, after the cremation of her father she always keeps his ashes in a Nescafé bottle, proudly showing them off to her friends. Nela's journey is interspersed with shocking, grotesque and funny incidents: her wanting to get immolated, her being punished because she has overtly protested to the way her dying father had been treated; her suffering violent harassment turning into rape during her train trip to her assignment; her seduction of a state prosecutor whom she threatens to blackmail by sending his wife photos of him naked; a funeral drinking party in the country in the presence of two agents of the Securitate, vividly shot with the tempo of a cabaret theatre.

During her teaching job assignment, filmed on location in the hyper-polluted town of Copșa Mică, the young woman eventually meets her masculine counterpart, Mitică Bostan, played by Pintilie's subsequent paradigmatic actor, Răzvan Vasilescu. He is an equally rebellious, outspoken and free-spirited young doctor, moving around at an incredibly fast pace and refusing brainwashing and 'normalisation'. This is what he tells Nela about the hospital where she ends up after he has freed her from her aggressors: 'I'll show you the patients' files. The silicosis rate is bigger than in Baia Mare [mining town in the north of Romania]. Forget about the handicapped, the alcoholics, malnutrition. All these are considered normal.'

Mitică is overtly confrontational with the hospital bureaucrats, both verbally (swearing constantly and using a vocabulary no translation could render faithfully enough) and physically, a fact which will lead to his temporary imprisonment. The 'odd' couple barely have the time to connect physically. They nonetheless become the perfect target for the secret police, the Securitate, who are soon spying on them as a couple and intruding upon their intimacy in the most unexpectedly tragicomic ways.[19]

Almost halfway through the film, once the Nela/Mitică binomial has been established, at least three subplots are introduced by Pintilie in a highly sophisticated way. First, there is the story of Titi, an illuminated, prophet-like patient whom Mitică unsuccessfully tries to save from death, but to whom he promises to keep his diary from the secret police and bury him in the countryside. Titi's picaresque last trip is taken in an open coffin set in a shaky truck and led by Nela and Mitică throughout the idyllic Transylvanian countryside. It is followed by the burial and funeral party at the priest's house, which assuredly is an anthology moment. Pintilie's tragicomic impulse is realised most impressively when Mitică explains to the party guests the way Romanians, especially those in the secret police, manage to lead a good life despite a difficult economic context: 'Take a look at them, they play James Bond, tracking us until we get here. On their way back they will play supermarket, with their cars filled with fresh country products. This is how Romanians manage to make ends meet nowadays.' The second thematic extension has to do with Nela's own personal trajectory. She is Pintilie's on-screen alter ego, fabulously played by Maïa Morgenstern: interviewing members of her family, such as her terminally sick mother (Leopoldina Bălănuța), to discover the truth about her father's ambiguous Communist past; taking hundreds of Polaroid snapshots in the most unexpected situations and displaying them all over her place. One of her models is Dudu, a slightly handicapped pupil, who seems to have a special gift for poetry. On being interviewed by Nela, his extraordinary self-portrait proves yet another expression of the picaresque nature of the ongoing narrative:

– What do you want to do for a living?

– Become a writer [...]

– You don't write memoirs at your age.

– Yes, but I wanted to write the story of my parents. My father is a factory worker and my mother a housewife... and a princess, one of her ancestors has ruled the country for four and a half years.

– So you're a nobleman?

– Yes, and my father is a Gypsy: mother was threatened with arrest, he saved her and she married him.

Thirdly, there is the film's epilogue: Pintilie himself has described it as yet another variant, following *Reconstruction*, of the biblical Massacre of the Innocents. Following planned military manoeuvres supervised by a helicopter on a huge hill, soldiers machine-gun a school bus filled with children aged

Fig 17. Precocious Dudu telling his story in *The Oak*

between six and nine. Some rebels who have taken the children as hostages ask the police to meet their demands, but they are totally ignored. A soldier tries to prevent the police from shooting but he is the first victim in a tragic, highly explicit slaughter episode with some scenes shot in slow motion.[20] Almost concomitantly, Nela has planned to bury her father's famous ashes under a splendid, venerable oak tree situated at the top

of a neighbouring hill. The breath-taking visual metaphor of the Adam-and-Eve-like couple, lying under the magnificent tree after escaping the absurd manslaughter, provides the final key to the film's international title. Obviously lampooning Communist ideas about 'normalisation', Mitică, his back against the almost biblical oak tree and still carrying a gun in his hands, is heard declaring: 'If we have a child it will be an idiot or a genius: if he is normal, I will certainly kill him with my own hands.'

A parallel can also be drawn between Pintilie's epilogue and the final biblical image of Andreï Tarkovsky's *Offret* (*The Sacrifice*, 1986): a long shot of Little Man watering the tree, yet another image of hope for a better future after a series of terminal events implying human sacrifice.

Pintilie described his own film as a 'journey through infernal circles, catastrophes which hang together [...] a catastrophe disappears only to make room for another, the last one being the massacre of the innocents' (Leonardi 2004: 79). When distributed in France, where the Cannes festival organisers had inadvertently forgotten to mention its screening in the official programme, the film was nonetheless acclaimed by critics (Jäckel 2001: 138). They heralded 'Pintilie's double return to his homeland and to cinema', 'a film arriving as an obvious necessity', and considered the filmmaker a clear-sighted witness of the 'Apocalypse according to the Balkans' (Jeancolas 1992: 16; Nevers 1992: 29).

Fig 18. Promising to start a new life under the mythical oak

The second film Pintilie shot in the 1990s, *O vară de neuitat* (*An Unforgettable Summer*, 1994), was another Marin Karmitz-initiated co-production, starring Kristin Scott Thomas in an emotionally challenging part, a somehow cosmopolitan parenthesis in his hectic career. Set in 1923, in a country which had just been reintegrated into frontiers, this is a costume drama, adapted from the short story *Salata* (*The Salad*) by exiled novelist Petru Dumitriu. The story focuses on the negative side effects experienced by a generous liberal Romanian family after violent Bulgarian ethnic minority frontier conflicts. It shows the descent into hell of two honest, liberal people whose intentions were more than honourable but who could not defy intolerance.

The autobiographical side of the project is not to be neglected. As Pintilie explains in *Bricabrac*, his family also belonged to a minority from Bessarabia, now part of Moldavia, which peacefully co-existed with other ethnic groups (e.g. Germans, Jews, Russians and Bulgarians). Born and raised in a family where tolerance and openness to the other were innate values, the director explains how the wild wind of history came along and shattered this pluri-ethnic harmony (Pintilie 2003: 390; Căliman 2000: 443).

The start of *An Unforgettable Summer* sticks to Pintilie's cherished double scene principle but is surprisingly conventional compared to the director's usual style. It introduces a voice-over that echoes the film's title in referring to 'that unforgettable summer', later to be identified as belonging to the elder child of the film's pivotal family. A spectacular opening scene backed by harpsichord chords from a Mozart piece reveals a horse leading a carriage at top speed towards an ineluctable destination, thus reminding one of *The Oak*'s similar prologue. Later on, an official party unfolds, while a Hungarian prostitute rebels because she has been asked to keep her distance. Racist invectives follow, and she even gets slapped, showing to what degree inter-ethnic relationships among Romanians, Hungarians and Bulgarians were difficult.

Among the guests are Marie-Thérèse von Debretsyn (Kristin Scott Thomas) and her husband, Captain Petre Dumitriu (Claudiu Bleonţ). Marie-Thérèse is of noble descent, half-Romanian, half-Hungarian, and raised in England, hence her 'Oxford' accent, which will prompt criticism and racist remarks. Her fragile, diaphanous appearance, with bobbed hair and jazz age glamour, masks a powerful consciousness, while her husband's character has no real depth. Though played by a gifted Romanian actor, the character Dumitriu is less credible, barely developed, and characterised by a rather ridiculous monocle.

Because his charming wife resists the advances of a military superior, lustful General Ipsilanti (Marcel Iureş), Dumitriu is transferred to a remote garrison of Dobroudja on the Romanian border, a kind of no man's land. Dobroudja has been claimed by Bulgaria and is infested with Macedonian rebels. However, the young wife is immediately attracted to the sandy environs, the desert landscape, and some stark mountains she relentlessly gazes at and compares to Mount Fuji.

Creating a fragile island of civilisation, Marie-Thérèse learns to accept, like and befriend the Bulgarian minority, who are asked to take care of her kitchen garden. Scott Thomas's fantastic emotional energy oscillates between ecstasy and pathetic despair. She tries to rebuild a charismatic world in the desert. Pintilie affectionately films her reading Proust, playing and accompanying her children on the harpsichord on music from Mozart's *The Magic Flute*, and standing next to a wonderful Venetian mirror, which will inevitably cause bad luck once it is broken by anarchist bandits.

But peace is fragile inside this allegedly idyllic context, and very soon the mirror will be shattered by stones thrown in protest by the anarchists, mud will be thrown against the walls of their house, bandits will start killing Romanian soldiers, and a

Fig 19. A perfect world in
An Unforgettable Summer

corpse will be found lying in one of their rooms. The heroine's attempt to assume command of her family, while also trying to save the hostages, fails: she is devastated, starts drinking and loses all faith. In reaction to the killing of border guards by Macedonian bandits, Dumitriu is ordered to execute the harmless Bulgarians. Almost on the brink of suicide, his career is ruined and he is forced to leave. Another massacre scene choreographed by Pintilie to serve the film's global design shows Dumitriu stoned by the hostages' widows.

The same voice-over from the beginning, belonging to one of their children, is heard; the narrator says that he will always 'keep fond memories of an unforgettable summer'. The Gogolian derision of Pintilie's earlier films seems to have been replaced by a blend of nostalgia and irony set against a tragic background.

An Unforgettable Summer was relatively popular with contemporary international audiences, being considered simpler and more accessible than the
director's previous films. It was presented in Cannes, this time in the official competition, and ran for eighteen weeks in Paris, with mixed reviews. It
was the first post-revolutionary Pintilie film to be distributed in Italy in 1995
(Ciment & Herpe 1994: 13–18). However, the film that 'Americans understood
best', according to its director, was not well received in his native Romania.
It hurt sensibilities because it dared show ethnic cleansing perpetrated by
native authorities and portrayed intolerance. Pintilie argued that his intention to depict a case of xenophobia was influenced by ongoing events in
ex-Yugoslavia, but also by the biblical Babel paradigm: when the babble of
tongues and dialects rose to Babelic heights, bloodshed ensued (Pintilie
2003: 391–408).

Another French co-production involving a myriad of media partners, *Prea
tirziu* (*Too Late*, 1996) proved much more challenging than the previous period
movie, apparently being intended to finalise the trilogy on the evils of totalitarianism initiated by *Reconstruction* and further developed by *The Oak*.[21] The
storyline was the first in Pintilie's filmography to deal with the post-Communist period: it follows young prosecutor Dumitru Costa (Răzvan Vasilescu),
entrusted with investigating the suspicious deaths of coalminers in the Jiu
Valley. The local authorities do everything to encourage Costa to abandon his
inquiry, as they have a lot to hush up: he will eventually end up as an exile in
Germany, as apparently nobody except himself is willing to reveal the truth.
Though conceived like a thriller, the intrigue is only a pretext for exploring the
meanders of both individual and collective post-Communist consciousness:
the film has thus been considered an ideological fable.[22]

In her essay '*Too Late*, or the Luciferian Temptation', Sylvie Rollet decrypts
the film as a parable about a new sub-species of politics, Romanian post-
Communism. Post-Communism appears as a demonic enterprise, refusing to
reveal truth in full daylight and preferring to remain in the underworld (Rollet
1997: 31). During a debate following the film's premiere in Paris, philosopher Alain Besançon read the film as a kind of modern *Germinal*, Emile Zola's
classic, underlining the fact that one of the main problems the film indirectly
approaches is that of general amnesia regarding Communism. 'Communism',
he argues, 'disappeared as a regime, not as a mentality' (Pintilie 2003: 412).[23]

The opening credit scene is yet another excursion in time. The year is 1996,
the place a German subway station, where an unidentified man's silhouette
is seen going down an elevator; he seems to hide some dynamite in a bag.
Next to him a female cellist whose face is hidden by her long hair is playing

for money. A Hollywood-like parallel montage then shifts us back in time. In a remote place near the sadly famous Jiu mining valley, a train runs at full speed, carrying prosecutor Costa on what will ultimately prove a very delicate mission. Another cut reveals a musical quartet playing inside a cosy living-room: we recognise the girl from the subway, the onscreen music actually featuring a quite unsettling theme from Dimitri Shostakovich's *String Quatuor* n° 8. They will cross Costa's path at several moments in the film, most significantly inside the mine itself, where they will play the main theme from Franz Schubert's *Death and the Maiden*. This prologue again confirms Pintilie's penchant for dual, albeit paradoxical universes.

While being introduced via an elevator to the almost nightmarish milieu of the miners' underground, Costa meets and is instantly attracted to topographer Alina Ungureanu (Cecilia Bârbora). He also learns from the miners about two mentally deranged identical twins, Ficht and Ferz: one of them has mysteriously disappeared, while the other is now in a mental asylum. The bodies of two other miners turn up in a disused mine shaft. Victims accumulate; apparently a man kills for food and the only indication is a mysterious, animal laughter. Everybody, including the miners and the authorities, becomes a suspect. Later in the film Costa will describe the mine as an 'extant ape reserve'.

In the same vein as the character played by Vasilescu in *The Oak*, Costa is sarcastic and unconventional, sexually aware, with just a touch of male chauvinism. Not many people are interested in the real truth about the mysterious mine murders, so the prosecutor will soon find himself alone and ridiculed by all. The exception is Alina, who happens to have been everybody's girl, but is now determined to stick with him. Their love-making scenes against a tropical kitsch wallpaper are alternated, in Pintilie's much-favoured tragicomic mode, with striking shots of bloody bodies excavated from the mine. The mine pit is under threat of closure and the corrupt local mafia is terrified by the way the prosecutor brings to light various truths, the main one being that one of the twins, Ferz, is probably the assassin hiding in the mine. In a strikingly naturalist scene, Costa inspects all the bearded miners, standing naked in a row, their backs against the gallery's walls.

During one ensuing scene, the miners demonstrate against the threat of the mines being closed down, while Costa watches the same event on a TV set. What first appears as a self-reflexive embedding is in fact the corresponding rhyme of a scene from *Reconstruction* mentioned before, where the ambulance reaching the football match is first seen on a TV set, only to be revealed in the nearby space through a swish pan. Later on there is a second *mise en abyme*: Costa will ask his investigators to show him different foreign TV broadcasts about the miners being mobilised by President Iliescu in June 1990 and clubbing the Bucharest students.

Despite telephone threats trying to persuade him to back off and a final order to suspend his investigations, Costa finishes his investigation and realises the homicide is related to members of the secret police from the past regime. But nobody will admit this: man has become a beast. This is what one realises when Ferz exits the mine,

Fig 20. Costa searching the miners in *Too Late*

following an explosion. Exile remaining the only alternative, Costa eventually escapes with Alina to Germany, and Ficht, the remaining twin, flees from the mental asylum for the same destination. A written explanatory title and a voice-over introduces us to the same images as those which opened the film. We now understand that the silhouette and the dynamite from the prologue are those of one of the twins. And the haunting music played by the cellist resonates in one's ear long after the film's ending.

Though present in competition at the 1998 Cannes festival, *Too Late* got mixed critical coverage in France, where it was distributed six months later, while the film was not granted wide distribution in Europe. Pintilie was criticised for insisting too much on the new post-dictatorial barbarism. However, what was clearly praised was the filmmaker's courage in depicting inconvenient truths. When the film premiered in Bucharest, respected contemporary directors such as Mircea Daneliuc and Stere Gulea explained to what extent their own subjects were highly influenced by the violent 1990 miners' upheaval. Later, Pintilie's film led to both philosophically grounded debates in Romania and violent criticism. Thus, columnist Cristian Tudor Popescu ends his highly provocative review of the film with the following imperative: 'Go back to Paris, Mr Pintilie, and leave us with our own problems'.[24]

With *Terminus Paradis* (*Next Stop Paradise*, 1998), an electrifying film and his second real love story, Pintilie the moralist was not ready to leave the country as some wished he would do. On the contrary, he widens the scope of his fresco of an agonising post-Communist Romania. He finally received international recognition, being awarded the prestigious Silver Lion at the 1998 Venice Film Festival. The screenplay is a mixture of two stories the director had initially submitted to Marin Karmitz. One is by atypical writer Radu Aldulescu, the other by Răzvan Popescu, who had already co-scripted *Too Late*. While the *amour fou* between Mitu (Costel Caşcaval), a marginalised pig-keeper, and Norica (Dorina Chiriac), a cunning waitress, will end in tragic vengeance through killing, overtly biblical references are meant to transform everyday misery into an allegorical message which defies time. Pintilie conceives some of the film's episodes as realistic counterparts to the Book of Job, human beings having turned into beasts. As suggested by the film's title, this time there is some mystery left in the message Pintilie wants to deliver. His *mise en scène* sticks to the double scene principle, meaning that the main narrative is backed by a secondary, symbolic one.

What strikes one as novel is the nature of the parallel montage, confronting and ultimately uniting humans and animals by way of a voice-over. While another quotation from Wagner serves as a powerful musical counterpoint, Mitu's voice-over is heard saying: 'there is no wiser animal than the pig… when Satan was chased by the son of man, he found refuge among the swine'. In the same line, Job, the biblical hero, better grasps the limits of his own material condition via his familiarity with pigs (Nasta 2005: 7).

The opening scene features the killing of the main hero, shown as a spectacular flash-forward, a device already used in *Reconstruction* and in *Too Late*. As in most Pintilie films, the audience is both intrigued and put off-balance. One watches a soldier being killed by mistake during a violent and surreal manhunt on the outskirts of Bucharest. As in *The Oak* and some pivotal scenes in *Too Late*, a helicopter is also part of the captivating visual network. One may infer that this is one of the most important symbols of military repression, still haunting Romanian post-Communist society.[25]

Retrospectively, Norica and Mitu meet casually over a drink at Papa Gili's (Doru Ana) roadside snack bar and spend the night together at the boy's place; Norica decides to move in with him, though she explains how her older boss has promised to wed her in the fall. The main plot is further complicated by a subplot involving Mitu's family. His brother Nicu (Şerban Pavlu) is back from the United States for a visit and the event is joyously celebrated with American Indian disguises and dances to Romanian rap rhythms. Nicu is doing the washing up in a Romanian restaurant, but Mitu is envious and jealous because Nicu made it in America. On their way back from the airport, a violent family argument causes a tragicomic traffic jam: we learn Mitu had to give up a similar immigration project to protect his father's political position.

In the meantime, Mitu has received a two-year enrolment order but is too proud to ask his father (Victor Rebengiuc) to intercede. Norica is dismayed by his attitude and returns to Gili's place. His tough military journey is orchestrated by a sadistic army instructor, Captain Burcă (Răzvan Vasilescu). Driven by his obsession to possess Norica, nothing will stand in Mitu's way. He thus steals a tank so as to literally destroy Gili's bar; he later shoots him during a grotesque love scene with Norica disguised as a cat. The discovery by the police of Gili's blood-stained body lying against the wall is – whether Pintilie intended it or not – a strong reminder of the image of Ceaușescu's corpse the whole world could see on TV almost ten years earlier. In the film's second part, the fugitive couple is tracked down with clock-work efficiency. During the film's unique moments of bliss, the fugitives go as far as summoning a country priest with a gun to give them the marriage blessing. They also spend some nice time attending the local fair, where they ironically pose against a New York skyline billboard, a piece of American myth heralding Pintilie's *Niki and Flo* (2003).

Fig 21. Norica and Mitu at the local fair in *Last Stop Paradise*

After a series of surrealist happenings, the lovers on the run, breathless, find refuge in a freight train. When they decide to part, Norica tells Mitu: 'I didn't have my period', thus letting him know she is expecting a child. Theirs is a similar project as the one envisaged by Nela and Mitică in *The Oak*.

The anticipated, though unusually arduous, capture and subsequent death of Mitu conforms to Pintilie's principle of the double scene. Norica carries his child in her womb and soon heads towards the church where he is to be baptised, in the midst of a sun-bathed, beautiful wheat field. This unusually tableau-like long shot is actually a 'paradise lost' image, which has already appeared in the film as a huge photo-poster at Mitu's place. The oxymoronic equation 'terminus = paradise' will thus be materialised.

The best critical reception came from Italy. The majority of essays insist on the social value of the film, 'a highly symptomatic radiography of a country still experiencing a great deal of confusion', in which Pintilie manages to fore-ground the now cynical, now heart-rendering humour of post-dictatorial times as well as the disastrous, violent passage to Western habits. The director was considered a fine observer of end-of-millennium upheavals, some of which also apply to other people and cultures (Leonardi 2004: 84). The most inter-esting review was by screenwriter and critic Tullio Kezich, who compares *Next Stop* to John Steinbeck's prose and fugitive heroes: he suggests that the film could be remade in Hollywood, praising Pintilie's generous anarchy and his vital spiritual energy (Kezich 1998: 32).

Last but not least, the domestic reception of *Next Stop* was, considering also the major Venice award, far better than that of the two preceding films. Poet Ana Blandiana, a key figure of the Romanian cultural scene, unreservedly praises Pintilie for representing the country within such a prestigious European film context as the Venice Festival:

Throughout this film, our image as a people has been defined as a mixture between the intention to exorcize evil and hate and the hope for a better world, where love would prevail. [...] He has been creating a work of art from the tragedy and truth of our epoch, with a lot of effort and difficulty. We will never know how to thank him enough for doing so.[26]

După-amiaza unui torţionar (The Afternoon of a Torturer, 2001) marked Pintilie's entrance into the new millennium in a very significant way. In terms of content, handling and style, it clearly appears to be one of the harbingers of what will be later labelled the Romanian minimalist trend.[27] Though unfolding mostly in an outdoor countryside location situated in the southern Romanian plain, The Afternoon of a Torturer is a chamber piece close to the theatrical Kammerspiel tradition: things are said and barely shown; stasis is preferred to action. Though deceptively simple, it is probably the director's most radical film since Reconstruction.

Adapted from Doina Jela's Drumul Damascului (The Road to Damascus: Confessions of an Ex-torturer), the film is conceived as a series of vignettes separated by breaks and flashes in time and focusing on the terrifying confession of a Communist ex-torturer of political prisoners.[28] The hero of Jela' s story is almost faceless, grotesque and absurd: Pintilie transfigures it poetically using some stylistic elements drawn from the Theatre of Cruelty (Dulgheru 2007: 2). An ex-political prisoner, the now retired professor (Radu Beligan) accompanies a female journalist (Ioana Ana Macaria) on her way to a delicate mission, that of interviewing his ex-torturer Franz Ţandără (Gheorghe Dinică). They travel by train, making what may be called a challenging journey to hell, a motif already present in Nela's trip to her job destination in The Oak and in prosecutor Costa's arrival by rail in Too Late. Characters obviously stand as symbols that need to be visualised. The professor relentlessly explains to his companion the difference between good and evil, the material and the immaterial world, eventually drawing opposed triangles echoing a sandglass on the compartment window. The young journalist is extremely naïve and not quite ready to start investigating crimes ignored for such a long time. The torturer embodies a post-Communist paradox, that of an inconvenient truth. His silhouette, holding a bunch of flowers in his hands, will first appear within an embedded triangle projection from the compartment window. Following the rhyme principle of the double scene, almost the same image will close the film, revealing that life goes on no matter what has been revealed.

Driving his guests to his barracks, while swearing over his old car, Ţandără explains he is now a beekeeper, an ancestral, highly noble occupation that is, according to the professor, a way of expiating his faults. The man is practically an illiterate, not being able to speak correct Romanian. He also tells them about his sick son Ticuţă, later to be revealed as a dangerous hooligan with nationalistic impulses. Ţandără almost feels responsible for the latter's illness and would sacrifice his own life to see his son cured. Once home, the journalist turns the tape recorder on and asks him to be

Fig 22. Ţandără welcoming his guests in *The Afternoon of a Torturer*

as natural as he possibly can, because they are preparing a documentary on the subject of Communist torturers. But Ţandără is tense and stops frequently, interrupted by the ringing phone (actually his nationalistic son threatening him for selling his secrets to strangers). He sees no obstacle to revealing his secrets and is apparently willing to confess his crimes, but he will need a *doppelgänger* to express his deepest thoughts.

Paradoxically, the general setup is quite idyllic: the main protagonists as well as Franz's slightly deranged, almost blind wife (Coca Bloos) are constantly facing the garden, more specifically a huge tree echoing the one from the final shot of *The Oak*. The theatrical principle of the embedded stage cherished by the director will soon be at work. It will echo similar interferences between present and past featuring in seminal films by Ingmar Bergman and Woody Allen.[29] Thus, during the whole confession, the film's audience almost simultaneously watches the ongoing action and mental images from the hero's macabre past: as in most examples of the same type, the images are only accessible to Ţandără and to us as viewers. His double is figured as a young boy who contemplates and acts at the same time, a kind of matrix for his childhood. Various tableaux will re-enact tragic scenes from the past in a playful way, by means of static, frontal shots.

Ţandără starts talking about his childhood: he seems to have been into crime ever since. He mentions to the journalist how he had a conflicted relation with his father, which led to the latter's murder and to a spell in jail when he was only fifteen. Then he recounts his recruitment by the Communist army. Phantasms and faces from the past are re-enacted every time under the tree: thus, a female torturer with whom he had an affair (Dorina Chiriac) appears as both angelic and demonic, childish and sexually aware. He remembers how satisfied his superiors were with his torture methods and how he was moved from prison to a psychiatric ward as a reward for his good work. Ţandără seems to have enjoyed his work without any sense of guilt:

What I have done no beast would have done.

In '51 when I was released you know what I did?

I said: No, I want to stay, which is to say I liked it, Madam.

(Pintilie 2001: 224)

Fig 23. Childhood musings in *The Afternoon of a Torturer*

Every challenging and sinister tale about one of the numberless victims is separated by a wipe. However, his testimony gets more and more confused, while the professor dozes off and almost falls asleep. Eventually Țandără's allegedly blind wife accuses the journalist of being a torturer, because she is too insistent, and the rebellious son makes an unexpected intrusion with a gang of menacing hooligans. The interview is over and Țandără drives his two guests back to the station. Ex-victim and retired executioner embrace, having become familiar with each other. The torturer has managed to resurface a past which many others have eluded by totally changing their identity, therefore dissimulating it forever. Though symmetrical with the beginning, the ending contains an allusion to the previously developed mental space of the torturer: two children get on the train at the same time, Țandără as the child and his midget aunt.

For Pintilie,

The tree is that of crime and horror [...] it is also the theatrical tree infiltrated by infernal elements, where Țandără watches spectres of the dead separated by curtains (white sheets hanged as laundry), while the interview goes on in the wings... The torturer builds up another penitentiary colony around his barrack and beehives surrounded by barbed wire: the house is a miniature concentration camp. (Pintilie 2004: 444)

Despite allowing for such a sophisticated symbolic reading, the film clearly leaves the impression of an authentic slice of life about a previously taboo subject, which had never been approached on-screen in such a manner. Its low-key acting, static shots, absence of musical score and unobtrusive editing will be found again in Pintilie's next film, *Niki and Flo*, yet another harbinger of the minimalist movement. *The Afternoon* was barely shown in Romania, being premiered at the Venice International Festival in 2001 and briefly distributed in France. It clearly stands among those underrated masterworks which still need to be rediscovered by audiences, critics and historians alike.

Pintilie's *Niki Ardelean, colonel în rezervă* (*Niki and Flo*, 2003), may be considered in terms of storyline as a partial sequel to *Next Stop Paradise* (Mancino 2004: 56). The film is narrated in a diary mode with no pre-existing score, being remarkably co-scripted by two key representatives of the upcoming contemporary Romanian minimalist trend, director Cristi Puiu and screenwriter Răzvan Rădulescu. A sarcastic, ironic, static, eventually tragic tale about new Romanians, the film confronts two symptomatic representatives of the social post-revolutionary upheaval with the departure for the US of a young couple within the 9/11 turmoil and with the death of an innocent victim. The latter is shown and remembered through photos and via a sepia home movie. The embedded film thus re-affirms Pintilie's strong belief in self-reflexive *mise en abymes*. The chronicle is regulated by significant dates indicated by titles and portrayed by means of static though perfectly orchestrated tableaux, focusing on ritualised events: a funeral and the ensuing mourning supper, Easter celebrations, and filmed recollections of a wedding.

Niki Ardelean (Victor Rebengiuc) is an old retired colonel from the Communist era who is now mourning his son Mihai (Marius Galea), accidentally struck down while trying to fix a dishwasher. After Mihai's funeral service, Niki, his wife Pousha (Coca Bloos) and their remaining daughter Angela (Dorina Chiriac) receive friends and family in their small Bucharest apartment. Among them are Eugen (Șerban Pavlu), Angela's fiancé, his father Florian/Flo Tufaru (Răzvan Vasilescu, in probably one of the most demanding roles of his entire career) and the latter's wife Doina (Micaela Caracaș). Shot in full frontal frames, Florian is hyperactive and seems in control of every detail and mourning accessory he is fixing up as a kind of master of ceremonies. Angela and Eugen take the opportunity of a family gathering to announce their decision to emigrate to the US, to seek a better life, as did Mitu's brother in *Next Stop Paradise*. An old-fashioned patriot, Niki is shocked by the news, especially as, we also learn, his daughter is pregnant. He represents the alienated subject, pathetic and marginalised, highly paradoxical because he is nostalgic, like many others, for the Communist times.

Puiu and Rădulescu's dialogue proves highly effective: 'America is extremely far from here, God knows what's expecting you up there', warns Niki; 'Niki', replies Doina, Flo's wife, 'from here to Satu Mare [town in Northern Romania] it is twelve hours by train. If you buy a return ticket, it's as if you'd been to the States twice. Do you realise this?' Flo's reaction is totally opposed to that of his in-laws. He thinks this is a very bright decision, most certainly because he himself is a pure product of a certain category of post-Communist, upstart Romanians: vulgar, eccentric, aggressive, seizing any opportunity, any small job to make money and have fun. Asked by the priest about his job, Florian is supported by his wife: 'I don't have a definite job... Florian is making pins, birthday and astrology cards, he knows a lot about zodiac signs, chiromancy, tarot, he can tell your fortune by cards or from your coffee cup'.

Two weeks later it is Easter time (April 14, as indicated by the title printed on a black screen), undoubtedly the most important religious event for Orthodox Romanians, but Eugen and Angela's thoughts are definitely elsewhere. They are actively filling in forms and preparing for their departure for the States. Paradoxical, almost shocking compositional shots reveal parallel activities inside Niki's apartment, proving to what extent cinematic space – here kitchen versus sleeping room – is used in accordance to what will later be considered as minimalist aesthetics.[30] While the old generation carefully paints the Easter eggs, prepares traditional dishes and lights candles for the mass, the younger one makes love in a totally unconventional way, Pintilie showing nudity and genitalia as quite ordinary. Florian will also help them choose and pack their most important pieces of furniture, leaving their room almost empty, except for a huge poster figuring the mythical Twin Towers.

Once they have seen them off to the airport on 'the 4th of July', as ironically indicated in the title, the American national anthem is heard in the background, Flo is dressed as a paratrooper (his bald head covered with adhesive tape after a stupid fall in his bathtub) and Niki almost collapses on the sidewalk. He and his ailing wife are left alone with their sadness and desolation. Like *The Afternoon of a Torturer*, *Niki and Flo* is yet another confrontation between a torturer and his victim. After having deprived Niki of almost everything, Flo exploits the emotional impact of carnival images from the filmed wedding. During one of his visits to their place, Flo is happy to show and comment on

the home movie he has been compulsively shooting. As a matter of fact, he has also been seen shooting during the first scenes of the film: the burial, the funeral party, the family at home, and so on.

Fig 24. *Niki and Flo*: after the children's departure for the USA

While watching the marriage film on their TV set, Niki and Flo have an argument about their totally opposing views on the way the Romanian army defeated the German troops on 23 August, and more generally on how recent Romanian history should be read. The powerfully rhythmic, sepia-coloured wedding report is yet another excursion in time and an opportunity for us, the audience, to get to know the deceased Mihai (Marius Gâlea), dancing like a clown. Showing the grandiose wedding celebration overflowing with food, speeches and dances filmed and commented on by Flo, both screenwriters perfectly synthesise the Romanian post-'89 zeitgeist. Despite the couple's declared intention to leave 'for a better life', what dominates is a mixture of nationalism and nostalgia for bygone times.[31] Flo's intrusive hand-held camera will soon echo the one in *Peeping Tom* (Powell and Pressburger, 1960): we will watch the bridegroom in a hot sex scene with Angela almost nude, his face covered with the bride's stockings, looking like a horror film freak. Dumbfounded Niki and his stultified wife will thus watch scenes of unbearable sexual explicitness on their small TV set.

A few weeks later, the collapsing Twin Towers are shown on the living room television set, but Angela's parents are so depressed they do not even watch the news any longer. A postcard received by Flo on his birthday from the States and read by his wife tells them all is well with their loved ones. Invited to Flo's 'Disney'-themed birthday party, stressed out Niki is offered a Mickey Mouse mask he grotesquely puts on. His mentally imbalanced wife fallen into infancy is also seen wearing a fairy mask.

Fig 25. Pousha rehearsing for Flo's
Disney party in *Niki and Flo*

On 25 October it's National Army Day, so Niki decides to wear his beautiful military outfit and leaves his place to pay a visit to Flo. He has taken a hammer along, concealed in a shopping bag: once at Flo's place he smashes his skull as if it were a piece of meat on the kitchen table. Florian's head, covered in blood and shot in close-up. is clearly a macabre reminder of Gili, the murdered bar owner lying against the wall in *Next Stop Paradise*. Fourteen years after the Romanian revolution, the dead dictator's over-mediatised phantom is still haunting Romanian cinema.

Says Pintilie:

> The origins of this film are easy to trace back: I read a six page treatment. It dealt with a crime that builds up slowly, inevitably. It is like an iceberg melting slowly but surely [...] This simple topic has been very exciting to deal with: the idea of picturing a misdemeanour in an unusual way. Why shouldn't a crime spring out of a banal, ordinary situation [...] Flo is a poor wretch, such a vile and pretentious character that the viewer is only half surprised to see him murdered at the end. *Niki and Flo* is not a political film, it is an absurdist fable, about a pathetic encounter ending up with a crime not easy to explain, almost incomprehensible. (Silvestri 2004: 108)

Though well received in Romania and acclaimed worldwide by critics, *Niki and Flo* was poorly distributed and barely shown in festivals over the world. Nonetheless, the film's powerful acting performances proved once more Pintilie's outstanding capacities as a director, even if some character traits are purposefully exaggerated. The film's minimalist *mise en scène*, its original use of confined space for narrative purposes and its highly sophisticated double-bind dialogue would soon turn into an undisputed characteristic of the Romanian New Wave. Appearing only on the closing credits as authors of the screenplay, Cristi Puiu and Răzvan Rădulescu will open up two years later, with *The Death of Mr Lăzărescu*, a path to international acclaim and recognition unique in the entire history of Romanian film.

Tertium Non Datur (2006) is Pintilie's last film to date and his shortest feature (39'). The film was freely adapted in 2005 from *The Aurochs' Head* (1945), a short story published posthumously by renowned Romanian mystic and writer Vasile Voiculescu: it was meant as a parable about fate, coincidence and pride in times of war, an allegory of survival at the beginning of Communism by an author who had been, like many others, unjustly imprisoned. In the Romanian historical framework, the Aurochs, an extinct animal in the bison family, is a powerful medieval symbol; in the film it is mentioned as the first token of liberation from Ottoman rule.

The action takes place in the Ukrainian desert during the spring of 1944, a few months before the Germans lost the war and Romania came under Soviet domination. A Romanian military unit is visited by two high-ranking German officials. During the meal, German Major von Klarenfeld (Tudor Aaron Istodor) astonishes his hosts by showing them he possesses the most expensive stamp in the world, the Aurochs' Head. According to him, only two Aurochs' Heads exist, the second one being owned by an American. The stamp inexplicably disappears, so the Romanian general (Victor Rebengiuc) orders an extensive body search; it is finally found at the back of a tin dish. The only one who refuses the search is Captain Tomuț (Sorin Leoveanu). After the departure of the Germans and a failed suicide attempt, Tomuț explains why he would not undress: he happens to own in a well-hidden place the third stamp – the one excluded by the Latin adage from the title (which means a third cannot exist). It is a gift from his mother, coming from an old Romanian *boyar* family, a kind of talisman he always keeps with him. However, so as to conform to the adage, he eventually burns his stamp with a lighter and symbolically leaves the assembly to get some fresh air.

Sticking to his principles, Pintilie changed some aspects and produced a screenplay where the initial meaning of the story is kept but more tragicomic aspects are added, ironically stressing the Romanians' tendency for nationalism and their difficult relationship to Europe as a political entity. Also, he introduces a new character, who tells the story in an ironic voice-over and makes critical remarks during the film, acting as a kind of alter ego for the director.[32] *Tertium*'s *mise en scène* echoes Pintilie's considerable body of theatrical work, featuring a perfect spatio-temporal unity. There are no ellipses, no flashbacks, no embedded images, Pintilie thus reinstalling a minimalist stylistic economy already at work in *The Afternoon* and later in *Niki and Flo*. The action unfolds during one day, mostly in deep long shots, inside a single three-dimensional performance space, actually a classroom transformed into a 'dining room' for the occasion. Props (a French window allowing the characters to step in and out, a table for twelve, a bundle of hay, chairs, cutlery, a world map) are destined to play an important narrative part. Given the film's format, form undoubtedly prevails over content.

In his review of the film, Yannick Lemarié sees *Tertium* as a 'triptych' with a three-part window opening on the outside, each part providing continuity and/or discontinuity effects. As in *Niki* the camera is often static, favouring a frontality through which several simultaneous actions can be followed. One can also distinguish three narrative moments conceived as tableaux: the meal, the 'striptease' and the captain's final confession (Lemarié 2007: 12).

Pintilie's central figure obviously is Major von Klarenfeld, a mixed-blood, European character reminding one of the Babel tower paradigm from the filmmaker's previous heritage film, *An Unforgettable Summer*. An Oriental-looking prince born in France and of Lithuanian descent, bearing a striking resemblance to Russian national poet Pushkin and eventually claiming Romanian origins, the Major will utter deliberately anachronistic lines, mostly in a quite artificial, rather clumsy French. As imagined by Pintilie, Western Europe's icons close to Von Klarenfeld's heart will thus range from French brothels, Veuve Cliquot champagne and Charles Trenet hits to Hollywood stars, such as Garbo and Dietrich. German diva Zarah Leander's voice serves as background score, coming from an off-screen car radio.[33]

From the moment the Major shows off the 'most expensive stamp in the world' as well as his ring bearing the same symbol, his references stop being anecdotal. He talks arrogantly and utters anti-Semitic comments about concentration camps, explaining how he has stolen the national emblem from a rich Jew. Eventually his xenophobia explodes: 'You are a country of Gypsy thieves'. Once the stamp suddenly disappears and the degrading body search is ordered, Pintilie stresses the highly grotesque nature of such an exercise, his camera shifting from the static, theatrical setup to an all-encompassing overhead shot. The table almost vanishes under hay and characters are filmed as if they were some kind of puppets. Surrounded by stark naked officers, the General himself turns extremely violent and aggressive and grudgingly undresses, though conscious of the humiliation he will have to experience.

Captain Tomuţ's threat to commit suicide if he is searched, followed almost instantaneously by the coincidence about the stamp which has been found, is yet another excursion into tragi-comedy typical of Pintilie. What interests Pintilie is creating a character which stands as an ironic challenge for a certain kind of Romanian mentality. Tomuţ speaks nationalist lines taken by Pintilie from philosopher E. M. Cioran: 'I want a Romania with the destiny of France and the population of China', thus reflecting a long-time obsession typical of marginalised countries. Before he exits the scene, the same Tomuţ will get a round of applause for his discourse from his fellow soldiers, as if they were all conscious this is only make-believe.

Irony pervades the final credits, as the director chooses another high angle to show the officers tidying up the room and then resumes the whole film in fast motion.

Meanwhile, an unusual additional piece of music is heard on the sound-track: a synthetic song, 'Tertium non datur', sung at the same accelerated speed by Ada Milea, a highly versatile contemporary poet and singer. The lyrics clearly represent another form of *mise en abyme*, projecting a small-scale narrative into the wider space of contemporary history with a capital H:

Let me lose my memory
Let me forget about useless victories
I want a delirious Romania
I want a country alive and well, not a cemetery
I want to breathe freely
Tertium non datur

Fig 26. The closing credits from
Tertium Non Datur

In a tribute to Lucian Pintilie, published on the occasion of the TIFF's (Transylvania International Film Festival) tenth anniversary, Michel Ciment compellingly wrote:

In the grand decade of the 1960s [...] Pintilie came to embody Romanian cinema almost by himself, before a young generation – which he helped hatch – started drawing the attention of the world [...] His body of work exhibits a rare coherence through ten feature films and a meteoric medium length film, his last achievement to date. It offers a very rare combination of moral reflection, visionary power and a sense of the grotesque [...] His entire cinema is carried by the refusal to forget, by the need to question history [...] And the greatness of his art comes from the alliance of opposites: an anchorage in the most material, even teratological reality and the philosophical speculation, the tragic thrill and the burst of laughter, the assumed theatricality, fluidity or syncopation specific to cinema. Pintilie: an essential contemporary. (2011: 72–74)

CHAPTER 8

The Films of Nae Caranfil
A Taste of Turn-of-the-Century
Sophisticated Comedy

The filmmakers of the Romanian New Wave have acknowledged its huge debt to Pintilie, the only internationally acclaimed Romanian director who continued his oeuvre after a long exile into the post-Communist era, while maintaining the same high artistic standards. This debt is evident, first, in the young filmmakers' quite generalised, albeit economically conditioned, refusal to produce big-scale spectacular movies: action films unfolding in exotic locales studded with national and/or international stars and lots of special effects, ideally backed by a fashionable score, with lots of easily recognisable musical hits. It is evident second, and somewhat implicitly, in their artistic credo: a strong belief in the virtues of textual and visual messages that are both very close to the Romanian ironic and absurdist psyche on the one hand and able to trigger an international audience appeal on the other.

However, the ongoing aesthetic '*parti-pris*' that has helped directors such as Cristi Puiu and Corneliu Porumboiu reach international recognition effectively emerged at the beginning of the new century, after what we may call a transitional phase, which has as its flag-bearers directors from the late 1990s such as Nae Caranfil. He is the only director with a constant production rate, combined with an international visibility (Nasta 2006a: 299, 2007b: 3).

In terms of subject matter, the transitional phase reveals a post-totalitarian chaotic society whose longing for the Western paradise is so strong that it breaks all existing barriers, overtly neglecting personal identity and integrity. Caranfil's acclaimed tragi-comedies about the difficulties of dealing with the Western dilemma set the tone as early as 1993 with his *Rashomon*-like tale about defection, *E Pericoloso Sporgersi* (*Sundays on Leave*, 1993). He stayed in the same vein with *Asfalt Tango* (*Asphalt Tango*, 1996), a less coherent road movie about young girls bound for Paris and being exploited by a female pimp. With *Filantropica* (*Philanthropy*, 2002), Caranfil went even further with a devastating, hyperbolic black comedy about a Bucharest mafia of beggars thriving through emotional manipulation, thus presenting to the audience the same mixture of social critique and devastating situational humour. Finally, in *Restul e tăcere* (*The Rest Is Silence*, 2007) he revisited the beginnings of Romanian film industry, via an authentic biopic about the director of the first feature-length Romanian film, *Independenţa României* (*The War of Independence*, 1913).

The son of respected film critic Tudor Caranfil, active both in the written press and on television during the Ceauşescu era, Nicolae (b. 1960) quickly took up the diminutive 'Nae', obviously trying to avoid any kind of confusion with the dictator's homonymous first name. His father's public and bedtime stories most naturally focused on films, and the cinephilia virus contaminated the son as early as his teenage years (Fulger 2006: 7–19). In addition, young Caranfil seemed to be gifted at creative writing, having a great facility for imagining comic sketches. Some of these were first published in his high-school journal and later on in the most irreverent Romanian post-revolutionary weekly, *Academia Caţavencu*. He also attended music classes, a training which would later be drawn on in writing the score of most of his films.

On graduating as a film director from the Theatre and Film Institute in 1984, from the class of seminal teacher Elisabeta Bostan, Caranfil worked as an assistant director, staged plays and did small parts as an actor. Refusing to shoot 'imposed' Communist subjects while trying to avoid censorship by carefully crafting encoded subjects, he directed only shorts, including *Frumos e în septembrie la Veneţia* (*Venice in September*, 1983) and *Treizeci de ani de insomnie* (*Thirty Years of Insomnia*, 1984), as well as *Backstage* (1988), an exercise in documentary filmmaking shot in a Belgian film workshop. His short-film output was quite interesting and reflected his penchant for humorous, absurdist situations as well as a constant obsession with 'closed spaces' to be found in most of his future films. Thus, in *Venice in September*, a group of Romanian tourists lucky to be in Venice are stuck in a hotel lobby and cannot get out because of torrential rain, thus echoing Luis Buñuel's similar plot-line from *El angel exterminador* (*The Exterminating Angel*, 1961).[1]

Thanks to a treatment accepted by the Selection Committee, the young director had the unique opportunity during such hard times to improve his training, by attending in 1988 the Creative Writing Session run by world-famous Hollywood screenwriting authority Frank Daniel at the Brussels Film Institute (a.k.a. INSAS). The political context of Ceauşescu's despotic *fin de règne* explains why Caranfil eventually chose to become a Belgian exile for two years, experiencing like most Westerners the Romanian revolution in front of a TV set.[2]

Back in Romania after the fall of Communism, Caranfil faced, as did most domestic directors, the difficulties of setting up a film project without international co-financing. Having already been asked to write a screenplay for French producers François Fries and Jean-Martial Lefranc during his western exile, he submitted his debut feature script initially called *Sundays on Leave* to the French CNC (National Counsel of Cinematography) and won the writing contest in 1992. Most importantly, both Pintilie and Caranfil benefitted from the ECO funding system, a French body created to finance co-productions with East European countries (Jäckel 2003: 148-9).

E Pericoloso Sporgersi (1992) is a film about dreams of escape of all kinds featuring many train journeys, hence its title. Caranfil employed the Italian version of the hackneyed formula *E Pericoloso Sporgersi* (meaning 'Don't lean out of the window'), which could be read on the window edges of European train compartments. As in Akira Kurosawa's polyphonic *Rashomon* (1950), the same story unfolding in a provincial pre-revolutionary Romanian town is told from three intertwined perspectives. The triptych – actually shot on location in three different towns, Bucharest, Caracal and Câmpulung Muscel – is a love triangle presented in three chapters named after the corresponding main character: I. The Student, II. The Actor and III. The Soldier.

Caranfil's tone is an ironic, mocking, eventually nostalgic and melancholy one, because he is providing not only an accurate account of the suffocating, grim declining years of Communism, but also his own personal story, the film being highly autobiographical.[3] In spite of a light tone, with lots of hilarious interludes, the subtext of *E Pericoloso Sporgersi* is an obviously dramatic, even tragic one. As evoked with a bright sociological ability by the young director, Communist dictatorship under Ceauşescu meant applying absurd birth rate standards, not being able to get central heating in public places because of economic restrictions and being denied any form of liberty, hence his characters' decision to leave this 'prison' for a better place.

A deceptively casual comedy which can also be read as a 'slice of life' including school, the military service and the travelling players' milieu, *E Pericoloso*

Sporgersi is extremely rigorous in its construction. According to Alex Leo Şerban, 'Not a single detail, a shot or a scene is left at random. The command of screenwriting is unusually good for a Romanian film-maker, as the hide and seek game the characters are meant to play oscillates between different temporal parameters' (Şerban 2009: 212–14). The second story starts earlier than the first one and so does the third one. Each of them takes over aspects from the previous one, withholding or, on the contrary, adding relevant information. The audience thus has to fill in the missing information, while being reminded of details already seen or heard.

The film's credits and opening scene unveil a rather classical setup with military barracks next to a deserted railway: young soldiers are obeying orders and watching departing trains, while a romantic score (by Anton Şuteu and Caranfil himself) tells us a lot about the general atmosphere of longing and ennui. Once the black screen introduces 'Chapter I: The Schoolgirl', Cristina (Nathalie Bonifay, a gifted French newcomer dubbed by Romanian actress Irina Movilă) instantly conquers the viewer with her charm and spontaneity, despite the strict uniform and compulsory hairband.

Pupils and teachers from her school seem to relish carrying out practical jokes and uttering verbal puns. For the first time in decades, Romanian audiences could identify with an authentic everyday language, banned from screens by Communist censorship for almost forty years. Classroom gags from Fellini's *Amarcord* (1974) or Allen's *Annie Hall* (1977) perfectly stand comparison with Caranfil. Thus, while Cristina recites her lesson in physics, the teacher intercepts other pupils exchanging prohibited 'Hungarian' contraceptive pills. This provokes uncontrolled laughter all over the class:

- How dare you bring contraceptives in class!
- These are not contraceptives, just vitamins, my grandmother brought them over from Hungary.
- This is nonsense Mînzatu. Are you familiar with our State and Party Demographic policy?
- Our party encourages... reproduction.
- Higher birth rate, Mînzatu, not reproduction. Nobody is asking you to reproduce yourself. A specimen like you is more than enough.

On having her pills confiscated, Mînzatu tells the teacher behind her back: 'I hope they're expired, so you'll have triplets'.[4]

Later, Cristina's everyday life is pictured in a series of narrative vignettes. Her small, packed home, the train journeys, the barracks where she visits her boyfriend Horațiu (Marius Stănescu) during his military service, and last but not least the provincial theatre, where she succumbs to the charms of a kind of Latin lover, actor Dino (George Alexandru). Memorable tragicomic moments, from a period dominated by bans of all kinds, are revealed by Caranfil with a particular gift for narrative pacing. Thus, while at home, Cristina's grand-father, played by the director's own father, critic Tudor Caranfil in a cameo appearance, complains about not being able to listen to Radio Free Europe, the banned radio station everybody was listening to. In a subsequent gag from another chapter, the performers put on Radio Free Europe by mistake instead of some Communist radio station, once again provoking laughter from the audience. A theatre addict, as many young girls of her generation were, Cristina is seen reciting in her room, and later on during her brief affair with the actor, lines from the highly popular poem 'Actors', by Marin Sorescu. These stand as a kind of *mise en abyme* for the whole story:

How naturally spontaneous – the actors!
With sleeves rolled up
How much better they know how to live our lives for us![5]

Once inside the universe of Horațiu's military service, Cristina realises to what extent he is both daring and immature. She is confronted by clownish young loafers, whose penchant for erotic games of all kinds is used in a comic way. Given the film's autobiographical subtext, the bespectacled, absent-minded, intellectualised Horațiu strongly resembles Caranfil himself. He will eventually prove far more subtle and complex than the other two characters, avoiding traps set for him and adopting a cynical attitude, despite his sincere love for Cristina.

The third narrative subplot focuses on the provincial theatre, its actors and the different plays they are meant to perform for the audience. Caranfil seizes another opportunity to lampoon a milieu where ideology and nationalism pre-vailed. Dino utters lines such as 'Marcela, now I can tell you the whole truth about myself: I'm a member of the Communist Party'; then we see him as the presumptuous hero of a nineteenth-century heritage drama in verse. Cristina literally falls under his spell: dream-like, blurred images backed by a pathetic score invade her. In the meantime, the other students/soldiers from the audi-ence are seen giggling at and relishing effective pranks, such as hanging fake rats from the balcony.

In the same vein, when the student and the actor accidentally meet next to the theatre's entrance, their dialogue exchange is inevitably marked by another series of puns.[6] When Caranfil decides to reveal the fact that Cristina has already spent a night in Dino's hotel room, the latter will tell her about his being fed up with his miserable provincial actor life and wanting to leave the country. When she looks for him the following day, the company has already left for another destination.

Shorter and less sophisticated than the first one, both the second and the third chapter provide variations and fill certain narrative gaps in a way no Romanian director had imagined before. Inside the bus leading them to the theatre, actor Dino and his fellow actors ironise provincial life under Communism. Says the bus driver: 'The beautiful town of Caracal we are entering is located next to the Danube and to the border with…' Actors are heard replying in chorus: 'Aus-tralia!' 'No, Yougoslavia, you fools!'

As in Welles's *Citizen Kane*'s (1940) duplicated opera sequence, Dino's version of the theatrical performance will include facts as they are seen from backstage, as well as the embedded gag about the Radio Free Europe signal replacing the official Romanian radio one. The audience will later be shown a non-point-of-view shot of the river Danube he is so eager to cross illegally. The love letters Cristina writes to him will be intercepted and laughed at by his alleged best friend, it being common practice under Communism for people to spy on other potential suspects. Last but not least, actors will be seen freezing, because of heating restrictions characterising the disastrous economic situation.

The soldier's chapter starts even earlier, in terms of timeframe, than the second one, most of its information having been passed on by Horaţiu only verbally to Cristina during their first meeting on leave. The highly autobiographical facts about an absurd despotic and coercive military milieu meant to terrorise young people are counterbalanced by an avalanche of funny moments.

The same soldiers who march intoning 'Proud country, corner of paradise' are happy to comment that Cristina is actually the main colonel's daughter. 'Who's that doll? Maybe she's his nanny, doing his laundry… She's not his sister, Miss Burlacu is the colonel's daughter, she's his chick…' The school girl pretending she does not want to have sex before marriage, Horaţiu's inmates set up an alternative wedding ceremony with prostitute Roxana, nicknamed Rexona after a highly coveted brand during Communist times.

Despite several elucidated mysteries, the most spectacular one being the revealed identity of Horaţiu as the person menacing Dino on the phone while he is in his room with Cristina, the final chapter opts for open endings. The soldier is set free from his service but does not know what to do next, given the hard times; the actor has managed to cross the Danube but maybe he will end up a taxi driver; the young girl is leaning outside the train window but we will never know what her next step will be.

Critical acclaim in Cannes in the Directors' Fortnight and prizes, mostly from French festivals, quickly followed for *E Pericoloso*. Though the film was shown almost two years later in the domestic circuit, it proved one of the few national hits of the early 1990s, a ray of hope in a very difficult post-Communist context.

Asfalt Tango (*Asphalt Tango*, 1996), Caranfil's second film, came up as another French co-production with several companies, including Les Films du Rivage and cinematographer-turned-producer Cristian Comeagă. It was not well distributed and fared less well at both the national and the international level. Post-Communist Romanian realities are presented in a highly cynical, sarcastic, albeit disenchanted way: there is no room left for nostalgia or for a kind of candid irony, as was the case with his first feature.

If the setup of this 'road movie' looks more conventional, revisiting the myth of young girls dreaming of a perfect marriage with the ideal French husband, in terms of manner and style it proves as original and dynamic as his first feature. Articulated differently in terms of editing, the same multiple story principle as in *E Pericoloso* is at work. Most performers are daring and sophisticated, including a surprising contribution by Charlotte Rampling as the 'Boss' of a band of joyous girls. According to Caranfil, the Anglo-French star accepted the part after being impressed by his debut feature.[7]

The narrative premise sets forth a sly and sophisticated French theatrical agent, Marion (Charlotte Rampling), who strikes a deal with her Romanian male counterpart Gigi (Florin Călinescu). The latter is charged to find eleven young and attractive Romanian girls ready to board a bus for Paris and act as prostitutes, under the lucrative cover of cabaret dancers. After quitting their different jobs and saying goodbye to family and boyfriends, the girls and their dictatorial agents set off on a picaresque journey. Their bus becomes the micro universe Caranfil had already hinted at in *E Pericoloso*, when showing the 'merry' travelling players in Dino's chapter. From the People's Palace, their point of departure, to the spectacular French National Day fireworks on the Champs Elysées, the film scenes offer the audience a chance to share with the characters a considerable number of road movie emotions thanks to classic pursuits, unexpected quid pro quos and last-minute revelations.

The journey is further complicated by a second subplot, which involves one of the girls' husbands, Andrei (Mircea Diaconu), who will do anything to bring back his reluctant wife Dora (Cătălina Răhăianu).[8] Eventually, Andrei will be manipulated by Marion so as to be disappointed by marriage as 'an institution': while at the point of asking for a divorce, he will nonetheless get caught and arrested by the Romanian border police.

The prologue and opening credits constitute an audio-visual *tour de force*, in the best classical Hollywood spirit. We are first confronted with a brief epigram on a black screen – actually a famous sardonic quotation by Groucho Marx: 'Marriage is a wonderful institution. But who wants to live in an institution?' A series of very quick shots further reveal marriage accessories from a shop window; they are dynamically backed by the first chords of the famous 'Chorus of Hebrew Slaves' from Verdi's opera *Nabucco*. Then there is an overlap sound cut to a real opera stage, revealing the source of the musical quotation. Cut to a loudspeaker in a dressing room from which the same chorus is heard, while a group of noisy young performers discuss their imminent departure for Paris.

The montage sequence is far from over, as we are shown another group of girls during a striptease session in a bar, as well as another young girl praying in her room to marry a rich Frenchman, the director ironically introducing organ sonorities to simulate a church-like atmosphere. This synthetic prologue literally paves the way for the credits, which unfold over a street walk and its asphalt, revealing an almost clichéd image of an attractive young blonde with a suitcase. This time the 'tango' from the title is heard on the score, an original composition by the same Şuteu and Caranfil as well as by a new Western collaborator, Rheinhart Wagner (Nasta 2007a: 3). In Verdi's opera, the chorus lines sung by exiled Jews actually express their longing for their lost homeland, while what we will be watching for more than an hour is how the travelling girls want to forget about their homeland and find their fortune in a better place. Caranfil's mastery of paradoxical humour is at work for most of the narrative. Thus, Felicia (Marthe Felten) declares she refuses to speak Romanian: 'I'll speak only French from now on. I consider Romanian a dead language', she tells her family.

Once the two agents, Marion, already disenchanted by the Romanian lack of discipline, and Gigi, a vulgar, mediocre, authoritarian macho, start their training inside the micro universe of the bus, every girl tells a story and reveals her total disillusionment regarding post-Communist Romania. Provocative, exuberant, confused or totally indifferent, they are meant to represent an authentic overview of Romanian youth. They fantasise about French icons such as Gérard Philipe and Jacques Prévert. As one of the characters says at a certain point in the film: 'You know what capitalist Romania means? Twenty-three million capitalists dying of hunger.' If the journey to the frontier means departing for a better world and unleashing dreams of escapism, the views chosen by the director of the Prahova Valley and of Transylvania reveal a beautiful though desolate country with picturesque people and locations.

In the meantime, Dora's husband Andrei has decided to track the bus, a pretext for Caranfil to emphasise the road movie aspect of the narrative. Keatonesque, slapstick-like gags, conceived as Balkan parodies, prove that even the most dramatic situation can turn funny. Hopping from an abandoned taxi into a stolen police car, our hero slowly but surely turns into a tough guy in spite of himself. Using self-irony, cynical Marion tries to persuade Andrei at several points to stop his quest. She manages to puzzle him and make him change plans during what may be called the film's embedded *mise en abyme*. The two of them are shot in a sophisticated pose on one of the hotel prosceniums where the girls are meant to perform. Marion – played with consummate skill by Rampling – encourages unskilled Andrei to dance the tango, providing yet another key to the film's title: 'a dance of violence, seduction and destruction of the other'.

Fig 27. Marion challenging
Andrei in *Asphalt Tango*

The film's final part is less homogeneous, and some scenes and gags seem redundant, but Caranfil carefully sets up two subtle endings, the first related to the main intrigue, the second to its subtext, tinted with a bit of nostalgic nationalism. Thus, caught in the trap of Marion's manipulative powers, Andrei will literally fall into the arms of Dora's colleagues, forgetting about his initial quest. In a rhyme echoing the initial marriage quotation by Groucho Marx, an imaginary flashback will ironically feature the bridal couple formed by Dora and Andrei, a priest putting handcuffs on his hands instead of a wedding ring. The ongoing narrative will switch back to real life, with frontier policemen repeating the same gesture for real. While the party girls head onwards for Paris, Felicia, the one who wanted so badly to forget her native language, eventually quits the bus and is figured as yet another 'girl with a suitcase'. She joyously whispers 'bullshit' in Romanian to Andrei the last time they catch a glimpse of each other.

Asphalt Tango had a limited distribution at home and abroad, though it has often been shown on television: it is definitely a film that needs to be reconsidered.

The made-to-measure Franco-Italian costume drama *Dolce far Niente* (1999) was a highly watchable 'foreign parenthesis' in Caranfil's career. Co-produced by television companies such as the Italian Tele Piu and the French France 2, the film was commissioned to be made by Caranfil by producer Antoine de Clermont Tonnerre. It followed the ambition of popular author Frédéric Vitoux to have his period novel *La comédie de Terracina* brought to the screen. The film features an entire well-known foreign cast and an efficient technical staff, except for one camera unit headed by a long-time Romanian Caranfil collaborator, cinematographer-producer Cristian Comeagă. Following complex distribution setbacks, *Dolce far Niente* never had its Romanian premiere and was only recently shown on national television.

The title comes from Stendhal's vision of Italian life during his brief journey at the beginning of the nineteenth century in Terracina, a small town next to Naples, where revolutionary bandits co-exist with an aristocratic family and with young composer Rossini. Henri Beyle (François Cluzet) – alias Stendhal – a young, not very daring adventurer who has not found his voice, is heard commenting in voice-over in a personal, not always convincing, diary mode on his stay at Count Nencini's (Giancarlo Giannini) place. There, two beautiful, rather amoral women, the Count's wife (Marguerita Buy) and her recently widowed cousin (Isabella Ferrari), will be seduced in turn by several aspiring lovers. Nencini is seen protecting anarchists close to the Risorgimento movement and fighting against Austrians for national independence. Among them there is young womaniser and future star Gioachinno Rossini (Pierfrancesco Favino), who is on the point of composing *Cinderella* for one of his mistresses. Beyle will soon find himself entangled in a complicated thriller with lots of twists and turns. He will eventually decide to return to Florence and start writing about his adventurous Italian stay.

The film's general tone is quite heterogeneous, Caranfil skilfully mixing vaudeville and drama. The rather conventional and clichéd plot oscillates between realistic, almost shocking moments and scenes of pure pastiche shot in the Cinecitta studios, brightened up by an ethnic Italian score. Beautifully shot locales indicated on a black screen change frequently because characters travel, hide and are even imprisoned in Naples, Terracina and Rome. *Dolce far Niente* got mixed reviews, the Italian press being more favourable than the French one. It did prove to what extent the Romanian director could deal with a cosmopolitan cast and technical staff, managing to avoid the Euro-pudding effect.[9]

Shot in only forty-two days with financial back-up from, as usual, French and European co-production partners such as Canal+ France and Eurimages, *Filantropica* (*Philanthropy*, 2002) has so far been Nae Caranfil's biggest domestic and international box-office hit. The recipient of numerous international prizes, the film also proves consistent in terms of theme and style, originating in yet another well-crafted screenplay.[10] Characters, situations, ironic reflexive devices, dynamic cutting techniques and effective language tricks are highly similar to the ones already developed by the director in his previous films. They are nonetheless meant to reach a wider audience, as they reference more popular topics involving fashionable attire and locales for post-Communist upstarts, as well as allusions to a familiar television channel talk show (Pro TV). The same Mircea Diaconu from *Asphalt Tango* is back in the saddle for a similar deceived hero position: his narrative voice nonetheless weighs much heavier, as the story is mainly told from his fluctuating viewpoint.

The film's indisputable novelty comes from its main storyline, which Caranfil admits to having taken from a 'news in brief' newspaper column: a writer having made money by composing texts for street beggars. The director confesses having imagined the film as a challenge to the highly stereotyped image of Romania, usually figured as the 'country of dogs, beggars and orphans', but also as a means to unveil, as was the case in *Asphalt*, the tragicomic consequences of savage capitalism in a chaotic Balkan environment. A Brechtian fairy tale, the film thus unveils a universe filled with traps and treachery.

The main plotline features Ovidiu Gorea (Mircea Diaconu), an aspiring writer and teacher for the well-to-do, who despite turning forty still lives with his parents. He is instantly seduced by and falls in love with Diana (Viorica Vodă), a sexy would-be model who is shooting ads on TV and who happens to be the sister of Robert (Cristian Gheorghe), one of his brash and troublesome pupils. Diana loves easy money and flashy clothes, and Ovidiu's meagre salary and unsold books cannot provide her with her lifestyle expectations. Diaconu plays the same type of apparently weak and helpless character, the paradigmatic ordinary Romanian who can only strike back when he manages to break the rules. Paradoxically, our hero is nostalgic for Communist law and order. He is disgusted by these students' vulgar language and amazed by the fact that their only way to communicate is via mobile phones, while he is unable to sell his book and make a living as a writer. He will soon become a variant on the *Blue Angel* professor Unrath, ridiculed by his pupils because he falls for a girl of their age. He meets by chance ex-political prisoner Pavel Puiuț, alias Pepe (Gheorghe Dinică), an 'affable sixtyish shark', as the *Variety* review rightly describes him, who specialises in concocting stories for beggars (Nesselson 2002: 26). His shadowy enterprise, deceptively and paradoxically called 'The Philanthropy Foundation', exploits beggars, as he invents stories to impress passers-by and then takes a great part of their profits.

Thanks to Pepe's unscrupulous but profitable solutions, Ovidiu is able to pretend to Diana he is a millionaire playboy. Pepe also involves him in another experiment in cheating the system. On different occasions, he re-enacts the sketch in which he is modestly married to Pepe's secretary Miruna (Mara Nicolescu) and celebrates his wedding anniversary in an expensive restaurant without being able to pay the bill, then cheats people into lending them money. Different rich mobsters offer to help until one day no one does, resulting in Ovidiu ending up disfigured after a fight. He is ready to testify during a renowned TV talk show, manipulating audience emotion to get people to provide financial help via a bank account. The negative spiral goes on as Ovidiu finds out he has been the dupe. In the same kind of ambiguous conclusion as in his previous films, the aspiring writer ends up with his confidant Miruna, the only one who has remained faithful to him all the way through.

Some extra comments on style, screenplay and *mise en scène* are necessary at this point. As in *Asphalt Tango*, some allegorical opening lines set up the highly critical tone of the upcoming story: 'Once upon a time there was a town, the inhabitants of which were divided into princes and beggars. In-between there were only vagabond dogs'. They provide an effective 'tie in' with the first restaurant sketch. We soon learn the ongoing scene is a recurrent one, actually part of Ovidiu's flashback confessions. Caranfil thus opts for yet another multiple scenario using duplication and repetition for ironic purposes.

In terms of visual and verbal *mise en scène*, Caranfil is close to the sophistication of Ernst Lubitsch: Ovidiu and Diana are seen almost missing each other on their first date at a bar called *Le Petit Paris*, while in the beggar's underworld headed by Pepe, everything seems to be perfectly timed because it is all counterfeit. Says Pepe to Ovidiu: 'Have a look at the Romanian state. Begging without getting anything. It's because they work with amateurs'. The larger than life portrayal of flashy Bucharest with luxury cars and restaurants, where Ovidiu acts like a cardboard prince, is deliberately contrasted with the miserable condition of the paupers. Caranfil thus indirectly provides a moral tale of modern times.

Fig 28. Caranfil as himself in *Filantropica*

The postmodern, self-referential vein equally cherished by the director is present on two distinct occasions. On the first, Ovidiu and Diana are in a discotheque where Caranfil, in a significant cameo appearance, performs in a playback Frank Sinatra's classic hit 'My Way'.

The second is larger in scope and is contained in the extended reality show sequence, quite similarly to Pedro Almodovar's 'interactive' handling of different audio-visual media in *Tacones lejanos* (*High Heels*, 1991) or *Kika* (1993). While Ovidiu's disfigured face is insistently shown in close-up on TV, different protagonists of the ongoing story tune in and testify from their respective homes.

Laughing at disaster brought him 113,000 attendances in Romania in three weeks, which may be considered a very good score, and numerous jury and audience prizes in his native country but also in Germany, France and Belgium. In addition, the film was chosen to represent Romania at the Oscars.[11]

Fig 29. The audience phones in during Ovidiu's reality show in *Filantropica*

Restul e tăcere (*The Rest Is Silence*, 2007), Nae Caranfil's filmic odyssey about the entangled circumstances which gave birth to the first important Romanian silent feature film, is actually one of his earliest projects. The original, discussed in chapter 1, *Independenţa României* (*The Independence War*, Grigore Brezeanu, 1912), is still preserved by the Romanian National Archive. The director started writing the story back in 1989, before the fall of Communism, after attending Frank Daniel's workshop in Brussels. Though his highly attractive screenplay was awarded prizes in Europe (Paris, 1998) and the USA (Los Angeles, 1999), Caranfil had to wait almost twenty years for his written lines to be brought to the screen.

Freely inspired by one of his own father's books on the beginnings of Romanian cinema destined for the general public, *The Rest Is Silence* was Caranfil's second period piece after the less-demanding *Dolce far Niente* (1981). Despite having benefited from the highest filming budget in post-Communist times, the director does not always seem perfectly at ease with non-contemporary locales and costumes, his caustic, sophisticated humour being less palpable than in his previous films. Nonetheless, for future generations, *The Rest Is Silence* will most certainly stand as the first whole-hearted, highly reflexive tribute from an accomplished filmmaker to his daring predecessors. Though almost a century separates them, Caranfil and his hero, aspiring director Grigore Ursache, eventually prove very close both in their passion for film and in their unusual perseverance in overcoming initially insuperable obstacles.

Another co-production between France and Cristian Comeagă's Bucharest-based Domino Film, the huge financing arrangement for *The Rest* also benefited from funds allotted by the Romanian CNC, by television investors and by a series of private partners. The result is a lavish wide-screen piece of entertainment running 140 minutes, which could only have been shot by national epic veterans such as Mircea Drăgan and Sergiu Nicolaescu during Communist times. Caranfil surrounded himself with a very professional technical staff. In terms of acting performances there are not many famous screen stars, the director preferring as usual to reveal new talent in secondary parts or cameo appearances.

Inspired by the real short-lived film career of short, hunchbacked theatre actor and film director Grigore Brezeanu, the existence of Grig (Marius Florea Vizante, already having played a spicy cameo part in *E pericoloso*) may be seen as the product of a miraculous Hollywood maverick. Caranfil opens the film with one of his customary reflexive twists: he casts himself as the theatrical assistant teacher exposing the ideal qualities of any aspiring actor, in front of a row of rather handsome young students. Grig suddenly breaks into the room, provoking an ironic grin, because he is not only late and totally unfit physically but also amazingly self-confident. Having failed to make the grade as an actor, Ursache is determined to make his other big dream come true: make the longest Romanian feature film ever produced, a 1912 reconstruction of the 1877 Independence War against the Ottoman Empire.

Combining authentic information taken from historical and literary sources with fictitious events derived from secondary sources, Caranfil seized a unique opportunity in the history of recent Romanian film, the opportunity to confront his daring hero with a multiplicity of turn-of-the-century media. Different subplots related to Grig's quest will thus develop in relation to performances in theatres, vaudeville fairs and operettas. The audience has access to the cinematic spectacle in its various forms: for example, rushes from scenes shot on location, surprising visual variations echoing animated cartoons, newsreel pieces and last but not least clips from the real existing film.

As it happens, most of the screenplay's narrative lines focus on the practice of filmmaking in a very consistent way. After what was figured in the initial screenplay as the opening scene, a very pompous, almost hilarious funeral service for a respected repertoire theatre actor, the director clearly suggests that a new artistic medium is knocking at the door.[12] The biggest and most famous cemetery in Bucharest, a Romanian equivalent of the famous Parisian Père Lachaise, offers Caranfil the perfect opportunity for a successful ensemble piece. In the most authentic Balkan tragicomic spirit, the sacred (priests reading the Orthodox mass, recitals and lamentations next to the grave) co-exists with the profane (aspiring actresses in tempting attires, Grig talking career issues with his father and journalists questioning the actor's young widow).

A cut to a journalist reporting in his office reveals the deceased's last wish had been to attend a film projection.[13] A few scenes later we learn he has bequeathed his garage to a shooting studio. Intrepid Grig is actively shown directing homemade silent films and giving technical indications. He is obviously 'l'homme orchestre', wishing to revive via moving shadows one of the most important pieces of national history in the most comprehensive way. Thus he will use famous poems, songs and dances from the national heritage tradition, while mobilising both the theatre companies and the official military and royal authorities.

Fig 30. 'Lights, camera, action' in *The Rest Is Silence*

Caranfil filled his screen subplots with fictionalised information mentioned in his father's book, but also with authentic facts validated by critics such as Bujor Rîpeanu and Valerian Sava in Romanian film history surveys (Rîpeanu 2004, I: 22-23; Sava 1999: 49-57). Brezeanu, alias Ursache, had thus first created the 'National Theatre Society for Animated Pictures' in collaboration with important actors from the Bucharest National Theatre, who co-scripted and acted in the original film. He also offered his services to Gaumont, one of the two most important European film production branches active in Romania, along with Pathé. In *The Rest Is Silence* the branch becomes 'Gaumonde' and is headed by Raymond Duffin (Samuel Tastet): problems arise because they steal the Romanian project and have it filmed by imposters from the Bucharest Jewish Theatre under a different name, *The War Against the Turks*.

Another important narrative thread was inspired by the flamboyant personality of Leon Popescu, businessman, landowner, producer and patron of the arts. He becomes Leon Negrescu (Ovidiu Niculescu) and is persuaded by Grig to invest in his unreasonable film project to the point of losing his mind. After a surprise visit to Negrescu's luxurious residence, Grig introduces the businessman to the world of moving pictures.[14]

A quite subtle meta-filmic sequence reveals Negrescu enthralled by those shadows animated by some mysterious 'God'. A provocative on-screen title suddenly reads: 'Leon, trust this young man'. The dumbfounded businessman is heard replying 'Yes, Father', revalidating Caranfil's passion for ironic winks. From that moment on, Negrescu becomes Grig's protector, substitute father and unconditional business partner. He goes as far as humiliating Grig's heavy-drinking caricatured father (Sandu Mihai Gruia, loosely inspired by real-life actor Ion Brezeanu), who despises his son, ignoring his real value and imagining his future only as a cloakroom custodian. Later, he will order that the alternative Gaumonde-filmed reels be burnt by the State Police authorities: the arson scene is spectacular and was chosen for one of the film's promotional posters. Caranfil does not hesitate to approach the highly sensitive issue of Romanian anti-Semitism: the local authorities criticise the fact that there are too many Jews in a film supposed to deal with an authentic episode from national history.

The third narrative thread is probably less convincing than the preceding ones, although it clearly stands as an obligatory plot point: Grig's on-and-off romance with a mysterious, highly attractive, frivolous young model, future actress and operetta singer Emilia (Mirela Zeța), who will be tragically devoured by flames at the end of the picture. As was the case with most male heroes from Caranfil's filmography, in *E Pericoloso Sporgersi*, *Asphalt Tango* and *Philanthropy* the relationship with a female counterpart is a complicated one, not being destined for a happy outcome. Emilia posing nude and innocently begging for a glass of water instantly fascinates Grig, but he is unable to overcome his shyness and seduce her.

Turning back to the first and foremost narrative vehicle, the much anticipated reconstruction of the film of the Independence War, Caranfil sticks to his tragicomic vein. Thus, for example, Romania's King Carol, having backed the whole film project and played a part in it, is represented in a satirical way. During an official meeting where Leon and Grig present their endeavour, a rather decrepit Carol (Alexandru Hasnaş) has difficulties understanding the director's position, ignoring the fact that such a profession exists: 'What's your job, young man, cinematographer, supervisor, producer?' Grig retorts, managing a perfect pun: 'I reign, Sire'.

Though the preserved silent epic has few close-ups, Caranfil simulates reframed and embedded shooting situations where soldiers and generals are scrutinised and given precise orders, helping deconstruct the creative enterprise in a refreshing way. Also, old army veterans invited to re-enact past events are turned into objects of ridicule, because they do not seem to agree on the way things happened during different key moments of the battle.

Irony also touches other media competing with film, such as theatre. Though it has been attested that the finalised epic resulted mainly from the efforts of the theatrical community, Caranfil makes a point of showing how Ursache wanted to get rid of a form of artificiality inherited from the theatre, notwithstanding the fact that using celebrated actors guaranteed the film would turn into a box office hit. A cameo appearance by veteran actress Ioana Bulcă (standing in for real-life stage 'goddess' Aristizza Romanescu) is yet another pretext for the kind of intertextual pirouette Caranfil is so fond of. She considers cinema 'distasteful' but still wants 'the moving shadow' of a great actress to be immortalised. Caranfil shows her as perfectly pathetic as a weeping mother of war victims, while in the 1912 picture the same actress played a nurse from the Red Cross.

Highly inventive cartoon strips building up a separate film fragment further enrich the diversified media material of *The Rest Is Silence*. Absent from the initial screenplay, the brief 'interlude in the form of a colourful cartoon strip', as described by *Variety*, recounts Grig's exploratory journey to Paris (Elley 2007). It is enlivened by Laurent Couson's Gershwin-style upbeat score. Thus Caranfil somehow anticipates the ongoing trend of using mixed media in order to figure film narratives in different ways.[15]

The new intertext includes Eiffel Tower views standing for Paris, a French cancan number, visits to prostitutes, and last but not least dealings with technical and distribution staff meant to help the dreamt project become a real film.

Fig 31. The animated clip about Paris in *The Rest Is Silence*

The film's last quarter is quite lengthy and deliberately pathetic. It includes the *War of Independence*'s much-awaited and acclaimed Bucharest premiere; the spectacular material and moral decay of Negrescu, who goes mad and is judged in court; and Grig's return to his theatre custodian position before his untimely death. However, a high degree of audience emotion is provoked by what is probably the best meta-textual pirouette of *The Rest Is Silence*. What people from the overcrowded movie theatre watch, alongside Grig and the surviving veterans, are authentic excerpts from the original 1912 production. Under the flickering lights of the projector, fiction and history become one. Courageous actors from the theatre who impersonated famous war heroes on screen, risking their fame and fortune, are now immortalised for good.

As in previous Caranfil films, the ending is conceived as a symmetrical round-up and provides an explanation of the film's title. Thus, 'The rest is silence', an overused final quote from Shakespeare's *Hamlet*, is alluded to at several moments in the narrative. The audience is supposed to measure the gap separating the old world of theatre from the pioneering motion picture universe. But when the director introduces it in the final shots, where Grig is attending a theatre performance, the quotation provides an interesting conjunction of contradictions. It clearly suggests that, almost a century later, despite misfortunes and catastrophes, those silent screen shadows have found a voice to speak up with.

Many national prizes were awarded to *The Rest Is Silence* on the occasion of the established Gopo Prize annual ceremony in Bucharest. Though shown in competition at the Locarno International Film Festival in August 2007, it got no prize: the rumour was it was considered more of 'a crowd pleaser' than an art film. Caranfil should be happy about this, as he has often declared he makes films for audiences, not for critics.

CHAPTER 9

Short Films on the Crest of the New Wave

With only a handful of isolated directors having received domestic and international recognition and only a few feature films produced on the brink of the new century, a decade after the end of Communism, Romanian cinema was still a 'white spot' on the map of world cinema (Corciovescu 2002).

However, starting in 2001, that spot became more and more visible for critics and audiences in the festival circuit, getting its 'primary colours' thanks to a previously neglected sub-genre, that of short films. This phenomenon had far-reaching consequences. Romanian shorts, mostly fictions presented by newcomers as part of the final phase of their university training or as totally independent projects, got recognition in high-profile competitions such as Berlin, Cannes and Venice, as well as in most European and US festivals showcasing this specific film category.

The now famous names of Cristian Mungiu, Corneliu Porumboiu and Cristi Puiu first reached the ears of film professionals when these filmmakers presented their brief audio-visual fictions on the brink of the twenty-first century.[1] Paradoxically enough, given their subsequent fame, they were far from being an isolated trio. In a two-year interval – roughly between 2002 and 2004 – Cătălin Mitulescu, Constantin Popescu Jr, Hanno Höfer and the late Cristian Nemescu, to list only the most salient names, also received international praise for their shorts.

The movement proved consistent over the whole decade, despite recurrent financing problems and the lack of visibility of such films at the domestic level. Thus, the films of the 'second generation' of New Wave directors, such as Radu Jude, Adrian Sitaru, Bogdan Mustață and Paul Negoescu, met with the same success. The latter rapidly turned to feature films thanks to intensive Western training sessions and financial back-up by specialised European institutions, such as Eurimages or the EU Media programme. Before trying to identify through relevant case studies the narrative and stylistic components which attracted such a generalised interest, one needs to focus on both the national and the international contexts which served as 'springboards' for these highly diversified personal profiles.

After a decade dominated by a relatively low domestic film output, often dependent on co-productions, in 2000 the Romanian National Film Office became the CNC (National Centre of Cinematography, depending on the Ministry of Culture) and offered filmmakers more concrete financing possibilities on the basis of bi-annual contests. Two years later, in 2002, a Cinema Law (n° 889) came into effect, extending the contest to short film screenplays alongside the usual features. Financing went up to 49% but decisions still favoured the commercial trend, dominated by old 'money-making' veterans such as Sergiu Nicolaescu.

An official protest letter signed by directors in 2002 revealed some of the dysfunctional aspects of the newly created Centre and required that young filmmakers be granted more financing for their final degree films or individual projects. More or less at the same time, several new production companies and firms backed by business enterprises or initiated by producers, filmmakers and cinematographers were added to the few existing ones, such as Constantin Popescu's renowned Filmex, co-producer of most Pintilie films.

Though domestic audience attendance rates and exhibition networks were shrinking more and more, film festivals became showcases for short films. International festivals were being offered packages of shorts to be distributed alongside feature films. Romanian cinema slowly but surely entered the world scene, mainly thanks to prizes received for fiction and documentary shorts, not only in festivals but also on the occasion of workshops and training sessions organised by the Cannes Cinéfondation, Dutch Hubert Bals Fund, and Berlinale Talent Campus.

How is this generalised interest and rapid recognition to be explained? Is there any link to be made with previous Romanian filmmakers and trends? Or have most of them an appeal precisely because they break from the past, striving to express themselves in a universally recognisable language? Both questions actually get an affirmative answer. Most stories are highly authentic and provide a minute scrutiny of ordinary human beings caught in the web of different social taboos dominating their daily lives. The post-Communist individual is clearly favoured over the collective, actions often unfolding at the margins, either at the periphery of a big city or inside provincial communities. Style-wise, however, they are not only influenced by Italian neorealism. Their naturalistic surface aims to portray the contrasting realities of savage capitalism, but this is often permeated by absurdist, ironic and even surrealist elements in the best Romanian literary and theatrical vein.[2]

Critics from all over the world also noted a lot of vigour and a great deal of honesty bringing 'new blood to world cinema', as well as a consistent desire to engage with alternative views as far as the Communist past is concerned. Also, the shorts produced roughly between 2001 and 2007 are related by a common passion for film in general and for the reflexive 'apparatus' in particular, being constantly ready to flush out pretence, asking questions more than answering them (Andrews 2008: 14–15).

Several interviews published in specialised media or on the occasion of international festivals revealed to what extent filmmakers such as Mungiu, Porumboiu, Mitulescu and later on Sitaru wanted to find new ways of making films and telling a story. They seemed to have clearly benefited from the heritage of role models such as Lucian Pintilie and of assisting foreign directors such as Bertrand Tavernier and Costa-Gavras, for films shot on location in Romania (Martinez 2007: 16–18). They also mentioned the natural influence exerted on them by famous world cinema auteurs as varied as Wilder, Fellini, Forman, Depardon, Kieslowski and Kaurismäki. The fact that they had been film buffs at different stages of their heterogeneous training somehow helped create a common denominator for their subsequent evolution. As a matter of fact, most of them did not start their career by entering the Film Directing Department of the Bucharest UNATC.

Once the films are subjected to close scrutiny, it becomes easier to distinguish some kind of a pattern, mid-way between what one may describe as postmodern pastiche and neo-modern minimalism. A good case in point is *Zapping* (2000), one of Cristian Mungiu's first shorts, made while still a film student, photographed by Oleg Mutu and co-produced by Filmex. It would later be shown on Canal+ France, after having received several national and international prizes.

The premise is rather simple: in a shabby apartment somewhere in Romania, a man obsessively zaps between his TV channels, despite his wife's complaints. A man from inside the TV will suddenly address him and explain to him some important principles of television zapping. *Zapping* has universal appeal because of an English-spoken reflexive opening. A voice-over is heard saying 'You can't stop it, nothing can stop it, it's coming', then different flashes inside the television set show a gun fight, until a reverse shot reveals the zapper, also called 'the husband' (Hanno Höfer), obviously an addict. Addiction presupposes loafing around with the remote control in front of the set, hence refusing any other occupation.

The willing suspension of disbelief is transgressed as in Woody Allen's *The Purple Rose of Cairo* (1985), when a character from inside the set, 'the remote control' (Ion Fiscuteanu), starts addressing the zapper and scolds him, inviting him to stop staring at stupid things. The husband does not understand how primary identification with the television screen has been transgressed and roles have been exchanged. 'Did you ever consider the question of how come you see me and I don't see you?' The Big Brother metaphor is thus very effectively presented as a moralising tale: 'Go take a walk instead of watching stupidly what I do'. The TV policeman checks inside the screen story and arrests the remote control in a very authoritarian way, because he advised people to read instead of watching TV. The husband hopelessly tries to prevent this, but the television policeman (Dorel Vişan) menaces the brash husband in an Orwellian way: 'soon you'll work for us and then I'll see you. This film ends here. Fun is over, next channel'. Instantaneous zapping is now activated from inside the remote control unit and the zapper immediately follows, getting back to his brainwashing habits, which make him watch indistinctively sex, violence and nationalistic epics. A closing Romanian credit song ironically sums up: 'Please turn on the TV, relax and tell me what you see while you're being brainwashed'.

Co-financed by the CNC and by Kodak Cine Labs, *Ajutoare umanitare* (*Humanitarian Aid*, 2002, 16') was made by Hanno Höfer, actor, music composer and collaborator of Mungiu. It tells the story of three young Westerners – actually the performers of Höfer's ethnorock band *Nightlosers* – who come to Northern Romania (Cluj region, Mărgău village) to bring some humanitarian aid, mainly medical supplies. They are welcomed with wine and food by the mayor and inhabitants of a small mountain village, to further underline the renowned Romanian hospitality.

The mayor (Ion Fiscuteanu) is very proud to welcome them in English, but otherwise dialogue is extremely sparse, almost absent. Different musical registers help the film pass from one feast to the other and slowly shift from traditional to modern music when dancing and flirting with local girls becomes a reality. Oleg Mutu's camerawork captures the village's authentic markers.

Repetition, not interruption or lack, is here the unifying style principle, ultimately provoking laughter in an almost burlesque way. Throughout the film's thirteen minutes, the humanitarian staff is ready to leave, and their truck is filled with lots of food in response to their aid. The 'goodbye shot' is a blend of popular music, bell-tolling and village noises. Höfer transgresses traditional closure principles: the intrigue goes on despite the credits being over. A long shot reveals an empty road while frontier customs verify the contents of the truck and empty the whole of it, in the best absurdist tradition. *Humanitarian Aid* won prizes in Clermont Ferrand, Montpellier and Cottbus.

Cristi Puiu's *Un cartuş de Kent şi un pachet de cafea* (*Coffee and Cigarettes*, 2003, 12') was made one year later, supported by Lucian Pintilie's creative film unit and co-produced by the Visual Arts Foundation. An old man enters a Bucharest restaurant and sits down next to a younger man who eats a lot and looks prosperous: he happens to be his son (Mimi Brănescu). Their conversation revolves around a job opening for the older man, out of work for the last two years. Actually the father (Victor Rebengiuc) brings along 'the coffee and the Kent [cigarette brand] carton' to bribe the future boss. The son complains this is only instant coffee, not real coffee, so he cannot offer it to the 'top guy'. 'It's like old times', the father concludes, 'with coffee and cigarettes'. 'Didn't you notice it's like old times, Father?' replies the son before they part and leave the place.

There is a minute attention to everyday objects, which are instantly turned into symbols. There are silences, frontal framing in long shots and no ellipses, and actors are obviously underplaying. The film won the Golden Bear for Shorts at the Berlinale in 2004, the main prize in the short film competition in Zagreb, and a Special Jury Prize in Syracuse in 2005.

Trafic (*Traffic*, 2003, 15') by Cătălin Mitulescu was also supported by the CNC and co-scripted by Andreea Vălean. It tells the story of Tudor (Bogdan Dumitrache), who, stuck in traffic on his way to a business meeting, has a twenty-minute break. He takes this opportunity to buy a nice young ad girl a cup of coffee, talk about his daughter and send the latter a funny picture of himself via his mobile phone.

The traffic jam opens up the film and will dominate it with a soundscape which foregrounds a chaotic urban Bucharest. Tudor is constantly framed through his rear-view mirror, driving nervously and talking on the hands-free mobile phone to his daughter. After having seen her briefly with her baby-sitter in a park, he learns she has mistakenly swallowed a hairpin and needs to go to the doctor. Inside his car once again, he promises his wife on the phone to be there on time, but is stuck in the jam. Exasperated, he gets out of the car and takes a taxi, continuing to comment on his actions on the phone. He finally meets his wife (Ana Bart). He notices an advertising girl dressed in red (Maria Dinulescu) in a POV shot. He looks at the phone and discovers a snapshot of his daughter, then stares back at the girl on the street.

Inside a bar, the businessman is seen taking a break and chatting with the advertising girl in a very blunt, casual way. An insert of Tudor's photo while making faces reveals a case of meta-filmic embedding and contraction of time. This happens to be a widespread twenty-first-century social metaphor: communicating via text messages, animated clips, drawings and photos on the mobile phone, unleashing emotional states otherwise difficult to express.

Fig 32. The wry father makes faces on the mobile for a sick daughter in *Traffic*

Tudor eventually leaves after throwing a final glance at the departing girl. All the car noises are foregrounded and there is an overlap sound cut covering the final credits (actually his station signal resembling a clock ticking).

The story is very complex considering it is so short, many aspects being only hinted at or suggested via the city traffic jam setting. After being selected in Cannes along with another short, *Bucharest-Vienna, 8.15* (2001), *Traffic* won Mitulescu the short film Palme d'Or in Cannes in 2004, as well as the Premiers Plans Angers Prize 2005 (First Film European Festival).

Călătorie la oraş (*A Trip to the City*, 2003, 19') was director Corneliu Porumboiu's final degree film for Bucharest University. On a spring morning the village teacher and the mayor's driver get ready for a trip to a nearby city to get a computer, which will enable them to set up an internet connection; they are also asked to purchase a special toilet that the mayor's wife has set her heart on. They soon realise everybody is busy celebrating an unnamed city's 854th anniversary. There are some pickpockets looming, so their mission turns highly risky, but they do eventually get home safe and sound. The opening shots reveal the meeting between the schoolteacher (Constantin Diţă) and the mayor's driver (Ion Sapdaru). A casual discussion about the computer they are going to purchase opens up unfathomed perspectives: 'We can create virtual worlds.' 'What's that?' 'For example we could build our village on the computer'.

Yet another mayor (Teo Corban) fakes work while oversleeping on his birthday. The community spirit in a Moldavian village is quite amoral, based on barter, theft and extra-marital relations. Humour derives from relishable dialogue quid pro quos: 'You're here for the fireworks.' 'No, we're here for the computer'. Irony is directed by Porumboiu against nationalist reflexes celebrating the country's glorious past instead of trying to create a better present. The celebration scene, with giant posters of co-founders of Romanian civilisation Trajan and Decebal, lampoons too much propaganda. The economic crisis is still a reality. When the young teacher goes to the restroom he is harassed by eavesdroppers, who steal his money.

An absurdist symmetrical ending anticipates Porumboiu's subsequent long feature *12.08: East of Bucharest* in its disenchanted tone: the teacher promises the driver that one day his son will be building virtual cities on the computer. Closing lyrics are clearly on the side of postmodern pastiche: the Moldavian band Zdob și Zdub, whose music opened the film, now sings

Fig 33. Lampooning celebrations in *A Trip to the City*

about Hollywood, Johnny Depp and other escapist dreams. The film won the second prize at the Cannes Cinefondation in 2004, where Porumboiu was subsequently invited for a writing session, as well as the short film contest in Montpellier the same year.

In Constantin Popescu's *Apartamentul* (*The Apartment*, 2003, 20') a man stands outside an apartment building smoking a cigarette before entering it. He takes the elevator, rings the bell and his wife lets him in. He takes out the garbage and lights another cigarette, while the woman, wearing an old bathrobe and rollers in her hair, prepares breakfast. He packs his suitcase for a short business trip after a careful shave in the bathroom, then leaves the apartment, wearing perfect business attire. He soon comes in again through another door, takes the elevator and rings another bell, that of his mistress. The same routine is repeated, except with a younger, trendier young woman and some modern equipment. The next day, after taking out the usual garbage to the miserable

outdoor bin, a similar high-angle shot of the elevator mechanism signals he is on his way back. But the early morning routine may be a false friend. He mistakenly rings his wife's doorbell and she stares at him flabbergasted, noticing he has put on his mistress's slippers with a pompom. The end song, accompanying an establishing shot of the whole apartment building, is 'What a Difference a Day Made', an American jazz hit from the 1950s.

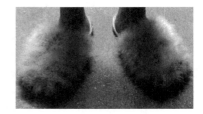

Fig 34. Wearing the wrong slippers in *The Apartment*

The Apartment, the title of which is a deliberate allusion to Billy Wilder's homonymous classic, thus proves a universal, prototypical tale of an adulterous episode with a tragicomic conclusion. Planning to deceive his wife, the husband is eventually caught in a trap he has himself set. Being totally devoid of dialogue, the film's entire meaning needs to be decoded by way of recurring visual elements but also with the help of a very effective soundscape. Every noise describing the daily routine from inside and outside the apartment is foregrounded and repeated in an almost surrealist way: the toaster, the alarm clock, the radio broadcast and the elevator mechanism almost turn into real-life characters.

As in most short and feature films from what will constitute the minimalist trend, there is no accompanying musical score. However, both incidental music occurrences – supposedly coming from the radio – are highly meaningful. The first one, called 'At Last' and sung by Etta James, is about the long-awaited bliss of finding real love: it backs the husband's first elevator trip, somehow anticipating his carefully dissimulated 'love trip'. The second one, a classic hit performed by Dinah Washington, frequently used in contemporary films, rounds up the story and goes on over the closing credits, adding up some indirect, ironic meaning. Its lyrics:

What a difference a day made
Twenty-four little hours
Brought the sun and the flowers
Where there used to be rain
My yesterday was blue dear
Today I'm part of you dear [...]

The lines refer to the happiness of finding true love at last in a more intricate way. Indeed, considering that the film's story also unfolds over twenty-four hours, from the morning he leaves his place to the morning when he returns inadvertently, one may infer that real time as such is irrelevant for capturing the story's ultimate meaning. What counts more is psychological time, the time the audience is invited to experience once the film is over. Thanks to the musical message, the tragicomic conclusion further creates a purely aesthetic, albeit universal kind of film emotion (Nasta 2008: 181–88).

The Apartment was awarded the Great Prize at the Venice Festival Short Film contest in 2004, as well as two important national awards: the Jury Prize at the TIFF (Transylvania International Film Festival, 2005) and the Best Screenplay prize at the newly created Danube Delta venue, Anonimul (2004). Popescu's subsequent well-crafted medium-length fictions *Canton* (2005) and *Apa* (*Water*, 2007) did not stick solely to contemporary topics, *Water* being a subtle adaptation of a Romanian army battle from the trenches, set in 1944.

In the same line, Popescu's highly controversial first feature, *Portretul luptătorului la tinerețe* (*Portrait of the Fighter as a Young Man*, 2010), is a daring tribute to the activities of right-wing partisan nationalists from the 1950s. Led by a charismatic partisan named Ogoreanu (Constantin Diță), they fought desperately against the repressive and sadistic Communist regime, taking refuge for several years in the Carpathian Mountains of Transylvania. The film's style is authentic, closer to documentary than to the minimalist vein developed in his previous shorts.

Despite the fact that a two-year production gap separates the two films, *Principii de viață* (*Principles of Life*, 2010) is Constantin Popescu's other feature issued the same year. It is co-scripted by Răzvan Rădulescu and Alexandru Baciu and very different from his previous *Portrait* in terms of narrative and style. A 'slice of life' about a middle-aged man unable to cope with inevitable setbacks caused by his family environment, the film, though filled with dialogue, is close to the cinematic spirit of the non-verbal *Apartment*. Behind the apparent control he boasts of every situation, the main hero is unable to really communicate and connect with people he loves and eventually grows violent and hysterical with his rebellious teenage son to no avail. The situation ends tragi-comically and the film seems to close where it began: Emilian and his recomposed family do leave for a vacation on the Bulgarian coast, but everyone inside the car is dead silent, the audience being left to interpret the film in multiple ways.

Radu Jude was part of the younger generation, having only graduated in 2003 from the UNATC, having read law at university. His second short, *Marea Neagră* (*Black Sea*, 2004), was chosen at the Berlinale Talent Campus screenings. *Lampa cu căciulă* (*The Tube with a Hat*, 2006, 23'), from a screenplay by Florin Lăzărescu, tells the story of seven-year-old Marian, who wants to see Bruce Lee on his old TV – but the set does not work. He and his father embark on a long and arduous journey to the city in order to fix it. Totally absurd, the narrative premise is only a pretext for describing a state of affairs: the miserable condition of Romanian post-Communist society. The director uses a child's spontaneity to bring forth important social messages about the generational gap being filled by access to new media, which nonetheless does not help people cope with parental disorder. Their trip starts from a derelict home, a barrack with water dripping from a badly protected roof, and goes on in an almost Tarkovskian way, filmed by Marius Panduru in dark blue tones suggesting an eternal night in early winter, with characters often barely visible.

The father (played by highly expressive actor Gabriel Spahiu, who specialised in secondary parts) asks his son (Marian Bratu) to help carry the television set covered by some plastic and a blanket: 'move on, don't stand there like a moron', he tells him, and goes on with some typical swearing at the situation. A truck eventually picks them up and they get to an improvised repair shop. He tells the guy he has no money, but it turns out there are no tubes left. The boy gets angry, afraid they will miss the six o'clock film. On their way back, the same difficulties in carrying the set and the rain and muddy roads only add to their pains. Once home, the son suggests they turn it on, and it ends up working. The room is all darkness, except for the set with a voice-over documentary on plants, which plays inside the empty living room over the closing credits.

The film's undisputable qualities are a minimalist *mise en scène*, spontaneous understated acting from the actors playing both the father and his son, with dialogue based on black humour, and sophisticated camerawork and sound design refusing any additional music. Produced like most shorts from the same period by HiFi, a Romanian film production company active since 2004 and headed by Ada Solomon, and co-financed by the Romanian CNC and by Romanian TV, *The Tube with a Hat* won a myriad of prizes in festivals all over the world. Adding to a series of European prizes (Cottbus, Bilbao, Trieste, Transylvania, and so on) was an unprecedented amount of awards won at different US festivals (Sundance, Los Angeles, San Francisco, and so on).

After another successful 'slice of life' short, ironically portraying the problems of a divorced couple confronted with the identity puzzle set up by their own four-year-old daughter, *Alexandra* (2008), Jude opted for a bittersweet, cynical comedy for his feature debut. Appreciated for its original screenplay at the Sundance Film Festival and acclaimed in Berlin, *Cea mai fericită fată din lume/The Happiest Girl in the World* (2009) tells the story of a young provincial girl who has won a car in a commercial campaign. She goes to Bucharest to claim her prize, only to become unhappy about her condition. It is a film with no stars, shot in a nonchalant realist way, featuring natural dialogue and purposefully lacking a traditional score.

Toată lumea din familia noastră (*Everybody in our Family*, 2012), winner of most 2013 Gopo prizes among other international ones, is the developed version of Jude's already discussed short *Alexandra* (2008). After an astute first feature conceived as a comedy but still focusing on dysfunctional families, in this hysterical episode sticking to the minimalist vein and echoing the rebellious spirit of Daneliuc, Jude proves a highly inventive and insightful observer of family dynamics. Marius Vizereanu's greatest stress factor is the imminent visit to the family where his five-year-old daughter Sofia lives with her grandmother (a very effective cameo appearance from stage legend Tamara Buciuceanu Botez), her mother and her new boyfriend Aurel. Marius wants to pick up Sofia to take her on a seaside outing. As soon as the camera enters the cramped flat with him, every emotion, sarcastic remark, threat or self-abasement is recorded in meticulous fashion. When it comes to family bonds the main character loses control: the boyfriend is tied up and the police are hopelessly knocking on the door, provoking laughter despite the domestic violence. After the carnage Marius simply walks away from the camera down a busy street. Shot largely in the confines of a unique location as many recent Romanian films recalling Bunuel's 'artificially' trapped characters from *The Exterminating Angel*, this kinetic drama is interspersed with flashes of dark comedy as modern stresses are shown to escalate into a conflict that spirals out of control, eventually into absurd violence.

Adrian Sitaru's short *Valuri* (*Waves*, 2007, 16') was far from being a debut, as it came after successful shorts such as *Biju* (2004) and *Trezeşte-te* (*Wake up*, 2006). *Waves* is probably one of the most complex contemporary Romanian shorts. During the film's climactic scene, the audience witnesses a foreign tourist's mysterious disappearance amidst the Black Sea waves.

The general atmosphere from the opening scenes is tense, the summer sun blazing mercilessly and vacationers of all sorts huddling together like sardines, as in most Romanian beach resorts. A middle-aged ordinary family sneers at a frolicking couple next to them, while Remus (Sergiu Costache), a young Gypsy boy, closely observes a beautiful blonde Swiss tourist (Karen Wallet). She asks the young man to watch her child and, once in the water with her inner tube, she gets entangled with Victor (Adrian Titieni), the middle-aged husband, who offers to teach her how to float over

Fig 35. A very special swimming lesson in *Waves*

the waves. While the young Roma boy tries to chat with her non-responsive child, the tourist, unable to float or swim, gestures for help, then plunges into the waves, never to appear again.

The amoral husband hurries away, pretending not to have noticed anything, and his wife tells him he needs a drink, because he looks nervous. In the meantime, Remus steals the foreign tourist's bag with camera and headphones and has fun taking photos; soon he realises her apparently disabled son also for some reason lies lifeless on the beach, and he runs away in the same cowardly way as the husband.

In terms of cinematography (Adrian Silişteanu), editing and *mise en scène*, the film is not minimalist. Thus, the opening is almost Hollywood-style, with quickly edited shots of the Roma boy walking among the crowd of vacationers. Sound mixing is very realistic and results in the development of autonomous auditory 'channels'. Direct sound combines dialogue, crowd noises, entertaining French music, radio football commentaries and mobile phone conversations. Such a soundscape brings forth lots of information about Romanian society on the brink of a new century.

Language comprehension quid pro quos, however, turn into a very effective screenplay device thanks to their minimalist use. Thus, the Roma boy answers in English and Italian while being addressed in French, which obviously provokes laughter. Similarly, when the middle-aged man accosts the tourist at sea he does it in Romanian: 'Nice weather today, with all these waves.' She answers in French: 'I'm sorry, I don't speak Romanian'. He asks her if she's French. 'No, Swiss', she says, to which he retorts, maintaining the linguistic misunderstanding: 'So you're from Sweden, in search of sunny weather'. After the closing credits we are confronted by another important New Wave characteristic of the minimalist trend, namely the fact that the action has a sequel, as was the case with *Humanitarian Aid*. Thus, in what one may call an 'open coincidence', runaway Remus accidentally stumbles over the middle-aged couple, who utter racist remarks such as 'get out of my way, damn black crow'. The film's finale is thus open, the viewer being invited to provide his or her own alternative conclusions. Co-produced, like most previous shorts, by the Romanian CNC, *Waves* also benefited from private financing from McCann Erickson, a company later involved in prize-winning projects such as Mungiu's *4, 3, 2*. It also won prestigious short competition prizes: the Pardino d'oro in Locarno 2007, Heart of Sarajevo 2007, Bayard d'or in Namur, Belgium, Best Direction at the Aspen Short Festival presented at Sundance in 2008 and best short at the Romanian Gopo Prizes in 2008.

One year later, Sitaru's much delayed fake thriller *Pescuit Sportiv* (*Hooked*, 2008) finally came out, the first Romanian film to exclusively use a subjective camera. A deliberate *clin d'oeil* to Polanski's classic *Knife in the Water* (1961), the film counters both the realist and the minimalist ongoing trends. As a matter of fact it verges on pure experiment, notwithstanding the theatrical, almost Brechtian relationship between stressed teacher Mihai, his girlfriend Mihaela and Ana, a prostitute met by accident during a countryside picnic. One is never fully informed about the relationships between the protagonists, and although there is a constant erotic undercurrent, emotions remain as ambiguous as the film's ending.

Two other shorts were completed by Sitaru in 2010, while waiting for financial support to shoot his next feature: they explore the often twisted relationships between people and pets, animals being pretexts for depicting human reactions. In *Colivia* (*The Cage*) a sick dove is brought home by a little boy raising new conflicts between father and son but also a possible 'reconciliation'. In the end the dove dies but the father/son relationship is saved. For the simplicity of execution, but also for very complex performances, *The Cage* won the Short Film Prize at the Berlinale. In *Lord* (2010), Toni 'specialises' in finding lost animals and then blackmailing their owners in order to obtain beautiful, large amounts of money. But one time, because of an old and ugly Pekinese he cannot get rid of, Toni is surprised to discover that strange and affectionate feelings are awoken in him.

Sitaru's second feature, *Din dragoste cu cele mai bune intenții* (*Best Intentions*, 2011), won two Leopards in Locarno and was inspired by personal events. Alex is in his mid-thirties but highly emotional and unable to accept his parents' mortality. When his mother is hospitalised after a stroke, his life suddenly changes after he rushes to the hospital to be at her bedside. At the hospital, he finds himself in a human zoo, full of unexpected characters and surprising events. Desperately trying to cope with this new situation, he is stuck between the well-intentioned advice of the doctors, his parents and his friends. Alex makes mistakes, tries to conspire against doctors, change medication, irony deriving from the fact he has the best intentions even when acting wrongly. The film is a cleverly choreographed psychological drama and presents itself as first-person cinema. While shot from different characters' points of view, it sides more and more with Alex. There is a lot of humour, mostly with the convalescing mother's roommates: one has had her face disfigured in an accident, so she is only seen wearing a cheap plastic bunny mask.

Romanian shorts have been following an ascendant curve, which does not seem to falter. Besides acting as effective laboratories for longer, more elaborate films, they frequently showcase the vitality and originality of emerging domestic or former exiled talents, getting the same international recognition as their predecessors. Examples of shorts dense and challenging both in subject matter and in style, often co-written or produced by established directors, are those bearing the signature of Anca Miruna Lăzărescu (*București-Berlin/ Bucharest-Berlin*, 2005), Miruna Boruzescu (*Carne/Meat*, 2006), Alexandru Mavrodineanu (*Lecția de box/The Boxing Lesson*, 2007), Paul Negoescu (*Acasă/ Home*, 2008) and Gabriel Sîrbu (*La drumul Mare/Life's Hard*, 2008).[3]

Bogdan Mustață's intriguing debut, *O zi bună de plajă* (*A Good Day for a Swim*, 2007) – about three young juvenile delinquents who break out of prison and start playing power games on the beach with a prositute – was awarded the Golden Bear by the Berlin Film Festival Shorts jury in 2008. Only three months later, Marian Crişan's minimalist tale *Megatron* (2008) won the Cannes Palme d'Or for Best Short Film. It takes the gifted director only fifteen minutes to tell the story of Maxim, an eight-year-old boy from the outskirts of Bucharest whose single mother takes him to a McDonald's for his birthday, where a Megatron robot awaits him. But the boy's deepest wish is to meet his estranged father, while the open ending does not satisfactorily meet his expectations. Crişan's subsequent first feature, *Morgen* (2010), tackled the sensitive issue of illegal immigration.

Providing further evidence of the ongoing vitality of the 'short' genre, as well as the emergence of a highly original 'feminine' trend, a couple of outstanding shorts were presented in festivals at home and abroad and fared quite well between 2009 and 2011.

Nunta lui Oli (*Oli's Wedding*, 2009) by newcomer Tudor Cristian Jiurgiu, is a bittersweet tale about scattered families abounding in witty dialogue lines. It deals with the impact of international communications via Skype. Alone in his kitchen, Dorel prepares for what seems to be a party. Actually, it's his son's wedding in the US: he is going to watch it through a webcam in the company of some of his son's friends, thus they are going to meet the bride and her father and will 'witness' the ceremony. *Trenul foamei* (*Hunger Train*, 2010) by Viorel Timaru, brings together two antagonist characters who eventually form a bond: a disrespectful and rebellious young man who doesn't have enough money for a train ticket and an elderly World War II veteran who succeeds in crossing the generation gap. Actually a real train which immediately after World War II carried people in need from Moldavia to wealthier parts of Tranyslvania, the transportation becomes a pretext for a road movie but also an excursion in time, the old veteran recounting tragic events. Beautiful photography (by Oleg Mutu) and a good command of acting mostly from newcomers are noteworthy, but what impresses most is again the mixture of sad stories with ironic and highly poetic situations.

Captivi de Crăciun (*Stuck on Christmas*, 2010) is Iulia Rugină's much praised graduation film, actually written by three women screenwriters, Ana Agopian, Oana Răsuceanu and Rugină herself. It tells the story of four characters who do not know each other and are forced to spend Christmas Eve together in a small and remote provincial train station, waiting for a train which is snowed up many miles away. As the hours pass and the train doesn't seem to arrive, they share with one another absurdity, hope, anger and despair and achieve through small but relevant gestures and minimalist dialogue intriguing bonds despite their obvious differences. *Oxygen* (2010) by Adina Pintilie premiered in Rotterdam 2010. During the Communist dictatorship, thousands of people risked their lives in the attempt to run from the country. *Oxygen* is inspired by a real case: a man who tried to cross the Danube illegally using an oxygen cylinder. Yet the facts are reinterpreted in a highly subjective vision. The film proves to be a poetic docu-fiction blending beautifully shot fiction and strange documentary-like archive footage in breathtakingly beautifully photographed visuals (greyish and colour-tinted industrial sites recalling Antonioni's recolouring of urban reality in *Red Desert*) and sounds of haunting quality with almost no onscreen dialogue.

Last but not least, *Apele tac* (*Silent River*, 2011), another short by Anca Miruna Lăzărescu, is a low-budget co-production almost entirely shot in Germany with a Romanian cast and shown at the 2011 Berlinale. The story is a true one, based on her childhood stories focusing on the obsession of escape and on the experience of a close family friend who crossed the Danube in the 1980s, hence it is similar in terms of story-line to *Oxygen*. Three characters embark on a risky escape adventure: two will manage, the third won't and the destiny of their families will be changed in unexpected ways. A lot of emotional tension is derived from a very good command of framing, lighting, direct sound and editing techniques and the director favors underplaying from very gifted performers.

Most examples reviewed here confirm the importance of shorts as a kind of rite of passage: they appear as an obligatory step and often serve as springboards for subsequent acclaimed feature-length films.

CHAPTER 10

Less is More

Puiu, Porumboiu, Muntean and the Impact of Romanian Film Minimalism

This chapter will focus on three of the most important representatives of the minimalist trend in Romanian cinema: Cristi Puiu, Corneliu Porumboiu and Radu Muntean. Their pioneering films were mainly produced between 2005 and 2007, coinciding with Romania's global success via what has been called the *4, 3, 2* phenomenon, to be dealt with in the next chapter.

Two authors, who also contributed to Pintilie's screenplay for *Niki and Flo*, are largely responsible for the creation of the minimalist model: Cristi Puiu and screenwriter/novelist Răzvan Rădulescu, from whose incisive and meta-physical writing technique almost all the important recent films originate. As often happens, their minimalism has its origins in the blend of the two figures' backgrounds: Puiu initially trained as a painter who wanted to fill the frame with striking, albeit ordinary details, and Rădulescu had a professional writer's gift for combining textual lucidity and absurdist hyperrealism with everyday life in a way that encouraged metaphysical decoding.[1]

Cristi Puiu's (b. 1967) first interest in the arts was painting. In 1992 he was admitted as a student at a visual arts school in Geneva; he soon switched to film studies within the same school and graduated in 1996. He returned to Romania and started writing and directing films, while also working as assistant and co-writer on two films by Lucian Pintilie, whose personal and professional contribution was crucial to Puiu's debut and his subsequent achievements.

Marfa şi banii (*Stuff and Dough*, 2001), Puiu's road movie co-scripted by Răzvan Rădulescu, was made before the short *Coffee and Cigarettes* (2003), so the latter cannot be described as a test for the former. On the contrary, *Stuff* appears as a 'rehearsal', containing many textual and stylistic elements to be developed later – in the subsequent screenplay for Pintilie's *Niki and Flo,* written by the same duo.

Stuff and Dough's depicted reality has a documentary flavour, direct sound and hand-held camera being there from the very beginning on the street where the hero's mother (Luminiţa Gheorghiu) is a busy saleswoman in her improvised boutique situated in her own apartment. Wise guy dealer Marius Ivanov (Răzvan Vasilescu) is supposed to meet her son, who is oversleeping. In the minimalist vein, there is no score, credits come in after 3 minutes and 50 seconds, discussions are low-key, and Silviu Stavilă's camera rapidly moves from one character to another. The dealer's conversation is harsh and blunt, and the mission consists in carrying some stuff (allegedly medicine) from Constanţa to Bucharest illegally, for a large amount of money. Ovidiu (Alex Papadopol) will be able to buy his own booth once the deal is completed. His disabled grandmother is realistically pictured. The black market milieu (parallel to the milieu his mother is involved with), but also the 'kitchen sink' atmosphere is what will characterise many Romanian contemporary narratives throughout the upcoming decade.

Three for the Road could be the film's alternative title, as Ovidiu is joined on the truck journey by his smart driver-associate Vali (Dragoş Bucur) and by the latter's girlfriend Betty (Ioana Flora). Filmed consistently inside the truck that becomes their micro-universe, the characters will become observers of the critical state of the Romanian nation. Punctuated by phone calls and on-and-off pursuits from mysterious aggressors, the four-wheel journey will include stopovers, police, radar controls and changes of itinerary that result in a lot of cross-country village and city outskirt views. Arriving at the destination is no big deal; there is nobody to welcome them in the first place and the three of them seem quite disillusioned, though no clear emotional reaction is represented: underplaying seems to be the rule and getting angry occurs far more often than feeling good.

Eventually, Doncea (Doru Ana) gathers up their stuff without engaging in any kind of conversation. On their way back home they come across the results of manslaughter, Ivanov's expected revenge: Ovidiu is seen staring flabbergasted at inanimate bloody bodies that the police have surrounded. The film's pay-off is probably its most innovative part: everything is implied, nothing is really explained. Ovidiu will not play the game again, even if there is tempting money at stake. With almost no dialogue, a rare thing in Romanian cinema up to that moment, Ovidiu just says goodnight to his exhausted mother. Fade out, with closing credits set to yet another Gypsy music score already heard at the beginning. The story's final message is there – easy money can trigger violent consequences in a world with no moral standards left – but a moralising attitude is totally absent, and so is any form of pathos or emotional outpouring. This is the main lesson Puiu will apply to his next film.

A harbinger for most domestic critics of the new Romanian cinema, the film won quite a lot of prizes and was selected for the Cannes festival *Quinzaine des réalisateurs* (Şerban 2009: 56).

There has been a lot of literature produced around the thematic virtues of *Moartea Domnului Lăzărescu* (*The Death of Mr Lazarescu*, 2005), Puiu's Dantesque journey featuring an old, retired, sick man, shunted from hospital to hospital until he slowly expires, thus revealing the dehumanising process of delayed medical treatment. In terms of style, however, Puiu's film is strongly reminiscent of minimalist techniques already present in Pintilie's *Niki and Flo*: recurrent use of long shots, lateral framing of tableau-like compositions, minute scrutiny of everyday, often non-spectacular details, a consistent refusal to use any score except some additional musical quotations within the opening or end credits, plus a constant challenging of audience emotional participation, through the lack of ellipses and the use of everyday small talk close to documentary 'live shooting'. Acting performances favouring underplaying, instead of the almost hysterical, aggressive overplaying which had characterised most Romanian films in the past, are part of a minimalist aesthetics identifiable in most contemporary films. Despite being a clearly original project, the script for *The Death of Mr Lazarescu* was first turned down by the National Centre of Cinematography; it was accepted for financing only after Puiu won the Berlin Golden Bear for his short in 2004 and wrote a letter of protest to the Ministry of Culture.

On being interviewed, Puiu explained the starting point was a real case he read of in the newspaper: around the year 2000 the ambulance brought an old sick man to six overcrowded hospitals that turned him down. As there was nobody at his place, he was literally left on the street with a drip administered by a nurse. He eventually passed away and the nurse received a jail sentence. The film's highly realistic 'making of' from the American DVD bonus features confirms Puiu's authoritarian directing and permanent focus on the extremely complex nature of human beings when confronted with solitude, suffering, pain and terminal illness. Everything in the filmed version of the event had to have a documentary value, a tribute – according

157

to Puiu – to Raymond Depardon's famous series *Urgences* from the early 1980s. Puiu further quotes as influences Eric Rohmer's *Six contes moraux* (*Six Moral Tales*), his similar project being entitled *Six Tales from the Outskirts of Bucharest* (Huber 2006: 7).

Simple credits on a black screen start accompanied by an entertaining hit from the 1960s by national icon Margareta Pîslaru ('Cum e oare, cum arată dragostea?/I wonder what love looks like?'): it is non-diegetic, as it will no longer continue once the visual story starts, while another song will be heard over the closing credits. The opening of Puiu's chronicle of an ordinary death reveals the same shabby, unglamorous interiors and characters as those appearing in most subsequent New Wave films; the rather static narrative setup is systematically rendered dynamic by witty, sarcastic dialogue mostly led by Mr Lăzărescu on the phone. During the telephone call he makes, textual and later on visual repetitions and variations on the same topic obviously echo Ionesco's theatrical legacy, a mixture of sarcasm and absurdist humour: 'Of course I drink [...] I drink on my own money'. From the moment we meet Lăzărescu (Ion Fiscuteanu) in pyjamas, wearing a nightcap and feeding his cat Mirandolina in his shabby apartment, the camera does not stop for a second.[2] The jittering of the camera will go on even when he sits down and starts explaining to an unseen emergency operator that he suffers from serious head and stomach pains despite the different kinds of medicine he mentions in great detail. Another theatrical influence emerges in this scene, the person at the other end of the line echoing the female character from Jean Cocteau's one-act monologue *La Voix Humaine* (*The Human Voice*, 1930), because the person is neither seen nor heard, while 'Lăzărescu Dante Remus' introduces himself in a highly articulate manner, providing his name, address, age and family condition. Given his solitary status, Lăzărescu listens and overhears television debates about the Romanian revolution and chats a lot with his two other cats, before calling again the emergency station for extra information about his past illnesses.

The hero's mytho-biblically significant name, 'Lăzărescu Dante Remus', echoes Dante's *Divine Comedy*, from which the screenwriters acknowledge having drawn their inspiration, the creation of Latin Rome, or the resurrection of Lazarus from St John's Gospel. It is meant to set up a double discourse about 'Hell on earth' which oscillates between the hyperrealistic depiction of pain and suffering and a sustained ironic, albeit symbolic mode. The same will apply for other characters' names, such as stretcher carrier Virgil, a paramedic called Beatrice, Doctor Anghel, close to 'angel', and the nurse's first name, Mioara, the diminutive of which, '*mioritza*', is the prototypical Romanian 'Mystic

Lamb' accompanying the dying shepherd, already discussed in earlier chapters (Nasta 2007b: 4).

The low-key lighting in the first sequence proves a constant stylistic feature, especially as the hospital odyssey will unfold at night, inside an ambulance or in overcrowded waiting corridors. The only identifiable source of bright light in Lăzărescu's home is the TV set, which is constantly on.[3] True to Pintilie's previously established *mise en abyme* paradigm, TV images shown and commented on anticipate the future parallels between Lăzărescu's personal journey into medical hell and a bus accident that turned the trauma centre 'into a slaughterhouse'.

The film's second sequence unfolds outside the flat on the same floor, where Lăzărescu rings his neighbours' bell to ask for extra medicine. The wife, Miki (Dana Dogaru), tells him she is convinced heavy drinking is the main cause of his pains, while the husband (Doru Ana) puts it plainly: 'Fuck this damn bottle, Romică' (diminutive for his second name, Remus), he tells him, thus adopting a highly familiar and vulgar tone. Once back in his flat with both neighbours trying to relieve his pain, Lăzărescu's condition worsens. The neighbours, after trying to diagnose the illness themselves, eventually decide to call the ambulance again. A black comic effect derives from the fact that, almost simultaneously, another neighbour (Ştefan Pavlu) pops in to suggest they should go and fetch some good wine from the countryside.

Eventually, medical assistant Mioara (Luminiţa Gheorghiu), from the emergency unit, arrives and demonstrates a command of the medical situation, revealing a matter-of-fact attitude, conveyed by the actor via an obviously underplayed style: 'You've been drinking a lot, this is why you're in such a bad state, I'll prepare you an injection and give you some medicine to relieve your stomach pains'. Once in the kitchen with Miki to prepare for his departure, Mioara learns Lăzărescu has been a widower for ten years and has a daughter who has emigrated to Canada and a sister Eva living in a remote town, so there is nobody with him, except for his three cherished cats, Mirandolina, Nushu and Fritz.[4]

Fig 36. The ambulance journey in *The Death of Mr Lazarescu*

The second essential locus of the film is the ambulance which drives Lăzărescu and his faithful nurse from one hospital to another, always making him and implicitly the audience believe they have finally reached the right place. The ambulance becomes the patient's second home. Lăzărescu is barely visible, though in constant dialogue with the medical assistant and with the driver facing the Bucharest nocturnal cityscape. The old patient is spoken to as if he were a disobedient small boy, most of his complaints being instantly brushed aside. Soon, however, every character tells his own personal story and relationships become more humane.

The first stop at Spiridon Hospital is a cruel depiction of medical indifference and aggressiveness, represented by blasé doctor Ardelean (Florin Zamfirescu), who, after diagnosing a serious case of ethylism, ironises every line Lăzărescu utters and suggests he should be transferred to the University Hospital. Hospital rooms turned into theatre scenes implicitly provide Puiu and Rădulescu the opportunity for innumerable puns, issuing from absurdist situations. Codes of social hierarchy are subverted: 'I thought I was the doctor here', says Ardelean after hearing the patient suggesting the medication which should be administered to himself. Discussions about the bus accident, already shown on TV, implicitly stress the fact that one man's condition is nothing compared to so many dead victims. Besides, doctors and nurses at different stages on the multiple hospital journey will be heard saying: 'Your liver will burst with drinking, pops', 'His liver is as big as the Parliament House', and so on. Such lines will come off as totally spontaneous, while actually every scene was carefully scripted.

Once at the University Hospital, Lăzărescu is unwanted, as most of the bus-accident victims are there. Mioara has to argue in the dark with swearing, exasperated doctors and exhausted nurses, while ambulance lights from the entrance are shown flashing around, suggesting an almost horror film atmosphere, the place filled with hurt victims lying on stretchers, looking like some anteroom of death. Stylistically, the sequence from the second hospital is one of the film's most dazzling and challenging ones. Puiu refuses classical editing with frequent cuts; he asked the cinematographer to move not before but after an action. During an unusually long shot, Mutu's camera constantly wanders from inside the consulting room to the waiting room and to different annexes, tracking all the characters, as if their actions were far more important than Lăzărescu's ever-growing pains. In figure 37, for example, the young female doctor is giving instructions to some other patients, Mioara is looking for help, and the neurologist Dragoş Popescu (Adrian Titieni) is just getting in through the door in the background.

Fig 37. *The Death of Mr Lazarescu*: scenes from the hospital

When the neurologist starts his check-up on Lăzărescu's capacities to react to different stimuli, Puiu and Rădulescu seize the opportunity to provoke laughter by means of puns and linguistic quid pro quos. 'Repeat after me', Popescu urges the hesitating old patient, who is already slightly delirious, and utters strange sentences: 'thirty-three storks on the roof of Kogălniceanu's house', 'follow my finger, do you see clear or double', and so on. Like most of the doctors featured in the film, Popescu has an offbeat humour which contrasts with the patient's critical condition. He strongly suggests a CT scan and they are off to another clinic, Filaret.

Once at the X-ray ward, Mioara meets a medical assistant who also happens to be a friend, good-looking Mariana (Monica Bîrlădeanu), with whom she engages in a personal discussion of marriage, sex and the emerging Romanian establishment. Shortly after, the almost incontinent Lăzărescu, who has also lapsed into incoherence, is introduced to the sophisticated tomography setup. Doctor Breslaşu (Mihai Brătilă) uses extremely colourful language to decode the deadly cells and a neoplasm he has found: 'good for Discovery Channel'. He thus urges Mioara to take the old man to the Filaret hospital

neurosurgery department: 'He's departing, poor pops, he needs immediate surgery so that he can die of cancer at his own place [...] unless you want me to get him directly to the crematorium'. Highly sarcastic turns of phrase thus unleash a kind of sardonic and morbid situational and verbal humour, typical of the Romanian blend of Latin and Balkan spirit (Eisenreich 2006: 24).

Fig 38. Delirious Lăzărescu disobeying the staff in *The Death of Mr Lazarescu*

Transferred to the Filaret Hospital, Lăzărescu grows weaker and cannot utter his name any more.

Fiscuteanu perfectly impersonates an almost paralysed character. This time he faces absurd bureaucracy and deliberate inefficiency. The medical staff turn him down for the surgery ward because there is no one from his close family to sign documents for him. Says the arrogant doctor Mirică (Mimi Brănescu): 'Hasn't he got a wife, a sister, a mistress?' Bagdasar, the fourth hospital, will be our hero's last stop. At this point, Puiu films and directs actors' performances so as to suggest everybody, including dedicated nurse Mioara, is exhausted at the end of the day. A female doctor and her nursing staff are barely audible as they speak in very low voices, and the general camera lighting and colouring favours dark blue and greyish tones in contrast to the previous strong artificial lights. Again, a point is made about the fact that the victims of the Săftica bus accident have priority over a drunk, unconscious old man.

As the end approaches, Mioara utters a sentence which confirms Ricoeur's meeting of *historical time* and *time of fiction*: 'We've been running around since 10pm… It's 3am… He needs an operation right away […] Our shift is almost over'. As Mioara, the loving, caring little lamb, says goodnight and exits the frame, doctor Anghel is being called off-screen, everybody waiting for his arrival. Two nurses take off his blue watch cap and pyjamas and meticulously shave off his grey hair. The scene appears as a kind of sacred ritual. The stark-naked original man, his body covered by a white sheet, is framed in a frontal

medium shot resembling Rembrandt's figuring of an agonised Christ after Calvary: he is close to becoming the Lazarus hinted at by his family name, before a quick last glance at the camera, actually at us, the audience.

Fig 39. *The Death of Mr Lazarescu*: exit Lazarus

The death, as heralded in the title, is always implied and never shown, but the film's conclusion confirms that no *deus ex machina* will manage to save him. Then the screen goes black and over the end credits we hear the opening lyrics of another hit from the 1960s, this time sung by Madeleine Fortunescu: 'When night is falling over the sea.' Story time and audience reception time are significantly blended into one single, highly intense emotional state (Sklar 2006: 63).

As decoded by Puiu himself, the film is about disappearance, about the extinction of a soul, a human being. 'Death', he argues, 'is a continuous process, from the moment we enter this world'. To Ryan Gilbey, the director revealed the novelty of the story's overall structure:

> I'm tired of the old forms of storytelling… of the traditional narrative, where we don't know what happens next. So I've tried with this film to move the accent from what's going to happen to how it's going to happen. Then the audience stops wondering where the story is leading and is forced instead to face the fact of what's on screen. (Gilbey 2006: 28)

In the 'Top Ten of Best Romanian Films' Puiu's film comes third, after *Reconstruction* and *The Forest of the Hanged* (Corciovescu & Mihăilescu 2010: 45). After receiving the important Un Certain Regard prize at the Cannes 2005 Film Festival, *The Death* got no less than forty-seven international prizes, among which was the BBC World Cinema award. *Sight and Sound* critics included it in the poll of the best films of the 2000s (held in February 2010). So did the 'American Critics Top 10', as well as equivalent polls organised by several French specialist journals. Alex Leo Şerban (2011: 5) subsequently categor-ised the New Wave films which were made after Puiu's achievement as 'ACP', meaning 'After Cristi Puiu'! *The Death* eventually became the first Romanian film to achieve international distribution on a relatively large scale, despite a totally non-commercial title.

> The film's international appeal moved beyond the cinema milieu, as it provoked reaction, debate and discussion among sociologists, philosophers and last but not least, specialists of the health care system.[5]

'This film happens to be Romanian', says Jean-Luc Douin in his chronicle in *Le Monde*. 'However, this does not come as a surprise, because its state of mind, the universe it depicts is close to two famous compatriots who had moved to France. Cioran, a nihilist full of irony, an apostle of despair... persuaded that there is something divine in each creature. And Ionesco, playwright of the absurd, of the ordinariness of human beings... of the anxiety to face death, the author of a farce about the difficulty of getting rid of a corpse' (Douin 2006: 26).

Five years later, Cristi Puiu's third feature, *Aurora* (2010), part of his six-movie series *Stories from the Outskirts of Bucharest*, is yet another film in which Puiu is eager to challenge his viewers, making many scenes difficult to watch. It is the story of an isolated divorcee with two daughters and a mistress, whose frustration with his ex-wife's family leads him to commit a series of murders. The slow-motion tragedy has Puiu directing himself as Viorel with a deliberately expressionless demeanour in the first part and with more sarcasm about his gradual downfall in the second, before the final confession sequence. Deconstruction of violence and examinations of the banality of evil follow the minimalist line, and so do the 'slow cinema' techniques: long takes and sparse dialogue, features of a varied strain of austere cinema that favours mood over event.

The movie covers one and a half days of a man's life in three hours, and there is a lot of ambiguity and mystery about his family and social status and his intentions. We see him repeatedly wandering and driving around the city, tracking with a hand-held camera from one apartment to another, the camera observing his gestures and elliptical dialogue. The director's complex performance suggests the tangle of emotions and thoughts going on in his disturbed mind, until he finally decides to confess his murders to the police in the same understated, precise, sarcastic manner. In terms of style, tension is built through absence, silences and banal exchanges before the gun goes off. Beyond his crimes not much happens. Puiu makes mannered dialogue sound strange: Viorel's much-awaited final confession inspires laughter for the sheer matter-of-factness of his performance. He contextualises what was missing from the beginning in an unhurried style, provoking laughter in spite of being a criminal, in the best tragicomic vein. The title *Aurora* is an oxymoron: most of the narrative unfolds at night or in barely lit environments, while the day he kills his in-laws and goes to the police to confess is a bright summer day. Another day breaks, despite murder. This is also the case for the end of *Lazarescu*, a chronicle of a death foretold, which is also about a kind of cathartic action.

Romania's other major representative of minimalism, who gained international recognition with his first feature film, is the already mentioned Corneliu Porumboiu (b. 1975). While sharing many style and content features with his contemporaries Puiu, Mungiu and Muntean, Porumboiu is most certainly unique in the way he revives on screen in an honest, sincere way the consistent Romanian tragicomic vein initiated by Caragiale and refined by Ionesco's Theatre of the Absurd. After spending his first years in his native Vaslui and after brief university training as a manager, Porumboiu fell for art cinema only in his early twenties after watching Fellini's *La Dolce Vita*. He shifted from economics to film school and was fascinated with authors from the tragicomic, bittersweet tradition, such as Chaplin and Forman (Fulger 2007: 160).

Besides the already discussed *Trip to the City* (2003), two other shorts proved important for Porumboiu's upcoming trajectory. In *Pe aripile vinului* (*Gone with the Wine*, 2002, 9′) a young peasant, Costel Adoagei (Constantin Diţă), confesses to the audience he wants to get away from what clearly appears to be an uneducated, vulgar, alcoholic milieu; he craves a job on a UK oil platform, hoping to never return to such misery. Following a compulsory medical check-up, the odds are against him: he is turned down because of a breath test which is positive for alcohol and will have to remain at home. Porumboiu already identifies crude post-Communist realities with a keen eye. The film got the jury's special prize at the 2003 Bucharest-based DaKino film festival and was selected for several foreign short film festivals.

The director's third important short film to be acclaimed both at home and in international festivals over the world was *Visul lui Liviu* (*Liviu's Dream*, 2003). Poignant and sombre with very few humorous touches, the film is very different in tone and subject matter from his previous features. *Liviu's Dream* includes footage of Ceauşescu's memorable speeches, hyperrealist slices of life portraying a corrupt younger generation lacking true values, and modernist dream sequences. A strange recurring dream forgotten in the morning is making Liviu (Dragoş Bucur) look differently at his friends and family. His night-time visions reveal the young man was born by mistake, his mother not being allowed to have an abortion. He will struggle to stay afloat during day-time scenes, but will not actually manage to avoid being amoral and making mistakes of all kinds.

The film's prologue opens with newsreel footage Porumboiu picked up from the Romanian television archives. It shows Ceauşescu's congress speech about punishing abortion with imprisonment via the 770 Decree, 'so as to help people build a bright new world', which is met with applause. Yet another male introduces himself and his family to the audience in a voice-over in an attempt to signify this is both a flashback and a summary of the present situation. Porumboiu acknowledges the fact that every time he uses a voice-over in his films literary influences are responsible for it in the first place. Liviu comments in an often ambiguous way on his everyday life and on his nightmarish visions.

The director relishes lampooning television as an intoxicating media, which offers up easy escapism to the Western world. We are also introduced to unemployed loafers who have their headquarters on the roof of an apartment building, echoing Fellini's *Vitelloni* (1953), and who have US mobster nicknames: Shadow, Fog and Midget. Harsh language, illegal market practices and prostitution are activities they all share in a quite detached way. Character direction and dialogue are so professional that overselling a wedding dress to a butcher in a slaughterhouse looks natural and eventually provokes laughter.

Liviu's final assessment is rather positive. Porumboiu eventually opts for the 'dream' world: the hero meets the brother he never had following his mother's forced abortion, a child with the voice of an adult, before shifting to a surreal landscape of his apartment building floating on a perfect blue sea. Four years before *4, 3, 2*, the spectre of abortion already haunts Romanian film. Though the ending is not entirely satisfactory and the film reveals to what extent Porumboiu was still hesitant as to what would be his next step, the exercise proved extremely helpful for his subsequent choice of minimalism as a style.

Liviu's Dream was rated the best film at the Transylvania IFF annual contest in 2004 and was selected for prestigious short film festivals such as Clermont Ferrand and Telluride (Colorado). While developing another project in the Cannes Cinéfondation 2005 residence, Porumboiu decided to change his initial screenplay and deal with a familiar topic unfolding in the town he knows best, his native Vaslui. *A fost sau n-a fost?* (*12:08 East of Bucharest*, 2006), his highly successful first feature film, eventually proves a very comprehensive study of the post-Communist psyche (Nasta 2007c: 62). A totally independent production written in a month and a half, lacking any CNC support, the film was co-financed by his own father's enterprises, and most of the crew worked for free.

Essentially dealing with a local TV broadcast that has to decide on whether or not there has been a simultaneous 1989 revolution in a small town in Moldavian Romania, this low-budget film first appears as one more story about what has become the main fuel for recent, unanimously acclaimed Romanian productions: the climactic moments preceding and following the dictator Ceauşescu's long-awaited though short-lasting *fin de règne*. However, Porumboiu revealed with a very sharp critical eye a post-totalitarian society painfully searching for new diamonds among the ashes of the past. In spite of a deceptively simple narrative line inspired by a real talk show the director watched in the late 1990s on a local Vaslui channel, the complexity of *12:08 East of Bucharest* has its roots in a very well-crafted screenplay, with dialogue obviously influenced by Romania's long-standing theatrical tradition and its consistent penchant for a corrosive, sarcastic humour.[6]

To begin with, the film's allegedly Shakespearian Romanian title posits an absurdist rhetorical question: *A fost sau n-a fost?*, literally meaning 'Was there or not?'; the latter becomes an overwhelming audio-visual refrain, answered in the most unexpected, hilarious, ultimately paradoxical ways. Once the viewer has watched the whole film, it becomes clear that the title is an abridged version of two rhetorical questions asked at different moments in the story. According to Mihai Fulger the question at the core of the TV talk show, 'Was there a revolution in our town?', gradually becomes 'Was there a revolution?' and ends up less optimistically positing a quite untranslatable 'Was there or not?' (Fulger 2010: 163).

Despite dynamic opening credits paced by an inventive ethno-folk clarinet solo, the narrative setup is unusually long (around forty minutes), the film having a two-act atypical structure quite different from the three-act classical one: until the TV show meant to provide an answer to the title question is finally launched, the viewer is somewhat puzzled by the lack of real action. After a long nocturnal establishing shot of the Christmas-light-lit town hall with its imposing tree and 1970s-style clock wishing its inhabitants a 'Merry Christmas', the camera wanders through the deserted, awakening city at dawn, strangely echoing Antonioni's modernist syntax of the early 1960s: the same shots will symmetrically close the film at dusk, with street lights going on and off against an almost sepia, chromatically de-saturated cityscape.

Vaslui is known as having served as an important administrative district in the north-eastern part of the country. Medieval leader Stephen the Great (1457–1504), a seminal historical figure due to his having defended the country against Ottoman invaders, had his headquarters there. His statue is seen looming in the centre of the town hall square and will be seen again as a comprehensive background image on the television studio poster. Porumboiu deliberately hides the city's name by means of the imposing Christmas tree to ensure the universal appeal of the story, which might have happened in any other Romanian provincial town.

Fig 40. The town hall square
Christmas lights in
12:08 East of Bucharest

The subsequent sequences reveal equally shabby interiors, describing the post-Communist poverty-stricken environment through stage-like frontal views inside three ordinary provincial apartments. Virgil Jderescu (Teo Corban), the local TV owner who desperately tries to call as many people as he can for the revolution anniversary show, is the definitive amoral provincial male. After a pre-revolutionary career as an engineer, he pretends to be both a respected journalist familiar with Greek philosophy and a good husband and father. A few scenes later he will be heard swearing and count-ing the money he refused his wife for his mistress, a moody blonde local news presenter who does not seem to care a lot for him. Mănescu (Ion Sapdaru), the disillusioned school teacher, is seen sleeping on his sofa because his wife cannot stand him any more: as in his previous cameo part in Porumboiu's short *Gone with the Wine*, he proves to be an alcoholic before we even see his face, while he is extremely ironic on the telephone: 'That's why you called, to ask if I had a hangover?' Finally, Pişcoci (Mircea Andreescu) is introduced in conversation with a young mother and her child desperately looking for the local Santa Claus. He stands as a living paragon for the pre-revolution-ary times, when he used to dress up for the town's children as *Moş Gerilă* (Father Frosty), any allusion to Christmas being prohibited. Later on he will be seen purchasing and parading in his Santa Claus attire in and outside of his apartment building, a humorous and colourful presence contrasting with the morose small-town atmosphere. Pişcoci's Christmas agenda includes a visit to a local Chinese bazaar-keeper called Chen, who happens to be everybody's friend in need: he sells Christmas attire and firecrackers to young children. Chen's verbal exchanges in Romanian with an Asian accent are worth all the verbal puns in the world.

In a way close to Luis Bunuel's surrealist taste for 'interruption as style', Porumboiu subsequently follows the three main characters chosen for the TV show through subtle cross-cutting that renders faithfully, through constant comic interludes, a chaotic but still witty and wry post-revolutionary country.

The bartender calculating Mănescu's drinking debts wonders 'what's the use in resuming talk about revolution?' The same disillusioned Mănescu hopelessly tries to calm down his undisciplined class by getting them to write a paper: 'I don't want to ruin your Christmas time, write about what you know, French revolution is ok, if nothing else works for you'.

Porumboiu's dynamic camera then tracks Jderescu on his way to the studio to attempt a show rehearsal with the deliberately unskilled cameraman Costel (Lucian Iftime), echoing Buster Keaton's *The Cameraman* (1927). A hilarious, brilliantly directed scene introduces a joyous young local band with a plump boy singing confidently in the foreground: 'Latino music is my life'. Jderescu scolds them for playing exotic tunes instead of the traditional Romanian Christmas carols. The Latino rehearsal music sung in Romanian has actually already been heard as incidental music in the opening credits and will be heard again, as hummed by the cameraman, as well as off-screen during the closing credits. Porumboiu makes very interesting use of these musical parameters, while sticking to the minimalist principles: there is no other score in the film and the band sounds are eventually mixed with snatches of dialogue.

A more dynamic editing pace further shifts the action to unexpected places. Mănescu is seen waiting in a hallway line for his monthly pay: after receiving his salary he gives back each his due debt.[7] Self-irony reigns at this point: 'Where do you celebrate New Year's Eve?' asks a guy from the line. 'Home', says the other. He retorts: 'I'll be celebrating it in Dubai with my boss, who's here next to me'. Outside, another series of establishing shots reveal miserable buildings with lamp posts in the centre and characters carrying unattractive trees. Following one of the film's rare ellipses, Jderescu and Pişcoci are heading by car to the studio, nostalgically echoing bygone white Christmases: 'Can't we stop at the market to pick up a tree?' the old man asks. They are later seen driving with three Christmas trees on the car's roof.

Starting half-way through the film, the pivotal show meant to answer the titular question first looks like a burnt-out soufflé. The studio looks so improvised one may think the familiar town hall poster in the background will fall off at any moment. The burlesque trainee cameraman is trying to frame them correctly but fails to do so, as they stand up, play with their pens or prefer to build paper boats. The three of them will be seen facing the audience with the town poster behind them for quite a while, making use of this epicentre whenever they want to visually endorse their arguments about how, when and where revolution occurred in their town. Porumboiu will thus implicitly reactivate Paul Ricoeur's already mentioned coincidence of *time of fiction* and *historical time*.

From this point on to the end, carefully scripted theatrical dialogue in the comic language vein of Caragiale and Ionesco abounds.

'Ladies and gentlemen, as you all know, today is a very important day. Sixteen years ago revolution started in Bucharest, so the question we'll try to answer in this broadcast is: did anybody rush to our town square before that crucial eight minutes after noon? ... I do think, dearest audience, we should do it, for the sake of truth.'

Fig 41. Piscoci, Jderescu and Manescu: the talk-show trio from *12:08 East of Bucharest*

Subsequent contradictory tragicomic phone interventions, made by local viewers from all social categories, eventually trigger multiple national and regional subtexts. They range from beaten-up clandestine Radio Free Europe listeners and popular tunes celebrating victory (e.g. 'olé, olé, we are done with Ceauşescu') to menacing verbal invectives from an ex-secret police agent now at the head of a flourishing business.

Thus, Mănescu confesses: 'I have to tell you there was not a soul in the market place [...] everything looked frozen, like the photo behind us, we started shouting and protesting [...] No, after a while we started to throw stones, tried to break the town hall open, still nobody around, then suddenly the Securitate turned up, I recognized one of them, Bejan, he worked for the secret police.' Bejan in person then calls to defend himself. After a couple more phone calls including one from their Chinese friend Chen, who dislikes the fact that 'you Romanians throw mud at each other', things appear to be reaching a dead end. Following a brief interlude, Mănescu and Pişcoci fear the audience is getting bored and threaten to leave the set as no real answers emerge. 'I think one of the gentlemen we heard made a very good point', says Jderescu. 'The flight from the Central Committee is like the Bastille for the French Revolution. If our town people came out after 12.08 this means there was no revolution in our town'.

Before the lights go off for good, the film nonetheless offers a second pay-off, welcoming tragic irony in the most typically East European vein. In a heart-rending tragicomic monologue, which is close to perfection in terms of minimalist underplaying, Pişcoci tells real and fictional audiences the story of his love for his deceased wife. We learn that they had planned a holiday at some Romanian spa, since Ceauşescu had promised them a 100 lei salary raise during his last speech. While Pişcoci hoped he could watch his usual *Laurel and Hardy* or *Tom and Jerry* afternoon entertainment, 'That very day some people appeared on TV to tell us the revolution had won'.

Similarly, a mother whose son really paid with his life sixteen years earlier does not seem to worry about unanswered questions: 'My son died near Bucharest on 23 December 1989. But I just called to say it's snowing', she is heard saying. 'Go out and enjoy, maybe tomorrow there will be mud again. Merry Christmas'.

Once the speakers have left the frame, the cameraman takes off the mikes and cleans the place. With only the town hall poster still visible onstage, we now hear his off-screen voice talking to himself or addressing an imaginary audience in an attempt to relativise the whole story: 'I should have shot everything in a fixed frame so people could hear them swearing and making up paper boats'. The same voice is commenting over the establishing shot revealing the shabby buildings and lamp posts from the opening scene, now rambling on without direction.

Porumboiu's minimalist perspective is not only tragicomic, it is also pioneering in its handling of the audio-visual medium in an unexpected way. Relating a provincial town such as Vaslui with a solid historical glow to an event with unprecedented consequences for the recent history of Romania could lead to a huge-scale epic about human valour revisited. Or paradoxically, it could lead to a major event being laughed at almost to the point of denial, in terms of both people's different actions and the way they are represented or recounted. The town hall epicentre is lit by a huge Christmas tree, indicating clearly that the time of the story is post-1989: electricity shortages imposed by Ceauşescu's sinister end of reign would have never allowed such lighting debauchery. In the same vein, the town's overall illumination system, beautifully rendered by Marius Panduru's sophisticated camerawork – with lights going on or off at precise moments of the day – clearly symbolises a concerted effort to catch up with Western standards.

Porumboiu used both setups, the town hall square and the lamp posts, as metaphors or in more complex terms as a *mise en abyme* for an imperfect revolution. Thus, collective memories rendered by talk show phone-in viewers and by the town's inhabitants provide ironic, albeit melancholy versions of the same event, as was the case with Akira Kurosawa's classic *Rashomon* (1950). The director thus faithfully pursues the self-reflexive vein at work in Daneliuc (*Microphone Test*), Tatos (*Sequences*), Pintilie (*Reconstruction*, *The Oak*, *Too Late*, *Niki and Flo*) and Gulea (*Bucharest, University Square*), as well as Ujică/ Farocki (*Videograms of a Revolution*), via their respective semi-documentary revolution 'reports'.

The perfect acting comes from experienced performers, most of them coming from the theatre, such as the trio formed of Corban, Alexandrescu and

Săpdaru. Porumboiu explains that he rehearsed a lot with the actors because he wanted each line to perfectly fit the show's general tone.[8]

12:08 East of Bucharest won the Cannes 2006 Caméra d'Or for an *opera prima* awarded by a unanimous panel headed by the Dardenne brothers. The latter were won over by the film's unflinching originality and its unprecedented comic impact. Besides getting the most important domestic prizes in 2006 and 2007, the film won more than ten international prizes in important festivals over the world.[9] It still enjoys consistent art-house, television and DVD distribution.

The critical reception both at home and abroad was as enthusiastic as the majority of festival jurors. Alex Leo Şerban considered it one of the most exciting post-Communist Romanian debuts and the best comedy since the fall of Communism. The critic chose an English title for one of his spicy reviews '(Less) Revolution Is (More) Fun'. For Şerban the director's overall minimalism dominated by static situations triumphs because it looks at a big, essential subject from an ordinary, small-town perspective, thus turning it into an auto-ironic parable of human endeavours (Şerban 2009: 266). French critics welcomed the film as a 'stunning, incisive debut on Romanian revolution as portrayed on television' (Azoury 2007: iv). Jacques Mandelbaum claimed that this remarkably modest and tragically absurd film represents the meeting of Gogol and Beckett (Mandelbaum 2007: 24).

In the UK ˇPorumboiu's film was described as 'A witty, incisive and very funny farce" and 'a black comedy with a subtle political edge'. In the US James Hoberman from *The Village Voice* found that *East of Bucharest* 'has a sly modesty that is reminiscent of the long-ago Czech New Wave, exhibiting a sense of film form that evokes the best of the rueful Czech comedies' (Hoberman 2007). A wonderful compliment indeed, considering that Forman was one of Porumboiu's inspirations while a film student.

Porumboiu's second feature, *Poliţist, adjectiv* (*Police, Adjective*, 2009) is a slow-moving police procedural with minimum action and dialogue unfolding in the same small town of Vaslui: stubborn policeman Cristi doggedly pursues a teenage high-school student suspected of hash possession, staking out and waiting for his suspect next to his home. The young detective will be confronted by a moral dilemma involving the boy's arrest and knowing that a future law will most certainly legalise the kind of practice he is accused of. In the meantime not much develops; Cristi writes down his minute police reports and argues with his wife about her listening to an insipid love song from the 1980s, the lyrics of which barely make sense. He also questions the meaning of law via an elusive final low-key discussion with his boss around the Romanian Academy dictionary: crucial words such as consciousness and police get multiple interpretations. In terms of cinematography there is a greyish predominance conceived by Marius Panduru, with many frontal tableau shots in long takes shot in real time, though the camera consistently tracks Cristi and there is no pre-composed music score, as in all other minimalist films.

The use of real time actually builds an invisible labyrinth around the hero, engaged, like the lead character in Robert Bresson's *Pickpocket* (1959), in complex body language that often does not need dialogue. In the most absurdist vein, the most important scene focuses not on a fact but on a verbal confrontation with his superiors, so as to prove that some rules are not legitimate. Words are devoid of their initial meaning once they are spoken, so images are stronger than words and transcend the story's initial realism. As in most minimalist films, understatement prevails.

The Romanian New Wave's third central minimalist figure is most certainly Radu Muntean (b. 1971). Unlike Porumboiu, Puiu and Mungiu, he loved film from an early age and started studying it as a first option, graduating from the Theatre and Film Academy as early as 1994 (Fulger 2006: 102). During his university training, he directed and was awarded prizes for both documentaries (*Şi ei sînt ai noştri/They Are Also of Our Skin*, 1992; *Lindenfeld*, 1994) and short fictions (*Ea/She*, 1994), which were part of student contests. There followed another series of well-received shorts and episodes for TV mini-series, *Tragica poveste de dragoste a celor doi* (*The Tragic Story of the Two*, 1996), produced by Romanian Television, already using a blunt, down-to-earth filming style. Soon after, Muntean was commissioned by the Romanian Visual Arts Foundation for a documentary on a community of Orthodox nuns, *Viaţa e în altă parte* (*Life Is Elsewhere*, 1996), which got a prize at the Locarno IFF Documentary Forum in 1997.

For almost a decade, filming became almost a daily habit for Muntean: he directed more than 400 TV commercials and musical video clips for reputable companies acclaimed for advertising domestic and international festivals. Only seven feature films were released two years after the fatidic year 2000, in which no Romanian film was produced. One of them was Muntean's debut feature, *Furia* (*Fury*, 2001, alternative title *Exit*). The production started as a private Media Pro studio initiative intended to be commercially viable and eventually also got official CNC support.

According to Radu Muntean, *Fury* was meant not as a portrait of a generation but as an authentic expression of his own fury, his rage against the violence and boorishness reigning in post-Communist Romania. Though less governed by minimalist principles than Muntean's subsequent films, the story time is nonetheless limited to twenty-four hours and incorporates Muntean's clip/commercial editing style. The different spaces of the ongoing narrative look very similar, being shot almost entirely in dimly lit places, the majority of scenes unfolding at night. This offers the ideal setup for vengeance scenes, easy sex, blackmail and, last but not least, violent criminality. Muntean's Bucharest appears as a huge suburb where low-life is predominant, the best place to do drug trafficking and illegal car rental and to indulge in different forms of tax evasion.

The director insisted on including at the core of the film's diversified cast an authentic Roma midget, highly popular singer Adrian *'copilul minune'*, meaning 'wonder boy'. He plays himself and seems to relish mixing it up with ex-cons, delinquents and recidivists. The merciless gang leader operating for Adrian is Roma mobster Gabonu (Adrian Tuli), a shaven-headed, tattooed giant, who prefers heavy swearing to everyday language.[10] The film's omnipresent protagonists are Bonnie and Clyde surrogates Luca (Dragoş Bucur) and Mona (Dorina Chiriac). There is also Luca's best friend Felie (Andi Vasluianu, whose nickname in the film actually means 'slice'), who will pay with his life for being an accomplice for illegal businesses. Both will be hired to control some car racing bets by Gabonu but will fail to obey his orders. The mobster will ask for his money back and some reciprocal vengeance with a lot of bloodshed will ensue.

As portrayed by Dragoş Bucur, who appears in subsequent Muntean and Porumboiu films and was already present in Puiu's *Stuff and Dough*, Luca is the epitome of the post-Communist middle-class youngster, who practises self-exclusion from his own milieu only because he wants to prove he is different from the old generation. A real daredevil, an independent spirit who handles difficulties easily, he is faithful to friends in need and quite easy-going with women. Revealed by Pintilie in *Last Stop Paradise* and successfully re-cast in his subsequent *Niki and Flo*, Dorina Chiriac as Mona is a victim of the same milieu, open to chance meetings of all kinds, sentimental and nostalgic for bygone times. When Luca falls for her, she simulates a mechanical doll, dressed up as Snow White amidst the performers at some popular fair, and later proves a mascot for a band of football supporters.

Despite colourful human fauna echoing Honoré de Balzac's *Human Comedy* (1842), *Fury*'s dominant tonality is extremely sombre from the opening shots to the very end. Muntean perceives no ray of sun within the universe he and his co-writer Mircea Stănculescu have chosen to depict, with the essential 'chiaroscuro' touch by experienced cinematographer Vivi Drăgan Vasile. From the beginning, Luca and Felie seem brainwashed by a debauched red-light milieu where swearing and beating are common practices. Their illicit dealings with mobster Gabonu often unfold next to a huge concert hall, where Adrian the 'wonder boy' simultaneously performs for and addresses a delirious audience. The versatile midget provides the film's text and intertext: we watch him singing, dancing, being interviewed about his future career plans, manipulated by Gabonu, who is in search of an ideal wife for Adrian, and spied upon by Luca inside an impressively kitsch Roma residence.

Managing to constantly shift from the hyperrealistic Roma entertainment world to the mobsters' underworld, Muntean's editing experience as a documentary filmmaker is clearly an added value. However, the most explosive sequences, backed by a very mobile camera and some rather intrusive electronic music,[11] are the ones showing Luca and Mona in action during their settling of scores. Luca avenges the death of Felie by killing Gabonu's perverted thirteen-year-old son during a birthday party. Fury's last manhunt sequence is close to the spirit of Arthur Penn's already mentioned Bonnie and Clyde (1967). Mona and Luca run away from the party, swimming through muddy waters: Muntean cuts to a railway location, suggesting the characters are off on a liberating journey. Later, a van picks up the fugitives, but the driver confesses he is an experienced rapist and wants Mona as his next victim. The very last image shows the red van at a distance in an ensemble shot with Luca hitting the rapist while the girl is heard shouting, yet another act of irrational fury. The closing credits unfold on the same image in freeze-frame.

Mihai Chirilov rightly describes Fury as 'A bomb dropped into the bed of a sick society on the verge of apocalypse, a desperate film about young people adrift in a world governed by money and a very courageous insight into the gypsy crime underworld' (Chirilov 2007). Though the film did not get the international acclaim it deserved, it proved a surprising domestic box-office hit, attracting no less than 60,000 viewers across the country and receiving a lot of domestic prizes.

Muntean's second feature, Hârtia va fi albastră (The Paper Will Be Blue, 2006), won the CNC script contest and was filmed in twenty-six days. While Fury dealt with the 'side heroes' of a marginalised society in a flamboyant, excessive manner, The Paper Will Be Blue is a minimalist tale about people at the core of the revolution facing an absurd, chaotic situation. It was co-scripted by a minimalist veteran, Răzvan Rădulescu, and by Alexandru Baciu: both have made use of a lot of existing archive material about the Romanian revolution.

The film depicts a famous night from the viewpoint of anonymous heroes, who wrote an important chapter of Romanian contemporary history. It is based on two sources: an authentic event drawn from Muntean's own experience as a soldier drafted into service in the town of Bacău during the revolution and a tragic killing, which occurred due to confusion between two armoured cars sent by the Defence Ministry to protect a military unit. It tells the story of a young military conscript, who is only months away from completing his military service when he is caught up and sacrificed in the dramatic events of 1989.

As was the case with Porumboiu's *12:08 East of Bucharest, The Paper Will Be Blue* is not just another film about revolution: it's a tragi-comedy, shot in the most authentic possible way, with uniforms and intervention vehicles lent by the Military Museum, from the standpoint of minor witnesses.

The story is not at all mild and nostalgic; on the contrary, its syntax renders the past strikingly present and realistic, avoiding ellipses and purposefully de-dramatising many hyper-mediatised events.

An opening daytime long shot is accompanied by hyperrealistic off-screen sounds, while two soldiers are shown coming out of an armoured car to light a cigarette. They are instantly killed. Again, unidentified off-screen voices are heard shouting: 'Hold your fire! Who's firing? I told you not to fire.'

Fig 42. The beginning is the end in *The Paper Will Be Blue*

There is a sudden cut in the opening credits, written with chalk on a blackboard and backed by walkie-talkie messages on the soundtrack about Ceauşescu the tyrant having left Bucharest.

The context changes abruptly, and only after a very long visually narrated night of chaotic combat does the story return to the car in daylight, making it clear that what we have been watching was a flash-forward and that one of the victims from the first scene was the film's main hero, militiaman Costi Andronescu (Paul Ipate). During subsequent scenes shot in a low-key nocturnal tone close to sepia or black-and-white photography and backed by a myriad of overlapping sounds from different sources, the militiamen inside the armoured car talk about a modified password and try to tune in to Radio Free Europe, in order to understand who is giving the orders to the supposed terrorists. The radio station, a means to provide information but also manipulate the listener, actually acts as a full-fledged character throughout the story. It clearly reminds one of the *mise en abyme* unleashed inside the improvised television studio of *12:08 East of Bucharest*.

Costi seizes a moment of inattention on the part of Lieutenant Neacşu (Adi Carauleanu) and impulsively decides to desert his post. He meets some loafers and civilians on a bus; they will further help him join the revolutionaries of the besieged National Television. Hyperrealistic dialogue including violent swearing, practical jokes and rough talk contributes to the feeling of immediacy about the ongoing events: 'Did they catch Ceaşcă?' (abbreviation for Ceauşescu meaning 'cup' in Romanian); 'What do you suggest, Rambo?'; 'Kill them all?'; 'Fuck it, I want to go there and fight'. Considered a deserter by his own squad, he is closely tracked by a highly mobile camera until he enters an ex-Communist activist's house in the company of Aurel (Andi Vasluianu), a Gypsy and occasional fighter later suspected to be an Arab terrorist. Costi is given a gun by captain Crăciun (Ion Sapdaru) and taught how to shoot until he is wrongly accused of terrorism.

Once inside the mythical Romanian TV station, the embedded reflexive paradigm is unleashed: while Costi's squad is desperately looking for him, the famous Committee for National Salvation is seen taking its position inside mini TV screens. Soldiers burst in to report that the police have identified Ceauşescu's car. *Time of fiction* and *historical time* keep coinciding.

Cross-cutting devices further reveal the lieutenant's squad resuming their discussion about a new password and searching for Costi everywhere around the capital, including the Parisian-looking Arch of Triumph. They end up at

the young man's small, shabby apartment, where his mother (Dana Dogaru) and his fiancée Angela (Ana Ularu) constantly watch the ongoing revolution on their TV set. Comic absurdity in violent times is rendered even more poignantly than in Puiu's or Porumboiu's films. 'Let's call a TV crew and film', says one of Costi's captors at some point. 'Let's watch TV, maybe we see him there', suggests his mother to his superior, who will almost forget he is there to look for a deserter.

Fig 43. The TV set of the main characters in *The Paper Will Be Blue*

A fake pay-off confronts the audience with Costi's unexpected release and return home, after Captain Crăciun asks him to identify himself on the phone to his lieutenant. Once home he asks for forgiveness for causing them such a scare. He kisses his fiancée goodbye because he has to reunite with his squad and promises to be back for New Year's Eve.

Back in the armoured car, a secondary auditory discourse is unleashed, with a lot of embedded action going on. Still maintaining an acting style which favours underplaying, the revolutionary for a day makes plans for his wedding. A walkie-talkie announcement eventually reveals the much delayed though often alluded to meaning of the film's title: 'Please identify yourselves with your password […] The paper will be blue'. The patrol does not have the same password as the army, so they all have to wait for another confirmation. Meanwhile, the young soldiers make plans for the future, dream about perfect cars and cigarettes and listen to hits on the radio. As was the case with Porumboiu's *12:08*, there is a perceptible hint of nostalgia for some good aspects of Communist times. The older generation is nostalgic about the beautiful music of the past, referring to appreciated Western singers such as Nana Mouskouri.

The film's astounding, symmetrical final twist comes as a shock. A voice is heard off-screen: 'Can we step out, just for a minute?' Through a brilliant rhyme effect, Muntean reveals the action we have been witnessing for more than an hour has actually been a flashback. Costi and Bobo (Tudor A. Istodor), who have been framed from a distance relishing their cigarettes in the first instance, suddenly become familiar when shown for a second time, because we now know their whole story. The real pay-off explains the prologue and introduces a stunning ellipsis in the most authentic minimalist vein. Then there is a fade-out, as in *The Death of Mr Lazarescu*, with closing credits introducing music for the first and only time in the film, with the partial exception of some barely audible hits on the car radio. Our emotional involvement with Muntean's ending is very close to a form of Aristotelian catharsis because of the musical quotation heard over the final credits. It is Nana Mouskouri's reworking of Giuseppe Verdi's famous operatic choir from *Nabucco* in her already mentioned hit: 'Quand tu chantes, je chante avec toi liberté / Quand tu pleures je pleure avec toi' ('When you sing, I sing with you liberty/ When you cry I cry with you'). It is a perfect oxymoron, because it clearly points to the innocent victim who wanted liberty so badly and had to pay with his life in such an absurd way (Nasta 2007b: 4).

According to Rădulescu, the decision to let the audience watch the same scene from two standpoints without revealing everything from the start came from him. He wished to maintain some mystery which would be solved at the end. By the time people realise who the victims are, there is no further explanation needed for the reaction of their family. The emotion is left for the audience to experience. They have to fill the gaps, once they are moved by the events already exposed: the fact that Costi had a family, a fiancée with whom he had wedding plans, and so on. The music from the closing credits is also Rădulescu's choice: some quite kitsch music he used to listen to as a child, by a Greek-born French *variété* singer who adapted a famous Italian opera hit, turning it into a perfect postmodern piece about liberty and sacrifice and a very effective authentic emotional trigger.[12]

Critics, who had seen the film both at home and on the festival circuit, praised Muntean's nerve and shooting precision, his pitch-perfect handling of such a major event in such a minimalist key and his exquisite command of actors who all look and speak very authentically. Most of them were, as already mentioned, film and theatre students at the beginning of their professional career. In her *Variety* review of the film, Leslie Felperin stresses the fact that 'the feature adeptly blends docudrama realism and wryly observed humour in a manner comparable to fellow Romanian Cristi Puiu's recent *The Death of Mr Lăzărescu*, and other local films, while offering yet another intimate-scaled, off-centre examination of the impact of 1989' (Felperin 2006).

The Paper Will Be Blue won many domestic prizes in 2006. It was part of the International Locarno Film Festival Competition, got two prizes from the International Sarajevo Film Festival, and was picked as Best Film at the Antalya Eurasia Festival. The Francophone Film Festival (Namur, Belgium) awarded it the Special Jury Prize the same year. Nonetheless, it was poorly distributed worldwide compared to other NRC films and had to wait for a second revival once it became available on DVD.

After the less convincing *Boogie* (2008), the story of a young father who, while at the coast with his pregnant wife and child, meets old friends who take him for a night out with unexpected consequences, Muntean's fourth feature, *Marți, după Crăciun* (*Tuesday, After Christmas*, 2010), is based on another brightly conceived screenplay by Alexandru Baciu and Răzvan Rădulescu. It tells the classic triangle story of infidelity, centring on Paul, a man torn between two women, his mistress, dentist Raluca, and his wife, Adriana, with whom he has shared a decade and a child: there is an agonising tension, as he has to leave one of them before Christmas.

The economical, minimalist style is subtle, consisting of a few dozen shots with the camera slightly moving, without anything essential missing. It deliberately feels like a voyeurist intrusion into the intimacy of characters, such as the opening sequence where husband and mistress are lying on the bed naked and kissing, as opposed to the final cruel testimony of a couple's implosion. Ordinary scenes are played out with attention to detail, emotional currents and ironies. The film's most accomplished moment in terms of *mise en scène* is the tableau-like frontally shot scene at the dentist's (where the mistress works), where they take their eight-year-old daughter to get her braces. When the film reaches its devastating final scene, the day specified in the title still lies in the future. Again the title is both a concrete indication and an allegory.

In the concluding scene around the Christmas tree, Adriana still hands Paul a present behind his back without turning around, conveying simultaneously the couple's familiarity and their heart-breaking disconnection. This is backed by another irony: Christmas carols are sung by children on the doorstep.

Though it lacks the political and ideological components of former films, the way it is dramatised refuses melodrama and turns it into something close to domestic tragedy. In terms of style, cinemascope seems to fit the intimacy, echoing Jean-Luc Godard's *Contempt* (1963), as Muntean's intention was to adopt this kind of voyeuristic mode while staying simple and unobtrusive and managing to express with a few movements complex feelings. Finally this is a morality play, despite its equivocal, ambiguous aspects, refusing to take sides and leaving the viewer to decide on the different issues at stake.

CHAPTER 11

The 4, 3, 2 Paradigm

Cristian Mungiu's Large-scale Phenomenon

Cristian Mungiu's *4 Luni, 3 săptămâni si 2 zile* (*4 Months, 3 Weeks and 2 Days*, 2007), the first Romanian Palme d'Or winner, certainly confirmed the triumph of the minimalist model in terms of acting, cinematography, editing and highly original soundscapes. It also highlighted one of the most controversial subjects of the Ceauşescu regime, illegal abortion and its tragic consequences on numberless female destinies.

Born in 1968, Mungiu first studied English and American literature and trained as a journalist and short story writer for various magazines. A graduate of the Bucharest Film School, he served as assistant director to Bertrand Tavernier (*Capitaine Conan*, 1996) and to Radu Mihăileanu (*Train de vie*, 1998) and directed a lot of commercials for public and private Romanian TV channels. Besides the already discussed *Zapping* (2000), he wrote and directed a number of very interesting shorts, either on his own or as part of collective international projects, and set up his own production company, Mobra Films, in 2003, with Oleg Mutu and Hanno Höfer as partners.

His most famous happened to be his graduation film, *Mâna lui Paulista* (*The Hand of Paulista*, 1999), followed by *Corul pompierilor* (*The Firemen's Choir*, 2000), *Nothing by Chance* (2000) and *Curcanii nu zboară* (*Turkey Girl*), conceived as part of the omnibus East European series *Lost and Found* (2005). Most of them were initially conceived by Mungiu as short stories: they were published either in their literary form or as screenplays available online, as early as 2003.[1] Despite highly realistic backgrounds, they all feature a mixture of surrealism, humour and reflexivity.

The Hand of Paulista (1999) could be labelled a 'foretaste' of *Zapping*: it is Mungiu's favourite among his shorts, having been selected for the 'Student Oscar'. A virulent satire of audience contamination by the 'telenovela virus', this short film effectively lampoons the universe of the mini-series *Avenida Paulista*, one of the most popular Brazilian *telenovelas* in Eastern Europe. Running on Romanian television in 1982, *Paulista Avenue* had a great impact on domestic audiences, conditioned to watch orthodox BBC adaptations rather than recent 'capitalist' tearjerkers. Its glamorous characters evolved in a perverted mob milieu at the heart of one of Sao Paulo's most fashionable areas. They were seen fighting, kissing and arguing in unusually ostentatious ways.

The young director exploited these aspects in a highly original way. Mixed lines often presented as subtitles such as 'Vitu estu minunatu' and 'Io voliu vediru lu filmu' ('Life is wonderful' and 'I want to watch the film'), using Romanian, Italian and French words with Portuguese endings, provoke instant laughter. The storyline and complex editing thus alternate embedded references to the series with two other 'real life' subplots: some beggars are busy commenting on the series as it is visible in a shop window, while at the same moment the shop's guard is held prisoner by an intrepid burglar who succumbs to his own fascination with the series. The ongoing Paulista story influences real-life characters to the point of making them utter the same hilarious multilingual lines.

Another short, *Nici o întâmplare* (*Nothing by Chance*, 2000), unfolds according to a thriller plot but verges on the absurd, featuring interesting narrative timing and minimalist dialogue. As in *The Hand of Paulista*, Mungiu seems to relish imagining unexpected exchanges and *quid pro quos* between an occasional thief and his supposed victim. The owner of the house is persuaded the burglar is the TV repairman he was expecting. Hoping to fare better, the thief knocks on another door 'by chance', only to come across the same host wearing different attire, and gets electrocuted while trying to fix another capricious TV set. Mysterious expressionist cinematography by Oleg Mutu and an electrifying score by Höfer add to the fake horror effect.

The Firemen's Choir (2000) is an obvious allusion to Milos Forman's *Hori, ma panenko* (*The Firemen's Ball*, 1967), not only in terms of the title, but also in tone and content. Assembled for the funeral of one of their colleagues, the Firemen's Choir is supposed to be actively rehearsing the instrumental centrepiece for the occasion. But their gathering in a picturesque countryside villa with a built-in theatre is only a pretext for unleashing some juicy secondary subplots. Embedded narratives featuring an inquisitive journalist, some foreign guests and a not-so-innocent young deaf-mute girl constantly challenge audience expectations. Mungiu swiftly handles interruption as style in a dense storyline, his dialogue already revealing a penchant for irony and macabre humour.

Four years later, Mungiu's more mature achievement is an episode from the collective film *Lost and Found* (2005) called *Turkey Girl*, its initial title reading *Curcanii nu zboară* (*Turkeys Don't Fly*).[2] Initiated in 2004 by Cologne-based producers and artistic directors from Icon Film, the project developed thanks to funding from the German federal cultural funds. The film had its premiere at the 2005 Berlinale Film Forum. Six Central and Eastern European post-Communist filmmakers from Bosnia, Serbia, Bulgaria, Romania, Hungary and Estonia were asked to film stories having as a common denominator the topic 'generation'.[3] Nevena Dakovic argues that

> The six films (four short narratives, a documentary and a cartoon) take on a wide range of cultural concerns that include the dreamy traditional past of Romania, the gloomy present of Hungary and the symbolic vision of an uncertain future in Bosnia. (Dakovic 2007: 57)

For Dakovic, Mungiu's *Turkey Girl* employs Kusturican magic realism to depict the visit of a peasant girl to her dying mother in a Bucharest hospital. Living in a remote village in the northern part of the country – actually shot on location in Transylvania, not far from Dracula's castle – Tatiana (Ana Ularu) is somehow 'far from the madding crowd': she spends most of her time training her pet turkey to learn the difference between a circle and a square.[4] She will have to quit an idyllic countryside for the harsh realities of Bucharest. Tatiana's mother being seriously ill, some extra 'payment' has to be handed over for the operation: besides money, it includes her beloved turkey. Mungiu shapes an ironic metaphor for a transitional society where tips still dominate the social system. Despite recommendations on how to handle such tips, the girl will do everything to set her animal friend free, to no avail. At several moments in the film Tatiana will be heard saying: 'I don't want him butchered by a stranger' and 'He knows a lot of things, he can tell the square from the circle'.

Once Tatiana is at the hospital, situational comedy in the best Romanian vein prevails. Tatiana is embarrassed by the whole thing, to the point of not being able to hand over the money and dropping the basket with the turkey in front of the doctor, during a spectacular pay-off scene. Ashamed and deceived, she ends up on the Bucharest streets at night with her turkey and her young military lover on leave. But Mungiu, efficiently backed by his regular camera operator Oleg Mutu, does not end their story here, as a second pay-off ensues. Tatiana's boyfriend shows her something she has never seen: the Parliament People's House fully illuminated at night, in a breath-taking long shot. In the foreground, the pavement features a round- and a square-shaped gutter: the turkey, who usually 'doesn't fly' now rushes to spot them, leaving the two humans in absolute astonishment. From the ashes of the past, a whole heritage district sacrificed to build the dictator's megalomaniac palace, a small film diamond emerges, thanks to the creativity of young, talented artists.

Mungiu's first feature-length film, *Occident* (*West*, 2002), is a bittersweet tragicomic portrait of youngsters yearning for a better future. Several sub-plots focus on characters who share common ground but whose actions are distributed over time in a highly arbitrary, intricate way throughout the narrative. The idea of dual paths and alternative trajectories, already present in Nae Caranfil's *E pericoloso*, is signified in the opening credits by means of double train rails filmed from a high angle. Similarly, titles printed on a black screen herald the multiple narrative principle of separate, though eventually intertwined, episodes.

In the first episode, 'Luci and Sorina', Luci (Alexandru Papadopol) is asked by Sorina (Anca Androne) to find a better job, which would enable them to improve their present condition and quit this miserable place. Their furniture has been thrown out of their flat in a shabby district and they are outside pondering their next steps. In a Bucharest cemetery, the superstitious couple is pictured waiting for a sign from Sorina's deceased father. She hesitates between staying and leaving the country, and waits for a sign from 'above' to indicate the right direction The surrealist tone is maintained, confirming Mungiu's penchant for such imagery, already present in his shorts. Luci finds a wedding ring and then a flying bottle hits him, leaving him unconscious on the ground. Sorina then hails a jeep to help her and introduces herself to a mysterious man called Jérôme.

The third sequence starts with a close-up of Luci's bandaged head: a subsequent effective narrative twist shows him being interviewed by an advertising company boss. Sequence four introduces us to Sorina's class and to her kindergarten director (Tora Vasilescu). The class is visited by a foreign guest, Michel (Michael Beck), a Belgian who would like to 'take some orphan children along'. Luci breaks in and wants to take her away because he has finally found a job. Dressed as a phone-shaped bear in his new advertising job, he meets a similarly costumed 'mobile telephone' girl (Tania Popa), later to be identified as Mihaela. A missed meeting with an ex-lover is a pretext for two 'lost' souls to get more familiar with each other. Mungiu further suggests that romance of the old-fashioned kind is totally inappropriate in contemporary Romania, where economic disillusion inevitably draws characters towards dreams of escapism to a better place. The film's pacing is extremely dynamic, proving to what extent Mungiu can handle many subplots in a limited time frame.

Back in the Bucharest World Trade Centre Mall, Mihaela has brought Luci a song he had been nostalgic about for quite a while: a very popular Communist hit from the early 1980s, sung by a children's choir, 'In the Year 2000 When We Won't Be Children Any More'.[5] At this point there is a clear touch of bitter irony introduced by Mungiu regarding the country's present situation, ten years after the end of the big Communist lie. Entertaining, easy to hum and with clearly over-optimistic lyrics, the song is first heard on earphones as an external source, then becomes diegetic and covers a series of domestic scenes related to each other in a contrasting montage. The second episode, 'Mihaela and Her Mother', unfolds in the same tragicomic vein. The opening shot is a strong reminder of Caranfil's harsh irony regarding 'arranged marriages' in *Asphalt Tango*. A ludicrous female mayor is seen marrying one couple after the other and explaining to Mihaela's mother that though her groom has not turned up, she cannot wait any longer as she has thirteen more marriages to declare. The coincidence principle seems to be governing the narrative. Mihaela's mother (Coca Bloos) will almost instantly turn to an unofficial 'underground' marital agency, revealing to her clients to what extent her daughter needs support in order to find the ideal Western husband. The same editing technique, alternating between Western fantasies and Communist nostalgia, prevails: Mungiu cuts to Luci singing yet another well-known tune along with Mihaela: 'I have my own pioneer tie and am very proud about it'.

The marriage agency episode is one of the most hilarious scenes from contemporary Romanian film. On entering the boss's office the hairdresser will be introduced to a vast choice of possible husbands: 'Where do you want the gentleman to come from? Europe, America, Asia?' The sequence during which Mihaela's family actively sets up the apartment for the Italian suitor's visit is also a precious piece of comedy. Luigi, the 'Italian' for whom Italian music and cuisine has been prepared, is actually black, a fact which causes disappointment among members of a Romanian society still relying on racist ideas.

The polyphonic aspect of the story is unusually complex: as in Caranfil's *E Pericoloso*, gaps in the previous episode are filled, but in a way that is in total contradiction to what the viewer might have expected. The third episode, which focuses on Mihaela's father, 'Nae Zigfrid and the Colonel', unfolds much quicker than the second one. The past catches up with the colonel, who is confronted by an incident which occurred before '89. An ex-convict now living in Germany and ironically called 'Nae Zigfrid' tells the colonel the story of Nicu, a young man crossing the Danube to reach liberty with an inflatable doll. He has now brought back his belongings to his best friend, Luci, including the doll, but they have been stolen at the airport. Eventually, the colonel suggests to Nae Zigfried that he take Mihaela along to Germany, because he is unhappy with her black suitor.

The film has three efficiently tied-in pay-offs. Sorina briefly embraces Luci before returning to her Frenchman as her final decision. Mihaela is taken along by Nicu's friend to Germany but wants to say goodbye to Luci before she goes. Luci remains home against all odds, a long high-angle shot revealing his lonely silhouette against the Trade Centre postmodern cityscape. Closing credits unfold, while what we hear is again the deceitfully optimistic 'Year 2000' hit.

Occident was supported by the CNC and by the Rotterdam-based Hubert Bals Fund, as well as by private financing. It received many prizes from festivals over the world.[6] It managed a fairly good domestic attendance rate for a Romanian film. People flocked to see the film, something that made Mungiu very happy because, as he mentioned in an interview for the Romanian Cultural Centre in London, this was one of his main goals when writing and directing the film:

> I drew on real stories… I can only tell stories that I know. I wanted it to be very realistic. I started to notice that many people around me were leaving the country, so it appeared to be obvious that this is the thing that interests everybody.[7]

Selected for Cannes' *Quinzaine des réalisateurs* with his first film, Mungiu understood everybody had high expectations for his future projects. After *West* and the already mentioned medium-length sketch *Turkey Girl* (2005), the director and a couple of young colleagues embarked on a long-term, multiple-episode film project, issuing from short stories about life under Communism, ironically called *Tales from the Golden Age*. While working on the project, a remark from a young reader had unexpected creative consequences. On reading the screenplay drawn from these stories he concluded that 'life under Communism seems to have been a lot of fun'. Mungiu thus decided to prove this was not always the case, surprisingly opting for a drama rather than a comedy, as was the case with his shorts and his first film, and for a chronological, simple storyline (Porton 2008: 36).

Choosing to tell the story of two young student girls who set up an illegal abortion in an extremely tough, Free Cinema style, Mungiu chronicles in an extremely accurate way the terror of everyday life during the last days of one of the most oppressive dictatorships in Eastern Europe. In the line of his predecessors, the director of *Patru luni, trei săptămâni şi două zile* (*4 Months, 3 Weeks and 2 Days*, 2007) overtly sticks to the minimalistic trend, as the film's detailed survey will aim to demonstrate: static, frontally framed long shots, refusal of any kind of ellipsis, frequent use of hand-held camera shooting, no score and underplayed acting.

A seminal documentary film most certainly played an important part in Mungiu's choice of the film's highly original subject. This was Florin Iepan's *Decreţeii* (*Children of the Decree*, 2004).[8] It contained an unprecedented amount of previously unseen archive footage on the Ceauşescu era. As summarised by Adina Bradeanu in her *Cineaste* survey 'Romanian Documentaries and the Communist Legacy',

> The film looks at the tragic intervention of the Communist state in the private sphere through Ceauşescu's infamous decree 770 of 1967, an Orwellian measure that criminalized contraception and banned abortion for all Romanian women under forty having less than four children. (Bradeanu 2007: 45)

Iepan's viewpoint sheds a lot of light on Mungiu's subsequent individually focused perspective. Thus, the documentary alternates personal interviews with important witnesses with stunning archive footage, a voice-over revealing how Ceauşescu set up a gigantic project, destined to literally reinvent a country and its people and turn them into world-famous individuals. The first highly publicised 'children of the decree' were born in 1968, Mungiu being one of them. However, the 'war between women and Ceauşescu' began after 1973, when the unusually high birth rate diminished and any form of illegal abortion was seriously punished, many doctors and abortionists – cynically labelled by one of the witnesses as 'serial killers' – having been arrested, tortured or imprisoned. Famous media people explain how they had illegal abortions performed in incredible circumstances, often with fatal consequences. Iepan does not hesitate to bring forth shocking images, almost unbearable to watch, the most striking one being that of a frontally framed foetus, an interviewed doctor explaining how failed abortions had fatal consequences for countless women.

In the early 1980s Ceauşescu imposed gynaecological tests to increase the birth rates in a country where people were queuing to buy their daily food, while he and his wife were visiting Disneyland. Ethnic minority cleansing and a high number of severely handicapped children are also part of the bleak picture figured by Iepan. After one sees such terrible images, the conclusion does not come up as a surprise. Once they became adults, some of the children born and celebrated during the glorious decree periods started the revolution which ultimately killed the dictator, often paying with their lives. The documentary eventually reveals that one of the killers of the Ceauşescu couple in the filmed trial was none other than 'a child of the decree'.[9]

Another event, less known though publicised in the Romanian press, occurred a few months before Mungiu started writing his screenplay. Dan Mihu, a Romanian writer and journalist, submitted his script in 2006 to an HBO jury of film professionals Mungiu was part of. The screenplay, called *Să iubeşti şi să tragi apa* (*To Love and Flush the Water*), got a prize at the TIFF (Transylvania Film Festival) and was published on the Internet but never became a film.[10] The story is set during Communism and focuses on courageous Ana, married and the mother of Mircea, who is cast out by her cowardly husband and has an illegal abortion at her mother's place in a remote provincial town. During her train journey home, she desperately carries along the foetus (hidden in her luggage) and is constantly spied upon by the secret police. Once home, she throws the unborn child into the toilet before flushing the water, hence the provocative title.[11]

As was the case with *West*, Mungiu confessed that he

> wrote about 17 versions of the script... When I write a script I use events from real life as imperfect as they may seem. The story figuring in the screenplay is quite similar to the one shown in the film: the person who told me the story 15 years ago referred to something which happened 20 years ago, so this is why I mention the year 1987 onscreen. Screenplay wise, my job was to transfer real destinies into fiction and trying to find out what really motivated each character. I had to make up the emotional background but not the motivation: motivation for the main character, Otilia, is solidarity, because life on the campus during Communism made people share everything and feel extremely close to each other [...] In the beginning I had two characters, they eventually became one because I needed an active character and a subjective perspective.[12]

The French journal *L'Avant-scène cinéma* published the film's edited script after shooting, accompanied by a series of interviews with Mungiu and his crew (Allon 2007: 3-10). Questioned about the origins of the subject, Mungiu explains how he perfectly remembers the atmosphere reigning among family and friends in relation to the abortion ban, so he went back to them and tried to collect as many stories as he could. He realised that several people who had been silenced for years by the terror of the regime now wanted to tell their own story. He also became conscious of the fact that such a topic was a good pretext to approach sensitive aspects of such a terrible period in Romanian history.

The script won the Romanian CNC contest in December 2006 and the shooting began right afterwards. Luckily, Mungiu managed to get extra financing from the Rotterdam Hubert Bals Fund, alongside the CNC, Mobra Films, his and Mutu's co-owned production company, Saga Films, and private financing from Mindshare Media and McCann Erickson. Romanian Television and the European cultural TV channel Arte joined the picture later on, so the film, which had run out of budget – because Mungiu shot more than expected and opted for the super 35 cinemascope format – eventually was ready for the Cannes pre-selection (Cieutat & Tobin 2007: 17).

After simple credits on a black screen, and an indication of place and time, 'Romania, 1987', the opening shot of *4 Luni, 3 săptămâni și 2 zile* is a frontal still life, a 'tableau', in pure daylight with snow seen falling in the window in the background. It also features a fishbowl on a table next to different objects. The metaphor of 'captivity' as figured by the fishbowl is quite striking at this point (Porton 2008: 36).

As in Puiu's opening of *Lazarescu*, Mutu's camera then tracks back, revealing the identity of an apparently anguished smoker listening to an off-screen conversation: Găbița (Laura Vasiliu).[13] The identification of the off-screen speaker is delayed, to be revealed later by the same jittering camera device: Otilia (Ana Maria Marinca) is finishing a phone call and asking for someone to feed the fish 'during her absence'. Otilia will be filmed looking for another colleague inside the dark corridors of the student house, where nudity in shower rooms, caring for kittens and collective tooth-brushing are shown in the most natural way. In terms of dialogue, despite its matter-of-fact tone, the entire sequence also contains other very relevant information about the Romanian Communist anti-abortion climate. Thus, the girls she meets in the lavatory will let her know that one of the female officers had noticed her absence at the monthly pregnancy test.

Visually, the sequence's most striking moment is a subjective tracking shot of Otilia walking along the dark corridor: the fluid hand-held camera filming only her back in motion is a strong reminder of the spectacular opening of the

Dardenne brothers' *Rosetta* (1999). The same type of one-take visual trajectory serving as a metaphor for her strong-willed, unflinching motivation will be repeated at crucial moments in the film. Otilia finally ends up at Ahmed's

Fig 44. The girls' dorm space in *4, 3, 2*

(Hazim E'Layan) place. He has a 'mini shop' full of Western brands, the most successful ones being used by students for barter and extra payment. Otilia will subsequently join another group of girls for a kind of open forum, a frontally shot collective tableau featuring their almost joyous trafficking to get birth control pills, missing food and foreign cosmetics.[14] As Constantin Pârvulescu argues, 'The dorm milieu is depicted as a world of solidarity, a protective matrix endowed with many features of a communist utopia' (Pârvulescu 2009: 3).

Ten minutes into the film, Otilia starts her outdoor journey into hell. She has been commissioned to search for the abortionist and to hand over the money. Different stopovers picture truthfully the overall reigning terror: thus, a bus ticket Otilia has forgotten to purchase becomes an issue. Once walking the university corridors to meet her fiancé, Adi (Alex Potoceanu), the young woman is secretive about her ongoing plans and consistently retains information.

She then goes to the Unirea hotel to check that the room reservation has been made: the conversation (framed frontally in a long shot, as will often be the case) with the overtly unfriendly and blasé attendant at the desk leads to the conclusion that no reservation has been made, and it is too late to get a room. Otilia continues her trajectory and goes to another hotel, Tineretului, with a pack of cigarettes as ammunition: she is desperate to find a room. Visually, a rhyme effect is created once the camera has changed position but maintains the same viewpoint, thus sticking to the minimalist repetition principle of suggesting more through less.

While Otilia is supposed to be looking for and meeting Mr Bebe (Vlad Ivanov), the chromatic signalling of the subsequent visuals is represented by variations on red. Both the gas station and the car in which the abortionist is waiting are patches of red in otherwise greyish, shabby street surroundings carefully captured by a distanced camera, a modernist technique to be found in Antonioni's famous *Il Deserto Rosso* (*The Red Desert*, 1964). According to Ioana Uricaru: 'The image was further desaturated through a bleach-bypass procedure in the developing of the negative and through the use of digital intermediates, a first in Romanian film production' (Uricaru 2008: 13).

Once engaged in a conversation about the meeting place and the missing abortion candidate, they are framed by the camera as almost immobile beings with neutral faces and low voices, though they are dealing with very serious issues. On their way to the hotel Mr Bebe asks Otilia to wait for him in the car for a few minutes, because he needs to talk to somebody: once outside, he approaches the entrance to a quite miserable apartment building and starts talking to an old person who is none other than his mother (Eugenia Bosînceanu).[15] Otilia watches from a distanced POV shot and overhears the conversation, as do we. What we understand from their exchange is that a friend has been queuing for the mother to get some sugar at the supermarket, revealing in a very subtle way the terrible end-of-reign economic crisis experienced by Romanian people of all generations.

Once Otilia and Mr Bebe get to the hotel, the same kind of subterranean terror prevails: hotel attendants ask for their papers, arrival and departure time, as if they were the police. However, the floor lobby they get to before knocking on Găbiţa's room is unusually luxurious and neat, clearly signifying such places were almost unused as few people could afford a room there. Mungiu and Mutu turn this space into a powerful symbol of secrecy and despair, introducing the fourth dimension – its ceiling – so as to further stress its particular autonomy.

Fig 45. Otilia and the abortionist knocking at Găbiţa's door in *4, 3, 2*

The first scene featuring the abortionist and the two girls is visually consistent with the frontal tableau principle, lacking almost any camera movement. The new triad confirms the anticipatory nature of the opening shots, with Găbiţa

Fig 46. Mr Bebe details the risks of illegal abortion in *4, 3, 2*

seated on her own bed, anxiously waiting for this crucial event.

It also acknowledges the importance of visual rhymes within the minimalist trend, since this is the second set of rhymes after the ones relating to the hotel desks. The upcoming dialogue, probably the most explicit and crude of the whole film, does not only set up some narrative lines which will be confirmed or contradicted. It also introduces the two girls and implicitly the audience to a frightening, almost horror-like 'failed abortion scenario', resulting in a highly critical health condition, court sentences, prison and eventually death. Though the information delivered by Mr Bebe is highly dense and dynamic (how he handles curettage, preferring it to abortion, what medicine to administer, the risks of calling the ambulance, and so on), his nuanced performance is clearly underplayed. His attitude is very determined, but he almost never raises his voice, almost whispering, except for a brief moment of yelling and cursing.

Serving as an explanation for the film's title, the upcoming moment reveals terror-stricken Găbița explaining she has an irregular menstrual cycle. 'You need to tell the truth', argues Mr Bebe, 'because these details are important, you're playing games with months. Four months, five months... After four months you're not done for abortion. They get you for murder, five to ten years.' Soon afterwards Mr Bebe will start his sexual blackmailing, putting the two girls under almost unbearable psychological pressure. After having heard from their side how much money they are ready to provide for such a risky business, he explains in the same totally non-emphatic manner, implying he has another kind of requirement, 'Did I mention money? You said we could work something out?'

Though dramatic tension is at its highest during these moments, both girls try to persuade him they can find more money provided that he will not ask for other favours. True to their minimalistic principles, Mungiu and camera-man Mutu do not reframe or cut to another setup, deliberately introducing framing errors, such as Găbița's beheaded silhouette. Finally, the girls are forced to accept and get ready for the proposed sexual agreement. Mungiu

Fig 47. Otilia in the pivotal bathroom scene of *4, 3, 2*

deliberately cuts to other spaces, where Găbița's and Otilia's desperate looks and gestures are framed in silent close-ups and back shots. Varying spatial parameters to unleash different types of audience anticipation is another governing principle of the minimalist aesthetic, reminding one of the Dardennes' similar techniques. The bathroom becomes a narratively relevant audio-visual domain, a refuge where intimate details are purposefully foregrounded, somehow anticipating the ultimate, unbearable revelation of the aborted foetus. Otilia's unusually long bathroom 'back shot' is probably one of the most meaningful in the entire film.[16]

Mungiu shifts to a different tonality and elegantly introduces one of the film's few ellipses, thus slightly diverging from the minimalist hyperrealist line: the sexual intercourse is not shown, the critical scene taking place off-screen. What we see are only images of the girls' crying, pain-stricken faces as reflected in the bathroom mirror. Later on, the off-screen space will be suggested by the sound of running water from the bathroom. Says Pârvulescu:

In depicting these abuses the camera rejects phallic cinematic conscience... visually the film peeps into the life of the others but it encodes the limits of such an
exploration by using a static and limited perspective. (Pârvulescu 2009: 5)

While Găbița prepares the bed for the abortion in an almost clinical way,
Otilia sneaks a look in the abortionist's suitcase, where she finds and opens
a Swiss army knife, which she will quickly put back with no other narrative
consequences. Mungiu argues: 'I try to leave approximate details irrelevant
or unaccomplished to make them seem more real in relationship to an event
going on over a single day'.[17]

Mr Bebe carefully prepares his abortion paraphernalia, starting right away
and giving precise instructions to a still terror-stricken Găbița. He goes as far
as explaining that the foetus must not be thrown in the lavatories or buried
in an easily identifiable place: 'Wrap it up nicely, take a bus, get off at a high
rise, go to the tenth floor and throw it down the rubbish chute. Understand?'
After carefully giving his last 'medical' instructions and mentioning he can be
reached on the phone in case of an emergency, Bebe wishes Găbița good luck
and leaves in the same casual, matter-of-fact way he arrived. The girls are left
to themselves, to their own fears and anxieties for the coming hours. Framed
by Mutu's camera in one of the film's rare profile close-ups, Otilia speaks up in
highly reproachful terms to Găbița, feeling betrayed and involved in a blackmail scenario she had never anticipated. She seems to finally accept that
Găbița had no alternative: they part, Otilia explaining she has to briefly attend
her mother-in-law's birthday party, but she promises to call and also advises
her not to move.

A series of apparently 'neutral' shots of an almost deserted town detail
her solitary streetcar journey and her arrival at the boyfriend's place. These
shots will later be matched by corresponding shots in a spatial rhyme: Otilia's
desperate nocturnal journey to the place where she will dispose of the foetus. Minimalism's propensity for inanimate elements acting as characters, in
this case the parallel streetcar shots, is a strong reminder of Michelangelo
Antonioni's pioneering use of objects and places to express psychological
tensions.

The 'supper sequence' at her boyfriend's place is an extraordinary digest
of Romanian society of the 1980s, actually the only moment in the film where
Communist times are explicitly alluded to. As a matter of fact it was co-scripted
by Răzvan Rădulescu, who mentioned that he and Mungiu purposefully modified the story's tonality, so as to clearly draw a line between Otilia's secret,
shared only by the audience, and the diegetic world surrounding her.[18] Adi's

parents introduce their relatives and friends to an absent-minded, highly anguished Otilia. These are mainly academics and doctors, all members of the Communist *Nomenklatura*: they will exasperate her both with harsh nationalistic remarks and with tips on how to succeed brilliantly, in a Communist Romania dominated by interdictions and restrictions. Reminding one of the priest's house feast scenes in Pintilie's *The Oak*, the small talk does not only centre on food as a sign of the social elite's alleged prosperity during extremely hard times. It also refers to issues such as prohibited churchgoing, job finding and the multiple ways to survive an absurd dictatorship. Nationalist friend Mr Rusu (Ion Săpdaru) first praises life and work in the countryside and military service, then asks the others to lend an ear to what Ceauşescu 'the wise one' says during one of his innumerable media interventions. 'Look at today's youngsters', says Rusu: 'Dorms, grants, Mum and Dad spoon feeding them... smoking in front of their parents, not experiencing army life, et cetera.' Trapped in a frontal perspective, Otilia stares at everybody in total confusion, while the camera has been framing them in the same position for more than six minutes.

Framed in a packed tableau format by Mutu's minimalist camera, this highly symbolic, unusually long (11') satirical sequence, which needed twenty takes and 500 metres of filming material, has often been cited in critical surveys as an undisputable stylistic *tour de force*. In terms of visuals, Mungiu set up various geometries of the seated guests until he reached their right position and the right filming distance. The scene makes innovative use of the off-screen space: gesticulating hands are shown and voices heard, and a phone is ringing (it might be Găbiţa), but the camera refuses to move so as to reveal their source/identity. Mungiu stressed when interviewed the fact that the greatest difficulty consisted in making distinctly audible different pieces of dialogue which were spoken almost simultaneously (Ciment & Tobin 2007: 17). Also, Otilia had to be both visually at the centre – as is the case with Jesus Christ during the 'Last Supper' – and aurally at the periphery of the ongoing conversation: in their agitation, the others often ignore her and one has to perceive her loneliness and the fact that her own thoughts are clearly elsewhere.

Fig 48. The supper scene in *4, 3, 2*

Unfolding in Adi's barely lit room, the next sequence is actually the film's first pay-off in scriptwriting terms. Asked why she looks so upset, Otilia reveals her well-kept secret. The same issues about risking prison if they are caught come up again, but Otilia confronts Adi with the fact that she herself might eventually need an abortion. The fearful young man is trying to reassure her, but Otilia remains very sceptical about it. In terms of both narrative and style the sequence is remarkably orchestrated. It positions Otilia as an extremely powerful female character who knows how to handle delicate matters and who values sacrifice for a friend in need more than her own personal relationship. Stylistically it also proves exquisite: they are shown almost as Chinese shadows, dark silhouettes whispering in a secret space, thus reinforcing the idea of the audience as an exclusive witness to the whole story.

The same obscurity, further symbolising Otilia's entering a black tunnel she will only exit once the film has ended, dominates the following night-time street sequence. This time subjective, almost jittering tracking shots follow the young woman on her way back to the hotel. Otilia's disarray is not only mental but also physiological: at a certain moment she is shown vomiting on a street corner. Once at the hotel she manages to rush upstairs and gets into a panic as her friend, who had not answered the phone call Otilia made during the supper scene, is not reacting and now seems inanimate among the bed sheets. The suspense is over once one discovers she was just sleeping. Găbița tells Otilia: 'I got it out. It's in the bathroom'.

What might be called the third bathroom occurrence is actually the most controversial moment in the film. It not only transgresses all taboos by explicitly showing the aborted foetus as an autonomous entity in a significant counter shot, it also proves consistent with the minimalistic aesthetics. A phone is ringing off-screen and Otilia asks Găbița to take the call. She tries to touch the foetus but only manages to stare dumbfounded at it before leaving the frame. The camera then pans slowly to reveal the foetus lying on the floor and frames it for almost two minutes: in the meantime, we hear the off-screen dialogue between Otilia and her friend, whom she is asking for a bag. The unbearable image thus turns into a reality one cannot elude. Ellipses and off-screen shots of delicate scenes are now stopped to leave a full view of the room. Mungiu and Mutu make it compulsory for us to go on watching, refusing to cut to another location. The girls will wrap the four-month-old dead foetus in white towels as if it were a new-born baby and Găbița will beg Otilia to bury it: 'Of course I won't dump it', Otilia answers confidently.[19] Symbolically speaking, this scene reflects the concrete result of Ceauşescu's absurd demographic policy. It needs to be watched as clearly and openly as was the dictator's killing in cold blood, broadcast worldwide in December 1989.

Asked about his choice to overtly show the foetus, Mungiu explained that they first shot extra material in the room with the girls looking for the bag and then decided to leave it all off-screen, to fit the film's 'bathroom effect' and concentrate on the dead infant. Says Mungiu:

It would have been an odd formal decision to avoid this shot. This was so much part of what was happening to her during this day. Since she spends the last thirty minutes dealing with what she experiences in the bathroom, you can't avoid showing the foetus… People tell me it's one minute, but it's only fourteen seconds, the length that was needed for her to deliver her lines. When I edited the film I realized this was part of the story and would have to remain. (Porton 2008: 4)

Back in the barely lit nocturnal environment, Otilia is beginning the film's last journey. The soundscape of this journey is more evocative than the rather vague visual parameters established previously. Eventually entering a barely visible apartment building, Otilia manages to get up the stairs and throws the parcel into the common garbage chute, the sound of the falling bag being deliberately foregrounded so as to compensate for the lack of vision. We hear her sob softly.

After a neutral long shot of the street at night which also introduces a brief ellipsis, Otilia is back in the lobby situated in front of her friend's room; again this is a four dimensional space framed as a tableau. As in Antonioni's films, the characters prove peripheral and pieces of furniture and neon wall lights are purposefully turned into highly symbolic figures. Thus, while she unsuccessfully knocks and calls her friend, the camera refuses to cut to her, preferring to keep the frontal distance. Otilia eventually returns to the main lobby, where the wedding has degenerated into a fight. Găbița, seated at a restaurant table in an adjacent room, is waiting for her. She is now smoking, confesses to being hungry and asks if the foetus has been buried. But Otilia doesn't answer, suggesting they had better never mention this topic again. While a wedding party goes on in the background and several silhouettes appear to dance joyously, the waiter details the 'wedding' menu in front of a blasé, disconcerted Otilia. The film's final cut on motion reveals her staring off-screen, maybe at some object or person situated off-screen, but most certainly at us, the audience, who have been sharing so much with her for the last couple of hours.

Mungiu explained that he wanted to end the film more or less in the same way he had opened it, as a kind of slice of life, a critical fragment of the existence of these two girls under Communism, showing how true friendship and solidarity were at work. Otilia and Găbița start sharing a terrible secret in their university dorm and are accomplices in a perilous enterprise. Otilia, the one who has sacrificed a lot to help her friend in need, ends up declaring 'let's never talk about it any more'.[20] Critic Magda Mihăilescu also identifies a circular structure, comparing the restaurant and its partying people in the background seen through a transparent partition to the aquarium from the opening shot, Otilia and Găbiţa sitting like isolated little fish caught in an evolving world, ignoring the terrible things which have been going on for the last few hours (Corciovescu & Mihăilescu 2010: 81).

As was the case with Puiu's *Lazarescu* and Muntean's *The Paper*, the final credits are backed by yet another hit from the 1960s, a duet performed by popular singers Angela Similea and Cornel Constantiniu, 'Te aud mereu' ('I'm Always Hearing Your Voice'). Defamiliarisation of a tragic issue by means of a musical counterpoint, arriving at the very end and echoing bygone times, once more proves an effective strategy. Mungiu also mentions the film is part of a *Tales from the Golden Age* series, a title ironically referring to the most nightmarish years of Ceauşescu's regime, when such slogans were frequently used.

Part of the main international competition at the 2007 Cannes Festival, *4, 3, 2* won the first Palme d'Or for a feature film in the history of Romanian cinema, the previous one having been awarded fifty years earlier to a short animated film, Ion Popescu Gopo's already mentioned *Short History*. Such a universally famous prize provoked an unprecedented series of chain reactions. These not only had an impact on the way the 'Romanian New Wave' became an indisputable reality for critics and audiences alike, but also – as was the case with *The Death of Mr Lazarescu* – improved the moral and social comprehension of controversial issues handled on-screen.

Besides Cannes, the film, its director and its main actress won more than fifty prestigious prizes, ranging from the Best European Film award, several Spanish Goya Prizes and the BBC film award to prestigious US awards emanating from the New York, Los Angeles and Chicago Film Critics associations, which chose it as Best Foreign Language Film, not to mention the domestic awards in most national festivals across the country. For Megan Ratner 'Mungiu's achievement is to have made a film both accurate to a specific place and time and a timeless illustration of the DNA-level damage such repression can wreak' (Ratner 2008). In his UK *Guardian* review of the film titled 'State of Denial', Peter Bradshaw writes:

> It all seems at once a very distant and a very recent era, I can't think of a film that has shown life in the Eastern Bloc more fiercely than this [...] Mungiu's film is a jewel of what is now considered the Romanian new wave along with Puiu and Porumboiu [...] On Marinca's face there is spiritual devastation or incineration. It was from wretchedness and rage such as this that bred the uprising that changed Romania and the world. (Bradshaw 2008: 9)

The Francophone reception (France, Belgium, Canada) of Mungiu's film most certainly represents a phenomenon reaching beyond the usual showcasing of a Palme d'Or product. Before standing ovations and ambulances for shocked people who fainted at the Belgian preview of the film in a packed 1750-seat concert hall, the French journal *Libération* paraphrased a famous Communist catchphrase about Ceaușescu: 'Genius of the Carpathians – Cristian Mungiu acknowledges the emergence of Romania on the world cinema scene'. The same journal is proud to have identified an obvious minimalist affinity with the Dardenne brothers, going as far as labelling Mungiu as their spiritual son: 'So the Dardennes seem to have a son: he is Romanian and his name is Cristian Mungiu' (Azoury 2007: ii–iii; author's translation).

Though *4, 3, 2* won the French National Education Prize (Prix de l'Education Nationale), Minister Xavier Darcos did not agree to finance the DVD edition in the first instance, fearing reactions from several anti-abortionist institutions after the Vatican's virulent criticism of the film.[21] The finally edited DVD/CD Rom – issued almost at the same time the film itself was distributed across the country – was meant to serve as a pedagogical tool to increase knowledge about abortion and its consequences in the context of East European Communism.

The worldwide acclaim of the press, which, thanks to the film's wide circulation in festivals, lasted for more than a year, was followed almost concomitantly by numerous side effects on the domestic level. The most salient one was Mungiu's *The 4, 3, 2 Caravan*, a documentary on a 'travelling cinema' crew trying to breathe new life into deserted movie theatres across fifteen Romanian towns. Directed by documentary filmmaker Sorin Avram in collaboration with two German cameramen and a journalist from Hamburg, the film proves an essential 'social act', combining interviews and screening setups. They eventually provide an exhaustive account both on the state of the nation and on its limited movie attendance, given very outdated projection conditions. The prologue titles explain that this is the first Palme d'Or in Romanian film history and in this same year, 2007, there are less than fifty cinemas in a country of over twenty million people, Romania having the lowest percentage of moviegoers in the EU. The German team is seen travelling on a minibus across the entire country, fixing the mobile screening material in movie halls, which seem to have been deserted and unequipped for quite a while. Over a white projection screen the film's final credits reveal the total number of viewers having benefited from the travelling caravan: 17,584.[22]

An authentic 'artist in the city', Mungiu did not only content himself with being honoured as a national hero 'back home' by high-ranking authorities and by ordinary people alike, grateful to have had their past terror mirrored in such an accurate and moving way. Besides initiating the 'Caravan' project, the director proved his attachment to his contemporary New Wave counterparts and continued to militate for better financing and film production facilities. As an economic corollary to the Mungiu phenomenon, the Romanian financial newspaper *Ziarul Financiar* listed the top ten businessmen giving a new start to Romania: they are called 'the 1968 Mungiu generation', yet another set of children of the decree.[23]

Interestingly enough, one year later, on the occasion of the 2008 Top Ten critics' poll designating the best Romanian films of all time, *4, 3, 2* was listed in fourth position, following Pintilie's *Reconstruction*, Ciulei's *Forest of the Hanged* and Puiu's *Death of Mr Lazarescu* (Corciovescu & Mihăilescu 2010: 65).

Conceived as the first episode of a series about life under Communism, Mungiu's ground-breaking *4, 3, 2* was followed in 2009 by a versatile shift in genre opting for a far milder approach to bleak life under Ceauşescu. *Povestiri din epoca de aur* (*Tales from the Golden Age*, 2009) is a portmanteau film containing six shorts (*The Legend of the Party Photographer*, *The Legend of the Chicken Driver*, *The Legend of the Greedy Policeman*, *The Legend of the Air Sellers* and *The Legend of the Zealous Activist*) presented in two series, all of them produced and written by Mungiu but directed by promising young directors such as Hanno Höfer, Răzvan Mărculescu, Constantin Popescu, Ioana Uricaru and Mungiu himself, the already discussed *Turkey Girl* having also been added to them. All stories are based on familiar urban myths and reveal Romanians' vitality and capacity to cope with hard times in unexpected ways. Miles away genre-wise from *4, 3, 2* their picaresque spirit proves to be closer to Mungiu's own previous shorts and to his first feature, *Occident*: light-hearted and funny, surrealist with hints of black humour, even melancholy despite the fact that they are set during the worst times of the Communist regime. Though not always getting the best results in terms of style, some are full of verve and sarcasm in the best Romanian absurdist tradition. Thus, in Hanno Höfer's *The Legend of the Party Photographer*, on the occasion of an official visit by President Giscard d'Estaing, the Party photographer is asked to modify the front-page picture by adding a hat on Ceauşescu's head, so that he will look as tall as his guest. Mungiu confessed he wanted to get closer to mainstream audiences, in the same way as Italian comedy directors did in the 1950s and 1960s with their multiple-episode films.

Finally, Mungiu's third feature *După dealuri* (*Beyond the Hills*, 2012) co-produced by France and Belgium, is a penetrating rendering of a real case of exorcism that took place in 2005 in a Romanian monastery, where a young orphan girl died in mysterious circumstances. The screenplay is a free adaptation of two non-fiction novels by journalist Tatiana Niculescu-Bran, who decided to reveal the dark side of an all-powerful institution in post-Communist Romania, the Orthodox Church. Overlty dealing with feminine hysteria and containing a subtle Lesbian subtext, it somehow becomes the Romanian modern variant of another East European paragon of the genre made fifty-years earlier, Jerzy Kawalerowicz's *Mother Joan of Angels* (1961). As in *4, 3, 2* the main narrative focuses on two young women who, while being very close to each other and ready for any kind of sacrifice, have a special relationship with a man (here, a priest) who will influence their decisions. Stylistically, Oleg Mutu's cinematography once again opts for single takes making sure the flow of each scene is preserved, thus creating ravishing contemplative 'tableaux » which recall Flemish or French seventeenth century paintings. Similarly, in terms of soundscape, voices and noises are foregrounded in highly original ways through the use of direct sound, and the minimalist lack of music invites the audience to a new kind of empathy with characters facing extreme situations.

The 2012 Cannes Festival Jury led by Nanni Moretti awarded both the Best Screenplay prize to Mungiu (who modestly declared the original subject did not belong to him) and that of Best Actress for two outstanding performers, newcomers Cristina Flutur and Cosmina Stratan. The supreme reward went to Michael Haneke's *Amour*, another tale about death, pain and sacrifice, clearly different in purpose and style. Mungiu looked dissapointed and he was right: *Beyond the Hills* is an absolute masterpiece and the Romanian director would have certainly deserved a second Palme d'Or.

CHAPTER 12

Making Films for Wider Audiences
Romanian Cinema Turns Global

If my main focus has been on contemporary art-house, mainly minimalist, non-commercial films which have received worldwide acclaim in spite of modest production costs and tight shooting schedules, other interesting creations from young, previously unknown creators of the Romanian New Wave emerged between 2003 and 2007, benefiting from previously non-existent shooting and production facilities.

Meanwhile, within the Romanian film industry, established auteurs previously discussed in more or less detail such as Dan Piţa, Mircea Daneliuc, Mircea Mureşan, Dinu Tănase and Nicolae Mărgineanu continued to be active, but unfortunately did not always manage to keep the same high artistic standards as in the past. In terms of both themes and style, films such as *Faimosul paparazzo* (*The Famous Paparazzo*, 1999) and *Binecuvântată fii închisoare* (*Bless You, Prison*, 2002) by Nicolae Mărgineanu, *Ambasadori, căutăm patrie* (*Ambassadors, Looking for a Country*, 1998) and *Sistemul nervos* (*The Nervous System*, 2005) by Mircea Daneliuc, *Femeia Visurilor* (*The Woman in Dreams*, 2005) and *Second Hand* (2007) by Dan Piţa, *Azucena* (2006) by Mircea Mureşan and *Damen Tango* (2003) by Dinu Tănase deal with the highly problematic post-Communist transition in a very chaotic, unaesthetic, often unconvincing manner. Stories about the corrupt Bucharest mob, prostitution at home and abroad, suicide, rape, adultery and illegal trafficking have been filling the centre stage, with little or no stylistic innovation. Less familiar names to non-domestic audiences such as Ioan Cărmăzan, who made *Raport despre starea naţiunii* (*Report on the State of the Nation*, 2003) and *Margo* (2005), Napoleon Helmis, who made *Italiencele* (*The Italian Girls*, 2004), and Şerban Marinescu, who made *Ticăloşii* (*The Bastards*, 2007), also active within the very popular television circuit, continued along the same lines. No great achievements have been made in the 'comedy' register either, except for very mediocre sequels to old hits by another veteran, Geo Saizescu – *Păcală se întoarce* (*Păcală Is Back*, 2006) – and a new film he also co-wrote and acted in made by his son Cătălin Saizescu – *Milionari de week-end* (*Week-end Millionaires*, 2004).

Veteran directors such as the one Şerban rightly calls 'the Romanian DeMille', Sergiu Nicolaescu (b. 1930), went on producing and directing genre films into the twenty-first century, mainly action and historical work of poor artistic quality but benefiting from solid financing. By way of example, Nicolaescu films include *Triunghiul morţii* (*The Triangle of Death*, 1999), about World War I military bravura; *Orient Express* (2004), where phantoms of an aristocratic multi-ethnic past co-exist with the present; *15* (2005), dealing with the destiny of a child born during the Romanian revolution; *Supravieţuitorul* (*The Survivor*, 2007), a political thriller with a convict who resurfaces to avenge his past, and so on. However, according to Şerban, the audience attendance rate for those films dramatically dropped from millions during the Ceauşescu era to less than tens of thousands (Şerban 2011: 5).

On a far more encouraging note, the common denominator for the 1970s generation – consisting of a majority of directors, screenwriters, actors, producers, festival directors, film editors, cinematographers, and so on, born roughly between 1970 and 1979 – was a consistent desire to experiment and exchange domains of competence in the field of short and feature filmmaking, thus confirming the 'wave' paradigm most critics have been questioning (Tramarin 2010: 17).[1] Also, following Cristi Puiu, who returned from a period of exile in Switzerland, directors such as Peter Călin Netzer and Ruxandra Zenide, born or educated abroad, returned to Romania and trained in film or made their debuts using effective co-production circuits, involving German, French or Swiss financing sources.

An exception in generational terms, because he was born in former Yugoslavia in 1960 and graduated from the Romanian Film Academy as late as 1991, Sinişa Dragin started his career as a news agency cameraman before directing shorts and documentaries. These paved the way to highly unsettling, dark parables shot in a striking style close to Kusturica and Tarr, but also to controversial French contemporary auteurs such as Gaspar Noé and Bruno

Dumont: *În fiecare zi Dumnezeu ne sărută pe gură* (*Everyday God Kisses Us on the Mouth*, 2001), which won the Tiger Award for first feature in Rotterdam (2002), and *Faraonul* (*Pharaoh*, 2004). The first has an unusually macabre subject matter, reminiscent of myths from Romanian folklore, the use of black-and-white image texture adding to its grimness and mystery. It tells the story of butcher and ex-con Dumitru (Dan Condurache), who becomes a kind of 'serial killer', witnesses the arson of his own house by a Gypsy woman and marries a deaf mute, magically turned into a white goose. For David Rooney, 'Dragin creates an arrestingly murky universe, brutally grim yet lightened by bitter humour and bizarre surreal touches' (Rooney 2002). Less convincing, *Pharaoh*, his second feature, is closer in theme and style to Romanian films from the 1990s about political prisoners, oscillating between documentary and fiction fragments. Costache Nicolau (Ştefan Iordache) is an elderly tramp whose prison years seem to resurface when a young TV reporter tries to solve the puzzle of his hellish Siberian journey.

Dacă bobul nu moare (*If the Seed Doesn't Die*, 2011), his third feature, makes no exception from the previous ones. A road movie with parallel stories about two aging fathers searching for their missing children, one Serbian the other Romanian, it mixes hyperrealist sequences with mystic, almost surrealist ones. His insistence on the grotesque side of events sometimes proves quite unbearable, though it is intended to document authentic tragic events related to prostitution and manslaughter inside the still tormented Balkan area.

Peter Călin Netzer (1975) emigrated to Germany with his parents during the Communist period, but returned to study film in Bucharest as a German resident. He directed his first important short, *Maria*, in 1997 and further developed the same subject for his homonymous feature-length debut in 2003. The film's main theme is based on the true story of an impoverished working mother of seven, abandoned by an unemployed alcoholic husband, who eventually turns to prostitution to save her family from starvation. After recounting her life to a local TV channel, which offers her an apartment as part of an advertising campaign, Maria meets an untimely death in a car accident, but her confession becomes available in the diary she has been secretly keeping.

Appearing as yet another bleak, vulgar and violent reflection on the tragic consequences of the post-Communist transition in the domestic sphere, the film actually proves a *tour de force* for a beginner. Netzer skilfully handles the different subplots involving the domestic and public spheres and manages to get outstanding acting performances from adults and children alike. As played by theatre actress Diana Dumbravă, who won the Best Actress prize in Locarno for her performance, the dual, complex character of Maria echoes the screen icon of the title character of Pasolini's *Mamma Roma* (1961). She has become part of the quite limited club of female characters who have been offered a main part in a Romanian contemporary film, next to Maïa Morgenstern's Nela from *The Oak* and Dorotheea Petre's Ryna, discussed later in this chapter. In her international survey *Moving People, Moving Images: Cinema and Trafficking in the New Europe* (2010), the only Romanian movie Dina Iordanova mentions is Netzer's, underlying the way it handles the destiny of a woman forced to enter the sex trade in a relevant, albeit universal manner. She compares the film to Italian, French and Canadian contemporary productions of the same calibre, thus acknowledging its perfect compatibility (2010: 105–6).

Six years after his impressive debut Netzer directed the equally praised *Medalia de Onoare* (*Medal of Honor*, 2009) in a totally different, albeit minimalist register. An ironic post-Communist story about a medal for heroic World War II achievements awarded to the wrong person, *Medal of Honor* is a perfectly performed subtle black comedy about missed opportunities, secrets and lies, difficult relationships and the hard way to gain back family esteem.

Netzer's latest contemporary social drama, *Poziția Copilului* (*Child's Pose*, 2013), starring Luminița Gheorghiu in her best performance to date, won the prestigious Golden Bear at the 2013 Berlinale. The director remarkably captures a domineering mother consumed by self-love, in her struggle to save her son who has caused the tragic death of a 14-year-old child in a highway accident. In a style still faithful to the minimalist vein, favouring hand-held camera, POV shots and only incidental pre-existing music, the film meticulously reconstructs the events of one night and the days that follow. Răzvan Rădulescu's perceptive screenplay reflects with tragic irony the moral turmoil of a prosperous middle-class woman tempted to resort to corruption through emotional blackmail.

Stylistic and thematic choices of other newcomers obviously go beyond the previously inescapable paradigm of the 1989 revolution, allowing audiences to become familiar with previously 'taboo' storylines. Thus, in Titus Muntean's thriller-like debut *Examen* (*Exam/Taxi or Limousine*, 2003), based on another true story, a womanising driver has been falsely accused and arrested for rape in the late 1970s. Once liberated, Săndulescu (Marius Stănescu) tries to find out the truth, while being interviewed for television by two film students as part of their final degree work. Terrible facts resurface, Muntean flashing back and forward in time to depict the brutality and violence of the Communist secret police (Grădinaru & Tudor 2007: 58–9). Though acclaimed only at the domestic level and barely distributed outside Romania, *Exam* is an effective variant on several Costa-Gavras films and on Wajda's paradigmatic *Man of Marble* (1976). This applies not so much to the subject matter, as political stakes are obviously less important than in the case of fallen Stalinist hero Birkut. Nonetheless, in terms of style and composition, the audience is challenged by the same framing narrative principle as the one practised by the Polish master. The students interviewing Săndulescu unleash a sophisticated network mixing present and past events, ultimately getting to the pessimistic conclusion: present-day audiences do not give a damn about Communist errors for which so many people have paid with their lives.

In *Ryna* (2005) a masculinised girl from the poverty-stricken Danube Delta takes up a new life after being sexually abused. Audiences from all over the world welcomed warmly the highly promising debut of Ruxandra Zenide, the only well-known female director of the RNW. Educated in Switzerland, where she studied international relations, Zenide eventually decided to take film courses in Prague and occasionally return to her native country for a filmmaking career. After two successful shorts, she managed to team up with other young Romanian directors and screenwriters. She asked Czech film and television screenwriter Marek Epstein to write the script and got financial backing for the *Ryna* project from France and from a Swiss French-speaking TV channel. Dorotheea Petre, still a student when cast in the main part, perfectly embodies in her acting style the dual nature of a beautiful teenager whose imposed masculine education and appearance (cropped hair and overalls) is due to her despotic father's longing for a son. Romanian cinema had rarely exploited such a topic in the past, no doubt because female directors, such as Malvina Urşianu and Elisabeta Bostan, had been forced to opt for narratives with less gender-issue relevance.

Unfolding in a rural community in the vicinity of Sulina, a godforsaken Danubian port, the film's plot oscillates between tough domestic scenes shot in a naturalistic manner and less oppressive, more engaging, collective ones. At home, Ryna's violent and alcoholic father (Valentin Popescu) operates a gas station where his daughter does most of the work as a trained mechanic. Following a highly symbolic hair-cutting session, Ryna's helpless mother eventually decides to leave home for a better life. The young girl nonetheless manages to develop her passion for photography, with the complicity of her good-natured grandfather (Nicolae Praida).

Zenide, assisted by Marius Panduru's outstanding camerawork, seizes the opportunity of such narrative interludes to foreground the Danube

Fig 49. Immortalising Danube Delta memories in *Ryna*

region's highly poetic universe, while also stressing the positive impact of natural cycles on otherwise 'Zolaesque' destinies. Events in the public sphere are dense and seem to be dealt with in a less homogeneous style. Once downtown, Ryna is metamorphosed and finds herself the object of several men's attention: the witty local young mail boy with whom she forms an innocent idyll, the corrupt mayor who will end up raping her savagely without being charged, and a French anthropologist with whom she will improve her French and share her dreams of escape.

Though not entirely satisfying at the level of narrative pay-off, the film's outcome reveals Ryna's strong-willed, atypical personality. She drops the charges against the rapist after having witnessed other falsely accused suspects and leaves town for good, during what appears to be an open ending. *Ryna* was shown in many different countries and won numerous prizes in 2005.[2] The enthusiasm was unanimous, and was shared by feminist audiences, who could add a new director and an astonishing actress to their filmography.

Finally, in Tudor Giurgiu's feature-length debut *Legături bolnăvicioase* (*Love Sick*, 2006), two student girls indulge in a heartfelt lesbian relationship that gets thwarted by an incestuous liaison. An authentic 'Jack of all trades', Giurgiu (b. 1972) had an artistic background close to Western standards, which went beyond directing shorts as well as numerous commercials. He served as an assistant to Caranfil and Pintilie, co-produced other RNW documentaries and fiction films, was director of Romanian Television between 2005 and 2009 and is still a leading figure of the Transylvania International Film Festival.

Literally meaning 'Sickly Liaisons', an obvious title variant of Choderlos de Laclos's classic *Dangerous Liaisons*, the film was the first ever made on the topic of lesbianism in Romanian cinema. It is based on a homonymous novel by Cecilia Ştefănescu, who co-scripted it with Giurgiu and Răzvan Rădulescu: the latter suggested an incestuous subplot involving brother and sister should be added to make the story appear even more controversial. As was the case with Netzer's *Maria*, which had its origins in a previous short film, Giurgiu had already approached sexual identity issues while making the graduation short *Singur(ă) pe lume* ((S)he Is Not Alone, 1995), in which a couple frequently disguise their boy as a girl because they did not manage to have a second child.

Love Sick interweaves the transgressive experiences of Bucharest-based Kiki/Cristina (Maria Popistaşu), her rebel brother Sandu (Tudor Chirilă, a popular Romanian rock singer and stage actor) and provincial Alex (Ioana Barbu).[3] A deceptive opening resembling more a TV series teaser than a feature film confronts us with glimpses of idyllic scenes between characters we are not yet familiar with, the editing technique seeming quite close to the commercials

Giurgiu had to shoot on a large scale before getting into fiction. However, things get better when Kiki's voice-over occasionally takes the lead: inter-weaving past and present, she confesses with a lot of frankness how she fell in love with her student/colleague Alex, while the latter also had to handle the transition from her provincial, rural origins to the more sophisticated and emancipated Bucharest circles.

Though the film's acting and general rendering of the contemporary Romanian atmosphere are quite realistic, with nudity issues being delicately handled, the scenes involving parents from both sides are often close to carica-ture and too theatrical. This is the case when Alex visits Kiki and her suspecting parents at their place. Later on, when the two girls elope to the countryside, one is compelled to witness the harsh contrast with Alex's simple but far more welcoming parents from the village of Pietroşiţa. A violent argument with a belligerent, incestuous brother Sandu, who unexpectedly resurfaces at Alex's place, precipitates a somehow strange, though plausible, ending. Kiki's tears and supplications do not succeed in changing her lover's mind: she has been deceived, and the final shot revealing sister and brother smoking together con-firms her deception. However, Kiki's final assessment stresses the unforgettable moments of a beautiful love story, and so does the correlative closing credit song, Chris Martin's 'Your Love Means Everything to Me'.Because it approached taboo issues, without any prejudice, Love Sick ranked as the first non-American title in the 2006 Romanian box-office, with 21,000 viewers (Duma 2007).

Undoubtedly, the two most salient directorial debuts to be considered in detail when entering the domain of non-minimalist, more commercially viable films are those of the aforementioned Cătălin Mitulescu and those of the late Cristian Nemescu. These have not only proved domestic hits but have also fared extremely well in terms of international recognition via festivals, cultural institute venues and DVD issues. Cătălin Mitulescu (b. 1972), whose already discussed Traffic (2004) won Romania's third short film Palme d'Or in Cannes, is another relevant case of a filmmaker interested in directing and writing but also financing his own and other young directors' films, hoping to reach wider audiences. After a few years spent navigating between different training posts and doing small jobs in different European countries, he graduated from the Film Directing Department in 2001 and directed two well-mounted student shorts, Bucureşti/Wien: 8:15 (2001) and 17 Minute întârziere (17 Minutes Late, 2002), distributed theatrically in Romania. Both got prizes in international festivals and were selected for the Cannes Cinéfondation sessions. Assisting renowned auteurs such as Dan Piţa, Mitulescu quickly proved both his facility for efficient filmmaking and his ability to play an active part in various areas of the business, motivated, as he confessed to critic Mihai Fulger, 'by films which can be read by everyone, as Charlie Chaplin did' (Fulger 2006: 116–28). His production company, Strada Film, soon turned into a family business, including his brother, Daniel Mitulescu, as an assistant producer and his one-time wife, screenwriter and playwright Andreea Vălean.

Echoing quite closely in subject matter and style Nae Caranfil's already discussed *E pericoloso sporgersi*, Mitulescu's first feature-length film, *Cum mi-am petrecut sfârşitul lumii* (*The Way I Spent the End of the World*, 2006) is a tale about seventeen-year-old Eva, who with her boyfriend accidentally breaks a bust of Ceauşescu in school during the last year of his rule. After a failed attempt to leave the country, she ends up a hostess on an international liner, while her younger brother, who was plotting to kill Ceauşescu with his friends, eventually witnesses the fall of the dictator on television. Paradoxically, a nostalgic, slightly nationalistic flavour characterises the film, implying that Ceauşescu's reign also has some good points, as there was considerable '*joie de vivre*' behind the totalitarian barricades. In terms of style, the visuals stress the country's uncontested beauties in a lyrical way, close to mainstream cinema (Nasta: 2007b).

Asked about the origins of and motivations behind his film, Cătălin Mitulescu explained that the screenplay by Andreea Vălean, himself and Bogdan Mustaţă[4] was an 'obligatory step', given that they needed to say goodbye to their past life and obsessions. The production setup of *The Way I Spent the End of the World* proved complex and once again confirmed that foreign pre-production and co-production backing is a necessity for achieving a big-scale project in twenty-first century Romania. The screenplay had already been selected for the US Sundance Film Festival, where it won the contest. Mitulescu's previous Cannes victories for his shorts and his experience as an associate producer (for the above discussed *Ryna*) allowed him to team up with the established French production company Pelléas Films and to get financing from Eurimages, Canal+ and the German Acht Frankfurt production company. He also managed to get such prestigious 'signatures' as Martin Scorsese's and Wim Wenders's on the credits (both figures acted as executive producers), and thus could hope to prove to audiences he already had an international profile.[5]

Though it may rightly seem a bit too idyllic and oversimplifying to Romanians having experienced harsh conditions at the end of the Communist period, the bittersweet atmosphere created by Mitulescu and Vălean manages to have universal appeal, as it gets very close to the 'Balkan fairy tale' paradigm. The latter has been a constant in the filmography of versatile East European director Emir Kusturica, for example, as early as his first international hit, *When Father Was Away on Business* (1985), up to the less coherent *Life Is a Miracle* (2005). In terms of storytelling, however, the film sticks quite close to Classical Hollywood principles: transparent narration with multiple storylines converging at the end via a satisfactory pay-off, recurring themes and motifs situated at pivotal moments, engaging characters from all generations carefully portrayed, implicative music at key moments, and so on. Last but not least, as its well-chosen title suggests, *The Way I Spent the End of the World* is yet another example fitting Ricoeur's and Aristotle's already discussed 'time and narrative' principle, mingling story time and history with a capital H in quite lively, though no less stimulating ways.

Setting up what may appear to be a frame narrative, both the film's prologue – purposefully set before the opening credits – and its closure feature Ceauşescu. He is first caricatured by an impersonator in what will prove a mental, oneiric episode from the subconscious of seven-year-old Lalaliu (Timotei Duma). During an official ceremony the young boy is seen receiving a huge piece of cheese from the dictator, invariably pictured with his astrakhan cap: he scolds him because he still has milk teeth and takes away the cheese, and a fight ensues. Later on, a rhyme sequence in Lalaliu's place, where his family witnesses the loss of a real milk tooth, further confirms that the opening scene was going on in the boy's mind. Also, Lalaliu's father (Mircea Diaconu) will further impersonate the dictator and his barking voice, promising 'another hour of TV broadcast about myself', a common outlet for Romanian families preferring laughter to tears in the face of adversity. Similarly, the film's first epilogue inevitably shows Ceauşescu's famous final discourse on a television set: an astute editing rhyme again reveals him to Lalaliu, happy to witness 'the end of the world' he has been so eagerly expecting.

In between, Mitulescu and Vălean will also tell the story of Lalaliu's cherished elder sister Eva (Dorotheea Petre). As indicated by one of the rare titles, the timing is crucial, as we are in '1989 Romania'. Though not as well drawn and humorous as in Caranfil's *E pericoloso*, the Romanian school atmosphere of the late 1980s is faithfully rendered. Besides practical jokes about suckered teachers who take some time to realise pupils are cheating, unconventional uniforms and national anthems, Mitulescu privileges powerful, highly explicit symbols that most viewers will be able to decode. Thus, while Eva and her 'official' boyfriend Alex (Ionuţ Becheru,) are hugging and making promises about lovemaking in the school corridor, the boy inadvertently breaks a bust of Ceauşescu after simulating a boxing match: here is a strong, though quite simplistic metaphor which heralds upcoming events. The urban neighbourhood in the Bucharest outskirts in which Lalaliu, Eva and their friends nurture dreams of escape obviously stands as a Balkan fairy-tale surrogate. Marian Țuțui rightly compares it to those created by Menzel or Kusturica, though the dialogue and overall tone are typically Romanian (Țuțui 2008: 220–21). An abandoned bus turned into a magic submarine will serve as the perfect vehicle for imaginary travels to distant places, but Lalaliu and his friend Tarzan (non-professional actor Valentino Marius Stan) will ask for a higher fee when leaving for Madrid, which is further away than Paris. Alexander Bălănescu's appropriate score, mixing accordion and cello, brings a touch of ethnic lyricism which reminds one of neorealist pictures in praise of communal life, such as Vittorio de Sica's *Miracolo a Milano* (*Miracle in Milan*, 1951).

Expelled from one of Bucharest's best high schools and implicitly from the mandatory Communist Youth Association for refusing to make compromises, Eva is eventually transferred to a bleak technical reformatory school. She is subsequently pictured as a silent female rebel both in school and at home, a social status which proves a contradiction in terms for Communist Romania. She goes as far as lying to her own brother, hospitalised after a serious flu, swearing she will never leave the country without him. At this point Mitulescu pulls out another very effective anticipatory image from his wizard's/director's hat. From his hospital bed Lalaliu gazes at a stamp featuring a big ocean liner, one very similar to the one Eva will embark on as a hostess at the end of the film.

Once Eva is at the new school, the audience will be granted an additional subplot by way of Andrei (Cristian Văraru), Eva's new colleague and neighbour, the son of a dissident who plans to swim to freedom across the Danube. Amidst a plethora of compulsory manual labour hours, school celebrations and song contests, Andrei will start flirting with Eva via a hard rock listening session. So as to prove official songs will always be part of the pre-revolutionary Romanian mind-set, Mitulescu resumes in the closing credits the song beautifully intoned by Eva during one of the rehearsals ('Țara noastră-i țara noastră/ Dulce pasăre albastră': 'Our beloved country/Such a sweet blue bird').

Fig 50. Lalaliu as perfect pupil in *The Way I Spent the End of the World*

Implicit nostalgia for happy moments despite hard times is palpable in the way the director films alternative universes in the neighbourhood: all generations attend a colourful christening party where they dance to the rhythms of a versatile band, joyously shifting from Romanian folklore to Gypsy tunes.

The film's second climactic episode – after the broken bust one – starts when Eva and Andrei plan their escape next to a railway line, again echoing Caranfil's heroes from *E peri-coloso*. Eva's first attempt fails, while Andrei makes it to Italy and sends photos, bubble gum and chocolate. Heartbroken after being deceived by Eva, Lalaliu attempts suicide by different means and puts the blame 'on Ceaușescu': in a tragicomic scene he is eventually saved by the handsome, piratical-looking character of 'Boulba Superman' (Corneliu Țigancu). Alongside Nea Florică (Jean Constantin), Boulba is part of an improvised warehouse network, reminding one of Kusturica's *Life Is a Miracle*, which will support the children naïvely plotting against Ceaușescu. Lalaliu glorifies the dictator, reciting official poems at school, while he prepares a catapult assault with his band of friends.

The kids put their miserable life aside and daydream by turning a piece of bubble gum into a huge balloon, swiftly led by Marius Panduru's camera through the whole neighbourhood.

In the film's final section, Mitulescu and Vălean provide the audience with a well-orchestrated revival of the discussed Aristotelian scenario, turning the fall of the dictator into an obligatory point of the narrated story. In the line of already discussed examples by Pintilie (*The Oak*, *Too Late*, *Niki and Flo*) and Muntean (*The Paper Will Be Blue*), but also the more documentary-oriented *Bucharest, University Square* and *Videograms of a Revolution* by Gulea and Ujică/Farocki, the core of the action is transferred to the medium of television, where archive images and fictitious ones eventually blend. However, Mitulescu's *mise en abyme* confronts the move of *historical time* to the *time of fiction*, in a way a wide range of viewers are liable to respond to (Ricoeur 1990, III: 127–41).

Thus, the improvised workshop where Nea Florică entertains the kids from the neighbourhood has a television set which will feature history in the making, via Ceaușescu's over-exploited last speech. When the image starts to tremble because revolution is on the move, another old neighbour is persuaded there is something wrong with the set and nervously bangs his fist over it. Consequently the *time of fiction* meets the television broadcast by means of an astute editing device: as a counter shot to Ceaușescu addressing the angry crowd, a black-and-white shot features Lalaliu proudly pointing at the dictator with his catapult.

From this point on cross-cutting between *historical time* and *time of fiction* becomes more predictable, Mitulescu's summary handling of

Fig 51. Ceaușescu's last speech on television

Fig 52. Lalaliu aiming at him in
*The Way I Spent the End of the
World*

the overall action being less convincing. Archive images broadcast by television thus range from the National Salvation Front mini-speech to the presidential couple's burial Mass on a snowy day. The film's rather predictable bittersweet epilogue opens up perspectives for a new world. A considerable leap in time confirms the validity of the rhyme principle, because the liner postcard has turned into a real image, and Lalaliu's voice-over further stresses the importance of a child's viewpoint. Eva is now a hostess on a foreign liner and carefully reads her brother's letters about life back home. A rather idyllic tableau features the whole neighbourhood waving to her: though she is asked to go on sending presents, the overall feeling, confirmed by the nationalistic song over the closing credits, is that there is no place like home.

Domestic critics judged the film and its conclusion in different ways. There was harsh criticism from some, mostly because Mitulescu oversimplifies Communism without being very critical about those times. Others praised the film for its optimistic approach, first and foremost for 'a long-awaited escape into a fantasy world where everyday life misery is not the only alternative, hoping to bring back to the theatres audiences fed up with films such as those directed by Pintilie' (Fulger 2006: 129).

For a distant observer, nonetheless, Romania appears as a world of tremendous vitality and warmth, despite very bleak times: clichés and stereotypes have been carefully used and characters and mood explored in a very perceptive way for a beginner. Dorotheea Petre's unusually multi-faceted and subtle performance received unanimous acclaim both at home and abroad. *The Way I Spent the End of the World* not only won the first acting prize for a Romanian actress in the history of Romanian films competing at Cannes, it was also selected as an Academy Award candidate, in a year when both Porumboiu and Muntean directed two other widely acclaimed debuts. This was also an achievement, considering that there had been no Romanian film proposed for such selection between 1997 and 2003. The film had good results at the domestic box-office and broke the audience record for a Romanian film at the 2006 TIFF in Cluj.[6]

Loverboy (2011), Mitulescu's less noteworthy second feature after a five-year interval, was also screeened in the 'Un Certain Regard' section of the Cannes Film Festival. It is a modern-day unconventional love story dealing with new forms of sex-trafficking but lacking any form of nostalgia. The narrative line is supposed to be hard-hitting: an attractive young hoodlum seduces girls before sending them abroad to prostitute themselves and inevitably falls in love with one of them with tragic consequences. However, screenplay-wise and in terms of style the film does not reach the intensity and appeal of the director's *opera prima*.

Cristian Nemescu's tragic, untimely death, alongside his sound engineer Andrei Toncu, in August 2006 at only twenty-seven, in a car crash on returning from a film viewing session, contributed to the creation of a larger than life myth around him and his unfinished feature film *California Dreamin' (Endless)*. However, the unanimous praise he got posthumously proved totally justified, and his contribution as a highly skilled director will remain quite unique in the context of the Romanian New Wave.

Nemescu (1979–2006) was born in Bucharest and grew up in an artistic environment that obviously had a strong impact on his future education and career options. Octavian Nemescu, his father, was active as a composer and music teacher at the Bucharest Conservatory, while his mother, Erica, used to work as a sound editor at Anima Film, the only animation film studio in the Communist period. In an interview for the Romanian journal *Esquire*, Nemescu's mother explains to what extent her son was fascinated by the moving puppets from the animation studio sets and what a perfect memory he had for the fairy-tale audio-visual universe (Lupşa 2007).

Both Nemescu's mother and his close friend and future film editor Cătălin Cristuţiu recollected interesting details about the aspiring director's constant passion for watching all sorts of films on a large scale, on television, DVD and at the movies. A real film buff, he memorised and assimilated every relevant image detail, from Hollywood blockbusters to established masters whom he cherished a lot, such as Cassavetes, Scorsese and Kubrick. However, he also had a penchant for European and US independent and art-house contemporary auteurs such as Krzysztof Kieslowski, Emir Kusturica, Lukas Moodysson, and Larry Clark.[7] Nemescu was admitted for outstanding creative qualities to the Academy for Theatre and Film aged eighteen, the year he graduated from college. He finished his training as early as 2003, after having already made four shorts as a student, surrounded by a 'trio' he relied on for his upcoming brief but dense journey into filmmaking: scriptwriter Tudor Voican, editor Cătălin Cristuţiu and sound engineer Andrei Toncu. He thus became the youngest active director of the Romanian New Wave. The shorts, both fiction and documentaries – *Kitschitoarele* (2000), *La Bloc oamenii mor după muzică (In Apartment Buildings People Are Crazy about Music*, 2000), *Mecano* (2001), *Mihai şi Cristina (Mihai and Christina*, 2001) – got important prizes both in student festivals across Romania and abroad.[8]

In Nemescu's graduating picture, *Poveste de la scara C* (*C Block Story*, co-scripted by Tudor Voican, 2003, 14′), the son of a modest Bucharest family (Alex Mărgineanu) makes frequent calls to an erotic hotline. The film's narrative was inspired by stories from Nemescu's own neighbourhood: it starts '*in medias res*', with the young boy listening to a voice which proposes all kinds of erotic services on the phone. The noisy, block-of-flats, 'kitchen sink' neorealist atmosphere is extremely convincing, including a promising chance meeting in the elevator with an attractive neighbour (Maria Dinulescu). The boy fantasises that the hotline voice is his neighbour's, but an effective editing cut to the offices reveals that he is actually talking to his own mother (Cătălina Mustaţă). The erotic hotline enterprise, with moans and sex simulations from different speakers pictured with their earphones, is a strong reminder of postmodern Egoyan and Almodovar films on contemporary voyeurism.

The audience eventually gets an interesting though almost frustrating pay-off: the boy's mother finds the phone bills and realises via some interesting mental flashes she had been talking to her own son, but the latter will probably never know what his mother's parallel job consisted of. As in Constantin Popescu's *The Apartment*, the final credit song is yet another US hit from the 1950s. This time we hear some lines from Perry Como's 1955 hit 'Papa Loves Mambo', the lyrics of which actually include a significant *clin d'oeil* to the film's double-bind narrative: 'Papa's looking for mama, but mama's nowhere in sight'.[9]

Similar issues involving illegal sex, prostitution and teenage abuse are at the core of Nemescu's second, more consistent short, *Marilena de la P 7* (*Marilena from P7*, 2006, 45′), again co-scripted by Voican, from a student exercise initiated by Cătălin Mitulescu. As in Radu Muntean's already discussed *Fury*, the audience faces a derelict underground Bucharest milieu, where an intolerant pimp (Andi Vasluianu) indulges in youth exploitation and corrupt money dealing. A storyline partly inspired by Nemescu's own teenage fantasies, the film features thirteen-year-old Andrei (Gabriel Huian), who meets and falls desperately in love with easy-going prostitute Marilena (Mădălina Ghiţescu). To impress Marilena, Andrei eventually steals his father's (Gabriel Spahiu) wages as a bus driver and later his trolley bus. However, deceived by her client and lover Giani (Cătălin Paraschiv), who cheated on her, the young girl commits violent suicide by cutting her veins: the boy is seen watching helplessly from behind a glass door.

Fig 53. A four-screen pursuit in *Marilena from P7*

The film's intricately structured narrative planes prove an obvious rehearsal for Nemescu's subsequent large-scale project, *California*. Andrei has different kinds of dreams about Marilena, both night fantasies and daydreams. Some of them contain hints of surrealism, others are conceived in a spectacular mode, with black-outs followed by blinding spotlights on a film set, where the young man imagines meeting the prostitute in flashy attire.

Andreï Toncu's sound design explodes the visual limits of a derelict yet very lively neighbourhood: it organically combines original music with source music, thus creating multiple sound spaces. An authentic Roma Elvis Presley impersonator, 'Elvis Romano' – actually a real-life icon of the Bucharest night club scene – performs both in Roma and in English heart-breaking standards such as 'Are You Lonesome Tonight?' In the style of Mike Figgis's almost experimental *Time Code* (2000), several split-screen occurrences are followed by four-screen shots at crucial moments in the film. The audience is thus able to either follow different actions unfolding simultaneously or to have a mixed perception of real and fantasy scenes on a single screen.

Backed by a more solid production setup, with both HiFilm producer Ada Solomon and Andrei Boncea from Media Pro involved, Nemescu had already proved himself an experienced director at twenty-six. Thus, *Marilena* was selected for the Cannes IFF 'Semaine de la critique' in 2006.[10]

Co-scripted by Nemescu and Voican with some additional English dialogue help from Catherine Lindstrum,[11] the narrative premise of *California Dreamin'* was inspired, as was the case with Puiu's *Lazarescu*, by a story cinematographer Liviu Mărghidan read in the miscellaneous column of a Romanian tabloid: an obscure station master from a small Romanian village next to the Black Sea stopped a US NATO convoy during the Kosovo war. According to the information provided by Media Pro Pictures, the main production company involved in the film's setup,

US Marine Jones is assigned to escort a train carrying NATO equipment headed for Yugoslavia: his mission is held back in the prototypical village of Căpâlnița by thorough station master Doiaru over a paperwork technicality. The actual reason why Doiaru stops the train is a very personal one, as shown by a series of recurring flash-backs [...] At the end of five intense days spent with various members of the village community, the train resumes its journey, leaving behind broken hearts, broken dreams and a civil war. *California Dreamin'* tells the poignant tale of the long awaited arrival of the Americans to Romania, after 55 mentality-altering years of crushed expectations.[12]

As was the case with his previous shorts, Nemescu included in the final script many previously used cinematic devices and situations, as well as auto-biographical details drawn from stories from his personal environment. He conceived the complex structure of his first and sadly last feature film in the best Hollywood 'cross-cutting' vein, alternating past and present, fantasy and reality, hilariously comic moments and utterly tragic ones. According to editor Cristuţiu, at the moment of his death, the non-finalised filmed material he left was three hours long and his intention was to make the film run for no more than two hours. If the version issued by the producers eventually reached two hours and thirty-five minutes, it is because the entire technical crew insisted on keeping intact Nemescu's spirit, bringing it to a watchable state without continuing the post-production job. Cristuţiu only took out the scenes he had fortunately previously discussed with the director, who had judged them unnecessary. No extra details were added, though according to the scripted version some scenes had still to be shot and no other director was hired to alter the auteur's 'unfinished' version.[13] This explains why the film seemed unpolished and overlong, 'sprawling shamelessly', for some demanding critics at home and abroad (Sarris 2009).

The first title of *California Dreamin'* states that 'On August 25, 2006 Cristian Nemescu (1979–2006) was killed in a car crash. You're about to watch the film just as it looked like at that time'. As indicated in a subsequent title, the black-and-white prologue unfolds in 1944 and shows a family fleeing the bombing announced on the radio; a boy, later to be identified as the younger version of the main hero, Doiaru, seeks protection from the bombs in a basement where an insert reveals a 'US made engine'. Then there is a cut to the TV news heralding anti-NATO movements: we are at the Ministry of Internal Affairs and 'NATO's calling'.

As in Caranfil's *E pericoloso sporgersi*, every new title appearing on screen will correspond to one or two pivotal characters, the action being structured around five days. From this point on, the intermingling of different time frames will enhance the unusual density of the narrative expressed in multiple ways. However, the present proves more expandable than the explanatory flashbacks, because it features mental images and wish fulfilment dreams belonging to the younger generation. Elise Domenach compares the flashbacks to the choir in Greek tragedy, because they comment on the ongoing action while building up the meaning of an event within both the individual and the collective subconscious (Domenach 2008: 32).

Another title, 'May 1999', followed by the image of a US cruiser in a long shot, introduces us to a very effective presentation of the American contingent.

Young, good-looking Sergeant David McLaren (Jamie Elman) is desperately trying to reach his US girlfriend on the phone, while his boss, Captain Doug Jones (Armand Assante), a self-parodic tough guy, orders his paratrooper soldiers to shout 'I'm proud' with a half-smile.[14]

A countryside road overlooking the Black Sea will lead the US soldiers to their Romanian homologues. Once in Căpâlniţa, the musical band welcoming them looks old-fashioned and ridiculous, echoing similar scenes from Kusturica's films. A double-bind, ironic translation from Romanian to English by soldier Marian (Andi Vasluianu) starts and will continue throughout the whole film, adding a light comedy flavour. We are introduced to obdurate stationmaster Doiaru (Răzvan Vasilescu), a surviving symbol of the damage caused by World War II, surrounded by provincial upstarts such as his over-sleeping daughter Monica (Maria Dinulescu) and caricature boyfriend Paul (Constantin Diţă). His attendant Stelică (Radu Gabriel) reports on how they are manipulating merchandise and special deals for the freight trains. An unexpected telephone call lets them know 'a train carrying NATO equipment will pass through your station'. Rebellious and free-spirited, Monica overhears the conversation and dashes to her room to pack her few belongings; she will eventually be caught on the train and sent back home.

Another subplot starts when the strike leader and trade union chief (Gabriel Spahiu) lets his protesters know that 'the time has come to make ourselves heard by manifesting against Doiaru'. Căpâlniţa's Mayor (Ion Sapdaru), however, refuses to rally the strikers because the American presence is a unique chance to showcase such a godforsaken place. The mayor seizes the opportunity to invite Jones and his contingent to the village's centenary party, an obvious reminder of Porumboiu's ironic celebration in A Trip to the City. Sarcastic humour prevails in the dialogue.

Doiaru is inflexible from the start. Later on, he explains to Monica that his rude behaviour is due to her mother having died when she was born, thus adding a touch of emotionally effective psychoanalysis. In school, Monica's captivating beauty explains why she is coveted by most of her local admirers: she gets love text messages from a certain Andrei, actually the son of the strike leader (Alex Mărgineanu).

A second flashback shows the young boy's family seeking refuge in the midst of bombardments. A black soldier photographed by a villager is seen landing in the countryside. Yet another allusion to the unfulfilled American expectations,

Fig 54. America has dinner with Romania in California Dreamin'

the same shot comes up as a significant binary editing rhyme in the present, the mayor showing some schoolchildren the photo and explaining: 'this is the first black man I ever saw in my life and I'll never forget how we, the simple Romanians, welcomed this man so warmly' (Lupşa 2007). Jones, whose sole obsession is meeting the deadline, pays several visits to Doiaru's office and offers some money to get things going, but the stationmaster refuses to be bribed. Though the two seem to get along quite well, the audience will subsequently grasp that Doiaru's aversion to Americans ('Fuck USA, NATO and Bill Clinton') has its roots not only in his troubled childhood but also in a form of disillusionment shared by millions of Romanians.

The brilliantly edited village party sequence is clearly the film's key point and a pastiche of early Forman, more specifically *Loves of a Blonde* (1965), in which initially shy young factory girls bond with some older men from a military contingent, with hilarious consequences. Here young Romanian village girls want intensely to bond with Americans because this has always been an enduring collective dream. As in Nemescu's shorts, skilful direction creates a very acute sense of community. Sequence highlights from the deliberately full-blown festive atmosphere include Elvis impersonator Nicky Valoare, the same Romano Elvis from Nemescu's *Marilena*; he will purposefully take over the 'Love Me Tender' standard. Monica and David eventually meet and start flirting, revealing to the audience they do not need linguistic skills in order to get along with each other.

While the young generation is having fun through overt sex and heavy drinking, the mayor challenges the US guests, making them visit an Eiffel Tower replica and an impressive villa echoing the *Dallas* TV series. The visit was actually shot on location at the Hermes Slobozia Ranch, an amusement park inspired by the US series.[15] At this point the narrative seems to falter, lacking a clear direction, but a short-circuit suddenly leaves the whole village in total black-out. A television commentator explains that an explosion caused no human or material losses, only panic; it appears to have been a projectile dating back to World War II. This was followed by a massive black-out of unknown origin. People feared it was a US Tomahawk projectile, which was meant to reach Yugoslavia but got here first.

A fourth flashback further shows Doiaru as a child, with his father promising him: 'before we get back the Americans will be here'. We hear Monica's voice explaining to David how her grandparents were arrested and imprisoned by the Communists because they had taken orders from the Germans. 'And the Americans never came back until the day before yesterday', she concludes. This actually sounds like one of the film's possible pay-offs. Soon afterwards, the mayor explains to a baffled crowd that their problem is Doiaru and manages to rally Jones to his cause. After waving goodbye to his Romanian 'escapade', David now manages to get his girlfriend from the States on the line. Monica and Andrei pursue their English lessons, one of them being about the lyrics that inspired the film's title, *California Dreamin'*.

All narrative lines eventually converge at the train station. Doiaru comes over with the police and violent combat ensues. Monica's father is badly hurt, while fireworks are set off. The American venue has thus met with a Romanian society where Communist evil seems to be deeply rooted and cannot be easily eradicated. Titles on a black screen indicate that the mission was actually superfluous because 'the radar became operational on June 9, 1999, but two hours earlier NATO announced a peace treaty with Kosovo and the bombardments ended'. An ambiguously optimistic epilogue intended as such by Nemescu shows Monica and Andrei meeting in a Bucharest bar and discussing classes and exams, then parting. The end credits once more feature the iconic hit 'California Dreamin'', sung by The Mamas and the Papas, a background tune already instrumental for Andrei when he declares his feelings.

Despite the length, a result of the director being tragically absent for the 'final cut', and a few scenes which seem unfinished, *California*'s polyphonic screenplay and its outstanding style reveal the film's unique potential to provide the audience with intelligent entertainment.[16] Much closer to the standards expected by mainstream audiences, more familiar with Hollywood than the more demanding films of the minimalist trend, Nemescu's first and unfortunately last feature filled the theatres and proved one of the rare authentic Romanian box-office hits. This proved almost a contradiction in terms in the Romanian film context, where the amount of domestic films which fare well at the box office has always been extremely limited. It also got a very successful European and US distribution, and its DVD edition is still popular both in art cinema and in more commercial circuits.

For Alex Leo Şerban, *California Dreamin'* was 'the most daring combination of genres ever attempted in Romanian cinema', blending a love story with a geopolitical one, magic realism with neorealism and leading to a convincing parable on national identity, without ever verging into clumsy details' (Şerban 2009: 283–85). In his London International Film Festival catalogue review, Nick Roddick notes that 'It is hard to believe that this epic satire, a rambunctious Balkan farce which shades into tragedy, is a first film' (Roddick 2007: 44). There was also praise for a 'screenplay filled with sharply witty observations, a hyper realistic cinéma vérité approach, a sophisticated essay and a critique of buffoonish war in the line of *Duck Soup*, *Catch 22* or *Dr Strangelove*' (Monder 2009).

California Dreamin' got many posthumous domestic and international prizes, the most important being the Un Certain Regard prize at the Cannes IFF 2007, the same year Mungiu was awarded the Palme d'Or for *4, 3, 2*.[17] The Jury's head, film director Pascale Ferran, initially did not want to judge 'an unfinished film', but eventually praised it for being a vivid, free and lively proposal for cinema, while in her *Positif* review Domenach compared the unfinished status of the film to that of Michelangelo's statue *David*, 'still caught in marble' (Domenach 2008: 32–33).

Nemescu's collaborator and long-time friend Yvonne Irimescu was responsible for the creation of the NexT International Short Film Festival in 2007. It was conceived to honour the memory of Nemescu and of sound engineer Toncu and has been attracting more and more interesting young filmmakers and films since. It is an important means to keep their brief but enduring legacy alive.

CHAPTER 13

Romanian Exilic and Diasporic Cinema
The Case of Radu Gabrea

Quite a few Romanian *émigré* actors, directors, cinematographers and producers from the first decades of the twentieth century have left a national imprint on their subsequent careers abroad or decided to return home from their exile for a short or extended period of time. Renowned early cinema performers such as Elvira Popescu (a.k.a. Popesco) and Alexandru Mihalescu (a.k.a. Mihalesco) had some domestic film and theatre experiences before embarking on successful French careers. Other contemporaries born in Romania and having chosen France or Germany as their second homeland, such as innovative *Kammerspiel* actor and director active in the early 1920s Lupu Pick, well-known actresses from the 1930s and early 1940s Pola Illéry (b. Paula Iliescu) and Janny Holt (b. Ecaterina Vlădescu-Olt), producer Emile Nathan (b. Tannenzaft) and screenwriter Benjamin Fondane (b. Barbu Fundoianu) only occasionally worked in their native country (Cantacuzino 1998: 250–76; Rîpeanu 2004: 235).[1]

According to Rîpeanu, the phenomenon of Hollywood artists (e.g. actors, directors and screenwriters) with origins in the Romanian region, 'that is ethnic Romanians, Hungarians and Germans and Jews born in Romania before World War I [...] is dominated by the fact that the majority of these people were very young emigrants who were only professionally trained *after* contact with the American film industry' (Rîpeanu 2006: 416).

The artists Rîpeanu is here referring to include classical Hollywood cinema melodrama and film noir specialist Jean Negulesco (who came to the US after attempting a painting career in Paris), producer John Houseman, director Lewis Milestone, screenwriter I. A. L. Diamond, and prestigious stars such as Edward G. Robinson (b. Emanuel Goldenberg), Johnny Weismuller (b. Johann Weissmüller) and Bela Lugosi (b. Bela Blasco), to list only the most salient ones. Rîpeanu rightly notes that, considering their 'young emigrant' status, these artists never set up a Romanian community in Hollywood as was the case with their German, Russian and French contemporaries and were never considered as a part of a structured 'immigration wave' fleeing Nazi or Communist regimes (Rîpeanu 2004: 236).

Romanian diasporic and exilic contemporary cinema has started resurfacing thanks to the increased accessibility of films produced, as very few critics and historians had the opportunity to watch and review films in their complete, uncensored form before 1989.

However, Romanian-born and educated filmmaker Radu Gabrea (b. 1937) is the most interesting case in point: his exilic multi-layered career as an *émigré* in Germany, and later on his return to post-totalitarian Romania, led to some very challenging creative work. Migrant Romanian cinema left its imprint in a German environment, thanks to an artist both attached to his roots and eager to adjust to a new environment. Once back in his native Romania, Gabrea continued to collaborate with his Western partners, helping create a new trend, which is still to be defined by film scholars, as it is neither 'in' nor 'out of' exile, but somehow in between (Nasta 2006b).[2]

Part of the Thaw generation that had temporarily reinstated Romanian cinema on the world map, Radu Gabrea initially trained as an engineer before entering film school. Gabrea's first film, *Prea mic pentru un război atât de mare* (*Too Small for Such a Big War*, 1969), was rightly considered an innovative variation on the theme of the young child confronted by the atrocities of World War II, as developed by Tarkovsky in his seminal *Ivan's Childhood* (1962).[3] It follows an orphan boy through his tragic experiences with a Western Front company whose soldiers are eventually killed, after pursuing Nazi troops across Romania, Hungary and Czechoslovakia. The metaphorical allegory of an outsider watching the way of the world while also being part of it has been a constant in Gabrea's filmography since then.

The striking opening sequence, with credits unfolding simultaneously, serves as a paradigmatic image for the director's entire work: we are introduced to young Mihai (Mihai Filip) playing hide-and-seek blindfolded, surrounded by other young boys in military attire next to target puppets, while some strange non-harmonic chords and musicalised noises are heard on the soundtrack.

The boy's apprenticeship on the mission he has to complete in a multi-lingual community oscillates between sombre war sequences and authentic moments of childish playfulness. Gabrea proved extremely skilled for a beginner in directing an experienced cast. War scenes are shot by Dinu Tănase's exquisite camera as if they were authentic tableaux. Spectacularly violent sequences alternate with lyrical, almost expressionist synesthetic moments; the rendering of

Fig 55. The opening credits of
Too Small for Such a Big War

natural locations and of the everyday life of Transylvanian inhabitants (mostly extras) has a documentary, true-to-life quality.[4] The film's pivotal scene occurs before the final capturing of Mihai by enemy troops. His fellow soldiers get to a castle where they all disguise themselves in the armour of medieval knights. One of them even takes a souvenir photo, but while Mihai has gone to look for the tripod they are all killed by a sudden German assault. When the boy comes back, he realises he is surrounded by immobile knights, resembling the lifeless statues surrounding them. Thanks to a daring visual syntax in tune with Western modernity and an expressive sound design, the director received very good critical acclaim and the Youth Jury prize at the 1970 Locarno International Film Festival.

After a brief period dedicated to shooting *Amintiri bucureştene* (*Memories of Bucharest*, 1970), which is probably one of the most comprehensive documentary archive collections of newsreel and home movies from Romania, covering forty years (1900 to 1940), and directing episodes of successful 'official' Romanian TV series such as *Urmărirea* (*The Chase*, 1971), Gabrea's next project was a successful, though controversial, autobiographical novel by Fănuş Neagu, *The Angel's Shout*, published in 1968. Bearing a less transparent biblical reference, the film's title eventually became *Dincolo de nisipuri* (*Beyond the Sands*, 1973), bearing the title of another story by Neagu.[5]

Like the four-part novel, the film spans twelve years and deals with the consequences of the clash between a Byzantine descendant, Prince Ipsilanti, and a community of delocalised peasants from Dobrudja, a deserted region next to the Black Sea. Hoping for a better life once they have crossed the Danube, the peasants wander from one village to another, turning into occasional bandits: one of them, Nicolae Mohreanu, is arrested and killed while trying to escape. A few years later, his son, Ion, tries to discover the truth and avenge his father. The only person who could help him unearth the truth is Nicu Jinga, a recluse nicknamed 'The Angel', but he is also killed before Ion manages to meet him. Says one of the characters: 'Our wandering was born out of deceit. I thought we were heading for a quiet life. It just proved the beginning of a greater suffering'. The tortured, excessive character of Ion (Dan Nuțu) is one of the film's multiple voice-over narrators, who move between violent and extremely sensual, overtly erotic scenes. Tita (Elena Racinede), an easy-going girl, breaks his heart and leaves him because he does not fit with her social ambitions. Once Communist times set in, Ion, the outcast, discovers that his father's mistress Vetina (Gina Patrichi) betrayed him, for fear of having to live in poverty. Deceived and desperate, he sides with a group of hysterical arms smugglers, only to end up having the same tragic destiny as his father.

On the opposite line, Ion's class enemy, Ipsilanti, an ageing aristocrat emphatically played by Emil Botta, has turned delirious and is constantly heard holding forth. He often emerges by way of sophisticated camera angles, pausing among elaborate mirrors and pieces of furniture, before a spectacular fire set up by peasants destroys what he himself describes as 'the golden remains of Byzantine emperors' (Grmek Germani 2000: 190).

Beyond the Sands' overall time and story structure is no doubt one of the most complex ever attempted in a Romanian film. There are at least four leaps backward and forward in time and three voice-over commentators (Ion and two highly articulate peasants, played by Ernest Maftei and Mircea Albulescu). They either address the main character, wanting to clarify moments from the past, or act as the alter egos of the camera. Gabrea resorts to third-person literary passages in order to express philosophical musings or to prophesise things to come: 'It was the madness of our world, born out of poverty and despair'. The visualised story also contains ethnographically relevant passages about religious events occurring before the triumphant arrival of the 'red flag regime'. Such is the case of the 'Holy Cross' purifying ceremony by the sea, backed by Orthodox Mass songs and containing breath-taking ensemble shots, which echo earlier East European religious pageants such as Jerzy Kawalerowicz's *Matka Joanna od aniołów* (*Mother Joan of Angels*, 1961).

Like *Too Small for Such a Big War*, *Beyond the Sands* features many moments of cinematic beauty, despite quite a few unpleasant instances of overly theatrical, almost hysterical acting. It is modernist in style and includes arbitrary flashes of sepia-like cinematography by the same Dinu Tănase, spectacular torch-lit night scenes and expressionist carnival moments, echoing medieval folklore. Considered by Mira and Antonin Liehm as one of the greatest East European achievements of the 1970s, its premiere was delayed and the film was only briefly shown. After being shelved, it only resurfaced in a 'director's cut' version in 1995 (Liehm 1977: 358; Rîpeanu 2005: 65). Consequently, Gabrea decided to leave Romania for West Germany.

Radu Gabrea's work in Germany between 1981 and 1989, including an adventure film produced in the US and shot on location in Chile, was characterised by a constant struggle between new forms of filmic expression and old, familiar ones. At the outset of the 1980s, after being forced to work as an engineer for a couple of years, the filmmaker managed, with the support of German film and television producers familiar with his previous work in Romania, to set up a German-Portuguese co-production, *Do Not Fear, Jakob* (*Fürchte dich nicht, Jakob*, 1981). Shot on location in the Portuguese Alentejo region, where Gabrea saw similarities with the surroundings of the original Romanian story, the film was well received by audiences and critics alike and managed to get a very good festival circuit distribution.

To Gabrea, who has maternal Jewish origins, the subject is extremely familiar, as the depicted intrigue echoes anti-Semitic attitudes some Romanians still have to deal with today. It is actually an adaptation of *An Easter Torch*, a cult novella by Caragiale, who also ended up as an exile in Berlin. Jewish merchant and tavern owner Leiba Zibal is the target of anti-Semitic insults and has to flee the pogroms with his pregnant wife, Sura, while also seeking revenge on George, an unfaithful servant who threatens him with murder. The unbelievable happens: afraid and desperate, Leiba/Jakob cuts the servant's hand with a torch of fire. By lighting the fire on an Easter night he saves his family, while also symbolically becoming a Christian, to his great dismay. Establishing a fast editing pace, Gabrea mixes collective 'folklore' scenes lit in chiaroscuro with a lot of ethnic music (conforming to his original tastes) and more personal, lyrical interludes. Almost entirely spoken in German with a few Portuguese background sonorities, the film features famous Austrian actor and singer André Heller in the main part and a lot of Portuguese extras.[6] *Do Not Fear, Jakob* was screened among other films at the 1981 Berlinale and hailed as one of the best German productions of that year.

Gabrea's second production in exile and undoubtedly his best-known film to date dealt with an extremely unorthodox subject, partly suggested by German producer Laurens Straub and co-written by Horst Schier: a fictitious slice of R. W. Fassbinder's controversial existence. Still shown in European and US art-house cinemas over the world, *A Man Like Eva* (*Ein Mann wie EVA*, 1984) risks a lot but succeeds. It has the late R. W. Fassbinder played by a woman, the extraordinary Eva Mattes, one of the director's former actresses. Only two years after his untimely death, Eva/Fassbinder is portrayed as a bearded, moody character with a woman's voice, wearing glasses and a leather jacket. He/she is in the process of shooting a version of *The Lady of the Camelias*. Eva is in love with both the male lead, Walter (Werner Stocker), and Gudrun (Lisa Kreuzer), the female one. During a carnival finale, Eva's tyranny and betrayals come to light with tragic consequences.

Most naturally, Verdi's *Traviata* sung by Maria Callas serves as a unique music quotation, establishing a strange analogy with Eva's personal chaos. A reflexive, recurrent *mise en abyme* interestingly echoes R. W. F.'s own dramatic fate, caused by his impossibility as a genius to separate his debauched bisexual life ('I love women too, but it is nicer to love men') from his professional one: the performers watch TV, look at the filmed rushes, re-shoot scenes, watch rehearsals, and so on. Gabrea uses a hyper-economical setting, almost a *huis clos*, which serves both as home to actors and as a theatrical film set. Dialogue often verges on the absurd. Tragic irony within the limits of a well-known reality is at stake, as the inaugural quotation from André Gide rightly anticipates: 'It is better to be hated for what one is, than to be loved for what one is not'. The exiled director again introduces the paradigmatic figure of the outsider watching a world where violent love and bloody vengeance co-exist.

After receiving unanimous international critical acclaim for *EVA*, including a Feminine Interpretation Prize for Eva Mattes at the 1984 European Film Festival, Gabrea did not in fact get interesting feature film proposals. He thus decided to embark on a parallel venture, a doctoral research project in film, while continuing to work for German television. The doctoral dissertation he presented at Belgium's Catholic University of Louvain resulted in one of the best books ever written on Werner Herzog, confirming the Romanian filmmaker's interest in 'otherness' both on the real and on the more transcendent planes (Gabrea 1986).

The second option Gabrea chose allowed him to remain 'in the picture'. Between the late 1980s and the early 1990s he directed and co-wrote films for television, most of them adaptations, unequalled as far as their artistic value is concerned. They constitute a perfect testimony to the exile's capacity to adapt to a country where the film industry often remained confined to the domestic distribution market. One of them, *Ein Unding der Liebe* (*A Strange Thing Called Love*, 1988), was adapted from German popular writer Ludwig Fels, starring Erich Bar, a talented character actor Gabrea would again cast, once out of exile. In the tradition of Fassbinder and Herzog, the plot tells the story of another outcast, an orphaned butcher in search of impossible love. He becomes a thief the day he learns that his prostitute mother had abandoned him to his spinster aunts. The German petty bourgeois milieu is very faithfully depicted, within the rather limited television constraints. The score is composed by another Romanian exile, Ştefan Zorzor.

Last but not least, in 1989, a few months before the long-awaited fall of the Berlin Wall, the multi-faceted Radu Gabrea also embarked on an audience-friendly US adventure, *The Secret of the Ice Cave*, written by versatile Hollywood author Mike Werb and shot on location in Chile. Starring, among others, Sally Kellerman, the film tells the story of treasure-seekers out to discover the secret located in a mysterious ice cave. Gabrea thus demonstrated he could handle the commercial film form, miles away from the European art-house one.

Having decided to reintegrate into the post-totalitarian Romanian film industry while still living partly in Germany, Gabrea realised that many things had to be reorganised after years of authoritarian regime: there were still state-regulated production units and the private production structures evolved in a very chaotic manner. Most of his colleagues sought refuge in the safer, less censored theatrical environment.[7] Appointed as the head of the National Film Office (before it became the CNC) from 1997 to 1999, Gabrea proved instrumental in providing German/Western know-how to Romanian film structures that needed it so badly. The director-producer was invited to teach at the university (1998–2000) and initiated several financing campaigns and contest sessions for aspiring and confirmed fiction and non-fiction directors of short and feature films. Gabrea promulgated the first independent film funding law (1999), seeking innovative funding solutions, both in the field of production and in that of film distribution. He took huge personal risks and condemned illegal financial operations in different media in relation to film.[8]

The director found it almost impossible to shoot a film in the 'new' Romania without West European financial support. In an almost paradoxical, though not completely surprising way, Gabrea reintegrated the production context of his exile period with a film for larger audiences, *Rosenemil* (1993). The film fits the 'Euro-pudding' category, being co-produced by Germany, France, Switzerland and Romania. A tragic love story between a kind-hearted prostitute and an adventurous upstart is quickly forgotten by a society in constant upheaval. Adapted from a novel by popular German writer Georg Hermann, the visualised story reveals a bygone, slightly idealised world, where Jews, Austro-Hungarians and Germans co-existed peacefully for a brief period of time, despite class conflicts. This *fin de siècle*, rather conventional melodrama is set in a colourful Berlin, but mostly shot in Romanian bourgeois mansions. Emil is played by the same Werner Stocker who acted in *EVA*, surrounded by stars such as Serge Reggiani and Dominique Sanda, as well as a lot of

Romanian actors in 'cameo' parts. Though *Rosenemil* fared quite well both inside and outside Romania, Gabrea had to wait another seven years before he could shoot his next three features, being forced to alternate, as he did at the beginning of his career, between TV films, documentaries and real feature-length films.

The filmmaker stepped into the new century directing docu-fictions acclaimed by Jewish communities over the world. The first, *Struma* (2001), co-scripted with politically active writer Stelian Tănase, tells of one of the most tragic events in the history of the Holocaust: the death of 768 Romanian Jews forced to flee for Palestine on the vessel *Struma* in February 1942. After being delayed for several months in Istanbul, the ship was torpedoed by a Russian submarine a few miles from the Bosphorus. Only one refugee, David Stoliar, a US citizen, survived and could tell their story. The narrative skilfully combines a voice-over quoting famous writers and poets of Jewish origin with fictitious homebound letters, invaluable archive footage, family photos and authentic Jewish music. History time and fiction time coincide through effective editing.

Noro (2002), the title a Romanian diminutive ironically meaning 'lucky', was Gabrea's next entirely Romanian post-exilic creation with domestic crew and production costs. It is a hyperrealistic, personal account of a heavily handicapped boy whose mother (Victoria Cociaş) desperately wants him to get an education and enjoy a normal existence. The social status of handicapped people had been almost taboo in the Romanian film context, so Gabrea was innovating in terms of subject matter. Young Tudor Necula is extremely convincing as Noro, frequently inviting the audience to share in his joy of life and the progress he is making, despite the difficulties he has to cope with. Thus, his ageing father (Dorel Vişan), a respected police officer, refuses to support his wife and son's efforts to reach normality and fears 'the talk of the town', resulting in inevitable private and public conflicts. An explicit tribute to Werner Herzog's most famous outcast, Kaspar Hauser (*Jeder für sich und Gott gegen alle/The Enigma of Kaspar Hauser*, 1974), to whom the film is dedicated, the narrative oscillates between realistic and more theatrical interludes and even uses some of Herzog's musical quotations.

Nonetheless, in terms of style, *Noro* does not manage to measure up to Gabrea's former achievements, hesitating between realistic, down-to-earth direction and far too pathetic, melodramatic instances, 'vampirized' as Şerban rightly notes in his review of the film, 'by too much music' (Şerban 2009: 47).

Gabrea's next project was once again related to his Jewish heritage. Conceived as a documentary, *Moştenirea lui Goldfaden – De la Iaşi la New-*

York (*Goldfaden's Legacy*, 2004) tells the true story of Abraham Goldfaden, 'The Jewish Shakespeare', known as the creator of the first professional Yiddish theatre in the Romanian city of Iaşi, as early as 1862. Goldfaden abandoned his rabbinical studies to write Yiddish folk songs, before joining forces with other performers to direct according to Yiddish traditions. Though he quickly became a hero for minorities in a tolerant and multicultural Romanian environment, Goldfaden's Yiddish performances were banned in 1883 and he was forced to emigrate to New York, gaining recognition only at the end of his life.

Shooting on location in Romania but also in Broadway, New York, Gabrea offers the audience lively, authentic testimonies in Romanian, English and Hebrew from renowned actors and artistic directors of musicals. Most of them acknowledge the importance of the Yiddish theatre revival, having benefited from Goldfaden's pioneering techniques. These consisted in mixing songs with improvised, often ironic spoken interludes. Having mentioned at a certain point that the exiles 'pretended once a week they were back in Romania', the director does not miss the opportunity to insert a Broadway poster, which most significantly echoes autobiographical elements: 'Discover who you are / remember where you're from'.

Still considering his commitment to Jewish-Romanian exilic and diasporic culture an artistic priority, Gabrea directed and co-produced another series of fascinating documentaries between 2006 and 2010. *Rumenyie! Rumenyie!* (2006), *Romania, Romania* (2008) and *Căutîndu-l pe Schwarz* (*Looking for Schwarz*, 2008) focus on the roots and traditions of popular music as a perfect repository for historical and personal events and emotions. Jewish bands and singers, filmed on location in New York, provide virtuoso performances of both Romanian and *Klezmer* folklore. Musicologists and artists based in the USA travel back to Romania to track their ancestors, while commenting on the incredible aspects of cultural convergence. In the same line, *Concerte de la Biserica Neagră* (*Concerts from the 'Black Church'*, 2009), features a series of classical music concerts composed by native Saxons from Transylvania and perceptively commented on by historians and performers alike.[9]

During the first decade of the twenty-first century, the director's fiction output proved equally consistent in terms of selected topics. It did not always appear innovative style-wise, his films often seeming closer to setups conceived for television. However, Gabrea has constantly aimed to bring to light historical, social and political aspects related to forgotten or seldom tackled issues such as Romania's Fascist occupation and anti-Semitic pogroms (*Călătoria lui Gruber/Gruber's Journey*, 2008), the exodus of Saxons from

Transylvania (*Cocoşul Decapitat/The Beheaded Rooster*, 2007) and the tragic consequences of the early Communist regime (*Mănuşile roşii/Red Gloves*, 2010).

Co-scripted by Răzvan Rădulescu and Alexandru Baciu, *Gruber's Journey* draws its inspiration from the war experience of the Italian author of *Kaputt*, Curzio Malaparte (played by Florin Piersic, Jr), who travelled to the north of Moldova in 1941, only to witness the devastating campaign of deportation of Jewish citizens. *The Beheaded Rooster*[10] and *Red Gloves* were adapted from two homonymous, highly successful novels by Saxon-born writer and minister Eginald Schlattner. Schlattner witnessed German minority upheavals in a multi-ethnic Transylvania, including the deportation of his own father to Russia. Unlike most co-nationals, Schlattner decided not to leave for Germany, despite having been arrested and given a very rough ride by Romanian Communist authorities. As a consequence both the novels and the screen versions offer an invaluable insight into the destinies of people from different ages and social milieus: their ordinary lives and beliefs will be shattered first with the rise of fascism and later as a consequence of the Stalinist totalitarian repression.

If Gabrea's four-decade career, spanning quite a number of fictions and documentaries and some important film endeavours, has not always measured up to the initial auteurist standards, deliberately opting for more general audience-oriented films, he nonetheless managed to acquire a unique status among Romanian filmmakers: that of an authentic European director, defying time through a constant desire to harmoniously blend relevant historical facts with entertaining fictions. 'Citizen Gabrea' would most certainly stand as a suitable nickname.

Conclusion

After difficult beginnings, uneven improvements, sparse moments of accomplishment during a short thaw, Stalinist-inspired state censorship control over all aspects of the film industry, and post-Communist difficulties in catching up with Western standards, several encouraging conditions marked a twenty-first-century revival of Romanian cinema. Over the last decade, the emergence of an authentic New Wave secured Romania more prizes in film festivals than any other country: Romania, a peripheral European country, has turned into a bright spot on the map of world cinema.

When I first started writing this book I had a different subtitle in mind, *Eastern Europe's Unexpected Cinderella*, the meaning of which is worth discussing at this point. In the mythic parable from the tales of Perrault and the Grimm Brothers, a young girl is deprived of her rights and mistreated by her stepsisters after the death of her mother. While working as a maid for her step-family and sleeping among ashes, she receives the magical aid of a fairy and gets to the royal ball, where she attracts the attention of the handsome prince. When she has to leave before midnight, she loses her small slipper, which becomes the key to proving her identity. Though she looks dirty and ragged, her elder sisters are unable to bar her way and the prince eventually marries the one who fits the small slipper.

Mutatis mutandis, though featuring interesting films and filmmakers, Romanian Cinema lagged behind its older and more experienced neighbouring Eastern European film industries for quite a while, striking back and catching up with most of them when least expected. This 'Cinematic Cinderella' clearly chose a narrow path, the 'minimalist' vein, to prove her originality and clearly looked for her main inspiration amidst the ashes of the Communist past. I thought that such a parable was more appropriate than other more popular but less relevant stereotypes associated with Romanian culture. A case in point is the myth of Dracula, a Western invention widely exploited in literature and film and only indirectly based on the medieval ruler Vlad the Impaler, (a.k.a. Vlad Dracul, meaning 'the Devil'), which actually did not attract many domestic filmmakers. However, I did not want to limit the recent Romanian 'fairy tale' paradigm to the minimalist phenomenon: this would have meant neglecting other equally interesting film phenomena from the past I have tried to deal with.

However, the present survey is by no means exhaustive. It only includes and analyses two or three specific titles from the very interesting Romanian film and television documentary vein, to which a separate book should be devoted. The names and essential works of Alexandru Solomon, who started as a fiction film cinematographer and later became an important author/producer (*The Great Communist Bank Robbery*, 2004; *Cold Waves*, 2007; *Kapitalism: Our Improved Formula*, 2010), Thomas Ciulei (*Facemania*, 1997; *The Flower Bridge*, 2008), the already discussed Florin Iepan (author of *Children of the Decree*, 2005; *The One, the Only the Real Tarzan*, 2004; and *The Fallen Vampire*, 2007) and Andrei Dăscălescu (*Constantin and Elena*, 2008) have been highly praised for their perceptive visions of Romanian past and present realities and need further discussion.

Similarly, the animated film tradition initiated by the famous Ion Popescu Gopo has continued to flourish after the fall of Communism. Thus, Anca Damian innovated with her first animated fiction *Crulic, drumul spre dincolo* (*Crulic, the Path to Beyond*, 2011), close in spirit and style to two other celebrated foreign animated films for adults, such as Marjane Satrapi's *Persepolis* (2007) and Ari Folman's *Waltz With Bashir* (2008). It proved to be the first widely acclaimed Romanian animated film in almost fifty years, since Gopo's Palme d'Or for his short animation *Short History*: it won more than 25 prizes in 130 festivals over the world and as a consequence was well-distributed in cinemas throughout Europe. Inspired by an authentic case, the film tells the real story of a 33-year-old Romanian falsely accused of theft and imprisoned while in Poland for work. Seeking to prove his innocence, Claudiu Crulic embarks on a long hunger strike but neither the Polish nor the Romanian authorities are ready to admit he is innocent, so he is left to die. As in Billy Wilder's *Sunset*

Boulevard (1957), the hero's life story is narrated by the character 'from beyond the grave', the voiceover being that of Vlad Ivanov. The story elegantly mixes animation techniques with real clips from TV news, paper inserts and photos, reminding one of Surrealist 'collage' techniques.

The concept of expanded cinema present in museums, urban and countryside locations has also proved a rapidly developing strain. Romanian-born, Amsterdam-based visual artist Călin Dan, author of video installations such as *RA* (1994–2000), *Sample City* (2003) and *Trip* (2006), is an interesting case in point.

When attempting to conclude a more or less comprehensive overview of Romanian cinema that has skimmed over the past to better understand the present, the fact that history repeats itself in specific spheres of the film industry does not come as a surprise. Thus, the spirit of the Buftea studios from the 1960s, the one-time Balkan Cinecitta, has enjoyed a consistent revival on the international plane thanks to the success of Castel Film Romania, a vast complex including one of the largest sound studios in Europe, offering much lower shooting and production costs than any similar Western or US structure and boasting 150 feature films in 17 years.

Mainstream international hits shot at Castel Film, with domestic crews and additional cast, include *Cold Mountain* (A. Minghella, 2003), *Borat* (S. Baron Cohen, 2006), *Pulse* (J. Sonzero, 2006), *Adam Resurrected* (P. Schrader, 2008) and *Mirrors* (A. Aja, 2008), as well as two films by Romanian-born director Radu Mihăileanu. The first one, *Train de vie* (*Train of Life*, 1998), resulted from a highly complex co-production setup (France, Belgium, Romania, Israel, the Netherlands) and was partly shot in Romania with skilled Romanian actors in cameos gravitating around a mainly French cast. Conceived as an effective tragicomic fable, it tells a story inspired by real facts from the Jewish-Romanian Holocaust history. Narratively and aesthetically designed to reach audiences worldwide, Mihăileanu's highly successful *The Concert* (*Le Concert*, 2009) also brought in Romanian locations and actors, while confirming the director's attraction to and facility in dealing with the tragicomic consequences of totalitarianism.

Acclaimed foreign films using Romanian locations other than the aforementioned studios have benefited from similar financial and technical facilities: *Capitaine Conan* (B. Tavernier, 1996), *Amen* (C. Gavras, 2002), *Youth Without Youth* (F. F. Coppola, 2007), adapted from an essential novel by Mircea Eliade, *Katalin Varga* (P. Strickland, 2009), and so on.

Concerned with Romanian social and ethnographic issues and partly shot in Romania with a Romanian crew but directed by foreign filmmakers, two categories of films also deserve some comment at this point. More than half a dozen contemporary Italian films feature convincingly Romanian characters confronted with the harsh realities of economic or illegal immigration. Prostitution, delinquency, blackmail and the broken lives of fragmented families are at stake in *Coverboy* (C. Amoroso, 2006), *Il resto della notte/The Rest of the Night* (F. Munzi, 2008), starring Romanian actress Laura Vasiliu, *Pa-ra-da/Parade* (M. Pontecorvo, 2008) and *Mar Nero/Black Sea* (F. Biondi, 2009), the latter featuring alongside Italian performers three important Romanian New Wave actors (Dorotheea Petre, Maïa Morgenstern and Vlad Ivanov) in challenging parts. The Romanian response to this sub-genre is Bobby Păunescu's controversial *Francesca* (2009), which got mixed reviews once shown in Italy: it dealt with the many vicissitudes of a young school teacher (Monica Bîrlădeanu) wishing to emigrate to Italy to start a new life but not being able to fulfil her dream.

The second category has to do with the Roma minority as pictured in the films of Tony Gatlif. Highly familiar with Romania, where three of his films unfold, the Roma director based in France rejected the negative assumptions associated with Gypsies, opting for a hybrid method that mixes moments of *ciné-vérité* with highly poetic audio-visual interludes. In *Latcho Drom* (*Gypsy Dream*, 1992), Roma cultural essentials of different countries are expressed via musical numbers, some sequences having been shot in Romania. *Gadjo Dilo* (*Crazy Stranger*, 1997) tells the story of a French musicologist (Romain Duris) who travels to Romania and ends up living in a Roma village after falling under the spell of a beautiful Gypsy girl (Rona Hartner). Mostly shot in the outskirts of Bucharest and backed by a Romanian production, the film is a unique opportunity to get familiar with multilingual verbal and highly original musical occurrences. Finally, in *Transylvania* (2006) Gatlif and his collaborator, ethnomusicologist Delphine Mantoulet, use Romanian locales to reveal hybrid, colourful aspects of Gypsy culture and folklore, including pagan rituals and religious customs.

Despite its international recognition and its effectively used production facilities, Romanian cinema is still faring poorly at home. Audiences inevitably prefer US box-office hits to national products and cinema attendance rates have not progressed as expected; neither have the viewing conditions been radically improved beyond the already operational mall multiplexes in the outskirts of big cities. However, film schools, European training workshops and festivals are flourishing all over the country, and the Romanian CNC is constantly trying to improve its selection and financing criteria. Critics at home and abroad are wondering if the New Wave is still a reality or whether we are witnessing the advent of a second wave, more diversified and less radical.

In the meantime, a newcomer like Florin Şerban has proved that original-ity and excellence in filmmaking are still on the Romanian cinema menu: his electrifying juvenile detention tale based on a screenplay by Cătălin Mitulescu and Andreea Vălean, *Eu când vreau să fluier, fluier/If I Want to Whistle, I Whistle* (2010), got the Silver Bear in Berlin and was enthusiastically received worldwide. Having Marius Panduru, a key figure in recent cinematography as director of photography and Nemescu's gifted collaborator Cătălin Cristuţiu as editor, *Eu când vreau sa fluier, fluier/If I Want to Whistle, I Whistle* (2010) is quite unique in terms of theme, morals and handling of the audio-visual universe. Despite being yet another story about difficult personal choices, there is nothing overtly theatrical or literary about the 'prison intrigue' it devel-ops. Mixing professional and nonprofessional actors, Şerban seems closer to European fictional hyper-realism and echoes the Dardenne brothers' 'juvenile delinquency' vehicles such as *The Promise* (1996) or *The Child* (2005). Silviu, the main hero, has almost finished his four-year sentence in a provincial town when things go wrong, once his younger brother lets him know their mother wants to take him along with her for a better life abroad. Self-destructive and stubborn, refusing to leave his brother in the hands of an unworthy mother, he plans an earlier escape. He takes Ada, a social worker, as a hostage during an unbearably violent assault against prison personnel. This mentally unbalanced 'rebel with a cause' eventually forces his way out of prison and surrenders after a brief chat with Ada. In *If I Want to Whistle, I Whistle*, no morals are advanced, there is no metaphysical background to rely on, no major historical issues to be dealt with.

One of the most atypical Romanian recent achievements is *Undeva la Palilula* (*Somewhere in Palilula*, 2012), the highly controversial cinematic debut of one of the most acclaimed Romanian theatre directors, Silviu Purcărete, known for his *mise en scene* featuring flamboyant visuals often conceived on a gigantic scale. A national variant of Kusturica's *Underground* shot entirely in an abandonned warehouse, it took more than three years to be finalised and was written by Purcărete, freely inspired by the real stories of a pediatrician who graduated during the Communist regime and was sent to work to a place in the middle of nowhere. The gynecologist's incursion into a dystopic space where paradoxically no children are born serves as a pretext for a baroque allegory of Romanian recurring myths and rituals, having Communist times as a background. Both scenography and lighting techniques echo theatrical conventions in a very unusual way and appear as a challenging alternative to a national cinema reputed almost exclusively for its realist vein. Purcărete's cast contains many well-known figures of the Romanian stage and screen, their performances echoing those from Pintilie's iconoclast screening of Caragiale's *Carnival Scenes*. Unfortunately, the screenplay lacks consistency and the over-abundant use of symbols and metaphors are almost impossible to decode for a non-domestic audience.

The present book started with a personal assumption based on mediatised historical facts: the Romanian dictator's entirely filmed fall and the ensuing 1989 revolution paradoxically contributed to the country's cinematic rebirth, fuelling an unprecedented amount of highly original audio-visual discourses. I have also attempted to situate events and images against a philosophical background, namely Paul Ricoeur's dichotomy between *historical time* and *time of fiction* with its conceptual extension, Aristotle's three-fold mimesis. A fictional universe, in this case film, draws its inspiration from real or imagined facts which are *prefigured*, then chooses a way to *configure* them and delivers the message to the audience, during the process called *refiguration* (Ricoeur 1980, I: 76).

Twenty years after the event that inextricably blended historical and fictional time on screen, Andrei Ujica's *Autobiografia lui Nicolae Ceaușescu* (*The Autobiography of Nicolae Ceaușescu*, 2010), a three-hour epic exclusively based on pre-existing found footage, revealed to the world that Romanian cinema had not only continued but changed and renewed itself. A new film category was born, still waiting to be defined: half-way between fiction and documentary, with real characters featured like puppets inside a perfectly orchestrated show and historical events unfolding as if they were part of a suspenseful thriller, comedy or tragedy. After watching more than 1000 hours of television archive material, including previously inaccessible home movies, Ujica decided to breathe new life into old images. Echoing Eisenstein's intellectual montage as well as the revolutionary polyphonic editing of Welles's *Citizen Kane*, the director mixes temporal parameters, starting with bits from the dictator's hasty trial and travelling back in time in the most unexpected ways. Twenty-five years of public and private events unfold with no voice-over comment, leaving the audience to decode and interpret a very special kind of autobiography.

Hopefully, sophisticated reconstructions of Romania's most celebrated dictator will be followed by new kinds of stories, inspired by other rich and original Romanian myths and legends. They will most certainly chase the tyrant and turn up some fairy queen…

notes

CHAPTER 1

1   CD (1999), *Taraf des Haïdouks*, Crammed Discs.
2   Zografi is an alter ego of Istrati, appearing in several novels. Another respected Istrati novel, *Kyra Kyralina*, was adapted twice by Russian (Victor Glagolin) and Hungarian (Gyula Maar) directors, its Romanian adaptation having been repeatedly delayed.
3   Gopo directed fantasy films and comedies and is particularly remembered for his adaptation of a very popular Romanian folk tale, *De-aş fi Harap Alb/The White Moor* (1965). He also served as head of the Romanian Film Directors' Association from 1968 to the year of his death, 1989.

CHAPTER 2

1   The *Cinema* monthly started in 1963 and continued until the 1989 revolution, on a very wide circulation basis, around 200,000 copies.
2   Liviu Ciulei and Victor Rebengiuc's on- and off-stage collaboration was a reality that lasted for more than forty years.
3   E.g. 'You are a poet of the asphalt who builds scaffolds instead of cathedrals'.
4   Until 1980 when he left for the USA.

CHAPTER 3

1   *Cinema*, n° 3, 1971, 11–55, author's translation.
2   The actor impersonating Michael was popular actor Amza Pellea. He was to become Nicolaescu's but also Ceauşescu's personal favourite, essentially because he came from the same region of Romania as the president, Oltenia. Pellea made practical jokes about his co-nationals, the 'Olteni', on a highly popular weekly television show featuring him as a familiar uncle called 'Nea Mărin'.
3   Played by Pellea's young daughter, future theatre and film actress Oana Pellea.
4   Backed by Romanian-born producer Raluca Nathan.
5   According to Călin Căliman, the name of the character is a composite made up of Toma Caragiu, the actor who plays Caratase, and Constantin Tănase (Căliman 2000: 238).
6   Caragiu died during the 1977 earthquake.
7   In an interview for the French newspaper *Libération*, published a couple of months after the Romanian revolution on the occasion of a film retrospective in La Rochelle, they both insist on the fact that *Water Like a Black Buffalo* was their neorealist

manifesto. They wanted to shoot their own *La Terra Trema* (L. Visconti, 1948), combining facts and fiction so as to build a new kind of film aesthetics (See Cazals 1990: 43; author's translation).

8 Mention should also be made of *Mai presus de orice* (*This Above All*, Dan Piţa and Nicolae Mărgineanu, 1978), another collective docu-fiction about the March 1977 Bucharest earthquake. This is a film that bears no comparison with *Water Like a Black Buffalo*: the idea of combining interviews with real victims, documentary footage and audio recordings of the earthquake with fictionalised fragments did not prove very successful. The hybrid status of the film is somehow frustrating for the viewer. Some real interviews seem overdone, such as the one featuring the bedridden victims from the hospital: 'when I heard on the radio that Comrade Elena and Nicolae Ceauşescu were coming, I knew we were saved'. This proves to what extent political brainwashing was much more effective seven years after *Water*. A voice-over comments about the respected intellectuals, artists and performers who were killed during the earthquake. The most heart-breaking sequence shows the over-crowded funeral service and obituaries for national star Toma Caragiu, whose outstanding theatre and film career is righteously praised. Several popular actors gather to talk about their missing colleague Caragiu.

9 Both Piţa and Veroiu continued their film career by alternating genres, whether they were contemporary thrillers or westerns in the Romanian style.

10 George Călinescu stands as Romania's most important literary critic from the first half of the twentieth century.

11 Costumes in beautifully harmonised pictorial tones are by Hortensia Georgescu, a constant collaborator of Veroiu's and also costume designer for big peplums by Sergiu Nicolaescu.

12 The film has two parts and lasts 142 minutes. Previous adaptations of Preda's work include *Desfăşurarea* (*The Development*, Paul Călinescu, 1954), *Porţile albastre ale oraşului* (*The Blue Gates of the Town*, a commissioned war screenplay by Preda directed by Mircea Mureşan, 1973), *Marele Singuratic* (*The Great Solitary*, Iulian Mihu, 1976), mostly on contemporary topics which did not have salient cinematic qualities.

13 Director Stere Gulea declared in a recent interview included on the film's DVD edition: 'It is not easy to talk about this film after twenty years, especially as many things happened in the meantime in Romania, so maybe I'm not the same person I used to be when I made the film. In doing this film I took a big risk, I had to lead a war in order to make this film. I did not want to stick to ideology and edulcorate things, make them look better, lighter, less harsh and realistic, as the authorities wanted me to. So using black and white and a minimalistic location setting was also serving the sobriety and integrity of Preda's masterpiece'.

14 As in Wajda's *Czlowiek z marmuru* (*Man of Marble*, 1977), with its shifting in and out of the present, and back to the Stalinist past.

CHAPTER 4

1 Almost every genre is represented in the chapter by a specific example, except for westerns. *Profetul, aurul şi ardelenii* (*Gold, the Prophet and the Transylvanians*, 1978)

and *Pruncul, petrolul și ardelenii* (*Oil, the Kid and the Transylvanians*, 1981), again co-directed by Veroiu, were actually films commissioned by the state and scripted by official film writer Titus Popovici. They seemed to have fared quite well in terms of attendance, being considered domestic box-office hits. These type of concessions enabled the directors to go on producing their more personal projects.

2   In order to survive decently in their everyday lives, Romanians were caught in a cobweb of social networking generically called *pile* (wangles): such relationships brought together people with important differences in social status. Besides food, people were fascinated by and craved goods such as blue jeans, coffee, deodorants, Western soap, perfume and fashion magazines and catalogues.

3   Screenwriter Mihnea Gheorghiu was asked to add some explanatory scenes and dialogues on the condition and revolt of peasants in this decaying world (Rîpeanu 2005: 120).

4   See Cazals (1990: 43; author's translation).

5   Ibid.

6   *Cinema*, n° 8, 1983, p. 3. Author's translation.

7   The film's storyline belongs to Grigore Bușecan and was clearly meant to show how exciting life in a Communist factory bachelor hostel could be. The film got the Silver Bear at the Berlin IFF in 1985.

8   Alex Leo Șerban, 'Retrocinemascop', in *Dilema Veche*, November, 1994. Author's translation.

CHAPTER 5

1   The film's screenplay was written by Timotei Ursu, a promising director who only made a few films and left Romania in the mid-1980s. Ursu's *Septembrie* (*September*, 1977) was considered a hit by the young generation because of shots of Anda Onesa almost nude on the beach.

2   For *Microphone Test*, editor Maria Neagu commented that they feared censorship constantly, so they sometimes mixed and added additional dialogue and scenes after the Party's censorship commission had previewed a first version. Here is an example: Gina Patrichi is found by her colleague and ex-lover Daneliuc in her apartment with another man, but one cannot distinguish the man in the dark in the first instance. A short scene showing how the half-naked man leaves the room was cut for official previewing purposes and reinserted afterwards (telephone conversation between author and Maria Neagu, 8 February 2009).

3   According to Neagu, the preview copy of the film was delivered without the Roma song, which was added afterwards.

4   Nicolae Iorga was murdered by the Iron Guard in 1940.

5   Chiaroscuro images will be a constant, cinematographer Călin Ghibu having taken Rembrandt as an inspiration and a reference for his brilliant visual compositions.

6   http://en.wikipedia.org/wiki/Glissando (10 March 2009).

7   Daneliuc has since then been writing novels, plays and short stories in the same vein.

8   See Andrei Gorzo, 'Intre cer si pămint', in *Dilema*, n° 516, 14 February 2003.

9   http://mirceadumitrescu.trei.ro/iacob.htm (8 March 2009).

10 Paul Goma (1990), *Patimile după Pitești*. Bucharest: Cartea Româneasca.
11 In a highly symbolic cameo appearance, Daneliuc himself stands as one of the allied officers giving strict orders to the prisoners in the start.
12 http://en.wikipedia.org/wiki/The_Eleventh_Commandment (5 January 2012).
13 Meaning literally 'baby', Bebe is a very common Romanian way to address someone affectionately. It is neither a diminutive nor a nickname.
14 Christina Stojanova, 'My Romanian Cinema', in *Kinokultura*, May 2007, www.kinokultura.com (10 March 2009).
15 Natalia Stancu, *'Senatorul Melcilor'*, http://www.mirceadaneliuc.ro/html/critica_senator3.html (5 January 2012).
16 Cristina Modreanu, Diana Popescu and Cristian Tudor Popescu, 'Premiul ALIA', http://www.mirceadaneliuc.ro/html/critica3.html (11 January 2012).

CHAPTER 6

1 Eugenia Vodă (1995: 171–223) explained that Daneliuc and a few others went as far as going on hunger strike in order to obtain autonomy. Andrei Pleşu, a very influential Romanian intellectual who had been appointed Minister of Culture, is said to have argued that the filmmakers lacked credibility and did not come up with a relevant project.
2 Şerban quotes as 'bad' examples of mediocre and kitsch productions two post-Communist films by Andrei Blaier, *Crucea de piatră/The Stone Cross* (1993) and *Terente, regele bălţilor/Terente, King of Swamps* (1995).
3 His subsequent films on contemporary topics, namely *Faimosul Paparazzo/The Famous Paparazzo* (1999) and *Schimb valutar/Exchange* (2008), were shot at ten-year intervals, restating the crude realities of a never-ending transitional period.
4 Mention should be made of *Memorialul durerii* (*The Memorial of Suffering*, 1991), a Romanian television documentary series about persecution, the labour camp system, anti-Communist resistance and the secret police, produced and co-ordinated by Lucia Hossu Longin and available on DVD.
5 The story was inspired by the careers of two well-known Romanian writers: Ion Caraion and Petru Dumitriu.
6 On this point see also Căliman (2000: 404–05) and Vodă (1995: 279–83).

CHAPTER 7

1 In an interview from the collective project *Lumière et Comp.*, French DVD edition from 2005.
2 To whom *Reconstruction*, his subsequent film, is dedicated.
3 Though acclaimed at home and abroad for his outstanding achievements, the presentation of his films in festivals as well as in the US and European distribution circuit has always been quite problematic and unpredictable, both for historical and economic reasons. However, in a country like France, where he has always been highly regarded, the almost complete DVD editions of his films have been available since 2003 thanks to one of his most efficient co-nationals and co-producers, Romanian-born Marin Karmitz.

4   George Littera, 'Interview with Lucian Pintilie', in *Cinema*, November 1965, 8-10.

5   *Reenactment* is an alternative English (UK) title for the film.

6   Marie-Odile Briot's essay 'L'irresponsabilité collective' is accompanied by two inter-
    views by Adrian Păunescu, translated from Romanian, in *Positif*, n° 123, January
    1971, 49-62.

7   The genesis of the Reconstruction 'project' has been at the centre of a docu-fic-
    tion co-directed by Armand Richelet-Kleinberg and Radu Dinulescu, *La Nostalgie
    de la Reconstitution/The Nostalgia of Reconstruction*, a first version of which was
    screened at the Underground Festival that took place in the Romanian town of Arad
    in May 2009. What the docu-fiction reveals is to what extent Pătrașcu and later on
    Pintilie wanted to be as close to reality as possible, both when depicting the facts
    by means of which he accuses the Communist procedures and when illustrating the
    modernist reflexive nature of the filming process.

8   Interestingly, there are two versions of this ending kept at the Romanian Film Archive,
    and this 'second version' has been confirmed by the sound engineer Andrei Papp
    to historian Bujor Rîpeanu. In the original one the song featured is the Western
    Bee Gees number 'Why Don't You Stop and Listen', and in the 'official' one meant
    for foreign distribution the song was replaced by a Romanian *variété* song by Dan
    Spătaru.

9   http://en.wikipedia.org/wiki/Massacre_of_the_Innocents (26 January 2012).

10 Pintilie provides the letter he had written to the Director of the Cannes Quinzaine
    des réalisateurs, Pierre Henri Deleau, in 1980, on the occasion of the section's 20th
    anniversary, explaining the reasons for his non-attendance: 'I have no memory
    of the screening in Cannes, of any meeting with other directors, of any anecdote
    because, intercepted by Gogolian state agents, your invitation never reached me.
    So it was only thanks to reported stories by those who had attended that I had learnt
    something about the screening of *Reconstruction*' (Silvestri 2004: 92).

11 Minutes from the conference on the Romanian New Wave organised by the author
    at the Belgian Film Museum in Brussels, 6 and 8 October 2007.

12 Michel Ciment, 'Les quarante ans de *Positif*' ('*Positif* at 40'), Locarno International
    Film Festival Catalogue, August 1992.

13 Alex Leo Șerban, 'Ramă în ramă în ramă în ramă', in *Contrapunct*, 19 October 1990,
    reprinted in Pintilie (2003: 335).

14 I thank Romanian television and Vlad Nedelcu for giving me access to the
    documentary.

15 As explained by Marin Karmitz on the French DVD (MK2 Editions, 2004) bonus fea-
    ture, the film has two versions, running 2h. 05 and 1h. 40, the latter having been
    judged more appropriate and easier to decode for an international audience.
    During his filmed 'Cinema lesson' Pintilie argues that no one before Karmitz, not
    even Ceaușescu in person, had dared impose cuts to his films. Both Pintilie and
    Karmitz tell the story of the film's complex production setup and of its difficult begin-
    nings, including an 'aborted' opening night at the 1992 Cannes Film Festival, where
    most critics were missing.

16 George Pruteanu, 'Implacabilul Mitică', http://www.pruteanu.ro/201croniciliterare-
    tot.htm (8 June 2009).

17 Writes Pintilie in the film's screenplay: 'Wagner's prelude accompanies the film's

credits tolerating or impeding the auditive interference with reality. A delicate balance which foreshadows most of the film's connections with reality... The camera is tracking up from a low-angle shot as if looking for somebody. A bizarre messenger. Our daily life' (Pintilie 1992: 259).

18 See DVD interview, MK2 Editions, 2004.

19 In the longer initial version of the film, the part played by the 'securitate' agent is indeed much more developed, clearly destined to be decoded by a domestic audience.

20 A character appears at this point in a car and Nela recognises her as being Ophelia, the young wife of Nedelcu, the *Securitate* agent, actually referring to a part that had been cut in the shorter version, so it is not comprehensible for the audience.

21 The film's co-production setup included MK2, Canal+, La Sept, Les Productions Traversière, Romanian Filmex and the Ministries of Culture from both countries.

22 The film originates from a short story by Răzvan Popescu: the writer, nowadays an important media authority in Romania, worked as a geologist in the Jiu Valley. He was highly familiar both with the mining environment and with the ideological controversy around the sadly famous Mining Raid of June 1990.

23 See the debate around the film retranscribed in *Bricabrac,* 410-17, author's translations.

24 Cristian Tudor Popescu, *Adevărul*, 1 October 1996, in Pintilie (2003: 425; author's translation).

25 Another possible explanation of the helicopter motif, also present in films by Daneliuc from the same period, is related to a historical highlight of the highly mediatised Romanian revolution: the dictator and his wife fleeing from the roof of the presidential palace with a helicopter on 21 December 1989.

26 See Ana Blandiana, film review in *România Liberă*, 19 September 1998, author's translation.

27 Thus, it features future director Cristi Puiu as counsellor/assistant director.

28 As a matter of fact Jela published more or less at the same moment *Lexiconul negru: Unelte ale represiunii comuniste/The Black Lexicon: Instruments of Communist Repression* (2001), containing 1700 entries about Communist torturers. Bucharest: Humanitas.

29 See also Jean A. Gili, 'L'Après-midi d'un tortionnaire: Confesser l'inconfessable', in *Positif*, n° 494, April 2002, 23-24, author's translation.

30 There are some very interesting remarks by screenwriter Rădulescu and by Pintilie himself about the use of space in *Niki and Flo*, re-transcribed from a debate on 'Space in Film' in *Secolul 21*, 32-35, author's translation.

31 The bridal couple dance and hum to the music of *Veronica*, a children's film hit from the late 1970s, as mentioned earlier.

32 Lucian Pintilie, *Capul de Zimbru* (*The Aurochs Head*), a screenplay inspired by Vasile Voiculescu's homonymous novella, published online in 2005, http://editura.liter-net.ro/carte/143/Lucian-Pintilie/Capul-de-zimbru-scenariu-dupa-Vasile-Voiculescu.html (23 March 2010).

33 Such comments are clearly absent from Voiculescu's original story. As will be the case with the 'nationalistic' last lines of the screenplay, they have been added by the director so as to correspond to the contemporary zeitgeist, the moment Romania

was knocking at the gates of Europe hoping to be accepted as an official member of the European Union.

CHAPTER 8

1 *Venice in September* got a Romanian debut prize and a second one at a French film festival in Tours (France).

2 This was a very unusual situation for a young East European director from the Communist era, Caranfil having most probably benefited from his father's privileged position within the Bucharest cultural scene. In an interview with the Belgian daily *Le Soir* he admits 'having been very lucky'. Marie Dussart, 'La Roumanie vue par un cinéaste: La population attend un miracle ou une catastrophe', in *Le Soir*, 20 December 1990.

3 In a user review for the film from the IMDb, entitled 'One of the Top-Five Romanian movies' and dated 9 February 2008, the film's second unit director declares that 'The military unit scenes are inspired by true events from our own army service, Caranfil's and mine, that we served in Caracal. Corporal Puşcaşu is a real person and Lieutenant Grecea is loosely inspired by our own commander, Lieutenant Burlacu. The exterior scenes of the theatre were shot next to the real People's Theatre in Caracal.'

4 The French unpublished version of the screenplay can be consulted at the Belgian Film Archive: Nae Caranfil, *Des Dimanches de Permission* (*Sundays on Leave*). Paris: La Compagnie des Images, 1992, 116 pages, author's translation.

5 See online translation of two pieces by Marin Sorescu by Adam Sorkin and Lidia Vianu, www.thebluemoon.com/4/fame/fame88sorescu.html.

6 'You're called Dino, like the one from the Flintstones?' 'Your name is Cristina Burlacu ["bachelor" in Romanian], which means you like bachelors?'.

7 Personal conversation with Nae Caranfil at the Mons International Film Festival (Belgium), March 2010.

8 Mircea Diaconu obviously specialised in playing deceived men. Thus, after *Asphalt Tango*, Caranfil would further 'recycle' him for a similar part in his fourth feature, *Philanthropy*.

9 Italian journals *La Stampa* (Lietta Tuornabuoni, 6 June 1999) and *La Reppublica* (Irene Bignardi, 30 May 1999) reacted quite positively to the film. The Belgian Francophone Film Festival awarded the film the Best Screenplay prize.

10 The only negative review was one signed by Gregory Valens in *Positif*, n° 406, June 2002, 43, criticising the fact that Caranfil offered a poor, negative image of Romania.

11 The film got six domestic prizes and six international ones (Mons, Paris, Bratislava, Wiesbaden, Wurzburg and Newport Beach).

12 Nae Caranfil, *The Rest Is Silence*, unpublished screenplay in English, 1999.

13 According to Bujor Rîpeanu, the character who served as an inspiration for the deceased is Petre Liciu, an important figure of the Romanian national theatre from the early teens, having been part of the initial 'Independence War' filming project before his untimely death.

14 This sequence was filmed on location inside two outstandingly preserved late

nineteenth-century Bucharest palaces, the George Enescu Memorial Museum and the Monteoru House.

15 Consider the wide acclaim for recent animated films for adults such as Marjane Satrapi's *Persepolis* (2008) and Ari Folman's *Waltz with Bashir* (2009).

CHAPTER 9

1 Cristi Puiu is somehow an exception because he had already directed a feature, *Marfa şi banii* (*Stuff and Dough*, 2001), to be dealt with in the next chapter.

2 See Adina Brădeanu's online introduction to the 2007 Romanian Film Festival: 'Past Imperfect, Future Continuous', Romanian Cultural Centre, London, http://rcc.evalde. com/filmfestival/2007/introduction.html (8 June 2010).

3 Romanian Company Metropolis Film released a DVD in 2008 containing five note-worthy shorts, called *5 Succese Mari pentru 5 Filme Mici* (*Five Big Hits for Five Small Films*). It includes the following shorts: *A Good Day for a Swim*, *The Boxing Lesson*, *Alexandra*, *Home* and *Waves*.

CHAPTER 10

1 Răzvan Rădulescu's track as a writer after graduating in modern languages and opera direction is rather impressive: before becoming a scriptwriter, he wrote nov-els, short stories, essays, poems, an opera libretto and last but not least several essential screenplays for the New Wave, to be dealt with in subsequent chapters. He co-directed his first short, *Networking Friday*, with Melissa De Raaf in 2008, and his first feature film, *Felicia, înainte de toate* (*First of All, Felicia*, 2010) was well received by critics and audiences alike.

2 Marian Ţuţui rightly compares the complicity between the ailing, retired old Lăzărescu and his cats to Umberto's concern for his dog in Vittorio De Sica's 1952 neorealist masterpiece *Umberto D* (Ţuţui 2008: 284).

3 On the same DVD, cameraman Oleg Mutu and his assistant Andrei Butică under-line the pictorial quality of single hand-held takes and long shots. Mutu stresses the value of natural light and the refusal to add extra lighting sources, even when Lăzărescu's apartment is barely lit.

4 After three weeks of rehearsals and thirty-nine intensive shooting days, the main actress, Luminiţa Gheorghiu, confesses in the bonus interview her fascination with the character of nurse Mioara as soon as she had finished reading the screenplay, because she realised to what extent she is the film's ray of hope, its leading light among the infernal circles. This acknowledgment gave her the strength and energy to inhabit almost every scene, from the moment she meets Lăzărescu to his untimely death, infusing the sequences with an extremely diversified palette of psychological states, as praised by Puiu himself in his comments: from indifference and matter-of-factness to a high degree of humour, complicity and tenderness in her relationship with the terminally ill patient.

5 Thus, on the US DVD bonus materials, Dr Fred Berlin goes as far as comparing the Romanian post-Communist health care system with the American one, explaining to what extent most issues approached in the films are universal. He praises the film's

outstanding lesson about human dignity and compassion and stresses the fact that even in the States there are still people lacking medical insurance, living in difficult conditions, without proper medication, and waiting for help in emergency rooms. Berlin claims educating the medical staff about human priorities, how to respond to peoples' sadness and suffering, is still an issue. In a similar line, Jean Luc Douin's review of the film in *Le Monde* argues that what Puiu is filming does not only apply to Romania, it also applies to the French emergency system as it revealed itself during the 2003 heat wave, 'a society despising its sick and elder persons'.

6   The proximity to Ionesco's Theatre of the Absurd is such that a French critic wrote that the story takes place in the playwright's birthplace, which is wrong, as Ionesco was born in the southern part of the country. In a personal email interview Porumboiu actually quotes Ionesco, Caragiale and Gogol as his favourite authors: he had been familiar with them and they had shaped his style before he started filmgoing on a regular basis. Personal email from 10 December 2010.

7   The film director's own mother and aunt and one of the co-producers are cast in small cameo appearances and seem to relish jokes about striking income differences between the new Romanians. According to Porumboiu such scenes were totally improvised on the set (Porumboiu's personal answers to the author's email questions from 10 December 2010).

8   Asked to recount their shooting experience with Porumboiu on the DVD bonus materials, the three actors explain in an informal way, seated as they were during the talk show, to what extent they enjoyed learning their lines for such witty, stimulating parts. Though it all sounds very spontaneous and characters had to pretend to be ignorant about TV conventions, the shooting was minutely prepared in order to lampoon the proliferation of numberless reality shows. The actors note that people from the festival circuit were persuaded the show was filmed during a single 40' session, while in reality they spent weeks rehearsing it (DVD released in the UK in 2008 by Artificial Eye).

9   Europa Cinemas Label – which allowed it to be distributed in fifty-nine countries – Golden Swann Copenhagen IFF, Gobbo d'oro, Bobbio Italy, Grand Prix Molodist Kiev IFF, Jury award in Bangkok, etc.

10 Muntean picked him up from the Bucharest Sfânta Vineri cemetery, where he served as an administrator.

11 The film's score is by the Electric Brother band.

12 Excerpts from seminar minutes on Contemporary Romanian Cinema, Brussels Film Museum, October 2007.

CHAPTER 11

1   See Cristian Mungiu, *7 Scenarii* (*Seven Screenplays*), Agenda liternet, www.liternet.ro, 2003; and Cristian Mungiu, *5 Povestiri* (*Five Short Stories*), booklet in the Romanian DVD edition, '4 ½ filme, 5 povestiri', Voodoo Films, 2010.

2   Mungiu later integrated it into the Romanian DVD edition of the omnibus series *Tales from the Golden Age* (2009).

3   *The Ritual*, by Nadejda Koseva, Bulgaria; *Birthday*, by Jasmila Zbanich, Bosnia; *Turkey Girl*, by Cristian Mungiu, Romania; *Short-lasting Silence*, by Kornél Mundruczó,

Hungary; *Fabulous Vera*, by Serb Stefan Arsenijevic; and an Estonian animated film, *Gene+Ratio*, by Mait Laas.

4   A fully-fledged 'character' in the film, the turkey, whose real name is 'Năstase', was trained by two professional animal trainers, the Neda couple, having already worked on the set of *Cold Mountain* (A. Minghella, 2003), an international production filmed in Romania. See 'Năstase, vedeta lui Mungiu', 2007, www.menonline.ro.

5   Score composed by Horia Moculescu.

6   Best picture at the Transylvania International Film festival, 2002, Best New Director Award in Leeds, Montpellier Nova Award, Best Film Prize in Mons (Belgium), etc.

7   http://www.romanianculturalcentre.org.uk/interviews/2006/09/cristian-mungiu/.

8   Co-directed by Răzvan Georgescu and co-produced by several foreign television companies.

9   The film *Children of the Decree* was included in the French DVD of *4, 3, 2*. Avant-scène du Cinéma and Bac Video, Collector Edition, 2007, also containing a DVD-ROM: wwwbacfilms.com.

10   http://editura.liternet.ro/carte/222/Dan-Mihu/Sa-iubesti-si-sa-tragi-apa.html. I am grateful to Cristina Corciovescu for providing this piece of information.

11   *Adevărul*, 27 May 2007. Mihu was interviewed by the press after Mungiu's unprecedented acclaim and victory in Cannes. He explained that he did not intend to sue the director for having 'stolen' his subject, after being part of the jury who awarded him the prize one year earlier. He wrote an email to Mungiu to which he never got an answer: he was simply asking him to validate the fact that Mihu's script inspired him to write a story about a similar case of illegal abortion during the Ceauşescu era. Mihu further commented on the fact that Mungiu had declared in Cannes: 'one year ago such a subject didn't even cross my mind'. Other members of the HBO jury stated that it is extremely difficult to confront an existing film with a similar idea that has not yet been turned into a film.

12   Romanian DVD edition released by Voodoo Films in 2007.

13   A Romanian diminutive of Gabriela: it could have been avoided, given the difficulty in pronouncing it as a non-native speaker, but it brings more realism and it suggests that she should be protected and treated as an innocent child.

14   On returning to their room, the young girl will notify Găbiţa that her father had called to say he is coming and the content of a secret plan will be further discussed. On one of the film's DVD bonus features, Mungiu shows the deleted scene of the father's visit: the latter is seen commenting on his daughter's needs in terms of food and laundry and explaining how he has even managed to buy a flat for her inside the building they inhabit. The director explains he cut the scene because he wanted to avoid any pathetic family moments which would provide more information than necessary, and thus transgress the minimalist rule.

15   There is another, albeit tragic, onomastic coincidence about the abortionist being nick-named 'Bebe', meaning 'baby'. It is actually a Romanian generic diminutive used for several first names, misleading for non-domestic audiences because many people are persuaded it is a family name.

16   It has been purposefully chosen for the Romanian DVD cover as well as for the poster presenting the film to Italian audiences.

17   French DVD bonus feature, interview with Cristian Mungiu, Bac Video, 2007.

18 During the 'Romanian Film Symposium' organised at the Brussels Film Museum, Rădulescu explained how Mungiu had conceived this as a salutary escape from the hotel room where such horrible things were going on. Rădulescu's childhood seems to have been dominated by the 'food issue' so common to all Romanian families: people constantly made provisions and were proud to boast about them on important occasions. The scriptwriter thus recounted his Easter meals in packed apartments, with discussions centring so much on what was being eaten that there was no room left for other topics.

19 This is a challenging face-to-face scene which has also served as an alternative promotional poster for the film.

20 In the French DVD 'deleted scenes' feature, two alternative endings to the final chosen one are featured. In the first one, Mungiu's camera shows the seated girls in a full frontal shot, zooms out and reframes the shot, revealing the restaurant window with snow falling, as in the opening shot. There is no off-screen look, no cut on motion. The second alternative reveals Otilia staring at somebody or something from afar, so that the interpellation effect is diminished and the reframed window and the snow are still there. The director eventually realised such endings would diminish the film's extremely powerful message and would depart from the consistent minimalistic aesthetics.

21 The Vatican's press organ *L'Osservatore Romano* condemned the film as being a 'sordid, talkative film… some scenes being unbearable for the common viewer'.

22 See French, Romanian and US DVDs containing the Caravan film and Sorin Avram, *Jurnal de Caravană* (*Caravan Diary*), www.4months3weeksand2days.com/blog/2007/10/08/jurnal-de-caravana-de-sorin-avram.

23 Sorin Pâslaru, 'Generația '68 a regizorului Cristi Mungiu restartează România', in *Ziarul Financiar*, 29 May 2007, author's translation.

CHAPTER 12

1 Tramarin (2010: 17) quotes the following names and birthdates for what he describes as 'Generation 70': Radu Muntean, 1971, Cătălin Mitulescu, 1972, Tudor Giurgiu, 1972, Constantin Popescu, 1973, Corneliu Porumboiu, 1975, Peter Călin Netzer, 1975, Florin Șerban, 1975, Ruxandra Zenide, 1975, Radu Jude, 1975, and Cristian Nemescu, 1979.

2 Best Film and Fipresci Award in Geneva, Best Film at the Women's International Film Festival in Bordeaux, Special Jury Award for main actress at the Manheim Film Festival, and so on.

3 Incidentally, both Sandu and Alex are alternative diminutives for the same name Alexandru/Alexandra, so as to further stress Kiki's bisexual inclinations.

4 Winner of the Golden Bear for Best Short in Berlin in 2008 with *O zi bună de plajă* (*A Good Day for a Swim*), from a screenplay by Mitulescu.

5 Scorsese and Wenders had been enthusiastic about his shorts and had read the screenplay for his first feature-length film.

6 It got the Youth Jury Award at the 2006 Valladolid Youth Film Festival and was shown in many festivals over the world (e.g. Toronto, Melbourne, Brussels, Helsinki). It is still frequently screened in Romanian cultural institutes as an illustration of recent film

production. Distribution sales for both the film copies and the DVD versions have been good in both Western and Eastern Europe, Japan, Australia and the US.

7   Personal email interview with Cătălin Cristuţiu, 2 April 2011.

8   CineMaiubit, 2000; DaKino, 2001; Best International Debut, IFF Message to Man, Russia; Public's choice, Milano Film Festival, Italy, 2001.

9   The film was produced by the Romanian Film School (UNATC), got a nomination as Best Short Film from the European Film Academy and received awards at the Angers (France) Premiers Plans International Film Festival, at the Zagreb IFF (Croatia, best short) and at the NYU Student Film Contest in 2004.

10 It got no less than six national and international prizes, at, among other places, the Transylvania Film Festival, 2006, Best Short Film prize; the Swiss International Film and Television Prize 'Cinéma tout écran'; and the International Art and Video Film Festival 'Syracuse' Best Short fiction prize. For detailed information on the film see also http://ro.wikipedia.org/wiki/Marilena¬_de_la_P7.

11 Following a conflict with the Romanian scriptwriters, Lindstrum's name does not appear on all distributed copies.

12 www.mediapropictures.com/californiadreaminendless/story.html 29/03.11.

13 Email interview with Cătălin Cristuţiu, 2 April 2011.

14 In the film's 'making of' by Claudiu Mitcu (2007), featured on the UK Artificial Eye edition, Assante is very enthusiastic about his contribution to the film: he argues he was rightly cast by young but brilliant Nemescu, who offered him a satisfactory part after several unsatisfactory ones. In the same vein, younger actor Jamie Elman confesses having been highly challenged by the contact with a completely different culture where the idea of miscommunication becomes a key issue.

15 See http://www.hermes-slobozia.home.ro/ (22 March 2011).

16 Cristuţiu mentions a whole nightmare dream sequence from the screenplay Nemescu had intended to shoot and introduce in the final version. Personal email, 2 April 2011.

17 For a complete list of prizes, including those from film festivals in Brussels, Rabat, Ibiza, Eurasia, London, Belgrade and Milan, visit the production company's website: http://mediapropictures.com/californiadreaminendless/awards.html (29 March 2011).

CHAPTER 13

1   Thus, mention should be made of two lost alternative-version films from the early 1930s produced in France at the Joinville/Paramount studios and involving Romanians, not all of them exiles at the time the films were released. These are the European version of *Paramount on Parade* (Charles de Rochefort, 1930), starring Pola Illéry, based on a screenplay by Benjamin Fondane, and *Televiziune* (Jack Salvatori,1931), featuring the same actress and screenwriter and with scenes shot in Bucharest by Jean Mihail.

2   Parts of this chapter are from 'Radu Gabrea, A Romanian Filmmaker in and out of Exile' by Dominique Nasta, unpublished paper presented on the occasion of the 'First International Conference on Migrant and Diasporic Cinema in Contemporary Europe', organised by Daniela Berghahn and Claudia Sternberg, Oxford, 6–8 July

2006.

3 The screenplay is by Dumitru Radu Popescu, inspired by a story by Colonel Aurel Petri.

4 Gabrea also introduces some fragments of authentic war newsreel footage.

5 Fănuş Neagu served as screenwriter for several Romanian films.

6 Gabrea also gave a 'dubbed' part to another familiar Romanian exile, Dan Nuţu, interestingly impersonating the village's fool. His brother, Şerban Gabrea, and Miruna Boruzescu are also credited as assistant art director and costume designer, respectively.

7 In 2002 Gabrea cast his wife Victoria Cociaş as 'Maria Callas – The Divine' in a convincing adaptation of Terence McNally's *Master Class*, which successfully toured in theatre festivals both in Europe and in the US.

8 '17 Miliarde de lei pentru cinematografia naţională', in *Adevărul*, 2737, 24 March 1999, 4; 'Peste 16 miliarde de lei au fost acordaţi pentru finanţarea de filme româneşti', in *Ziua*, 1478, 3 May 1999, 4.

9 In 2011 Gabrea merged *Looking for Schwartz* and *Concerts from the Black Church* into a single film called *Două lumi în muzică* (*Two Worlds in Music*, 2011).

10 A Romanian, German, Austrian and Hungarian joint production co-directed by Marijan David Vajda.

filmography

4 Luni, 3 săptămâni şi 2 zile (*4 Months, 3 Weeks, and 2 Days*, Cristian Mungiu, 2007)
15 (Sergiu Nicolaescu, 2005)
17 Minute întârziere (*17' Minutes Late,* Cătălin Mitulescu, 2002)

A 11a poruncă (*The 11th Commandment,* Mircea Daneliuc, 1991)
A fost sau n-a fost (*12:08 East of Bucharest,* Corneliu Porumboiu, 2006)
Acasă (*Home,* Paul Negoescu, 2008)
Această lehamite (*Fed Up,* Mircea Daneliuc, 1994)
Actorul si sălbaticii (*The Actor and the Savages,* Manole Marcus, 1974)
Adela (Mircea Veroiu, 1985)
Afacerea Protar (*The Protar File,* Haralambie Boroş, 1955)
Ajutoare umanitare (*Humanitarian Aid,* Hanno Höfer, 2002)
Alexandra (Radu Jude, 2008)
Allo, Hallo (Ion Popescu Gopo, *1963*)
Ambasadori caută patrie (*Ambassadors Seek Country,* Mircea Daneliuc, 2003)
Amintiri bucureştene (*Memories of Bucharest,* Radu Gabrea, 1970)
Amor Fatal (*Fatal Love,* Grigore Brezeanu & Aristide Demetriade, 1911)
Apa ca un bivol negru (*Water like a Black Buffalo,* Andrei Cătălin Băleanu, Dan Piţa,
    Mircea Veroiu, Petre Bokor, Youssouf Aidabi, Stere Gulea, Roxana Pană, Iosif Demian,
    Dinu Tănase, Nicolae Mărgineanu, 1970)
Apartamentul (*The Apartment,* Constantin Popescu, 2003)
Apele tac (*Silent River,* Anca Miruna Lăzărescu, 2011)
Asfalt Tango (*Asphalt Tango,* Nae Caranfil, 1996)
Astă seară dansăm în familie (*Tonight we Dance at Home,* Geo Saizescu, 1972)
Aurora (Cristi Puiu, 2010)
Autobiografia lui Nicolae Ceauşescu (*The Autobiography of Nicolae Ceauşescu,* Andrei
    Ujica, 2010)
Aventuri la Marea Neagra (*Adventures at the Black Sea,* Savel Ştiopul, 1970)
Azucena (Mircea Mureşan, 2006)

Balanţa (*The Oak,* Lucian Pintilie, 1992)
Baltagul (*The Hatchet,* Mircea Mureşan, 1969)
Bela Lugosi: Vampirul căzut (*The Fallen Vampire,* Florin Iepan, 2007)
Binecuvântată fii inchisoare (*Bless You Prison,* Nicolae Mărgineanu, 2002)
Boogie (Radu Muntean, 2008)
Brigada Diverse în acţiune (*Brigade Miscellaneous,* Mircea Drăgan, 1971)

Brigada lui Ionuţ (*Ionuţ's Brigade*, Jean Mihail, 1954)
Bucharest-Vienna, 8.15 (Cătălin Mitulescu, 2001)
Bucureşti-Berlin (*Bucharest-Berlin*, Anca Miruna Lăzărescu, 2005)
Bucureşti, Piaţa Universităţii (*Bucharest, University Square*, Stere Gulea, co-directed by
    Vivi Drăgan Vasile and Sorin Ilieşiu, 1991)
Bucureşti/Wien: 8:15 (Cătălin Mitulescu, 2001)

Călătoria lui Gruber (*Gruber's Journey*, Radu Gabrea, 2008)
Călătorie la oraş (*A Trip to the City,* Corneliu Porumboiu, 2003)
California Dreamin' (Endless) (Cristian Nemescu, 2006)
Captivi de Crăciun (*Stuck on Christmas*, Iulia Rugină, 2010)
Carne (*Meat*, Miruna Boruzescu, 2006)
Cartierul veseliei (*The Gaiety District*, Manole Marcus, 1967)
Casa din vis (*The House from a Dream*, Ioan Cărmăzan, 1991)
Cătuşe rosii/Odessa in fiamme (*Odessa in flames*, Carmine Gallone, 1942)
Căutîndu-l pe Schwarz (*Looking for Schwarz*, Radu Gabrea, 2008)
Cel mai iubit dintre pământeni (*The Most Beloved of Earthlings,* Şerban Marinescu,1992)
Cea mai fericită fată din lume (The Happiest Girl in the World, Radu Jude, 2009)
Child's Pose (*Poziţia copilului*, Peter Călin Netzer, 2013)
Ciuleandra (Martin Berger, 1929)
Ciulinii Bărăganului (*Bărăgan Thistles*, Louis Daquin, 1957)
Cocoşul Decapitat (*The Beheaded Rooster*, Radu Gabrea, 2007)
Codin (*Codine*, Henri Colpi, 1963)
Cold Waves (Alexandru Solomon, 2007)
Colivia (*The Cage*, Adrian Sitaru, 2010)
Columna (*Trajan's Column*, Mircea Drăgan, 1968)
The Concert (*Le Concert,* Radu Mihăileanu, 2009)
Concerte de la Biserica Neagră (*Concerts from the Black Church*, Radu Gabrea, 2009)
Concurs (*Contest*, Dan Piţa, 1982)
Constantin şi Elena (*Constantin and Elena*, Andrei Dăscălescu, 2008)
Corul pompierilor (*The Firemen's Choir*, Cristian Mungiu, 2000)
Croaziera (*The Cruise,* Mircea Daneliuc, 1982)
Crulic, drumul spre dincolo (*Crulic: The Path to Beyond*, Anca Damian, 2011)
Cu mîinile curate (*With Clean Hands*, Sergiu Nicolaescu, 1972)
Cum mi-am petrecut sfârşitul lumii (*How I Spent the End of the World*, Cătălin Mitulescu,
    2006)
Curcanii nu zboară (*Turkey Girl*, part of the *Lost and Found* collective film, Cristian
    Mungiu, 2005)
Cursa (*The Long Drive*, Mircea Daneliuc, 1975)

Dacă bobul nu moare (*If the Seed Doesn't Die*, Sinişa Dragin, 2011)
Dacii (*The Dacians,* Sergiu Nicolaescu, 1966)
Damen Tango (Dinu Tănase, 2003)
De ce trag clopotele, Mitică? (*Carnival Scenes*, Lucian Pintilie, 1981)
Decreţeii (*Children of the Decree*, Florin Iepan, 2004)
Desfăşurarea (*The Development,* Paul Călinescu, 1954)

Diminețile unui băiat cuminte (*Mornings of a Sensible Youth*, Andrei Blaier, 1966)
Din dragoste cu cele mai bune intenții (*Best Intentions*, Adrian Sitaru, 2011)
Dincolo de nisipuri (*Beyond the Sands*, Radu Gabrea, 1973)
Dincolo de pod (*Beyond the Bridge*, Mircea Veroiu, 1976)
Do Not Fear, Jakob (*Fürchte dich nicht, Jakob*, Radu Gabrea, 1981)
Dolce far niente (*Sweet Idleness*, Nae Caranfil, 1999)
Drum în penumbră (*Through Dusky Ways*, Lucian Bratu, 1972)
Duhul aurului (*Lust for Gold*, Dan Pița & Mircea Veroiu, 1974)
Duminică la ora șase (*Sunday at Six*, Lucian Pintilie, 1965)
După dealuri (*Beyond the Hills*, Cristian Mungiu, 2012)
După-amiaza unui torționar (*The Afternoon of a Torturer*, Lucian Pintilie, 2001)

E Pericoloso Sporgersi (*Sundays on Leave*, Nae Caranfil,1993)
Ea (*She*, Radu Muntean, 1994)
Ediție specială (*Special Edition*, Mircea Daneliuc, 1977)
Ein Mann wie EVA (*A Man Like Eva*, Radu Gabrea, 1984)
Ein Unding der Liebe (*A Strange Thing Called Love*, Radu Gabrea, 1988)
Erupția (*The Eruption*, Liviu Ciulei, 1957)
Escadrila Albă (*The White Squad*, Ion Sava, 1942)
Eu când vreau să fluier, fluier (*If I Want to Whistle, I Whistle*, Florin Șerban, 2010)
Eu sunt Adam (*My Name is Adam*, Dan Pița, 1996)
Examen (*Exam*, Titus Muntean, 2003)

Faimosul paparazzo (*The Famous Paparazzo*, Nicolae Mărgineanu, 1999)
Faleze de nisip (*Sand Cliffs*, Dan Pița, 1983)
Faraonul (*Pharaoh*, Sinișa Dragin, 2004)
Felix și Otilia (*Felix and Otilia*, Iulian Mihu, 1971)
Femeia visurilor (*The Dreamt Woman*, Dan Pița, 2005)
Filantropica (*Philanthropy*, Nae Caranfil, 2002)
Filip cel Bun (*Filip the Kind*, Dan Pița, 1974)
Francesca (Bobby Păunescu, 2009)
Furia (*Fury*, Radu Muntean, 2001)

Gadjo Dilo (*Crazy Stranger*, Tony Gatlif, 1997)
Gioconda fără surîs (*Gioconda Without that Smile*, Malvina Urșianu, 1967)
Glissando (Mircea Daneliuc, 1984)

Haiducii (*The Haidouks*, Dinu Cocea, 1965)
Haiducii (*The Outlaws*, Horia Igiroșanu, 1929)
Hârtia va fi albastră (*The Paper Will Be Blue*, Radu Muntean, 2006)
Homo sapiens (Ion Popescu Gopo, 1960)
Hotel de lux (*Luxury Hotel*, Dan Pița, 1992)

Iacob (Mircea Daneliuc, 1988)
Ilustrate cu flori de câmp (*Postcards with Flowers*, Andrei Blaier, 1974)
În fiecare zi Dumnezeu ne sărută pe gură (*Everyday God Kisses us on the Mouth*,

Sinişa Dragin, 2001)
În sat la noi (*In Our Village,* Jean Georgescu & Victor Iliu, 1951)
Înainte de tăcere (*Before There Was Silence*, Alexa Visarion, 1978)
Începutul adevărului: Oglinda (*The Mirror*, Sergiu Nicolaescu, 1993)
Independenţa României (*The Independence War*, Grigore Brezeanu, 1912)
Înşir-te Mărgărite (*Spin a Yarn*, Grigore Brezeanu & Aristide Demetriade, 1911)
Intre oglinzi paralele (*Between Facing Mirrors*, Mircea Veroiu, 1978)
Italiencele (*The Italian Girls*, Napoleon Helmis, 2004)

Kapitalism: Our Improved Formula (Alexandru Solomon, 2010)
Kitschitoarele (Cristian Nemescu, 2000)

La Bloc oamenii mor după muzică (*In Apartment Buildings People are Crazy About Music*, Cristian Nemescu, 2000)
La drumul Mare (*Life's Hard*, Gabriel Sîrbu, 2008)
La moara cu noroc (*Mill of Good Luck,* Victor Iliu, 1956)
Lampa cu căciulă (*The Tube with a Hat*, Radu Jude, 2006)
Latcho Drom (*Gypsy Dream*, Tony Gatlif, 1992)
Lecţia de box (*The Boxing Lesson*, Alexandru Mavrodineanu, 2007)
Legături bolnăvicioase (*Love Sick,* Tudor Giurgiu, 2006)
Legiunea străină (*The Foreign Legion*, Mircea Daneliuc, 2008)
Lindenfeld (Radu Muntean, 1994)
Lord (Adrian Sitaru, 2010)
Loverboy (Cătălin Mitulescu, 2011)

Ma-ma (*Rock'n Roll Wolf*, Elisabeta Bostan, 1974)
Maiorul Mura (*Major Mura,* Ion Timuş, 1928)
Mâna lui Paulista (*The Hand of Paulista,* Cristian Mungiu, 1999)
Manasse (Jean Mihail, 1925)
Mănuşile roşii (*Red Gloves*, Radu Gabrea, 2010)
Marele jaf comunist (*The Great Communist Bank Robbery*, Alexandru Solomon, 2004)
Marfa şi banii (*Stuff and Dough*, Cristi Puiu, 2001)
Margo (Ioan Cărmăzan, 2005)
Maria (Peter Călin Netzer, 2003)
Marilena de la P 7 (*Marilena from P7*, Cristian Nemescu, 2006)
Marţi, după Crăciun (*Tuesday, After Christmas*, Radu Muntean, 2010)
Meandre (*Meanders,* Mircea Săucan, 1966)
Mecano (Cristian Nemescu, 2001)
Medalia de Onoare (*Medal of Honor*, Peter Călin Netzer, 2010)
Megatron (Marian Crişan, 2008)
Mere Roşii (*Red Apples*, Alexandru Tatos, 1976)
Mihai şi Cristina (*Mihai and Christina,* Cristian Nemescu, 2001)
Mihai Viteazul (*Michael the Brave*, Sergiu Nicolaescu, 1971)
Milionari de week-end (*Week-end Millionaires,* Cătălin Saizescu, 2004)
Mitrea Cocor (Victor Iliu & Marietta Sadova, *1952)*
Moartea Domnului Lăzărescu (*The Death of Mr. Lazarescu*, Cristi Puiu, 2005)

Morgen (Marian Crişan, 2010)

Moromeţii (*The Moromete Family*, Stere Gulea, 1987)

Moştenirea lui Goldfaden – De la Iaşi la New-York (*Goldfaden's Legacy*, Radu Gabrea, 2004)

Nebunia capetelor (*Facemania*, Thomas Ciulei, 1997)

Nepoţii gornistului (*The Bugler's Grandsons*, Dinu Negreanu, 1953)

Niki Ardelean, colonel în rezervă (*Niki and Flo*, Lucian Pintilie, 2003)

Noiembrie, ultimul bal (*November, the Last Ball*, Dan Piţa, 1987)

Noro (Radu Gabrea, 2002)

Nothing by Chance (Cristian Mungiu, 2000)

Nunta de piatră (*The Stone Wedding*, Dan Piţa & Mircea Veroiu, 1973)

Nunta lui Oli (*Oli's Wedding*, Tudor Cristian Jiurgiu, 2009)

O noapte de pomină (*A Night to Remember*, Ion Şahighian, 1939)

O noapte furtunoasă (*A Stormy Night*, Jean Georgescu, 1942)

O vară de neuitat (*An Unforgettable Summer*, Lucian Pintilie, 1994)

O zi bună de plajă (*A Good Day for a Swim*, Bogdan Mustaţă, 2007)

Occident (*West*, Cristian Mungiu, 2002)

Omul zilei (*The Man of the Day*, Dan Piţa, 1997)

Orient Express (Sergiu Nicolaescu, 2004)

Oxygen (Adina Pintilie, 2010)

Păcală (Geo Saizescu, 1974)

Păcală se întoarce (*Păcală is Back*, Geo Saizescu, 2006)

Pădurea Spânzuraţilor (*The Forest of the Hanged*, Liviu Ciulei, 1965)

Pădureanca (*The Forrest Maiden*, Nicolae Mărgineanu, 1986)

Pas în doi (*Paso Doble*, Dan Piţa, 1985)

Patul conjugal (*The Conjugal Bed*, Mircea Daneliuc, 1993)

Pavillon 6 (Lucian Pintilie, 1972)

Pe aripile vinului (*Gone with the Wine*, Corneliu Porumboiu, 2002)

Pepe şi Fifi (*Pepe and Fifi*, Dan Piţa, 1994)

Pescuit Sportiv (*Hooked*, Adrian Sitaru, 2008)

Podul de flori (*The Flower Bridge*, Thomas Ciulei, 2008)

Poliţist, adjectiv (*Police, Adjective*, Corneliu Porumboiu, 2009)

Polul Sud (*South Pole*, Radu Nicoară, 1991)

Porţile albastre ale oraşului (*The Blue Gates of the City*, Mircea Mureşan, 1973)

Portretul luptătorului la tinereţe (*Portrait of the Fighter as a Young Man*, Constantin Popescu, 2010)

Poveste de la scara C (*C Block Story*, Cristian Nemescu, 2003)

Povestiri din epoca de aur (*Tales from the Golden Age*, collective portmanteau five-film project, co-directed and co-produced by Cristian Mungiu, Hanno Höfer, Ioana Uricaru, Constantin Popescu and Razvan Mărculescu, 2009)

Prea mic pentru un război atât de mare (*Too Small for Such a Big War*, Radu Gabrea, 1969)

Prea tirziu (*Too Late*, Lucian Pintilie, 1996)

Principii de viață (*Principles of Life*, Constantin Popescu, 2010)
Privește înainte cu mânie (*Look Forward in Anger*, Nicolae Mărgineanu, 1993)
Proba de microfon (*Microphone Test*, Mircea Daneliuc, 1980)
Puterea și Adevărul (*The Power and the Truth*, Manole Marcus, 1972)

RA (Călin Dan, 1994–2000)
Raport despre starea națiunii (*Report on the State of the Nation*, Ioan Cărmăzan, 2003)
Răscoala (*The Uprising/Blazing Winter*, Mircea Mureșan, 1965)
Răsună valea (*The Valley Resounds*, Paul Călinescu, 1949)
Răzbunarea haiducilor (*The Revenge of the Haidouks*, Dinu Cocea, 1968)
Reconstituirea (*Reconstruction/Reenactment*, Lucian Pintilie, 1969)
Restul e tăcere (*The Rest is Silence*, Nae Caranfil, 2007)
Rochia albă de dantelă (*The White Lace Dress*, Dan Pița, 1989)
Rosenemil (Radu Gabrea, 1993)
Roumanie, terre d'amour (*Romania, Country of Love*, Camille de Morlhon, 1931)
Rumenyie! Rumenyie! (*Romania, Romania*, Radu Gabrea, 2006)
Ryna (Ruxandra Zenide, 2005)

Să mori rănit din dragoste de viață (*To Die Wounded by Love for Life*, Mircea Veroiu, 1983)
Sample City (Călin Dan, 2003)
Scurtă istorie (*A Short History*, Ion Popescu Gopo, 1956)
Se aprind făcliile (*Torches Are Lighted*, Ion Șahighian, 1939)
Second-hand (Dan Pița, 2003)
The Secret of the Ice Cave (Radu Gabrea, 1989)
Secvențe (*Sequences*, Alexandru Tatos, 1982)
Senatorul Melcilor (*The Snails' Senator*, Mircea Daneliuc, 1995)
Și ei sînt ai noștri (*They are also of our Skin*, Radu Muntean, 1992)
Singur(ă) pe lume (*(S)he is not Alone*, Tudor Giurgiu, 1995)
Sistemul nervos (*The Nervous System*, Mircea Daneliuc, 2005)
Stare de fapt (*State of Things*, Stere Gulea, 1994)
Ștefan Luchian (Nicolae Mărgineanu, 1981)
Stop cadru la masă (*Snapshot Around the Family Table*, Ada Pistiner, 1982)
Struma (Radu Gabrea, 2001)
Supraviețuitorul (*The Survivor*, Sergiu Nicolaescu, 2007)
Suta de lei (*One Hundred Lei*, Mircea Săucan, 1973)

Tănase Scatiu (*A Summer Tale*, Dan Pița, 1976)
Țara Moților (*The Land of the Motzi*, Paul Călinescu, 1939)
Terminus Paradis (*Next Stop Paradise*, Lucian Pintilie, 1998)
Tertium Non Datur (Lucian Pintilie, 2006)

Ticăloșii (*The Bastards*, Șerban Marinescu, 2007)
Toată lumea din familia noastră (*Everybody in our Family*, Radu Jude, 2012)
Trafic (*Traffic*, Cătălin Mitulescu, 2003)
Trahir (*Betrayal*, Radu Mihaileanu, 1993)

Train de vie (*Train of Life*, Radu Mihăileanu, 1998)
Trenul fantomă (*Phantom Train/Ghosts in the Train*, Jean Mihail, 1933)
Trenul foamei (*Hunger Train*, Viorel Timaru, 2010)
Trip (Călin Dan, 2006)
Triunghiul morţii (*The Triangle of Death*, Sergiu Nicolaescu, 1999)
Tudor (Lucian Bratu, 1964)

Ultimul cartuş (*The Last Bullet,* Sergiu Nicolaescu, 1973)
Un cartuş de Kent şi un pachet de cafea (*Coffee and Cigarettes*, Cristi Puiu, 2003)
Un film cu o fată fermecătoare (*This Charming Girl*, Lucian Bratu, 1966)
Unde la soare e frig (*Sunny but Chilly*, Bodgan Dumitrescu, 1990)
Undeva în Est (*Somewhere in the East*, Nicolae Mărgineanu, 1991)
Undeva la Palilula (*Somewhere in Palilula*, Silviu Purcărete, 2012)
Unicul, adevăratul Tarzan (*The One, the Only, the Real Tarzan*, Florin Iepan, 2004)

Valuri (*Waves*, Adrian Sitaru, 2007)
Valurile Dunării (*The Danube Waves*, Liviu Ciulei 1959)
Vânătoarea de vulpi (*Fox Hunting*, Mircea Daneliuc, 1980)
Venea o moară pe Siret (*The Mill on the River Siret*, Martin Berger, 1931)
Veronica (Elisabeta Bostan, 1972)
Veronica se întoarce (*Veronica is Back,* Elisabeta Bostan, 1973)
Viaţa e în altă parte (*Life is Elsewhere*, Radu Muntean, 1996)
Videogrammen einer Revolution (*Videograms of a Revolution*, Harun Farocki, Andrei
    Ujică, 1992)
Visul lui Liviu (*Liviu's Dream*, Corneliu Porumboiu, 2003)
Visul lui Tănase (*Tănase's Dream*, Constantin Tănase, Bernt Aldor, 1932)
Visul unei nopţi de iarnă (*A Midwinter Night's Dream*, Jean Georgescu, 1944-1946)
Vulpe Vânător (*Fox: Hunter*, Stere Gulea, 1993)

Zapping (Cristian Mungiu, 2000)

bibliography

Allon, Yoram (2002) 'Focus on the "Other" Europe', http://www.kamera.co.uk/features/new_europe_ff_2002.html (6 June 2009).

Allon, Yves (2007) 'Entretien avec Cristian Mungiu', in *L'Avant-scène cinéma*, June 2007, n° 563, 3-11.

Althabe, Gérard (2001) *L'homme et la société*. Paris: L'Harmattan.

Andrews, Nigel (2008) 'Catching the New, New Wave', in *Financial Times Magazine*, January 2008, 6-8.

Audé, Françoise (2003) 'Niki et Flo: Vous pouvez clouer' and Franck Garbarz, 'Comme un exercice de musique de chambre: entretien avec Lucian Pintilie', in *Positif*, n° 512, 29-33.

Azoury, Philippe (2007) 'Il est fou ce roumain: *12:08 A l'Est de Bucarest*', in *Libération*, January 10, iv.

_____ (2007) 'L'horreur est roumaine', in *Libération*, 29 August, ii-iii.

Blaga, Iulia (2003) *Fantasme şi adevăruri: O carte cu Mircea Săucan*. Bucharest: Hasefer.

Blümlinger, Christa (2004) 'Slowly Forming a Story while Working on Images', in Elsaesser, Thomas (ed.) *Harun Farocki: Working on the Sightlines*. Amsterdam: Amsterdam University Press.

Boia, Lucian (2001) *Romania: Borderland of Europe*. London: Reaktion Books.

Bourdeau, Emmanuel (1998) 'Terminus Paradis', in *Cahiers du cinéma*, n° 528, 74-76.

Bradeanu, Adina (2006) 'Microphone Test', in Iordanova, Dina (ed.) *The Cinema of the Balkans*. London: Wallflower, 171-81.

_____ (2007) 'Romanian Documentaries and the Communist Legacy', in *Cineaste: Special Supplement on Contemporary Balkan Cinema*, vol. 32, n° 3, 45-46.

Bradshaw, Peter (2008) 'State of Denial: *4 Months, 3 Weeks and 2 Days*', in *The Guardian*, 11 January, 9.

Briot, Marie-Odile (1971) 'L'irresponsabilité collective', in *Positif*, n° 123, 49-62.

Căliman, Călin (2000) *Istoria filmului românesc, 1897-2000*. Bucharest: Ed. Fundaţiei Culturale Române.

Călinescu, Alexandru (1998) *Interstiţii*. Iaşi: Polirom.

Cantacuzino, Ion (1965) *Momente din trecutul filmului românesc*. Bucharest: Meridiane.

_____ (1968) 'L'évolution historique du cinéma roumain', *Revue Roumaine d'Histoire de l'Art*, 5, 189-208.

Caranfil, Tudor (1981) *În căutarea filmului pierdut*. Bucharest: Meridiane.

Cazals, Patrick (1990) 'Cordée roumaine à La Rochelle', in *Libération*, 6 July, 43.

Chirilov, Mihai (2007) 'You Can Run, But You Cannot Hide: New Romanian Cinema', in

Kinokultura: Special Issue on Romanian Cinema, May 2007, http://www.kinokultura. com/specials/6/chirilov.shtml (8 October 2010).

Cieutat, Michel and Yann Tobin (2007) 'Entretien avec Cristian Mungiu: Une façon franche de filmer', in *Positif*, n° 559, 17–21.

Ciment, Michel and Noël Herpe (1994) 'Entretien avec Lucian Pintilie. Retrouver la grâce' and '*Un été inoubliable*: Le charme discret de Babel', in *Positif*, n° 401-2, 13–18.

____ (2011) '10 Films by Lucian Pintilie: An Essential Contemporary', in *APERITFF, Ten Years of New Romanian Cinema*, special edition, official publication of the Tranyslvania International Film Festival, Bucharest: The Romanian Cultural Institute, 72–74.

Codrescu, Andrei (1991) *The Hole in the Flag: A Romanian Exile's Story of Return and Revolution*. New York: William Morrow.

Corciovescu, Cristina (2002) 'Romanian Cinema', in Ian Hayden Smith (ed.) *International Film Guide*. London: Wallflower Press, 249–250.

Corciovescu, Cristina and Magda Mihăilescu (eds) (2010) *Cele mai bune 10 filme româneşti ale tuturor timpurilor*. Iaşi: Polirom.

Dakovic, Nevena (2007) '*Lost and Found*', in *Cineaste*, vol. XXII, n° 3, 57–58.

Daneliuc, Mircea (1997) *Pisica ruptă*. Bucharest: Univers.

Darras, Matthieu (2007) '12: 08, A l'est de Bucarest et trois courts-métrages: Techniques de survie', in *Positif*, n° 551, January 2007, 7–11.

Deaca, Mircea (2011) *Camera Secundă: Articole şi studii de film*. Timişoara: BrumaR.

De Baroncelli, Jean (1965) '*La forêt des pendus*', in *Le Monde*, 27 May.

Dobrincu Dorin, Vladimir Tismăneanu and Cristian Vasile (2007) *Raport final al Comisiei Prezindenţiale pentru Analiza Dictaturii Comuniste din Romania / Final Report of the Presidential Commission in Charge of the Analysis of Communist Dictatorship in Romania*. Bucharest: Humanitas.

Doinaş, Ştefan Augustin and Alex Leo Şerban (eds) (2001) *Secolul 21: Filmul*. Bucharest: Uniunea Scriitorilor & FCS21.

Domenach, Elise (2008) '*California Dreamin'*', in *Positif*, n° 563, 32–33.

Douin Jean Luc (2006), 'Dante dans l'enfer des urgences: *La mort de Dante Lăzărescu*', *Le Monde*, 11 January, 26.

Dulgheru, Elena (2007) 'Two Insights into the Romanian Goulag', http://www.kinokultura.com/specials/6/dulgheru.shtml (8 October 2010).

Duma, Dana (2007) 'Are We Still Laughing when Breaking with the Past', http://www.kinokultura.com/specials/6/duma.shtml (8 October 2010).

Durandin, Catherine (1995) *Histoire des Roumains*. Paris: Fayard.

Eisenreich, Pierre (2006) '*La mort de Dante Lăzărescu*: L'indésirable' and 'Entretien avec Cristi Puiu: Filmer l'acte de la création initiale', in *Positif*, n° 539, 24–30.

Elley, Derek (2007) '*The Rest is Silence*', in *Variety*, 27 August, 108.

Elsaesser, Thomas (ed.) (2004) *Harun Farocki: Working on the Sightlines*. Amsterdam: Amsterdam University Press.

Felperin, Leslie (2006) '*The Paper Will Be Blue*', in *Variety*, 22 August 2006.

Fulger, Mihai (2006) *Noul val în cinematografia românească*. Bucureşti: Grup editorial Art.

____ (2010) '*A fost sau na fost*: Cum se ratează istoria la periferie şi cum începe o carieră de autor', in Corciovescu, Cristina and Magda Mihăilescu (eds), 2010, 146–62.

Gabrea, Radu (1986) *Werner Herzog et la mystique rhénane*. Lausanne: L'Age d'Homme.

Garbarz, Franck (2004) 'Guardare in faccia il male', in Silvestri, Silvana and Giovanni Spagnoletti (eds) *Guardare in Faccia il Male: Lucian Pintilie, Tra cinema e teatro*. Faces 01: 40° Mostra Internazionale del Nuovo Cinema. Pesaro: Revolver Libri, 29–36.

Georgescu, Vlad (1985) *Romania: 40 Years* (1944–1984). New York: Praeger.

Gilbey, Ryan (2006) 'Chasing the Ambulance: *The Death of Mr Lazarescu*', in *Sight & Sound*, August 2006, 28–30.

Gili, Jean A. (1994) '*Les Dimanches de permission*: chronique ordinaire de la vie provinciale', in *Positif*, November 1994, 39–40.

____ (2002) '*L'Après-midi d'un tortionnaire*: Confesser l'inconfessable', in *Positif*, n° 494, 23–24.

Gorzo, Andrei (2006) 'În tot şi-n toate, *Cum mi-am petrecut sfârşitul lumii*', *Dilema Veche*, September 2006, http://agenda.liternet.ro/articol/3232/Andrei-Gorzo/In-toti-si-n-toate-Cum-mi-am-petrecut-sfirsitul-lumii.html (23 June 2011).

Grădinaru, Ariadna and Dragoş Tudor (2007) *The Young, The New, The Daring: Best Romanian Feature Film Debuts*. Bucharest: Romanian Cultural Institute.

Grmek Germani, Sergio (2000) 'Romania, Reconstructions of the Tears', *Trieste Film Festival Catalogue*. Trieste: Alpe Adria Cinema, XII Edizione, 153–219.

Harrington, Joseph F. and Bruce J. Courtney (1991) *Tweaking the Nose of the Russians: Fifty Years of American-Romanian Relations*. New York: Columbia University Press.

Hoberman, James (2007) 'The Revolution Must Be Televised', in *The Village Voice*, 29 May, http://www.villagevoice.com/2007-05-29/film/the-revolution-must-be-televised (9 December 2010).

Huber, Christoph (2006) 'A Tale from the Bucharest Hospitals: Cristi Puiu on *The Death of Mr. Lăzărescu*', *Cinema Scope*, spring 2006, 7–14 (part of the Tartan Video DVD booklet).

Iordanova, Dina (2001) *Cinema of Flames: Balkan Film, Culture and the Media*. London: British Film Institute.

____ (2003) *Cinema of the Other Europe: The Industry and Artistry of East Central European Film*. London: Wallflower Press.

____ (ed.) (2006) *The Cinema of the Balkans*. London: Wallflower Press.

Iordanova, Dina, William Brown and Lechu Torchin (eds) (2010) *Moving People, Moving Images: Cinema and Trafficking in the New Europe*. St. Andrews: St. Andrews Film Studies.

Jäckel, Anne (1999) 'The Grand Theatre of the World: The Films of Lucian Pintilie', in *Cineaste*, December 1999, 27–29.

____ (2001) 'Romania: From Tele-Revolution to Public Broadcasting, National Images and International Image', in *Canadian Journal of Communication*, vol. 26, n° 1, 131–41.

___ (2003) 'La recherche d'un modèle culturel en Europe: Le Royaume-Uni et la Roumanie', in Sojcher, Frédéric and Jean-Pierre Benghozi (eds) *Quel modèle audiovisuel européen?* Paris: L'Harmattan, 148–9.

___ (2006) '*Michael The Brave*', in Iordanova, Dina (ed.) *The Cinema of the Balkans*. London: Wallflower Press, 75–85.

Jeancolas, Jean-Pierre (1992) '*Le chêne*: Zéro moins trois', in *Positif*, n° 379, September 1992, 16–17.

_____ and Françoise Audé (1998) 'Terminus Paradis: Un lyrisme très intense' and 'Je ne veux plus dialoguer avec le mal: Entretien avec Lucian Pintilie', in Positif, n° 452, 25–30.

Jela, Doina (1999) Drumul Damascului. Bucharest: Humanitas.

Jones, Michael S. (2006) The Metaphysics of Religion: Lucian Blaga and Contemporary Philosophy. New Jersey: Farleigh Dickinson University Press.

Kezich, Tulio (1998) 'Abel si traveste da Godard, Pintilie "sogna" Steinbeck', in Corriere della Sera, 10 September, 32.

Lefort, Gérard (1998) 'Le monde sans pitié de Pintilie', in Libération, 7 October.

Lemarié, Yannick (2007) 'Tertium non datur: Celui qui dit non', in Positif, n° 551, 12–15.

Leonardi, Francesca (2004) 'L'accoglienza critica del cinema di Pintilie in Francia e in Italia', in Silvestri, Silvana and Giovanni Spagnoletti (eds) Guardare in Faccia il Male: Lucian Pintilie, Tra cinema e teatro. Faces 01: 40° Mostra Internazionale del Nuovo Cinema. Pesaro: Revolver Libri, 74–87.

Liehm, Mira and Antonin J. Liehm (1977) The Most Important Art: Soviet and Eastern European Film After 1945. Berkeley, CA: University of California Press.

Lupşa, Cristian (2007) 'Nemescu, Viaţa ca un film', in Esquire, online edition, http://esquire.ro/articole/reportaje/nemescu-viata-ca-un-film.html (7 September 2011).

Mancino, Antonio Giulio (2004) 'Le stelle di striscio: requiem rumeno del sogno Americano', in Silvestri, Silvana and Giovanni Spagnoletti (eds) Guardare in Faccia il Male: Lucian Pintilie, Tra cinema e teatro. Faces 01: 40° Mostra Internazionale del Nuovo Cinema. Pesaro: Revolver Libri, 55–59.

Mandelbaum, Jacques (2007) 'Bilan moral d'une révolution: 12:08 A l'est de Bucarest', in Le Monde, 10 January, 24.

Martinez, Dominique (2007) 'L'étoile de chacun: Table ronde roumaine', in Positif, n° 551, 16–18.

_____ (2007) 'La saveur de la Moldavie: Entretien avec Corneliu Porumboiu', in Positif, n° 551, January, 9–11.

Mihăilescu, Magda (2004) 'L'uomo senza identita', in Silvestri, Silvana and Giovanni Spagnoletti (eds) Guardare in Faccia il Male: Lucian Pintilie, Tra cinema e teatro. Faces 01: 40° Mostra Internazionale del Nuovo Cinema. Pesaro: Revolver Libri, 37–46.

Modorcea, Grid (2004) Dicţionarul filmului românesc de ficţiune. Bucharest: CNC/Cartea Românească.

Monder, Eric (2009) 'Film review: California Dreamin', in FilmJournal.com, January 23, http://www.filmjournal.com/filmjournal/content_display/esearch/e3i6e3ab16ed8-b79d8ba6d0546f6de54b58 (30 March 2011).

Nasta, Dominique (2000) 'Cinema Romeno', in Gian Piero Brunetta (ed.) Storia del Cinema Mondiale: L'Europa/Le cinematografie nazionali, vol. III. Turin: Einaudi, 1459–93.

_____ (2004a) 'Musique, écoute et valorisation du son: de Starewitch à Tim Burton', in Nasta, Dominique and Didier Huvelle (eds) (2004) New Perspectives in Sound Studies. Bruxelles: PIE Peter Lang, 56–66.

_____ (2004b) 'Lucian Pintilie e il rinovamento modernista europeo degli anni sessanta', in Silvestri, Silvana and Giovanni Spagnoletti (eds) Guardare in Faccia il Male: Lucian Pintilie, Tra cinema e teatro. Faces 01: 40° Mostra Internazionale del Nuovo Cinema. Pesaro: Revolver Libri, 47–54.

____ (2005) 'Mythopoïétique et cinéma contemporain: Trois cas de l'Est européen', online essay in *Proceedings of the 2nd International Congress on European Contemporary Cinema*, CICEC, Barcelona, Pompeu Fabra University, 3 June, http://ocec.eu/pdf/2005/nasta_dominique.pdf (2 May 2012).

____ (2006a) Entry on *Nae Caranfil* in Brunetta, Gian Piero (ed.) *Dizionario dei registi del cinema mondiale*. Torino: Giulio Einaudi, vol. I, 299–300.

____ (2006b) 'Radu Gabrea, a Romanian Filmmaker in and out of Exile', unpublished paper, First International Conference on Migrant and Diasporic Cinema in Contemporary Europe, Oxford, July 2006.

____ (2007a) 'Musiques migratoires dans la Roumanie post-totalitaire: réceptacles esthétiques en quête de reconnaissance', unpublished paper, International Conference on Film Music, Sorèze, Université de Toulouse, February 2007.

____ (2007b) 'The Tough Road to Minimalism: Romanian Contemporary Film Aesthetics', in *Kinokultura: Special Issue on Romanian Cinema*, May 2007, 1, http://www.kinokultura.com/specials/6/nasta.shtml (8 October 2010).

____ (2007c) '*12:08 East of Bucharest*', in *Cineaste: Special Supplement on Contemporary Balkan Cinema*, vol. 32, n° 3, 62–63.

____ (2008) 'What a Difference a Day Makes, Twenty-four Little Hours: Esquisse pour une théorie de l'évocation musicale au cinéma', in Danblon, Emmanuelle and Mikhaïl Kissine (eds) *Linguista sum, Mélanges en hommage à Marc Dominicy*. Paris: L'Harmattan, 181–87.

____ (2012) 'Continuity, Change and Renewal in Romanian Auteur Films: From *Reconstruction* (1969) to *If I Want to Whistle I Whistle* (2010)', in *Film International*, vol. 10, n° 1, 34–56.

Nesselson, Lisa (2002) '*Philanthropy* by Nae Caranfil', in *Variety*, 1 July, 26.

Nevers, Camille (1992) '*Les Voleurs*: entretien avec M.Morgenstern et R. Vasilescu' and 'Nela et l'odyssée', in *Cahiers du cinéma*, n° 457, 27–29.

Niculae, Ion-Vasile (2008) *Catalogul Cinematografiei Româneşti, 2000-2008*. Bucharest: CNC.

Niculescu, Adrian (2002) '25 de Ani de la Mişcarea Goma', in *Observator Cultural*, 113, 23 April 2002, 4–7.

____ (2010) 'Evenimentele din iunie 1990', in *Revista Institutului Revoluţiei Române din Decembrie, Caietele Revoluţiei*, n° 4-5, 35–85.

Pârvulescu, Constantin (2009) 'The Cold World Behind the Window: *4 Months, 3 Weeks and 2 Days* and Romanian Cinema's Return to Real-existing Communism', in *Jump Cut*, n° 51, spring 2009, http://www.ejumpcut.org/archive/jc51.2009/4months/index.html (26 June 2009).

Pavel, Laura (2006) 'Eliade and His Generation: Metaphysical Fervour and Tragic Destiny', in *Journal for the Study of Religion and Ideologies – Special Issue: Remembering Mircea Eliade*, 15, 5–19.

Pethö, Agnes (2005) 'Chaos, Intermediality, Allegory: The Cinema of Mircea Daneliuc', in Imre, Aniko (ed.) *East European Cinemas*. New York: Routledge.

Pintilie, Lucian (1992) *Patru scenarii*. Bucharest: Albatros.

____ (2001) '*După-amiaza unui torţionar*: Fragmente din scenariul filmului', in Doinaş, Ştefan Augustin and Alex Leo Şerban (eds) n° 10–12, 224.

____ (2003) *Bricabrac*. Bucharest: Humanitas.

____ (2005) *Capul de Zimbru* (*The Aurochs Head*), a screenplay inspired by Vasile Voiculescu's novella, published online in 2005, http://editura.liternet.ro/carte/143/Lucian-Pintilie/Capul-de-zimbru-scenariu-dupa-Vasile-Voiculescu.html (23 March 2010).

Popescu, Cristian Tudor (2011) *Filmul surd în România mută: Politică şi propagandă in filmul românesc de ficţiune.* Iaşi: Polirom.

Porton, Richard (2008) 'Not Just an Abortion Film: An Interview with Cristian Mungiu', in *Cineaste*, vol. 33, n° 2, 35–39.

Potra, Florian (1979) *Profesiune: Filmul.* Bucharest: Meridiane.

Privett, Ray (1999) 'The Revolution Was Televised: Farocki and Ujica's *Videograms of a Revolution*', in *Central Europe Review, Kinoeye*, vol. 1, n° 17, October 1999, http://www.ce-review.org/99/17/kinoeye17_privett.html (9 June 2009).

Ratner, Megan (2008) 'Stunted Lives: On *4 Months, 3 weeks and 2 days*', in www.brigthlightsfilm.com, n° 59.

Ricoeur, Paul (1990) *Time and Narrative* (trans. K. McLaughlin and D. Pellauer), 3 vols. Chicago: University of Chicago Press.

Rîpeanu, Bujor (2004) 'Quelques considérations sur le cas roumain', in Irène Bessière and Roger Odin (eds) *Les Européens dans le cinéma américain: Emigration et Exil.* Paris: Presses Sorbonne Nouvelle, 235–8.

____ (2004/05) *Filmat în România: Un repertoriu filmografic*, vol. I, 1911–69; vol. II, 1970–79. Bucharest: Universitatea Media.

____ (2006) 'Romania', in Phillips, Alastair and Ginette Vincendeau (eds) *Journeys of Desire: European Actors in Hollywood.* London: BFI, 416.

Rîpeanu, Bujor and Cristina Corciovescu (1996) *1234 Cineaşti Români.* Bucharest: Ed. Ştiinţifică.

Roddick, Nick (2007) '*California Dreamin'* (*Endless*)', in 51st London International Film Festival Programme. London: BFI, Time Out, 44.

Rollet, Sylvie (1997) 'Lucian Pintilie: Un cinéma en état d'urgence' and '*Trop tard* ou la tentation luciférienne', in *Positif*, n° 431, January 1997, 27–30.

Roof, Judith (1992) 'Romania', in Slater, Thomas J. (ed.) *Handbook of Soviet and East European Films and Filmmakers.* New York: Greenwood Press, 309–41.

Rooney, David (2002) '*Everyday God Kisses Us on the Mouth*', in *Variety*, 6 February 2002, http://www.varietyultimate.com/search/?search=dragin+rooney&startYear=2001&endYear=2002 (7 April 2011).

Sarris, Andrew (2011) '*Peace, Love and Understanding*', review in *New York Observer*, January 2009, http://www.observer.com/2009/o2/peace-love-and-understanding (29 March 2011).

Sava, Valerian (1999) *Istoria critică a filmului românesc contemporan*, vol. 1. Bucharest: Meridiane.

____ (2011/12) *O istorie subiectivă a tranziţiei filmice*, vols 1 and 2. Piteşti: Paralela 45.

Semo, Marc (2003) 'Ils sont fous ces roumains: Dans le Bucarest postcommuniste, *Niki et Flo*, une fable sadique de Pintilie', in *Libération*, 24 September.

Şerban, Alex Leo (2006) *De ce vedem filme.* Iaşi: Polirom.

____ (2009) *4 Decenii, 3 ani si 2 luni cu Filmul Românesc.* Iaşi: Polirom.

____ (2011) 'What Next?', in *Film Comment*, January/February 2011, 4–7.

Silvestri, Silvana and Giovanni Spagnoletti (eds) (2004) *Guardare in Faccia il Male Lucian*

Pintilie, Tra cinema e teatro. Faces 01: 40° Mostra Internazionale del Nuovo Cinema. Pesaro: Revolver Libri.

___ (2004) 'Intervista a Lucian Pintilie', in *Guardare in Faccia il Male*, 16-28.

Sklar, Robert (2006) *'The Death of Mr Lazarescu'*, in *Cineaste*, vol. 3, summer 2006, 62-63.

Stoil, Michael J. (1974) *Cinema Beyond the Danube: The Camera and Politics.* Lanham, MD: The Scarecrow Press.

___ (1982) *Balkan Cinema: Evolution after Revolution.* Michigan: Ann Arbor/UMI.

Stratton, David (2003) *'Niki and Flo'*, in *Variety*, 26 May 2003.

Taboulay, Camille (1993) 'Cannes '93: *E pericoloso sporgersi'*, in *Cahiers du Cinéma*, n° 469, 33.

Tatos, Alexandru (1994) *Pagini de jurnal.* Bucharest: Albatros.

Tismăneanu, Vladimir (2003) *Stalinism for All Seasons: A Political History of Romanian Communism.* Berkeley: University of California Press.

Töke, Lilla (2006) *'Stone Wedding'*, in Iordanova, Dina (ed.) *The Cinema of the Balkans.* London: Wallflower, 127-136.

Tolu, Mihai (ed.) (1998) *Producţia cinematografică din România 1897-1970 Filmografie adnotata*, 2 vols. Bucharest: Alo, Bucureşti.

Tramarin, Achille (2010) *Il cinema romeno dopo la fine del mondo*, Universita degli studi di Padova, Dipartimento di Romanistica.

Tuţui, Marian (2006) *'Forest of the Hanged'*, in Iordanova, Dina (ed.) *The Cinema of the Balkans.* London: Wallflower, 33-41.

___ (2011) *Orient Express: The Romanian and Balkan Cinema.* Bucharest: Noi Media Print.

Uricaru, Ioana (2008) *'4 Months, 3 Weeks and 2 Days*: The Corruption of Intimacy', in *Film Quarterly*, vol. 61, n° 4, summer 2008, 12-17.

Vasile, Aurelia (2011) *Le cinéma roumain dans la période communiste: Représentations de l'histoire nationale.* Bucharest: Editura Universităţii din Bucureşti.

Vodă, Eugenia (1995) *Cinema şi nimic altceva.* Bucharest: Editura Fundaţiei România Literară.

Young, Benjamin (2004) 'On Media and Democratic Politics: Videograms of a Revolution', in Thomas Elsaesser (ed.) *Harun Farocki: Working on the Sightlines.* Amsterdam: Amsterdam University Press, 245-71.

index